David T. Runia, D. Litt. (1983) Free University, Amsterdam, is Professor of Ancient and Medieval Philosophy at the University of Leiden and C. J. de Vogel Extraordinary Professor of Ancient Philosophy at the University of Utrecht. He has published extensively on Philo, including *Philo of Alexandria and the* Timaeus *of Plato* (1986) and (with R. Radice) *Philo of Alexandria: an Annotated Bibliography* (1988, 1992²), both published by E. J. Brill, Leiden.

PHILO AND THE CHURCH FATHERS

SUPPLEMENTS TO

VIGILIAE CHRISTIANAE

Formerly Philosophia Patrum

TEXTS AND STUDIES OF EARLY CHRISTIAN LIFE
AND LANGUAGE

EDITORS

J. DEN BOEFT — R. VAN DEN BROEK — A.F.J. KLIJN
G. QUISPEL — J.C.M. VAN WINDEN

VOLUME XXXII

PHILO AND THE CHURCH FATHERS

A COLLECTION OF PAPERS

BY

DAVID T. RUNIA

E.J. BRILL
LEIDEN · NEW YORK · KÖLN
1995

The paper in this book meets the guidelines for permanence and durability of the Committee on Production Guidelines for Book Longevity of the Council on Library Resources.

Library of Congress Cataloging-in-Publication Data

Runia, David T.
    Philo and the church fathers : a collection of papers / by David
T. Runia
        p.   cm. — (Supplements to Vigiliae Christianae, ISSN
    0920-623X ; v. 32)
    Includes bibliographical references and indexes.
    ISBN 9004103554 (cloth : alk. paper)
    1. Philo, of Alexandria.   2. Philo, of Alexandria—Influence.
3. Christian literature, Early.   4. Theology—History—Early church,
ca. 30-600.   5. Theology—History—Middle ages, 600-1500.
I. Title.   II. Series.
B689.Z7R8645   1995
181'.06—dc20   95-15212
                                                                CIP

Die Deutsche Bibliothek - CIP-Einheitsaufnahme

[Vigiliae Christianae / Supplements]
Supplements to Vigiliae Christianae : formerly Philosophia
Patrum ; texts and studies of early Christian life and language.
– Leiden ; New York ; Köln : Brill.
    Früher Schriftenreihe
    ISSN 0920–623X
NE: HST
Vol. 32. Runia, David T.: Philo and the church fathers. – 1995
Runia, David T.:
Philo and the church fathers : a collection of papers / by David
T. Runia. – Leiden ; New York ; Köln : Brill, 1995
    (Vigiliae Christianae : Supplements ; Vol. 32)
    ISBN 90–04–10355–4

                    ISSN   0920-623X
                    ISBN   90 04 10355 4

to
Eric and Lorna Osborn

CONTENTS

PREFACE

When scholars in various disciplines belonging to the humanities make use of the extensive corpus of Philonic writings, they seldom stop to think about how it came to happen that these precious documents were preserved for posterity. Philo was an Alexandrian Jew, but his writings and thought fell out of favour in his own Jewish tradition. They were preserved through the efforts of early Christians, who decided that these works could assist them in developing their own distinctive kind of thought. This process of reception and selective appropriation was the focus of my research in the period from 1987 to 1993, resulting in the publication of the monograph *Philo in Early Christian Literature: a Survey*, published in 1993 by Van Gorcum (Assen) in their series Compendia Rerum Iudaicarum ad Novum Testamentum (III 3) in conjunction with Fortress Press (Minneapolis).

In this book I attempted to give a fairly comprehensive coverage for the period up to 400 AD. As was observed in the preface, the theme was very broad, and hitherto largely unresearched in a systematic fashion. Many a time I had to resist the temptation to delve more deeply into particular aspects of my theme. But I did not always resist. As a result a number of essays were published in journals and other collective works which complement various aspects of that book. In particular mention should be made of the inaugural lecture given in Utrecht in 1992, in which I attempted to place the results of my research in a broader philosophical and theological perspective. It now appears for the first time in an English translation. In consultation with the editors of this series Professors J. C. M. van Winden (Leiden) and J. den Boeft (Amsterdam-Utrecht) and with Drs. H. van der Meij (Brill) it was decided that it would be a worthwhile idea to collect these scattered essays together and put together a companion volume to the monograph mentioned above.

The papers in this volume have been reset. The original pagination has been inserted in square brackets in the text (except in the case of the first chapter). The original place of publication and various comments on the text of the papers are given in a section of Addenda et corrigenda at the end of the volume (p. 250–261).

Asterisks in the margin of the text refer to comments in this section. Before reading each chapter, the reader is advised to consult the opening remarks in that section, where I say a little more about what led me to write the paper in the first place.

I would like to thank the following editors and publishers for give me permission to reprint the papers contained in this book: Prof. S. Cohen (Brown University) for chapters 2, 8, 9, 12, 14; Dr. E. Lovering jr. (Society of Biblical Literature) and Mr. D. Ford, Scholars Press, Atlanta, for chapter 4; Mr. P. Peeters of Peeters Publishing House, Leuven, for chapter 6; Dr. J. Dinter, Köln, for chapter 10; Drs. C. J. Visser of Kok Publishing House, Kampen, for chapter 11.

This volume is dedicated to my mentor and friend, Eric Osborn (Queens College, Melbourne) and his wife Lorna, in celebration of more than a quarter of a century of shared interest and collaboration in the field of ancient and patristic philosophy.

Leiden, Easter 1995

ABBREVIATIONS

1. Philonic treatises

Abr.	*De Abrahamo*
Aet.	*De aeternitate mundi*
Agr.	*De agricultura*
Anim.	*De animalibus*
Cher.	*De Cherubim*
Contempl.	*De vita contemplativa*
Conf.	*De confusione linguarum*
Congr.	*De congressu eruditionis gratia*
Decal.	*De Decalogo*
Deo	*De Deo*
Det.	*Quod deterius potiori insidiari soleat*
Deus	*Quod Deus sit immutabilis*
Ebr.	*De ebrietate*
Flacc.	*In Flaccum*
Fug.	*De fuga et inventione*
Gig.	*De gigantibus*
Her.	*Quis rerum divinarum heres sit*
Hypoth.	*Hypothetica*
Ios.	*De Iosepho*
Leg. 1–3	*Legum allegoriae* I, II, III
Legat.	*Legatio ad Gaium*
Migr.	*De migratione Abrahami*
Mos. 1–2	*De vita Moysis* I, II
Mut.	*De mutatione nominum*
Opif.	*De opificio mundi*
Plant.	*De plantatione*
Post.	*De posteritate Caini*
Praem.	*De praemiis et poenis, De exsecrationibus*
Prob.	*Quod omnis probus liber sit*
Prov. 1–2	*De Providentia* I, II
QE 1–2	*Quaestiones et solutiones in Exodum* I, II
QG 1–4	*Quaestiones et solutiones in Genesim* I, II, III, IV
Sacr.	*De sacrificiis Abelis et Caini*
Sobr.	*De sobrietate*
Somn. 1–2	*De somniis* I, II
Spec. 1–4	*De specialibus legibus* I, II, III, IV
Virt.	*De virtutibus*

2. Journals and series

ALGHJ	Arbeiten zur Literatur und Geschichte des hellenistischen Judentums
ANRW	*Aufstieg und Niedergang der römischen Welt*
C-W	L. Cohn and P. Wendland (and S. Reiter), *Philonis Alexandrini opera quae supersunt*, 6 vols. (Berlin 1896–1915)
CPG	*Clavis Patrum Graecorum*
CPL	*Clavis Patrum Latinorum*
CRINT	Compendia Rerum Iudaicarum ad Novum Testamentum
CSEL	Corpus Scriptorum Ecclesiasticorum Latinorum
EPRO	Études préliminaires aux religions orientales dans l'Empire romain
GCS	Die griechischen christlichen Schriftsteller
G-G	H. L. Goodhart and E. R. Goodenough, 'A General Bibliography of Philo Judaeus', in E. R. Goodenough, *The Politics of Philo Judaeus* (New Haven 1938, repr. Hildesheim 1967²) 125–321
JThS	*The Journal of Theological Studies*
Lampe	G. W. H. Lampe (ed.), *A Patristic Greek Lexicon* (Oxford 1961)
LCL	Loeb Classical Library
LSJ	H. G. Liddell, R. Scott , H. S. Jones (edd.), *A Greek-English Lexicon* (Oxford 1940⁹)
PAPM	*Les œuvres de Philon d'Alexandrie,* French translation under the general editorship of R. Arnaldez, J. Pouilloux, C. Mondésert (Paris 1961-92)
PG	Patrologia Graeca, ed. J. P. Migne
PL	Patrologia Latina, ed. J. P. Migne
PLCL	*Philo in Ten Volumes (and Two Supplementary Volumes)*, English translation by F. H. Colson, G. H. Whitaker and R. Marcus, 12 vols., Loeb Classical Library (London 1929–62)
RAC	*Reallexikon für Antike und Christentum*
R-R	R. Radice and D. T. Runia, *Philo of Alexandria: an Annotated Bibliography 1937–1986* (Leiden 1988)
SC	Sources Chrétiennes
SPhA	*The Studia Philonica Annual*
TLG	Thesaurus Linguae Graecae
VC	*Vigiliae Christianae*
WUNT	Wissenschaftliche Untersuchungen zum Neuen Testament

CHAPTER ONE

PLATONISM, PHILONISM, AND THE BEGINNINGS OF CHRISTIAN THOUGHT

Inaugural address
University of Utrecht*

Rector Magnificus,
Members of the Board of the C. J. de Vogel Foundation
 for the Study of Ancient Philosophy,
Ladies and Gentlemen

Point of departure for my address this afternoon is a number of passages in the church father Augustine which relate to the biblical text Exodus 3:14–15. When Moses hears that he is being sent by God to the children of Israel in Egypt, he asks God the following question: when I say 'the God of your fathers sends me to you', and they say 'what is his name?', what should be my reply. The answer he receives is in the words of the Latin Bible which Augustine read:[1] *ego sum qui sum; sic dices filiis Israel: qui est, misit me ad vos* (I am who I am; thus you will speak to the children of Israel: he who is has sent me to you). Now please allow me to put you at ease. I am well aware that this biblical text suffers from over-exposure. It is, for philosophers at any rate, the best-known text in the entire Old Testament, and I would not dream of taking this text on its own as the subject of my address. This text, however, has a sequel in verse 15 which is much less well known: God spoke again to Moses: *haec dices filiis Israel: dominus deus patrum vestrorum, Deus Abraham, Deus Isaac, et Deus Jacob misit me ad vos; hoc nomen mihi est in aeternum; et hoc memoriale meum in*

---

* This inaugural address was delivered in the historic location of the Aula of the University of Utrecht on the 1st April 1992, when I formally accepted the invitation to the extra-ordinary chair of Ancient philosophy in the Faculty of Philosophy, with as special area of study the Platonist tradition in relation to early Christianity. The chair is endowed by the C. J. de Vogel Foundation for the Study of Ancient Philosophy.
[1] The text that Augustine reads here is more or less that of Jerome's Vulgate translation.

generationem et generationem (you will speak these words to the children of Israel: the Lord God of your fathers, the God of Abraham, the God of Isaac, the God of Jacob has sent me to you: this is my name in eternity, and this is my remembrance from generation to generation). What I first want to do is focus attention on the fact that in no less that five quite lengthy passages Augustine makes a
* *distinction* between these two divine pronouncements.[2]

In his commentary on Psalm 101:25 it is the words of the Psalmist *in generatione generationum anni tui* (your years are in the generation of generations) that cause Augustine through verbal association to recall the text Exodus 3:15. The years of God indicate his eternity. God's eternity is his substance, for he possesses nothing that is in any way changeable, no past, no future, only the present conveyed by the verb *est* (he is). This is the God who sends Moses forth. He asks the name of the One who is sending him. His request is not left unfulfilled, for the question is sound: it is posed not out of *curiositas* (curiosity) but out of a *necessitas ministrandi* (a need to minister to his people). My name, Moses learns, is the great *est*. But what is a man in comparison with this great *est*? How can he be a participant in it (*particeps eius*)? *Noli desperare, humana fragilitas,* do not despair, o human fragility: I am the God of Abraham, and the God of Isaac, and the God of Jacob. You have heard what I am for myself; hear also what I am for your sake.[3] In the case of Psalm 121 it is the words in verse 3, *Jerusalem cuius participatio eius in idipsum* (Jerusalem, whose participation is in it itself) and especially the difficult term *idipsum* (it itself) which induce Augustine to reflect on God as 'Being itself' and give our two texts a similar interpretation.[4] In the case of Psalm 134 the pretext for the discussion is different again. In verse 3 we read: 'Praise the Lord because he is good; sing psalms to his Name, for it is pleasing.' God takes the weakness of mankind into account: *ego sum qui sum* is my true, eternal name, but you do not understand it. For this reason I give you my temporal name, *Deus Abraham et Deus Isaac et Deus Iacob.* But at the same time this is my name *in aeternum* (to eternity, as in the biblical text), because it leads man to eternal life. The patriarchs were not eternal, but God

---

[2] The texts are too long to cite in their entirety, or even to paraphrase adequately.

[3] *Enarr. in Psalmum* 101, 2.10, CCL 40.1445.14–55; see also 2.14, 1449.36–46.

[4] *Enarr. in Psalmum* 121, 5, 1805.11–54.

has made them such: they had a beginning, but they will not experience an end.[5] In two of his sermons as well Augustine develops the distinction between the two divine names: the one is a *nomen incommutabilitatis* (name of immutability) or a *nomen substantiae* (name of substance), the other a *nomen misericordiae* (name of mercy, i.e. towards mankind).[6]

Above his bookcase filled with the works of Augustine Isidore of Seville placed the epigram: 'he who claims to have read you entire is a liar'.[7] The texts I have just cited did not gain my attention as the result of an extensive exploration through the mighty *œuvre* of the bishop of Hippo. In this context it is entirely appropriate to indicate where I did come across them, namely in an article written by the late Professor C. J. de Vogel, who in 1958 published an important essay on 'Antike Seinsfilosofie und Christentum im Wandel der Jahrhunderte'.[8] In a sensitive *In memoriam* in honour of this remarkable scholar, her successor to the Utrecht chair wrote: 'In fact it is quite apparent that De Vogel had mastered the entire terrain of Greek philosophy'.[9] The same can also without doubt be said for the equally daunting field of Patristic philosophy. She has set an example that inspires us to emulation, even if few of us will be under the illusion that we might be able to match her achievement.

There is, however, another question we might wish to pose: does this exegesis of Exodus 3:15 occur for the first time in Augustine, or did he take it over from an exegetical predecessor? It is remarkable fact that, although Exodus 3:14 is cited by the church fathers on numerous occasions,[10] the following verse receives almost no attention at all.[11] And with regard to the *distinction* that Augustine makes between the pronouncements in the two texts the situation is even more striking. This exegesis is, as far as I can tell, not found in any

---

[5] *Enarr. in Psalmum* 134, 6, 1942.9–43.

[6] *Sermo* 7.7, CCL 41.75.156–194; *Sermo* 2.5, PL 46.825–6.

[7] PL 83.1109, cited by Brown (1972) 25.

[8] De Vogel (1958) 8–9; the same texts are cited in *eadem* (1973) 249–51.

[9] Mansfeld (1986) 293–294.

[10] Extensive analyses of the patristic use of Ex. 3:14 can be found in the diverse articles in Vignaux (1978).

[11] This can easily be checked for Greek authors up to the 4th century in *Biblia Patristica*, Aa. vv. (1975–91). The question is complicated by the fact that Ex. 3:6 strongly resembles 3:15 and sometimes replaces the other text, also in Augustine.

church father before Augustine (with one partial exception which I shall mention later[12]). A comparable interpretation is found, however, in an author who is in fact no church father, but who for a long time was regarded as such *honoris causa*, namely the Jewish exegete and philosopher Philo of Alexandria.

Twice in his extensive corpus of writings Philo explicitly distinguishes between the divine pronouncements in Exodus 3:14 and 3:15.[13] In his *Life of Moses*, written for a broad public, he gives the following paraphrase: 'First tell them [i.e. your people] that I am the he who is, so that they may learn the distinction between being and non-being, and also be taught that no name at all properly describes me... But if through their natural weakness they seek a title, reveal to them not only this, that I am God, but also that I am the God of the three men whose names express their excellence, God of Abraham and God of Isaac and God of Jacob.'[14] The second passage, located in the allegorical treatise *On the change of names*, gives a deeper philosophical analysis. God as Being is not comprehensible to the human mind. This also means that no name can properly be predicated of him. God's nature is to be, and not to be spoken of. But in order that the human race should not be deprived of a title for the One who is supremely good, he grants through misuse of language, as if it were a proper name, the title 'Lord God of the three natures of teaching, perfection and practice, Abraham Isaac Jacob.' Philo here connects the statement in Exodus 3:15 with the words in Exodus 6:3, which he interprets as 'I appeared to Abraham and Isaac and Jacob as their God, but my proper name I did not reveal to them'.[15] In the *Life of Abraham* there is a third text relevant to our subject, but here only the text Exodus 3:15 is dealt with. God honours the patriarchs by joining his name to their names: God of Abraham and God of Isaac and God of Jacob, that is to say, instead of the absolute the relative. God himself is in no need of a name,

---

[12] See below n. 78.

[13] For Philo's writings I use the standard abbreviations as listed in Runia (1986) xi.

[14] *Mos.* 1.75–76. This passage is paraphrased in turn by Ps.Justin, *Coh. ad Gr.* 21.1, 51.1–9 Marcovich, but the reference to Exodus 3:15 is not taken over. Both passages are then excerpted by Johannes Damascenus, *Sacra Parallela* cod. Cois. 276, f.223ᵛ; see Cohn-Wendland (1896–1915) 3.137, Marcovich (1990) 51.

[15] *Mut.* 11–14; on this highly complex passage see my analysis at Runia (1988) 76–78. The terms teaching, perfection and practice refer to Philo's standard allegorical schema for the patriarchs.

but nevertheless he grants to the race of men a suitable appellation, so that they will not be deprived of hope and kindness.[16]

What, we may now ask, is the relation between the two authors we have cited so far? As is well known, it cannot be maintained that our North African church father had a really extensive knowledge of literature from the Greek-speaking East.[17] But Philo is certainly not totally unknown to him. In the work written against the Manichean Faustus in about 398 he names Philo expressly as a *vir liberaliter eruditissimus, unus illorum, cuius eloquium Graeci Platoni aequare non dubitant* (one who belongs to the Jewish camp, a man of exceedingly wide learning, whose style the Greeks do not hesitate to equate with Plato's).[18] But, in spite of this positive verdict, to which we will re-turn in a moment, the tenor of Augustine's report is for the most part negative. Philo is a prime example of what happens if one, just like Faustus, does not interpret the Old Testament in a Christo-centric manner. Take for example the exposition of the design and measurements of Noah's ark. These he interprets allegorically in terms of the proportions of the human body. For a little while all goes well, for Christ too had a human body. But when he comes to the door which is made in the side of the ark, things goes badly wrong for our Jewish exegete. He dares to explain this door in terms of the lower parts of the body, which have the function of removing urine and excrement. This is quite unacceptable. If he had crossed over to Christ, he would have perceived that the door is a symbol of the sacraments of the church, which streamed out of Christ's side on the cross.

The passage to which Augustine refers is found at the beginning of the second book of Philo's work *Questions and Answers on Genesis,* which in its entirety has only been preserved in an Armenian trans-lation.[19] How did the Latin church father come to know about this passage? The German Patristic scholar Altaner was convinced that Augustine had read Philo in a Latin translation.[20] He draws our

---

[16] *Abr.* 51.

[17] Courcelle (1969) 196ff.

[18] *Contra Faustum* 12.39 (text printed at Cohn-Wendland (1896–1915) 1.cv; for the dating see Brown (1967) 185.

[19] *QG* 2.1–7; Augustine refers to the same text without naming the source at *De civitate Dei* 15.26.

[20] Altaner (1941).

attention to the fact that there is still extant a Latin translation of
Book VI of this work, which is dated to the fourth century. Originally
the translation must have covered more of the work, and was consulted by Augustine.[21] This conclusion was energetically contested by
Courcelle, who tried to demonstrate that Ambrose was the intermediate source. Augustine would have known that the bishop of
Milan had taken over an enormous amount of material from Philo,
including the explanation of the door of the ark which Augustine
found so distressing. Criticism of Philo is thus meant as indirect
criticism of Ambrose, who in Augustine's view too easily appropriated non-Christocentric allegorical exegesis for his own use.[22] But
about ten years ago an unexpected development took place. The
original Greek text of precisely these seven Questions on the ark of
Noah turned up in a manuscript on Mt Athos. The scholar who
edited this discovery, Paramelle, was able to show on philological
grounds that it was highly probable that Augustine made use of a
translation that adhered closely to the original Greek text.[23]

Nevertheless it would be premature to conclude that the positive
remark about Philo that Augustine gives at the beginning of the
passage under discussion is based on a thorough study of his work. It
is in fact taken over from the short biographical sketch written by
Jerome in his *De viris illustribus*, where Philo, together with Seneca
and Josephus, receives a place of honour among the leading figures
of early Christianity. It is in Jerome's work that we also read for the
first time the striking *bon mot* which apparently circulated among the
Greeks and to which Augustine makes an allusion: ἢ Πλάτων
φιλωνίζει ἢ Φίλων πλατωνίζει (either Plato philonizes or Philo
platonizes). Jerome gives a free translation and adds a brief
comment: 'Either Plato follows Philo or Philo follows Plato, so great
is the similarity of thought and style.'[24] Naturally it would be quite
naive to think that the church fathers were unaware that Philo lived
long after Plato, and that it was quite out of the question that Plato
should in any way be indebted to him. What the *bon mot* wishes to say

---

[21] See also the edition of this work by Petit (1973), en esp. 1.7.
[22] Courcelle (1969) 197–198 (written in 1943), and returning to the same
subject (1961).
[23] Paramelle (1984), esp. 111–121.
[24] *De viris illustribus* 11; cf. also the biography of the evangelist Mark, where
Philo is described as *disertissimus Iudaeorum* (§8.4). On this *bon mot* see further
Billings (1919) 2, Runia (1991a) 315.

is something like the following: the resemblances between the two great thinkers is so marked that it is difficult to determine who is the master and who is the pupil. We might compare the often quoted remark that Marsilius Ficino, the founder of the Florentine Academia Platonica, was an *alter Plato*. Because the names Plato and Philo are rather similar, it was possible to use the verbs derived from them to make an elegant play on words. The denominative verb πλατων-ίζειν is rare.[25] Such verbs indicate that the language, style, or views of another group or person are taken over: compare ἑλληνίζω, ἀττικίζω, and closer to home, ἀριστοτελίζω (used by Strabo of Posidonius).[26] I am in disagreement with Dörrie when he claims that these verbs generally have a negative connotation, and that in the case of our *bon mot* Philo is *accused* by the church fathers of being a Platonist.[27] But there is a difference of opinion among them whether the *bon mot* only applies to *style*, or whether it also refers to the *content* of their thought. We observe that in this respect Augustine silently corrects his source Jerome. The similarity has to do with *eloquium* (language or style), not *sensus* (thoughts).[28]

It is apparent, dear listeners, that at the end of the fourth century various church fathers, both in the East and in the West, were aware of two facts: firstly, that there was an affinity between the writings and thought-world of Philo and the Platonist tradition; secondly, that Philo had featured in some way or other in the beginnings of Christian thought. This result brings us at last, via a long but hopefully not uninteresting detour, to the subject that I wish to broach in my oration this afternoon: *to what extent may we affirm that the Jew Philo played an important, or even a decisive, role in the development of Christian thought?* Ever since the completion of my dissertation on the subject of Philo's Platonism, this related theme has been one of the focal points of my research. The ceremony this afternoon seemed a excellent occasion to present to you a number of the results that I have reached.

My theme has certainly not received an excessive amount of attention in recent times. Nearly every introductory work on Philo

---

[25] Elsewhere only in Origen, *Contra Celsum* 4.83.

[26] *Geog.* 2.3.8; cf. also ἡρακλειτίζω in Aristotle *Met.* Γ 5, 1010a11 (on Cratylus).

[27] Dörrie (1972) 509–510; the term he uses is 'Vorwurf'. Sandbach (1985) 80 concludes that these words indicate 'conscious imitation'.

[28] See above at n. 18.

ends with the statement that his works were preserved because they were taken up in the Christian tradition. If the matter had been left in the hands of his fellow Jews, these works would have been swept away by the effects of time and decay, together with almost the entire rich tradition of Jewish-Alexandrian literature.[29]

But the question is much less often regarded from the other point of view: what did it mean for the development of Christian thought that, at the moment that the early Christians began to re- flect on what their faith meant, there already existed in their direct proximity a solid tradition which had for some time been engaged in a confrontation of biblical tradition with Greek philosophy? Partly this relative neglect can be explained by the fact that it concerns an awkward question which has proved difficult to tackle properly. Other reasons might also be given. But fortunately there have also been exceptions. Because I am pressed for time, I will now only mention the patrona of the chair which I am taking up.

In the monumental third volume of her *Greek Philosophy*, written in the years from 1953 to 1959, Professor De Vogel pays a surprising amount of attention to the thought of Philo, even though the subject of Patristic thought is entirely excluded from her collection of texts. Partly the reason for this is that Philo is an important wit- ness to what she still called 'Prae-Neoplatonism' (now usually called Middle Platonism).[30] But this is not how she begins her treatment:[31] 'With Philo a new element comes into the history of philosophy, namely Revelation. Since, however, Philo was an Alexandrian Jew of Hellenistic culture, bred in the Greek philosophy of his age, the question arises as to what prevails in his thought: either Revelation in Scripture or Greek philosophy.' Her way of formulating the problem betrays, in my view, the strong influence of Jewish-Ameri- can historian of philosophy, Wolfson. In his magisterial two-volumed study published in 1947 Wolfson defended the thesis that Philo was the father of medieval philosophy, which he rather idiosyncratically defined as the system of religious philosophy established by Philo and destroyed by Spinoza, in which reason is subordinated to faith.[32]

---

*   [29] This fascinating story has as yet not been told in an accessible way. For a brief account and a chronological diagram see Runia (1991b) 43–47.
     [30] De Vogel (1950–59) 3.353–376.
     [31] De Vogel (1950–59) 3.353.
     [32] Wolfson (1947) *passim*, and esp. 87–199. The thesis is applied to the philo- sophy of the church fathers in a subsequent study, Wolfson (1956). This work

Professor De Vogel criticizes this view, and also criticizes Philo himself, because the distinction which he made between natural Reason and Revelation (her capitals) was not clear enough. Some thirty years later, however, in her last extended article entitled 'Platonism and Christianity' she returned to this subject. Her attitude to Philo is now much more positive. Philo stands at the beginning of a new era. The church fathers took over many of his ideas, not only various fundamental philosophical themes, but also the insight that philosophy is not just an affair of the intellect only, but engages one's entire religious or spiritual life.[33]

The position of Professor De Vogel illustrates a paradoxical fact. Even though Philo is often regarded as a theologian rather than a philosopher (but this largely depends of course on how one understands the terms),[34] in scholarly discussions it is precisely the historians of philosophy who tend to attribute to him an important role in the development of Christian thought, whereas the historians of theology are much more reticent, or even remain wholly silent. It would be easy to give examples of this,[35] but we must press on.

But before I return to our main question, there is still one matter that briefly requires out attention. Earlier I remarked that our question is rather awkward and difficult to tackle. Why is this the case? The difficulty of determining the role that Philo played at the beginning of Christian thought and the widely divergent answers that are given to this question result from the fact that a conflict can very easily arise between an historical and a systematic approach to the question. As I observed earlier, the Philonic corpus was saved from total destruction by the efforts of the early Christians. It would

---

begins with a perspective on the beginnings of the Christian movement as seen—in a highly speculative manner—through the eyes of Philo.

[33] De Vogel (1985) 7–18. See also her concise history of patristic philosophy, (1970) 14 (my translation): 'Philo, who in his own person brought Jewish faith and Greek thought together in a profound spiritual unity'.

[34] Bousset-Gressmann (1926) 445 name him 'the first theologian', Daniélou (1961) 'the first theologian of transcendence'.

* [35] For example the Australian theologian Eric Osborn, who in his fine monograph on the beginnings of Christian philosophy, Osborn (1981), scarcely mentions Philo. Christian philosophy begins with the speech of Paul in Acts of the Apostles. Philo is only important if you look at the terms and not at the arguments (241ff., with sound criticisms of Wolfson). In an article on Philo and Clement, Osborn (1987) 36, he cites the view of Chadwick (1966) 142 that Clement makes frequent 'minor borrowings' from Philo, but that 'his main problems are different from Philo's and are approached from quite a different angle.'

seem obvious, to start with an investigation into the preservation and reception of Philo's works in this tradition. The first step then must be to distinguish between a *direct* and an *indirect* line of transmission. The *direct* line is the more easily dealt with. Philo is first explicitly mentioned and cited by Clement of Alexandria, who appropriates large sections of his writings.[36] After that he is referred to in a large number of Patristic authors. The dissemination of Philonic ideas in Patristic authors is greater than is often thought. But here too there are considerable problems. Very often direct citations are not a very sound guide to the way sources are exploited in Patristic works. An extreme case is furnished by of Ambrose, who uses Philo on about 600 occasions—often in a way that we would regard as plagiarism—, but only refers to him on a single occasion.[37]

But it is not very likely that all these fathers made a direct and intensive study of Philo's works. Another possibility is that his ideas were transmitted in an *indirect* manner. This occurs especially via the Alexandrian tradition of Clement, Origen and Didymus, and to a lesser degree via the works of the brothers Basil and Gregory of Nyssa, which were later extensively read in Byzantium. Above all Origen's great (but lost) *Commentary on Genesis* is thought to have played a central role in the appropriation and transmission of certain Philonic philosophical themes in the exegetical tradition.[38] It is a remarkable and little observed aspect of both the Hellenistic-Jewish and Christian exegetical tradition that names of individual exegetes are seldom mentioned, in marked contrast to the Rabbinic tradition, but also to that of the Platonist commentators, where names of predecessors occur on almost every page.[39] This means that later interpreters often had no idea of the actual origin of ideas that they report and utilize. Thomas Aquinas, for example, will not have known, when he cites the *De fide* of John of Damascus in his chapter on the divine names in the *Summa Theologia*, that the Greek church father took over a term from one of the Philonic passages on Exodus 3:15 that we cited at the outset of our address.[40]

---

[36] See now the excellent analysis by Van den Hoek (1988).

[37] I derive the statistic from Lucchesi (1977) 7; see also the extensive monograph of Savon (1977), and his summary in Savon (1984).

[38] E.g. in the reference to *Hebraei* in Calcidius and Nemesius.

[39] See some inadequate remarks on this at Runia (1986) 505.

[40] *Summa Theologiae* I, 13.11, where Thomas cites *Expositio Fidei* §9. This passage reads in the original Greek: δοκεῖ μὲν οὖν κυριώτερον πάντων τῶν ἐπὶ θεοῦ λεγομένων ὀνομάτων εἶναι ὁ ὤν, καθὼς αὐτὸς χρηματίζων τῷ Μωσεῖ ἐπὶ τοῦ ὄρους

Now, if the difficulties we face were confined to the unravelling of a direct and an indirect tradition, then matters would still be reasonably under control. But there is a further complication. Before we reach Clement there are a number of early Christian writers who do not mention by Philo by name, and whose writings do not allow us to prove beyond all reasonable doubt that they had read his books. Yet they do mention themes that are so closely related to Philonic thought that some kind of relationship cannot possibly be denied.[41] The same can be said—with all due caution—of the New Testament.[42] For this reason I am compelled to propose a *third* tradition, which I call the *broader* or *general* tradition. This third line of transmission is caused by the fact that Philo was without doubt the greatest and best-known exponent of Hellenistic-Jewish thought, but he did not stand alone. The anonymity of the exegetical tradition means that he is indebted to a broader current of thought, which also exercised an influence outside the direct line of his works.[43] Because this rich literature has almost entirely disappeared, we are unable to reconstruct its precise contours, and are left guessing as to the influence it may have had.

What should one do in this situation? If I take only the direct and indirect line of transmission, I will be leaving out of consideration a number of important stimuli for the appropriation of explicitly Philonic material in the subsequent tradition. On the other hand I cannot simply attribute the broader tradition to Philo, not only because this would be irresponsible from the historical point of view, but also because it would then be easy to lose sight of what is

φησιν· «εἶπον τοῖς υἱοῖς Ἰσραήλ, ὁ ὢν ἀπέσταλκέ με». ὅλον γὰρ ἐν ἑαυτῷ συλλαβὼν ἔχει τὸ εἶναι οἷόν τι πέλαγος οὐσίας ἄπειρον καὶ ἀόριστον. The expression κυριώτερον πάντων τῶν ἐπὶ θεοῦ λεγομένων ὀνομάτων is to be explained via Philo *Mut.* 11–14, which John cites in his *Sacra Parallela* (see above n. 14).

*   [41] This entire question will be dealt with in greater detail in my study *Philo and Early Christian Literature: a Survey*, which will be published soon. Especially in the case of Justin and Theophilus the question whether they knew of and used Philo is extremely delicate. On Philo and Theophilus see now the study of Martín (1990a).

[42] For example the εἰκών christology in the Epistle to the Colossians and the notable dualism of the Epistle to the Hebrews, which in my view cannot be *entirely* explained in eschatological terms.

[43] Since Bousset (1915) it has been customary to speak of an Alexandrian school, although in my view this should not be understood in any kind of institutional sense. Recently Philo's relation to earlier exegetical traditions has been thoroughly researched by Tobin (1983) and Goulet (1987). I cannot accept all the conclusions of these two studies; see my discussions in Runia (1986) 556–558 and (1989).

specifically Philonic. The solution which I tentatively suggest this afternoon is the distinction between Philo and Philonism. Philo, we have seen, is the most important and most vital representative of a wider movement, in which the biblical tradition was first brought in direct contact with the philosophical thought that was developed in Greek culture. In actual fact this movement goes back at least as far as the translators of the Septuagint. They made various striking choices, which certainly would have been different without the philosophical tradition in the background, as for example in the case of the divine name ὁ ὤν (he who is).[44] It is on account of this
* wider background that I have adopted the term Philonism, and not the name Philo, in the title of my address.

We now finally return to our question, now posed in a slightly modified form: to what extent did Philonism play an important role in the development of early Christian thought? It is possible in my view to give at least four answers to this question. It goes without saying that these can now only be presented and discussed in very general terms.

(1) At the end of his most well-known work, *De opificio mundi*, Philo names five δόγματα (doctrines), knowledge of which is a guarantee for a pious and felicitous life: that God exists, that He is One, that he created the cosmos, that this cosmos is unique just as its Maker, and that He always exercises providence for what he has made.[45] Goodenough once called this passage 'the first creed of history', and recently Mendelson has ventured to speak of a 'concept of orthodoxy' that is essential to the preservation of Jewish identity.[46] Might it be legitimate to see Philonism as the origin of a *dogmatism* that was to distinguish Christianity from subsequent (Rabbinic) Judaism and also from pagan thought? In my view a distinction is required here. Philo is not a dogmatician in the manner of an Athanasius or a Basil, or even of an Origen.[47] He does not regard

---

[44] See Hengel (1974) 162–163 and notes; Harl-Dorival-Munnich (1988) 255–258. This pre-Christian process of hellenization is recognized by Bos (1991) 90–91.

[45] *Opif.* 172.

[46] Goodenough (1940) 43; Mendelson (1988) 29. For Wolfson (1947) 1.164 this passage supplies five of the eight articles of his 'preamble of faith'. It is striking, however, that for four of the five Philo delivers arguments in their support.

[47] On the background of the concept 'dogma' in the early Christian tradition

himself as subjected to something like an ecclesiastical tradition, a *regula fidei*, but rather as connected to a tradition of exposition of the Mosaic philosophy, a tradition in which he claims for himself no more than a modest role. On the other hand he is an intellectual, to use a slightly anachronistic modern term, with a tendency towards an intellectual re-interpretation of his religious heritage. He takes Plato as his model when he is prepared, in theory at least, to ban certain directions of thought.[48] The *praxis* of being Jewish is not to be neglected, but it is less important than the *theoria.*

(2) Photius, the learned ninth-century Patriarch of Constantinople, tells us in his *Bibliotheca* that he read various Philonic treatises, very many of which contained interpretations that forced scripture into an allegorical mode. Starting from this man, he continues, the entire allegorical method of reading scripture began to pour into the church.[49] This observation is essentially correct, and even more so if we broaden Philo to Philonism.[50] The writings of Philo furnish the church fathers with numerous allegorical themes and schemes, especially in the area of physical (or cosmological), psychological and moral exposition. Augustine too, as we saw, recognizes Philo's use of the allegorical method. Despite our modern reservations towards this method,[51] it is wise not to overlook its attractive aspects. These are primarily two in number. The first is only too well known: it allows the interpreter to connect up with and exploit contemporary philosophical ideas.[52] The second is more subtle: it also allows the interpreter to preserve at least partly the narrative element of the biblical text, but then at the more general

---

see the analysis of O'Cleirigh (1980) 205–210. In n. 49 he cites Fascher (1959) 6: 'Man darf wohl sagen, daß Philon in der Hellenisierung des AT und des Judentums so viel vorgearbeitet hat, daß die zweite und dritte Generation der Christen schon ein Feld bereitet fand, auf dem die Hellenisierung der Lehre Christi als 'Dogma' fortgesetzt werden konnte'. This is in itself correct, but formulated too generally.

[48] Compare *Spec.* 1.327–345 with Plato *Laws* X, esp. 885b.

[49] *Cod.* 105, 2.72.9–11 Henry: τὰ πλεῖστα πρὸς ἀλληγορίαν τοῦ γράμματος ἐκβιαζόμενα· ἐξ οὗ, οἶμαι, καὶ πᾶς ἀλληγορικὸς τῆς γραφῆς ἐν τῇ ἐκκλησίᾳ λόγος ἀρχὴν ἔσχεν εἰσρυῆναι.

[50] For allegorical interpretation in the period from the Apostolic fathers to Clement see Hanson (1959) 103–117.

[51] They have lessened in postmodern literary theory.

[52] Recent studies in Pépin (1987) 7–40, Dawson (1992) 73–126. Dawson affirms: '...for Philo allegorical interpretation is an effort to make Greek culture Jewish rather than to dissolve Jewish identity into Greek culture.' The philosophical aspect is here insufficiently taken into account.

level of the quest of the soul for God.[53] On the other hand, the role of allegory should not be exaggerated. Its role is primarily *instrumental*. Even in the case of the great allegorizer Philo it is possible to discern a reaction against excesses in his Alexandrian environment. It is very significant, for example, that he refuses to allegorize God himself.[54]

(3) We draw closer to the epicentre of our question when we observe that Philo (together with others before and after him) takes the crucial step of selecting the Platonic paradigm[55] of being and becoming, immutability and change, knowledge and ignorance as the system of thought most suitable for the task of expounding and interpreting the truth revealed to Moses. In my dissertation I defended the thesis that Philo is no Platonist. Both the requisite loyalty and the feeling of obligation to incorporate as many as possible of the details of the system are missing.[56] I still believe this view is correct. But at the same time I added that Platonism remains for Philo a pillar of his thought which, if removed, would cause the whole edifice to totter and perhaps even collapse. This complex attitude—no loyalty, but often admiration, occasional hostility, but time and time again demonstrable dependence—is also characteristic of how Platonism would fare in early Christian thought.

(4) But not all has yet been said. In my view we have to take still one more step before we can get the Philonic contribution to early Christian thought in full perspective. This can be made clear by focusing on one striking example, the case of Clement of Alexandria, who, as we saw, was the first Christian to refer to Philo by name. According to tradition he was born in Athens. We cannot be sure of this, but what it symbolizes is very probable, that he learnt his philosophy before he became a Christian.[57] After long *Wanderjahre*

---

[53] Well seen by Dawson (1992) 122–124; but his claim (3–4) that allegory always has a narrative element goes too far. In physical allegory, for example, it is wholly absent.

[54] See esp. the radical analysis of Goulet (1987) and my observations in Runia (1989) 596. On pp. 154, 259, 386 Goulet demonstrates that in texts such as *Leg.* 3.222, *Migr.* 128, *Fug.* 168 remnants can be detected of an interpretation in which God is taken to represent the ὀρθὸς λόγος.

[55] It seems to me legitimate to take over the Kuhnian term, even though I am well aware that it is far from clear how it should be applied to ancient thought and that it has been used in many different ways.

[56] Runia (1986) 518–519.

[57] For Von Campenhausen (1963) 26 the information *is no more* than symbolic, but Méhat (1966) 43 rightly points out that this too is not certain.

he found the master whom he sought, Pantaenus, teacher in the Alexandrian church. Presumably it was here that Clement made acquaintance with the works of Philo. What did he learn from them? Not his Platonism, for that he already knew well enough. What he learnt was how a link could be established between Platonist ideas and the contents of scripture. It is this, I submit, that forms the greatest contribution of Philonism to the beginnings of Christian thought. It showed how insights from the Greek philosophical tradition could be localized in the authoritative words of scripture. For Philo scripture was limited to the books of Moses. In his choice of the Platonist paradigm it would seem that the following four clusters of texts from these books played a decisive role:

(a) the title of the first book of the bible, Genesis, and the striking similarities between the Mosaic creation account and the Platonic cosmogony in the *Timaeus* and in Platonist handbooks;[58]

(b) the creation of man 'according God's image' in Gen. 1:26–27;[59]

(c) the encounter of Moses with God (or his angel) on Mt Horeb and the revelation of the name 'I am he who is';[60]

(d) the texts that describe Moses' ascent of Mt Sinai, where he has intimate contact with God, but is not allowed to see his face.[61]

It is noteworthy that for all these texts the allegorical method of interpretation was not of decisive importance.

I summarize the results so far. The history of Philonism in the church fathers is the process in which a long sequence of apologists and theologians takes over themes and ideas from Philo and the broader Hellenistic-Jewish tradition. These ideas are seldom *abstractly* philosophical. They are connected to the exposition of the biblical text or—as occurs later—introduced in polemical dogmatic discussions. In this process of appropriation a bass note of Platonist thought nearly always makes its presence felt. It reminds me of the Scottish bagpipes I used to hear when I attended a Presbyterian school as a boy. The droning note of the bass did not attract much attention, but it was always there.

---

[58] Extensive analysis in Runia (1986); see esp. 92–94 on *Opif.* 12.

[59] See Runia (1986) 334–340, 471–472.

[60] Philo's exegesis of Ex. 3:14 is analysed by Starobinski-Safran (1978). According to Martín (1990b) 153 the exegesis of this text forms the nucleus of Philo's thought.

[61] For Philo's exegesis of Ex. 20:21 and Ex. 33:13–23, as given esp. at *Post.* 8–21, 168–169, *Spec.* 1.32–50, see Montes-Peral (1987) 150 and *passim.*

A further question cannot now be avoided: what should we think of this development and its consequences? The question is indissolubly tied to the problem of the Hellenization of Christianity, in which— remarkably enough—a Jewish tradition acts as pacemaker for the Hellenization. Here, as we all know, the verdicts are sharply divided. The two extremes are represented by the liberal theologian Harnack, for whom this process was 'bedauerlich aber notwendig',[62] and the orthodox believer De Vogel, for whom it was no less inevitable, but the result of providential intervention.[63]

I agree with these two great scholars that in retrospect the process of Hellenization was inevitable. By this I do not wish to say that it could not have gone differently. This is a matter of pure speculation. What I want to emphasize is that Christianity could not have become the Christianity that we know, if it had not accepted the challenge posed by Greek philosophy with its trust in a world-view based on rational thought.[64] Harnack's position is untenable, because it means one has to saw off the branch on which one is sitting.[65] The process of Hellenization took place, but it did not penetrate to Christianity's heart. This heart is to be located in the Gospel, and within it, at the cross of Jesus Christ. This nucleus stays out of the reach of both Philonism and Platonism.

But there is the further question that should be posed: once the challenge had been accepted, was it inevitable that the choice would be made in favour of Platonism? Professor de Vogel was profoundly convinced that this was the case. But we might reply that the statement 'I am he who is' is by no means the only pronouncement in the Bible which might be used for foundational purposes. One thinks of others such as God is fire, God is One, God is spirit, God is light, I am the truth, to name merely the most familiar.[66] The first two are located in the Septuagint, and so were available to Philo. It is most striking that he never explicitly cites or even alludes to the first

---

[62] Harnack (1909) 1.20–21, Meijering (1985) 20–21.

[63] Cf. for example her statement in De Vogel (1977) 96 (my translation): 'The revelation of God in Christ has been made known to us in Greek. The transition from a Semitic language to Greek is made in the New Testament itself, and was thus part of God's salvation plan.'

[64] Excellent formulation of this view recently by Adriaanse (1991) 83.

[65] This also applies to his attempt to defend it by introducing the distinction between the role of the historian and the theologian (cf. Meijering (1985) 21).

[66] Deut. 4:24, Deut. 6:4, John 4:24, 1 John 1:5, 1 John 4:8, John 14:6.

words of the *shema*.[67] And it occurs only once that he ventures to cite the second text, that God is a consuming fire, arguing that as fire God is constructive, not destructive, i.e. he completely uses up the elements as material for his creative work. It seems to me that Philo must have felt uneasy about this interpretation, even though it tries valiantly to remove the danger of Stoic materialistic theology by describing the creative process in Platonic terms. It remains an isolated passage.[68] Clement follows him in his general approach, arguing that this text only gives a image of God's activity or power.[69]

Why then did Platonism win out? I find the historical or historistic answer that the *Zeitgeist* scarcely gave the first Christians any other option unsatisfactory.[70] A comparison with the beginnings of Islamic thought is in this respect highly instructive. The first Arabic philosophers, the Asharitic school of the *Mutakallimun* chose not to follow the path of Plato and Aristotle, but opted for a philosophy which combined a rigorous conception of divine omnipotence with a purely atomistic theory of the natural world.[71] The church fathers could have gone in different directions, but preferred to follow the Platonist path which Philonism had opened up for them.

Why was this path so attractive for them? Partly I go along with Meijering, when he argues that Platonist ontology, with its emphasis on the immutability of the highest Being, gave expression to the conviction of God's faithfulness and reliability, that He *is* from eternity and will not abandon the works of his hands.[72] In Philo's case, however, another conviction was even more important in my view, and it exerted a powerful influence on the church fathers after him, namely the conviction of God's *exaltedness*, or, to express it in

---

[67] I do not see an allusion at *Spec.* 1.30, as suggested by *Biblia Patristica*, Aa. vv. (1975–91), Supplément 83.
[68] *De Deo* 7. See the commentary of Siegert (1988) 103ff., who adduces *QE* 2.47, where Philo denies that fire belongs to God's essence.
[69] *Ecl. Proph.* 26, 144.10–19 Stählin-Treu, cited by Siegert (1988) 103.
[70] Cf. Meijering (1974) 27: 'Als kinder ihrer vom platonischen Geist geprägten Zeit waren die Kirchenväter... genötigt, das Credo so zu interpretieren, dass es ihrem eigenen Platonismus... nicht all zu sehr widersprach.'; cf. also Armstrong (1980) 79: 'The most important part of intellectual self-definition in relation to Hellenic culture undertaken by educated Christians from the second century onwards was the determination of what they could accept and what they must reject in contemporary Platonic-Pythagorean tradition.'
[71] Summary of their doctrine at Maimonides, *Guide of the Perplexed* 1.73. Exhaustive analysis in Wolfson (1976).
[72] Meijering (1968) 186–189; but his psychologizing remarks on Athanasius are less successful.

more philosophical terms, his *transcendence*. God, as he really is, is known only to himself (and to his Son, as the church fathers would immediately add, because the latter is ὁμοούσιος). God's essence is not accessible to man. What the human mind can comprehend is disclosed to it. In almost aphoristic terms Philo places this view in God's mouth, when Moses asks him to reveal himself: χαρίζομαι τὰ οἰκεῖα τῷ ληψομένῳ (I bestow what is appropriate for the one who is to receive it).[73] The Cappadocian father Gregory of Nyssa was strongly attracted to Philo's exegesis of Moses' double ascent up the mountain, and takes over the idea that God's essence transcends all forms of creaturely knowledge.[74] But Gregory gives the interaction a greater dynamism than we find in Philo:[75] 'Moses beseeches God to appear to him, not according to his capacity to partake, but according to God's true Being... The munificence of God assented to the fulfilment of his desire, but did not promise any cessation or satiety of the desire... Thus what Moses yearned for is satisfied by the very things which leave his desire unsatisfied. He learns from what was said that the Divine is by its very nature infinite, enclosed by no boundary.'

Gregory goes further than Philo in the correlation that he posits between God's transcendence and his infinity (in Philo the ancient *horror infiniti* has not yet been surmounted).[76] He does retain the central thesis of Philonism that God is Being, and is not *beyond* being, as promulgated in the Neoplatonism that he knew so well. This is not just a matter of loyalty towards scripture, but also has philosophical significance. If the Origin of all things is beyond being, then the relation to that which is after the Origin, created being, is endangered. If the Origin is true Being, then he remains in the fullness of his essence unreachable,[77] but his knowability is

---

[73] *Spec.* 1.43.

[74] See *De vita Moysis* 2.162–163; Gregory emphasizes, with reference to John 1:18, that this applies not only to man, but to every rational creature.

[75] *De vita Moysis* 2.230, 232, 235–236, citing the translation of Malherbe-Ferguson (1978).

[76] Convincingly demonstrated by Mühlenberg (1966) 58–64. Contra, for example, Armstrong-Marcus (1960) 10: 'The Greeks are very shy of attributing infinity to God, though it seems to us naturally and necessarily implied by this way of thinking. The Christians, in this following Philo the Jew of Alexandria, speak of God as infinite without any hesitation or qualification.' Compare the text of Johannes Damascenus cited in n. 40, where he speaks of 'an unlimited and infinite ocean of being'.

[77] All the church fathers agree on this (but contrast Eunomius cited in n. 79).

guaranteed through his relation to that which comes after him. What we have here is the metaphysics of 'self-disclosure'.[78]

It is clear that further problems lurk in the background here. Firstly there is the problem of the acceptability of the *analogia entis* that this philosophical approach assumes. I cannot possibly embark on this question now. Secondly we might wish to conclude that in this tradition of Philonism, which Gregory for the most part wishes to take over, there is a tendency to a far-reaching intellectualism, that is to say, that the primary goal is to gain knowledge of God, and not to encounter him in a personal relationship. A third problem does not affect Philo, but it does concern Christian thinkers who follow in his footsteps: can a meaningful relation be discovered between God's revelation to Moses and the heart of the Christian religion such as we described it earlier? But I have to short-circuit our discussion. It is opportune, I believe, to return to the theme which we commenced this address, the interpretation of Exodus 3:14–15 in Philo and Augustine.

My thesis was, as you will recall, that with one partial exception Philo and Augustine stand alone in their development of the idea that there is a distinction to be made between the two divine pronouncements in verses 14 and 15. The exception is partial because it concerns a passage in Basil, where he is almost certainly dependent on Philo.[79] Basil is attacking Eunomius, who was subsequently to be condemned for heresy, on account of his assertion that he was able to gain knowledge of God's essence.[80] God did not disclose his essence or his proper name to the patriarchs, Basil answers, but he allows himself to be called God of Abraham and God of Isaac and God of Jacob on account of their perfect excellence (διὰ τὸ εἰς πᾶσαν ἀρετὴν τέλειον; implicit, of course is the contrast with the

---

[78] I avoid the term 'revelation' because it has become so threadbare.

[79] *Contra Eunomium* 1.13, 218.11–220.6 Sesboüé-Durand-Doutreleau. The translation in this edition (Sources Chrétiennes 299) of Basil's comment on v. 15, 'biensûr, il leur a révélé ce qu'est sa substance', could lead to confusion if it is not realized that the words are meant ironically. The dependence on Philo is suggested by the following: (i) the striking connection made with Ex. 6:3 (cf. *Mut.* 13), and (ii) the emphasis on the perfection of the patriarchs (cf. *Abr.* 48–55).

[80] See also his notorious statement, cited by Socrates Ecclesiaticus, *HE* 4.7, PG 67.473B-C, = fr. 2 Vaggione, that 'God does not know his own essence better than we can know it'. According to Wiles (1989) this statement focuses on the same question, whether Ex. 3:14 expresses his essence: Eunomius thinks that it does, his Cappadocian opponents think that it does not.

puffed-up pretensions of his opponent). This presentation does not go quite as far as what we find in Philo, for whom the patriarchs are above all *symbols* of excellence in the form of the three natures of learning, perfect aptitude and training.[81] In the case of Augustine, however, the tone and timbre are quite different, because he is pro-foundly aware of the weakness and insufficiency of human know-ledge. The name 'God of Abraham and God of Isaac and God of Jacob' does not only indicate a relation, but is also a name of mercy. 'Because you are unable to reach me, I will come down to you. Fix your hope on the seed of Abraham'.[82] Philo too spoke of hope, as we saw,[83] but the change that Augustine introduces runs entirely parallel with his criticism of Philo's allegorical interpretation. What he emphasizes is the Christocentric element, precisely that which—unavoidably, of course—was lacking in his Jewish predecessor. According to Madec Augustine's originality in his interpretation of Ex. 3:14–15 lies precisely in the combination of ontology and soteriology.[84] This may be so, but we should not make the mistake of overlooking the philosophical component of the theme.[85] If it is difficult, or rather, impossible for man to grasp God's essence[86]—and this is Augustine's deepest conviction—then it is precisely in his relation to us that he makes himself known. This occurs above all

[81] Cf. *Abr.* 52–55, where Philo first carefully notes that the pronouncement could concern 'pious men'. But a few lines later he continues by stating that the words τὸ αἰώνιον ὄνομα indicate that we have to do here not with mortal men but eternal capacities. A quite different interpretation of 'eternal' is given by Aug-ustine at *Enarr. in Ps.* 134.6, 1942.40: *hoc*, inquit, *mihi nomen est in aeternum*, non quia aeternus Abraham, et aeternus Isaac et aeternus Iacob, sed quia Deus illos facit aeternos postea sine fine...

[82] *Enarr. in Ps.* 121.6, 1806.51: ego descendo, quia tu venire non potes. *Ego sum Deus Abraham, et Deus Isaac, et Deus Jacob.* In semine Abraham spera aliquid... (free translation).

[83] *Abr.* 51: μὴ ἀμοιρῶσιν ἐλπίδος χρηστῆς.

[84] Madec (1978) 139.

[85] In my view this occurs in Mayer (1986) 22–23, who interprets Augustine's distinction between the two pronouncements in terms of 'Gottes Wesen'and his 'Heilshandeln in der Zeit'. The claim 'trotzdem culminiert die Selbstoffenbarung Gottes nicht in der Benennung dessen, was Gott in alle Ewigkeit is, da es dazu nach A's Auffassung keiner Offenbarung bedürfte: «etsi hoc non diceret, intellegeretur» (en. Ps. 134.6)' is based on a faulty interpretation. What God does not have to say is *that* his name is *eternal*. But what he is in eternity man can only learn from God, and then only partially.

[86] Cf. *Enarr. in Ps.* 134.6, 1942 13, quia ipsum proprie esse menti humanae difficile erat capere; and *Enarr. in Ps.* 121.5, 1806.51, percipere non potes quod est idipsum (also *Sermo* 7.7, CCL 41.76.174–188).

through his Son, who for the church fathers, as we must constantly recall, is fully present in the Old Testament as well.

Finally you will no doubt wish to hear from me whether Augustine was or was not directly indebted to Philo. We saw earlier on that Augustine did have some acquaintance with Philo's work. But the three passages in Philo where the distinction between the two divine pronouncements is made do not belong to those parts of his *œuvre* which we know Augustine to have read. An obvious solution presents itself. Augustine derived this interpretation from Ambrose, who did read and digest large parts of the *corpus Philonicum.* But nowhere in the extensive works of Ambrose do we find what we are looking for: the first pronouncement on God as Being is cited a number of times, but the second 'relational' pronouncement is never mentioned.[87] It is always possible to speculate further. For example, did Ambrose use the theme in a sermon when Augustine was present? But speculations like this are of little help. Perhaps you will lose patience with me, for it is a cardinal methodological mistake to deduce *propter hoc* from *post hoc.* Philo and Augustine, both great and fertile minds, could have easily reached similar interpretations quite independently of each other (as we have seen, they are not
* identical). Indeed, this is quite well possible, and I cannot prove the contrary. But I do not wish to end my address on this negative note. I conclude on the basis of the question that we have examined today that the philosophical and theological framework within which Augustine's interpretation has to be placed has its origin in pre-Christian Philonism. The example we have studied demonstrates how Philonism made a powerful contribution to the development of Christian thought.

---

[87] Madec (1978) 129–132; cf. esp. *Ep.* 8.8, where it looks like Ambrose deliberately avoids citing Ex. 3:15.

Bibliography

AA. VV. (1975–1991): *Biblia Patristica*, 5 vols. and Supplément (Paris).

ADRIAANSE, H. J. (1991): 'Met God zonder 'God'?', in H. M. VROOM (ed.), *De God van de filosofen en de God van de Bijbel* (Zoetermeer) 74–98.

ALTANER, B. (1941): 'Augustinus und Philo von Alexandrien: eine quellenkritische Untersuchung', *Zeitschrift für Katholische Theologie* 65: 81–90; reprinted in *Kleine patristische Schriften*, Texte und Untersuchungen 83 (Berlin 1967) 181–193.

ARMSTRONG, A. H. (1980): 'The Self-Definition of Christianity in Relation to Later Platonism', in E. P. SANDERS (ed.), *Jewish and Christian Self-Definition*, Vol. 1, The Shaping of Christianity in the Second and Third Centuries (Philadelphia) 74–99.

ARMSTRONG, A. H. & MARCUS, R. A. (1960): *Christian Faith and Greek Philosophy* (London).

BILLINGS, T. H. (1919): *The Platonism of Philo Judaeus* (diss. Chicago).

BOS, A. P. (1991): *In de greep van de Titanen: Inleiding tot een hoofdstroming van de Griekse filosofie* (Amsterdam).

BOUSSET, W. (1915): *Jüdisch-Christlicher Schulbetrieb in Alexandria und Rom: literarische Untersuchungen zu Philo und Clemens von Alexandria, Justin und Irenäus* (Göttingen).

BOUSSET, W. & GRESSMANN, H. (1926): *Die Religion des Judentums im späthellenistischen Zeitalter* (Tübingen 1926³).

BROWN, P. (1967): *Augustine of Hippo: a Biography* (London).

——, (1972): *Religion and Society in the Age of St. Augustine* (London).

BRUNN, E. ZUM (1978): 'L'exégèse augustinienne de "Ego sum qui sum" et la "métaphysique de l'Exode"', in VIGNAUX (1978) 141–164.

CAMPENHAUSEN, H. VON (1963): *The Fathers of the Greek Church* (London).

CHADWICK, H. (1966): *Early Christian Thought and the Classical Tradition: Studies in Justin, Clement, Origen* (Oxford).

COHN, L. & WENDLAND, P. (1896–1915): *Philonis Alexandrini opera quae supersunt*, 6 vols. (Berlin).

COURCELLE, P. (1961): 'Saint Augustin a-t-il lu Philon d'Alexandrie?', *Revue des Études Anciennes* 63: 78–85.

——, (1969): *Late Latin Writers and their Greek Sources*, English translation of French edition 1948² (Cambridge Mass.).

DANIÉLOU, J. (1961): *Message évangélique et culture Hellénistique aux IIe et IIIe siècles* (Tournai).

DAWSON, J. D. (1992): *Allegorical Readers and Cultural Revision in Ancient Alexandria* (Berkeley).

DÖRRIE, H. (1972): 'Was ist „spätantiker Platonismus"? Überlegungen zur Grenzziehung zwischen Platonismus und Christentum', *Theologische Rundschau* 36: 285–302; reprinted in *Platonica Minora* (München 1976) 508–523.

FASCHER, E. (1959): Artikel 'Dogma II (sachlich)', *Reallexikon für Antike und Christentum* 4: 1–24.

GOODENOUGH, E. R. (1940): *An Introduction to Philo Judaeus* (New Haven, Oxford 1962²).

GOULET, R. (1987): *La philosophie de Moïse: essai de reconstruction d'un commentaire philosophique préphilonien du Pentateuque*, Histoire des doctrines de l'Antiquité classique 11 (Paris).

HADOT, P. (1978): 'Dieu comme acte d'être dans le néoplatonisme: à propos des théories d'É. Gilson sur la métaphysique de l'Exode', in P. VIGNAUX (1978) 57–63.

HANSON, R. P. C. (1959): *Allegory and Event: a Study of the Sources and Significance of*

Origen's Interpretation of Scripture (London).

HARL, M., DORIVAL, G. & MUNNICH O. (1988): *La Bible grecque des Septante du Judaïsme Hellénistique au Christianisme ancien* (Paris).

HARNACK, VON A. (1909): *Lehrbuch der Dogmengeschichte*, 3 vols (Tübingen 1909⁴).

HENGEL, M. (1974): *Judaism and Hellenism: Studies in their Encounter in Palestine during the Early Hellenistic Period*, English translation of German edition 1973² (London).

HOEK, A. VAN DEN (1988): *Clement of Alexandria and his Use of Philo in the Stromateis: an Early Christian Reshaping of a Jewish Model*, Supplements to Vigiliae Christianae 3 (Leiden).

LUCCHESI, E. (1977): *L'usage de Philon dans l'œuvre exégétique de Saint Ambroise: une 'Quellenforschung' relative aux Commentaires d'Ambroise sur la Genèse*, Arbeiten zur Literatur und Geschichte des Hellenistischen Judentums 9 (Leiden).

MADEC, G. (1978): 'Ego sum qui sum de Tertullien à Jérôme', in VIGNAUX (1978) 121–139.

MALHERBE, A. J. & FERGUSON, E. (1978): *Gregory of Nyssa The Life of Moses*, The Classics of Western Spirituality (New York).

MANSFELD, J. (1986): 'In memoriam C. J. de Vogel', *Algemeen Nederlands Tijdschrift voor Wijsbegeerte* 78: 293–294.

MARCOVICH, M. (1990): *Pseudo-Justinus Cohortatio ad Graecos De Monarchia Oratio ad Graecos*, Patristische Studien 32 (Berlin-New York).

MARTÍN, J. P. (1990a): 'Filon Hebreo y Teofilo Cristiano: la continuidad de una teologia natural', *Salmanticensis* 37: 302–317.

——, (1990b): 'Ontologia e creazione in Filone Alessandrino: dialogo con Giovanni Reale e Roberto Radice', *Rivista di Filosofia Neo-scolastico* 82: 146–165.

MAYER, C. (1986): Art. 'Abraham', *Augustinus–Lexicon* (Basel–Stuttgart) 1: 10–33.

MÉHAT, A. (1966): *Études sur les 'Stromates' de Clement d'Alexandrie*, Patristica Sorbonensia 7 (Paris).

MEIJERING, E. P. (1968): *Orthodoxy and Platonism in Athanasius: Synthesis or Antithesis?* (Leiden 1974²).

——, (1974): 'Wie platonisierten Christen? Zur Grenzziehung zwischen Platonismus, kirchlichem Credo und patristische Theologie', *Vigiliae Christianae* 28 (1974) 15–28; reprinted in *God Being History* (Amsterdam 1975) 133–146.

——, (1985): *Die Hellenisierung des Christentums im Urteil Adolf von Harnacks*, Verhandelingen van de Koninklijke Nederlandse Akademie van Wetenschappen, Afdeling Letterkunde 128 (Amsterdam).

MENDELSON, A. (1988): *Philo's Jewish Identity*, Brown Judaic Studies 161 (Atlanta).

MÜHLENBERG, E. (1966): *Die Unendlichkeit Gottes bei Gregor von Nyssa: Gregors Kritik am Gottesbegriff der klassischen Metaphysik*, Forschungen zur Kirchen- und Dogmengeschichte 16 (Göttingen).

O'CLEIRIGH, P. (1980): 'The Meaning of Dogma in Origen', in E. P. SANDERS (ed.), *Jewish and Christian Self-Definition*, Vol. 1. The Shaping of Christianity in the Second and Third Centuries (Philadelphia) 201–216.

OSBORN, E. F. (1981): *The Beginning of Christian Philosophy* (Cambridge).

——, (1987): 'Philo and Clement', *Prudentia* 19: 35–49.

PARAMELLE, J. (1984) *Philon d'Alexandrie: Questions sur la Genèse II 1–7: texte grec, versions arménienne, parallèles latins*, Cahiers d'Orientalisme 3 (Geneva).

PÉPIN, J. (1987): *La tradition de l'allégorie de Philon d'Alexandrie à Dante: études historiques* (Paris).

PETIT, F. (1973): *L'ancienne version latine des Questions sur la Genèse de Philon d'Alexandrie*, volume I édition critique, volume II Commentaire, Texte und Untersuchungen 113–114 (Berlin).

RUNIA, D. T. (1984): 'History in the grand manner: the achievement of H. A. Wolfson', *Philosophia Reformata* 49: 112–133; reprinted in RUNIA (1990).

——, (1986): *Philo of Alexandria and the* Timaeus *of Plato*, Philosophia Antiqua 44 (Leiden).

——, (1988): 'Naming and knowing: themes in Philonic theology with special reference to the *De mutatione nominum*', in R. VAN DEN BROEK, T. BAARDA and J. MANSFELD (edd.), *Knowledge of God in the Graeco-Roman world*, EPRO 112 (Leiden) 69–91; reprinted in RUNIA (1990).

——, (1989): 'Review of R. Goulet, *La philosophie de Moïse*', *Journal of Theological Studies* 40: 590–602; reprinted in RUNIA (1990).

——, (1990): *Exegesis and Philosophy: Studies on Philo of Alexandria*, Variorum Collected Studies Series (London).

——, (1991a): 'Philo of Alexandria in Five Letters of Isidore of Pelusium', in D. T. RUNIA, D. M. HAY and D. WINSTON (edd.), *Heirs of the Septuagint. Philo, Hellenistic Judaism and Early Christianity: Festschrift for Earle Hilgert*, Brown Judaic Studies 230 [= *The Studia Philonica Annual* 3] (Atlanta) 295–319. (= below Chapter 9).

——, '(1991b): 'Witness or Participant? Philo and the Neoplatonic Tradition', in VANDERJAGT, A. – PÄTZOLD, D. (edd.), *The Neoplatonic Tradition: Jewish, Christian and Islamic Themes*, Dialectica Minora 3 (Köln) 36–56 (= below Chapter 10).

SANDBACH, F. H. (1985): *Aristotle and the Stoics*, Cambridge Philological Society Supplementary Volume 10 (Cambridge).

SAVON, H. (1977): *Saint Ambroise devant l'exégèse de Philon le Juif*, 2 vols. (Paris).

——, (1984): 'Saint Ambroise et saint Jérôme, lecteurs de Philon' in , *Aufstieg und Niedergang des römischen Welt* II 21.1 (Berlin) 731–759.

SIEGERT, F. (1988): *Philon von Alexandrien Über die Gottebezeichnung "wohltätig verzehrendes Feuer" (De Deo): Rückübersetzung des Fragments aus dem Armenischen, deutsche Übersetzung und Kommentar*, Wissenschaftlichen Untersuchungen zum Neuen Testament 46 (Tübingen).

STAROBINSKI-SAFRAN, E. (1978): 'Exode 3, 14 dans l'œuvre de Philon d'Alexandrie', in P. VIGNAUX (1978) 47–55.

TOBIN, T. H. (1983): *The Creation of Man: Philo and the History of Interpretation*, Catholic Biblical Quarterly Monograph Series 14 (Washington).

VIGNAUX, P. (1978): (ed.), *Dieu et l'être: exégèses d'Exode 3, 14 et de Coran 20, 11–24*, (Paris).

VOGEL, C. J. DE (1950–59) *Greek Philosophy: a Collection of Texts*, 3 vols (Leiden).

——, (1958): *Antike Seinsphilosophie und Christentum im Wandel der Jahrhunderte* (Baden Baden).

——, (1970) *Wijsgerige aspecten van het vroeg-Christelijk denken: kleine geschiedenis van de Patristische en vroeg-Middeleeuwse wijsbegeerte* (Baarn).

——, (1973): 'Plato in de latere en late oudheid, bij heidenen en Christenen', *Lampas* 6: 230–254.

——, (1977): *De grondslag van onze zekerheid: over de problemen van de kerk heden* (Assen).

——, (1985): 'Platonism and Christianity: a Mere Antagonism or a Profound Common Ground?', *Vigiliae Christianae* 39: 1–62.

WILES, M. (1989): 'Eunomius: hair-splitting Dialectician or Defender of the Accessibility of Salvation?', in R. WILLIAMS (ed.), *The Makings of Orthodoxy: Essays in Honour of Henry Chadwick* (Cambridge) 157–172.

WOLFSON, H. A. (1947): *Philo: Foundations of Religious Philosophy in Judaism, Christianity and Islam*, 2 vols. (Cambridge Mass. 1968[4]).

——, (1956): *The Philosophy of the Church Fathers: Faith, Trinity, Incarnation* (Cambridge Mass. 1970[3]).

——, (1961): *Religious Philosophy: a Group of Essays* (Cambridge Mass.).

——, (1976): *The Philosophy of the Kalam* (Cambridge Mass.).

CHAPTER TWO

PHILONIC NOMENCLATURE

*to David Winston**

Introduction

It is one of the commonplaces of modern Philonic scholarship that
Philo is known under two names, Philo Alexandrinus (or Philo of
Alexandria) and Philo Judaeus (or Philo the Jew). As an example we
may adduce Valentin Nikiprowetzky's magisterial monograph *Le
commentaire de l'Écriture chez Philon d'Alexandrie*, which was written as a
kind of Prolegomena to the reading and study of Philo.[1] It commences with two introductory chapters on Philo's Hellenic and
Judaic background which are pointedly given the titles Philo

---

* This piece of research was suggested by a conversation I had with David
Winston in Washington in November 1993, when we were attending the Philo
Seminar as part of the annual AAR/SBL meeting. David asked me whether
Jerome was the first to call Philo 'Judaeus'. I said I thought this was correct, but
could not say for certain. At almost the same time as this article will appear in
print, David will withdraw from active teaching duties at the Graduate Theological
Union in Berkeley, where he has been Professor of Hellenistic and Jewish studies
for nearly 30 years. By means of this article I would like to wish him a blessed and
fruitful period of retirement.
[1] See the remarks at *SPhA* 1 (1989) 6, and note the title of the final chapter,
'Prolégomènes à une étude de Philon'.

Alexandrinus and Philo Judaeus respectively.[2] It would certainly be a very interesting exercise to examine how these two titles have been used in Philonic scholarship during the past century and a half. But that is not my aim in this essay. What I want to do is to look at the background of these and other titles, which, as we shall see, in certain (but not all) respects go as far back as antiquity. The subject of my enquiry is Philonic nomenclature. I wish to examine the labels which are given to Philo in our ancient sources in order to signify him as the historical and literary personage which he was.

By way of introducing our topic, it will be worthwhile briefly to look at Philo's actual name. Φίλων (usually *Philo* when transcribed into Latin)[3] is one of the more common personal names in the Greek-speaking [2] world.[4] In Egypt the name occurs at least 80 times in papyri, and indeed 9 times in the Zeno archive alone.[5] It is one of the Greek names most frequently found among Jews.[6] In Rome too it occurs on numerous inscriptions.[7] It is hardly surprising, therefore, that the name was carried by a large number of men of some fame or prominence in antiquity. Pauly-Wissowa's *Realencyclopädie* lists no less than 66 Philos.[8] Of these about 15 (other

---

[2] Nikiprowetzky (1977) 12–49.

[3] The ending -ων indicates that it was originally a name derived from the adjective (used as a noun) φίλος, i.e. 'dear', in Dutch 'lieverd'; cf. Kühner–Blass (1890–1904) 1.1.476, 1,2.281, and compare Ἀγάθων (from ἀγαθός, = 'goodie'), Τρύφων (from τρυφή, = 'sweetie' or 'softy'), and indeed Πλάτων (from πλατύς, = 'broad one'), Σίμων ('flat-nosed one'). Another possibility, to which my colleague G. Mussies drew my attention is that it is a hypocoristic (shortened form) of a longer name such as Φιλοδῆμος etc.

[4] Cf. the long list at Pape-Benseler (1911) 1630–31 and now the much longer list in Fraser-Matthews (1987) 472–473 (315 exx. covering only a small part of the Greek world).

[5] In the papyri, cf. Preisigke (1922) 465 (at least 30 exx.), Foraboschi (1967) 2.1.322 (at least 50 exx.); for the Zeno archive see Pestman *et al.* (1981) 436–7.

[6] Cf. Royse (1991) 11 n. 49, who refers to CIJ 1.xix and its indices. See further Mussies' analysis of Jewish personal names, (1994) 243ff., where Philo would fall in category c4 (Jewish Greek names with no Hebrew equivalent). In a private communication Mussies suggests to me that Philo's name might have had its origin in a theophoric name such as Theophilos or Philotheos. In Egypt, however, surprisingly few Jewish inscriptions and papyri have been found containing the name Philo; cf. CPJ 3.195, Horbury–Noy (1992) 2–3 (but many more indexed on p. 331 for Cyrenaica).

[7] Solin (1982) 2.740–742, 63 exx., largely based on the Corpus Inscriptionum Latinorum.

[8] See RE XIX 2 (1938) 2526 – XX (1941) 60, with additions at Supplbd. VIII (1956) 469, X (1965) 534. Shorter list at *Kleine Pauly* (Munich 1975) 4.770–777 (by various authors). See also the impressive list in Fabricius (1795) 4.750–754, 46 in all, but with various inaccuracies, including a Philo Pythagoreus from Clement

than 'our' Philo) achieved prominence in art, literature or philosophy, as indicated in the following list:

GREEK
    Philo of Athens, sceptic philosopher (4th c. BC), = RE (37)
    Philo of Megara, dialectical philosopher (4th c. BC), = RE (39)
    Philo of Eleusis, architect (4th c. BC), = RE (56)
    Philo of Herakleia, paradoxographer (3rd c. BC), = RE (42)
    Philo of Byzantium, engineer (3rd–2nd c. BC), = RE (48),
        various writings extant
    Philo of Larissa, Academic philosopher (1st c. BC), = RE (40),
        extensively reported in Cicero
    Philo of Tarsus, doctor/pharmacologist (1st c. AD), = RE (47)
        fragments extant
    Philo of Gadara, mathematician (early 2nd c. AD), = RE (50)
    Philo of Byzantium, paradoxographer (4th–6th c. AD), RE
        (49), work on seven wonders of the world extant [3]
PHOENICIAN
    Herennius Philo of Byblos, historian (1st–2nd c. AD), excerpts
        extant (in RE see under Herennios (2), but often just called
        Philo)
JEWISH
    Philo the Epic poet (2nd c. BC), = RE (46), fragments extant
    Philo the Elder, historian (2nd–1st c. BC), = RE (46)
CHRISTIAN
    Philo, bishop of Carpasia (4th c. AD), = RE (29), excerpts
        extant
    Philo the Presbyter (5th c. AD), = RE (31), translator of the
        Latin Canons of Nicaea
    Philo the historiographer (5th–6th c. AD?), = RE (30),
        fragments extant.

Nearly all these men will have left behind writings which survived for a longer or a shorter time. In practice 'our' Philo was most likely to have been confused with either the Jewish or the Christian Philos,

---

(who is of course a double for 'our' Philo). It may be suspected that the name declined in popularity in later antiquity: in the last two volumes of *PLRE* (Jones-Martindale-Morris), covering the years 395–641, only one Philo occurs.

but confusion with other Philos was also easily possible. This question of confusion of names has been touched on by James Royse in his splendid monograph on spurious Philonic texts.[9] He points out that Eusebius was aware of the possibility of confusion when at *Praep. Evang.* 1.9.20 he introduces Philo of Byblos and explicitly warns his reader that he was not ὁ ᾽Εβραῖος. Clement of Alexandria most likely confuses Philo with the older Jewish historian of the same name when he states at *Str.* 1.141.3 that 'Philo himself also recorded the kings of the Jews, but differently than Demetrius'. The phrase Φίλων καὶ αὐτός suggests that he has the most famous Philo in view, who has indeed already been introduced earlier in the same book (see further below).[10] In modern times there was much confusion between the various Philos, but all such problems seem to have been sorted out. For example, Goodhart and Goodenough in their list of Philonic manuscripts cite 5 mss. 'containing a *Catena on the Song of Songs* in which Philo is cited'. But this work must be attributed to Philo the bishop of Carpasia, as Royse has shown. Finally, while on this subject, we might note that there is yet another, less ancient Philo who can also cause confusion, namely a dialogue-[4]partner with that name in David Hume's famous *Dialogue concerning Natural Religion* (1779).[11]

The chief interest of our subject lies not in these confusions, but rather elsewhere. The study of the way Philo was referred to can yield important insights into the reception of Philo's writings and thought in the ancient world. Because in the period of antiquity Philo was mentioned only by Christian authors in the extant material at our disposal (with the single exception of Josephus), the results must necessarily be confined to the reception of Philo in the Christian tradition. But it hardly need be said that this tradition was richly varied and underwent many developments in the period of nearly a millenium which we shall be studying. So our subject may well allow us to discover nuances in the way Philo was regarded and received in this period. Moreover this Christian reception remained

---

[9] Royse (1991) 11–12, and esp. n. 49.

[10] If this is correct, it would contradict Royse's assertion in the note just cited that 'only modern scholars have actually assigned texts from another Philo to Philo of Alexandria'. To complicate things further, C-W in their invaluable collection of ancient testimonia at 1.lxxxxvi assert wrongly that Clement had Philo of Byblos in mind.

[11] Doubtless suggested by Philo of Larissa. This character is a bother when one searches electronic data-bases.

highly influential until the gradual emancipation of Philonic studies from the stranglehold of orthodox theology in the period from the 17th to the 19th century. I have given an overview of the reception of Philo in the early Christian tradition in a recently published monograph.[12] The subject of how Philo is referred to is raised on a number of occasions in that study, but not treated systematically. So this article should be regarded as a supplement to the material presented there.

Before we commence with the presentation of the evidence at our disposal, it will be worth our while to dwell briefly on a question of methodology. A distinction needs to be made, I believe, between a *title* and a *description*. Titles are what interest us most. By a title I mean an epithet which is added to a name in order to specify and make clear the person to whom the name refers. The reader is supposed to *recognize* or *recall* who is being talked about. A description, on the other hand, has the primary purpose of *introducing* the figure concerned to the reader for the first time, or perhaps of *jolting* a memory which is scarcely expected to recall the name. For this reason a description is generally longer than just a single epithet, drawing attention to a number of defining characteristics. Nevertheless there is a clear connection between the two. Both attempt to typify a person, and thus can show very succinctly and very clearly how he or she is regarded and categorized. Descriptions, because they are somewhat fuller, allow us to fill in the background of the epithets used in titles. In our investigation, therefore, it is necessary to take both titles and descriptions into account. [5]

The evidence

It is time now to present the evidence. The following list attempts to give all the more important passages in Patristic and related literature in which Philo is given a title or an introductory description. The list is based on a considerably longer list of all references to Philo in Christian literature up to 1000, the date which we have also set for the current investigation.[13] Comparison of the two lists shows that there are a large number of texts in which Philo is not given any kind of title. For example Origen refers to Philo three times, but

---

[12] Runia (1993); see also further *SPhA* 6 (1994) 90–110.
[13] See Runia (1993) 348–356, and further below in this volume, pp. 228–239.

each time assumes that the reader knows who he is. Didymus the
Blind in his commentaries cites Philo's name on six occasions without feeling the need to give him a title. But there are a large number
of authors who do provide nomenclature, as will appear in the
following list. The list is given in approximate chronological order.
Wherever possible I cite the original Greek or Latin text, and add a
literal translation in brackets.[14] This list will then be the basis of the
discussion of the evidence in the rest of the article.

LIST OF PHILONIC TITLES AND DESCRIPTIONS

JOSEPHUS (37–c. 100)
> *Antiquitates Iudaicae* 18.8.258: Φίλων ὁ προεστὼς τῶν Ἰουδαίων τῆς
> πρεσβείας, ἀνὴρ τὰ πάντα ἔνδοξος Ἀλεξάνδρου τε τοῦ ἀλαβάρχου
> ἀδελφὸς ὢν καὶ φιλοσοφίας οὐκ ἄπειρος (Philo, the leader of the
> embassy of the Jews, a man respected in every way, brother of
> Alexander the Alabarch, and not unskilled in philosophy).

CLEMENT OF ALEXANDRIA (c. 150–c. 215)
> *Str.* 1.72.4: ὁ Πυθαγόρειος Φίλων (the Pythagorean Philo).
> 2.100.3: ὁ Πυθαγόρειος Φίλων τὰ Μωυσέως ἐξηγούμενος (the
> Pythagorean Philo giving exegesis of the works of Moses).

* PSEUDO-JUSTIN *Cohortatio ad Gentiles* (between 220 and 300)
> §9.2: οἱ σοφώτατοι Φίλων τε καὶ Ἰώσηπος, οἱ τὰ κατὰ Ἰουδαίους
> ἱστορήσαντες (the most wise Philo and Josephus, who have re-
> counted the history of the Jews).
> cf. §13.4: παρ' αὐτῶν τῶν περὶ τούτων ἱστορησάντων σοφῶν καὶ
> δοκίμων ἀνδρῶν, Φίλωνός τε καὶ Ἰωσήπου (from the wise and re-
> putable men themselves who have recorded these matters, Philo
> and Josephus). [6]

ANATOLIUS of Alexandria, bishop of Laodicaea (died c. 280)
> cited at Eusebius *HE* 7.32.16: Ἰουδαίοις ... τοῖς πάλαι καὶ πρὸ
> Χρίστου ... ἐκ τῶν ὑπὸ Φίλωνος ... λεγομένων ([this was known] to
> the Jews who lived long ago and even before Christ, [as you can
> read] from the writings of Philo).

EUSEBIUS OF CAESAREA (c. 260–339)
> *Eccl. Hist.* 2.4.2: Φίλων ..., ἀνὴρ οὐ μόνον τῶν ἡμετέρων, ἀλλὰ καὶ
> τῶν ἀπὸ τῆς ἔξωθεν ὁρμωμένων παιδείας ἐπισημότατος. τὸ μὲν οὖν

---

[14] For further details on the editions used etc. see below pp. 228–239.

γένος ἀνέκαθεν Ἑβραῖος ἦν, τῶν δ' ἐπ' Ἀλεξανδρείας ἐν τέλει διαφανῶν οὐδενὸς χείρων ... (Philo, a man most distinguished not only among (lit. of) our people but also among (lit. of) those motivated by an outside (secular) education (i.e. pagans). By descent he was a Hebrew from ancient times, inferior to none of the prominent people in authority in Alexandria); cf. 2.5.4 Φίλων ... ἀνὴρ τὰ πάντα ἔνδοξος ... καὶ φιλοσοφίας οὐκ ἄπειρος (Philo, a man distinguished in every respect, and not unskilled in philosophy).

Praep. Evang. 1.9.20 Φίλων ... ὁ Βύβλιος, οὐχ ὁ Ἑβραῖος (Philo of Byblos, not the Hebrew); 7.12.14: Ἑβραῖον ἄνδρα ... Φίλων (a Hebrew man ... Philo); also 7.17.4: ὁ Ἑβραῖος Φίλων (the Hebrew Philo); cf. further 7.20.9, 11.14.10, 11.15.7, 11.23.12.

Also 13.18.12: ὁ τὰ Ἑβραίων πεπαιδευμένος Φίλων (Philo, learned in matters concerning the Hebrews).

EUSEBIUS OF EMESA (c. 300–359)

Frag. in *Catena in Genesim ad* Gen. 2:6: Φίλων ὁ Ἑβραῖος (Philo the Hebrew).

GREGORY OF NYSSA (c. 338–c. 395)

Contra Eunomium 3.5.24: ὁ Ἑβραῖος Φίλων (the Hebrew Philo); same epithet at 3.7.8.

PS. CHRYSOSTOM (387)

In sanctum Pascha sermo 7.2: σοφοὺς Ἑβραίους οἷον Φίλωνα καὶ Ἰώσηπα (Hebrew sages such as Philo and Josephus).

RUFINUS (c. 345–c. 410)

Latin translation of Eusebius' *Eccl. Hist.* (see above); note the following additions to the source: 2.4.2 Filo insignissimus scriptorum (Philo, most distinguished of writers), 2.17.1 a viro disertissimo Filone (by Philo, a most eloquent man).

JEROME (347–420)

Adv. Iov. 2.14: Philo vir doctissimus (Philo, a very learned man).

Comm. in Amos 2.9: Philo vir disertissimus Hebraeorum (Philo the most eloquent of the Hebrews); same description at *Comm. in Hiezech.* 4.10b.

De vir. ill.: 8.4 Philon disertissimus Hebraeorum (Philo the most elo[7]quent of the Hebrews); 11.1 Philon Iudaeus, natione Alexandrinus, de genere sacerdotum ... (Philo the Jew, Alexandrian by birth, of priestly descent ...).

Ep. 22.35.8: Philo Platonici sermonis imitator (Philo, imitator of Platonic diction).

Ep. 29.7.1: Iosephus ac Philo, viri doctissimi Iudaeorum (Josephus and Philo, most learned men belonging to the Jewish people).

Ep. 70.3.3: de Philone ... alterum vel Iudaeum Platonem (Philo, a second or Jewish Plato).

Liber Hebr. nom. pref.: Philo vir disertissimus Iudaeorum (Philo the most eloquent of the Jews).

Praef. in libr. Sal.: Iudaei Philonis (of the Jew Philo).

THEODORE OF MOPSUESTIA (c. 350–428)

Treatise against the Allegorists, 14.28 Van Rompay: 'Philon, un juif'.[15]

LATIN TRANSLATOR OF PHILO (c. 375–400)

Title of translation of *De vita contemplativa* (cf. C-W 6.xviii): Philonis Iudaei liber de statu Essaeorum, id est Monachorum, qui temporibus Agrippae regis monasteria sibi fectrunt (Philo the Jew's book on the way of life of the Essenes, i.e. monks, who in the times of King Agrippa made monasteries for themselves).

AUGUSTINE (354–430)

Contra Faustum 12.39: Philo quidam, vir liberaliter eruditissimus unus illorum (i.e. Iudaeorum) (a certain Philo, a man of exceedingly great learning, belonging to that group (of Jews [introduced in first line of paragraph])).

ISIDORE OF PELUSIUM (c. 370–c. 435)

*   *Ep.* 2.143: Φίλωνα, καίτοι Ἰουδαῖον (Philo, though a Jew)

Ep. 3.19: Φίλων ὁ θεωρητικώτατος καὶ Ἰώσηπος ὁ ἱστορικώτατος (Philo, highly versed in contemplation, and Josephus, highly versed in history).

Ep. 3.81: Φίλων ... ἄνθρωπος Πλάτωνος ἢ ὁμιλητὴς ἢ ὑφηγητής (Philo, a man who was either disciple or instructor of Plato).

PS.PROCHORUS (fl. 400–450)

Acta Johannis 110.9: ἄνθρωπος Ἰουδαῖος, ὀνόματι Φίλων, ἐπιστάμενος τὸν νόμον κατὰ τὸ γράμμα (a Jewish man named Philo, who knew the Law according to the letter); cf. also 112.4 ὁ Φίλων ὁ ἀκαμπὴς καὶ φιλόνεικος (Philo the inflexible and contentious (sc. interlocutor)).[8]

JULIAN OF ECLANUM (386–c. 454)

at Augustine *Contra sec. Jul. resp.* 4.123, PL 45.1420: illos Hebraeos, Sirach vel Philonem (those Hebrews, Sirach or Philo).

---

[15] Van Rompay, the translator of this text, informs me that the Syriac probably translates Φίλων, Ἰουδαῖός τις. All discussions of texts preserved in Syriac in this article are based on collaboration with my esteemed colleague, for which I offer him once again my sincerest thanks.

SALAMINIUS HERMIAS SOZOMEN (c. 400–c. 460)

Eccl. His. 1.12.9: Φίλων ὁ Πυθαγόρειος (Philo the Pythagorean).

CATENA IN GENESIM, CATENA IN EXODUM (c. 450–500)

passim under the headings Φίλωνος, Φίλωνος ἐπισκόπου, Φίλωνος Ἑβραίου (of Philo, of Philo the Bishop, of Philo the Hebrew).

CASSIODORUS (487– c. 580)

Inst. Div. Litt. PL 70.1117B: a Philone doctissimo quodam Iudaeo (by Philo a very learned Jew).

ANONYMOUS ARMENIAN TRANSLATOR OR GLOSSATOR (c. 550?)

Praef. in libr. Philonis De prov. vii: magnae sapientiae vir Philo Israelita fuit (Philo, a man of great learning, was an Israelite).

ISIDORE OF SEVILLE (c. 570–636)

Etymologiae 6.2.30: Iudaei Philonis (the Jew Philo).

BARḤADBŠABBA ᶜARBAYA, bishop of Ḥalwan (c. 600)

Cause of the Foundation of the Schools, 375.15: 'Le directeur de cette école et l'exégète fut Philon le Juif'.

ANASTASIUS SINAÏTA (c. 610–c. 700)

Viae dux 13.10.1: ἀπίστου Ἰουδαίου Φίλωνος τοῦ φιλοσόφου (the Jewish unbeliever Philo the philosopher), ὁ μιαρὸς Φίλων (the detestable Philo).

CHRONICON PASCHALE (c. 650)

PG 92.69A: Φίλωνος τοῦ παρ' Ἑβραίοις σοφοῦ (of Philo the sage among the Hebrews).

PS.SOPHRONIUS (c. 700?)

Greek translation of Jerome, *De vir. ill.:* 12 [= Jerome 8], Φίλων ὁ τῶν Ἰουδαίων ἐλλογιμώτατος (Philo, the most eloquent of the Jews); 21 [= Jerome 11] Φίλων Ἰουδαῖος, τεχθεὶς ἐν Ἀλεξανδρείᾳ … (Philo the Jew, born in Alexandria…).

JOHN OF DAMASCUS (c. 675–c. 750)

Prol. in Sac. Par. PG 95.1040B: ἀπὸ τοῦ Φίλωνος καὶ Ἰωσήπου συνταγμάτων … Ἑβραῖοι δὲ ἄμφω καὶ λόγιοι ἄνδρες (from the treatises of Philo and Josephus … both were Hebrews and men of learning).

ARMENIAN TRANSLATOR OF EUSEBIUS' *CHRONICLE*

Chronicle, p. 213: 'Philo from Alexandria, a learned man, was prominent'.

GEORGE SYNCELLUS (died after 810)

Ecloga chronographica 399.6: ὡς Φίλων Ἰουδαῖος ἐξ Ἀλεξανδρείας διάγων ἱστορεῖ (as Philo the Jew from Alexandria recounts at some length). [9]

ANONYMOUS Syrian commentator of the works of Gregory of Nazianzus (8th or 9th century)
At the end some quotations are found from other writers, among
them two quotations from 'Philo the Hebrew', fol. 98a and 144a
in ms. London, Brit. Libr. Add. 17,147.[16]

PHOTIUS, patriarch of Constantinople (c. 820–891)
Bibliotheca cod. 103: Φίλωνος τοῦ Ἰουδαίου (Philo the Jew); cf. 105
Ἀλεξανδρεὺς τὴν πατρίδα.

ANASTASIUS incertus (9th century)
In hexaemeron 7, PG 89.961: Φίλων ὁ φιλόσοφος καὶ τῶν ἀποστόλων
ὁμόχρονος (Philo the philosopher and contemporary of the
apostles).

ARETHAS, archbishop of Caesarea (c. 850–c. 940)
Comm. in Apoc. 1, PG 106.504: Φίλωνι τῷ θεωρητικωτάτῳ Ἰουδαίῳ
ἀνδρί (Philo the Jewish man most versed in contemplation).

ANONYMOUS list of exegetical authorities (date unknown, no earlier
than the 9th century)[17]
Exegesis Psalmorum 29.1: Philo philosophus spiritualis (Philo the
spiritual philosopher).

SOUDA (c. 1000)
s.v. Ἀβραάμ: Φίλων, ἐξ Ἑβραίων φιλόσοφος (Philo, a philosopher
from the Hebrew people).
s. v. Φίλων: Φίλων Ἰουδαῖος, τεχθεὶς ἐν Ἀλεξανδρείᾳ ... (cf.
Sophronius above).

Analysis of the evidence

There are various ways in which this list could be analysed. Each
author could be dealt with in turn. But this method would lead to
results that were rather fragmented. In my discussion of the
evidence I will use a more systematic approach. The nomenclature
used for Philo will be presented under nine headings.

(1) Philo a man of learning

If we survey the group of texts as a whole, the first impression is
that a large number of them emphasize Philo's great learning. This

---

[16] The work is unedited; information given by Wright (1871) 439b, 440a.
[17] List found in some mss. of an East-Syrian Psalm Commentary as well as in
one branch of the ms. tradition of the *Gannat Bussāmē* (Garden of Delights), a
commentary on the East-Syrian lectionary; see Vandenhoff (1899), Chabot (1906)
491–492, Reinink (1977) 125, n. 74.

tendency commences with Josephus, who regards him as 'not un-skilled in philosophy', a description which is unclear, and to which we shall return. For [10] Ps.Justin Philo is a sage (σοφός) or most wise (σοφώτατος). The same general epithet returns in two authors dealing with Paschal questions, Ps.Chrysostom and the *Chronicon Paschale*.[18] Eusebius emphasizes the great distinction of both his sacred and his secular learning (παιδεία); the latter aspect is again emphasized on one occasion in the *Praeparatio Evangelica*, a work that gives quotations from no less than nine Philonic treatises.[19] According to the Armenian translator[20] Philo was a man of great wisdom. The greatest emphasis on Philo's learning, however, is found in Jerome, who refers to it on six separate occasions (similar descriptions found in Rufinus and Augustine are very likely depen-
* dent on him). Jerome is the first (together with Isidore) to record the proverb 'either Plato philonizes or Philo platonizes', interpret-ing it as referring to the similarity of both thought and style.[21] Against this background we can understand why sometimes Philo's learning is praised in a general way (note especially *doctissimus*, *eruditissimus*), but on other occasions special emphasis is placed on his eloquence (*disertissimus*, cf. ἐλλογιμώτατος in the translation of Jerome's account in Ps. Sophronius). If Philo is a second or Jewish Plato, and an imitator of Plato's style, then eloquence can hardly be denied him. That Philo was a distinguished (and prolific) writer is noted only by Rufinus, who adds this information to his translation of Eusebius.[22] A final text that emphasizes Philo's learning is found in Johannes Damascenus, who draws extensively on Philo in his *Sacra Parallela*.[23] The Greek epithet λόγιος which Johannes uses probably refers to learning in general rather than just to his eloquence. Other passages among our texts refer to more specific aspects of Philo's learning. These we shall now examine separately under the next three headings.

---

[18] On the use of Philo in the Easter controversies see further Runia (1993) 231–234.

[19] List at *ibid.* 223.

[20] Or glossator; see further below n. 73.

[21] On this proverb see further Runia (1993) 4, 208, 313–314, 323.

[22] The three biographical accounts in Eusebius, Jerome and the *Souda* indicate this feature at greater length, because in each case a long list of Philo's works is given.

[23] On Philo in the *Florilegia* derived from Johannes see further Royse (1991) 26–27.

(2) Philo as historian

One of the reasons that Philo was a valuable source for Christian writers was that he furnished much historical information, not only about early Pentateuchal times, but also concerning the crucial events at the time of and just after Jesus' death. Various writers point out that he was a contemporary of the apostles (e.g. Anastasius incertus in the 9th century). In the descriptions cited above, this aspect is explicitly brought forward by [11] only one author, Ps. Justin, whose aim is to convince his pagan readers about the antiquity of the Jewish-Christian tradition. On both occasions he connects Philo with the other great Jewish author who wrote in Greek, Josephus.[24] The connection with Josephus occurs in four other Christian sources: Ps.Chrysostom, Jerome, Isidore, John of Damascus. Of these all but one join them together and describe them as learned. The exception is Isidore, who distinguishes between them, calling Josephus a supreme historian and Philo a supremely speculative thinker. We return to this text under (4).

(3) Philo the philosopher

φιλόσοφος and φιλοσοφία are notoriously ambiguous words. In later antiquity they can refer to Greek philosophy, but just as easily to the Christian faith or to the practice of biblical exegesis.[25] So when Josephus, the first author to mention Philo, says that he was 'not unskilled in philosophy' we may wonder what he is specifically referring to. I suspect that it is to 'Greek' or 'pagan' philosophy. Jewish observers, and perhaps also those outside the Jewish community, will have noted how deep a knowledge of Greek philosophy is presumed by Philo's literary *œuvre*. But there is no way of being sure, since Josephus, not unlike Philo (on whom he probably to some degree

---

[24] On Josephus' reception in the Christian tradition see now the excellent survey in Schreckenberg (1991) 3–148. There are significant parallels with the process of Philonic reception. But he does not give a systematic analysis of (i) the relation to Philo, or (ii) the specific nomenclature used for Josephus. In the Syrian tradition there is an interesting, if wholly erroneous, connection made between the two by Bar-Hebraeus (13th cent.) in his *Chronography* (p. 49 Wallis Budge): 'And at that time Felix, the Eparch of Egypt, was sent, and he afflicted the Jews for seven years, and because of this ambassadors were sent to Gaius that they might break him, namely Josephus, the wise man, and Philo the Hebrew philosopher, who was from Alexandria.'

[25] Cf. Malingrey (1961) 99ff. and *passim*, *PGL* s. vv., Görgemans (1989) 619–620.

depends),[26] regards Greek philosophy as posterior to and dependent on Jewish philosophy or wisdom, which in his view is to be
equated with fundamental Jewish religious convictions centred on
the Law.[27]

In the case of Clement of Alexandria, the first Christian author to
refer to Philo, there can be no doubt whatsoever that the title he
uses, Philo the 'Pythagorean' or 'follower of Pythagoras', refers to
Greek philosophy. In Clement's day the Pythagoreans were a
recognized philosophical 'school' (αἵρεσις), even if in practice there
was little to distinguish them from Platonists.[28] Nevertheless it is
once again not easy to deter[12]mine what Clement means by the
epithet.[29] Given the contexts—in the first passage Philo is cited in
order to prove the antiquity of 'Jewish philosophy', in the second it
is expressly stated that he is 'giving exegesis of the writings of
Moses'—it is to my mind not likely that he means that Philo was a
member of the Pythagorean school. It is possible that he is alluding
to Philo's great knowledge of this area of Greek philosophy, as
Eusebius was to do a century later when he introduces Philo in his
Historia Ecclesiastica and states that he 'showed a special zeal for the
study of Plato and Pythagoras'.[30] Another possibility is that there
were aspects of Philo's thought and exegetical practice, e.g. his
extensive references to numbers and their symbolism in his exegesis,
that reminded Clement of Pythagorean philosophers.

Remarkably Clement's epithet returns once more in the extant
tradition, namely in the 5th century historian Sozomen's account of
the early monastic movement. Where did Sozomen, who was of
course heavily indebted to earlier material, get it from? Recently it
has been suggested that the above-mentioned passage in Eusebius
was his source.[31] I regard this as rather unlikely, since why would he
choose the school of one philosopher at the expense of that of the
other (which was in fact more famous)? A few pages earlier (1.1.12)
Sozomen informs his reader that he wrote a short account of the
history of the Church up to the time of Constantine in two books, in

---

[26] See esp. *C. Ap.* 1.162ff., 2.168, and further Pilhofer (1990) 193–206.
[27] Cf. *TDNT* 9.182–184, Mason (1991) 185f. (with further references).
[28] As noted by Whittaker (1987) 115.
[29] The question remains surprisingly unaddressed in Van den Hoek's excellent
monograph on Clement's use of Philo, (1988). I intend to deal with this question
* in greater detail elsewhere. See further my remarks at (1993) 136, 147, 150.
[30] *HE* 2.4.3: ὅτε μάλιστα τὴν κατὰ Πλάτωνα καὶ Πυθαγόραν ἐζηλωκὼς ἀγωγήν.
[31] In the note by Sabbah in Grillet-Sabbah-Festugière (1983) 166.

which one of his sources was 'Clement' (in addition to Eusebius).
He may mean the *Pseudo-Clementina*,[32] but he may also mean Clement of Alexandria,[33] whose lost *Hypotyposeis* contained much quasi-
historical material on the apostolic age.[34] If so, then this work of
Clement may be his source for the Philonic epithet which he uses.[35]

Another reference to Philo as philosopher is implied in the
famous proverb on Philo's Platonism cited by Jerome and Isidore of
Pelusium, which has already been discussed under (1) above, especially if the [13] imitation involved is taken to refer to thought as well
as (or rather than) style.[36]

In a number of very late documents the epithet 'philosopher' returns.[37] Anastasius the Sinaite, a rabid defender of orthodoxy, uses it
in most pejorative fashion, connecting it with the fact that Philo was
a Jew and an unbeliever (how much worse can one be!).[38] In the
Souda Philo is introduced as a 'philosopher from the Hebrew
people' in connection with the lemma on Abraham. The implication is that 'philosopher' here has to do with biblical interpretation.
There are a number of other texts pointing in the same direction,
which we will discuss in more detail under the next category.

(4) Philo the exegete

Only in one text is Philo directly referred to as 'exegete' (though
more as a description than as a title), namely in the Syriac writer
Barḥadbšabba ᶜArbaya, who regards him as founder of the Alexandrian school of exegesis, and the one whose example led the great

---

[32] As argued at *ibid.* 116.

[33] As concluded by Bidez-Hansen (1960) 458.

[34] On this work, which was sighted as late as 1779, see Duckworth–Osborn
(1985), esp. 74–77, where it is noted that Eusebius made use of Clement's
material.

[35] And so this may be evidence in favour of the view that Eusebius' story about
the origins of the Alexandrian church and the Philonic monks there was derived
from Clement, as I suggest at (1993) 7. Sozomen's description of the early monks
is, however, taken entirely from Eusebius; cf. *ibid.* 229.

[36] Resemblance of thought is explicitly stated by Jerome in *De vir. ill.* 11.7 (and
taken over in Ps.Sophronius and the *Souda*) and it strongly implied at *Ep.* 70.3.3.
Isidore of Pelusium too implies it at *Ep.* 3.81, as I observe at (1991) 315.
Augustine, however, in his only mention of Philo at *C. Faustum* 12.39 emphasizes
only the stylistic resemblance, and perhaps implicitly denies the similarity of
thought (but he does emphasize Philo's learning).

[37] Note also the 13th cent. text of Bar-Hebraeus cited above in n. 24.

[38] At (1993) 210 I note that this is the most negative text on Philo in the entire
tradition.

Origen astray.[39] Other texts, however, point towards the same aspect of his literary activity. Clement, as we saw, calls Philo a 'Pythagorean', but immediately adds that he gives exegesis of Mosaic scripture. The next relevant text is the letter of Isidore (*Ep.* 3.19) in which he is called ὁ θεωρητικώτατος. What is the contemplation (θεωρία), we may ask, in which Philo is so highly versed? When explaining the epithet Isidore states that Philo 'turns almost the entire Old Testament into allegory', so that there can be no doubt that the epithet refers especially to the practice of allegorical or 'speculative' exegesis.[40] Exactly the same epithet is used five centuries later by Arethas when referring to Philo's praise of the hebdomad (i.e. in O*pif.* 89–127).[41] In the Syriac tradition Philo's name occurs in a long and rather disorganized list of *nomina doctorum patrum orthodoxorum* together with the title *philosophus spiritualis*. Philo appears to be the only [14] non-Christian in the list, but is included as a member of the exegetical tradition[42] The title certainly refers to his exegetical activity. If the author has Philo's allegorizing in mind, it may be equivalent to the Greek φιλόσοφος θεωρητικός. We note, however, that the 9th century Anastasius incertus speaks in similar terms about the early 1st and 2nd century exegetes who 'spiritually contemplated the Paradise story' (πνευματικῶς τὰ περὶ παραδείσου ἐθεώρησαν), so it is also possible that the term may be equivalent to πνευματικός.[43]

(5) Philo the Hebrew

It is time to turn to a quite different aspect of our theme, the use of titles and descriptions to indicate Philo's descent. With one

---

[39] See *ibid.* 269–270. The words 'and exegete', deleted in the Scher's translation, have been reinstated by Van Rompay.

[40] See translation and comments on this text at Runia (1991) 310–312.

[41] Arethas writes ἐν λόγῳ αὐτοῦ τῷ εἰς τὴν κατὰ Μωυσέα φιλοσοφίαν, where we might suspect that the last word is substituted κοσμοποιίαν in the title of *Opif.*

[42] The only other figure in the list earlier than the 4th century is Origen. In passing we note that Philo is described as philosopher in the following Syriac text taken from the *Anonymi auctoris Chronicon ad annum Christi 1234 pertinens* (translation at Chabot (1952) 100): Pilatus autem post tribulationes quae ei acciderunt, seipsum necavit, ut scripsit Philo philosophus. The text is later than our cut-off point, but doubtless contains earlier material (the information is clearly—and mistakenly—taken from Eusebius *HE* 2.7.1).

[43] Text at C-W 1.cix. Johannes Damascenus in the Prologue to his famous *Sacra Parallela* calls Philo and Josephus λόγιοι. The content of this work is primarily theological and philosophical, so presumably Johannes had these aspects of Philo's writings in mind when he wrote this passage.

exception the relevant texts can be divided into two groups, those
that describe Philo as 'the Hebrew' (ὁ Ἑβραῖος), and those that
describe him as Jewish or 'the Jew' (ὁ Ἰουδαῖος). In our sources the
first group begins with Eusebius of Caesarea, the man who did more
than anyone else to place Philo on the Christian map. For Eusebius
Philo is 'a Hebrew by descent'. Elsewhere too he consistently refers
to Philo by this epithet. Other 4th century texts in Eusebius of
Emesa, Gregory of Nyssa, Ps.Chrysostom all use the same title. It is
used by Jerome too (but less frequently than the other title *Iudaeus*
—twice as opposed to five times), and also by the opponent of
Augustine, Julian of Eclanum. The author of the *Catena*[44] employs it
towards the end of the 5th century, as do four later writers (author
of the *Chronicon Paschale*, John of Damascus, an Anonymous Syriac
writer, and the *Souda* once). We shall see in the following section,
however, that this epithet is used less than that of Philo 'the Jew'.

What do Christian authors mean to say when they call Philo 'the
Hebrew'? The relation between the epithets Ἑβραῖος and Ἰουδαῖος
is by no means straightforward, and has so far been insufficiently researched.[45] One must be careful not to over-interpret the evidence.
The [15] terms may be used in a neutral fashion, without any particular overtones. It is possible, however, to draw broad lines of
division between the two terms. Philo's own usage is revealing in this
respect.[46] He uses Ἑβραῖοι as a term to describe the ancient lineage
of the Jewish nation going back to the Patriarchs, or he relates it to

---

[44] On this author see below p. 46.

[45] Three studies should be mentioned: Kuhn–Gutbrod (1965), Arazy (1977),
Tomson (1986). All three examine three names, Ἰουδαῖοι, Ἰσραήλ, Ἑβραῖος. The
first examines primarily Jewish (including Hellenistic–Jewish) and New Testament
evidence, as does the third, which moreover attempts to apply sociological criteria
to the subject. Only the second takes into account Greco-Roman and Patristic
usage, but the analysis given in this unpublished work is rather primitive and
parochial. It is remarkable that Feldman (1993) in his compendious work on Jew
and Gentile does not touch on this issue at all. A full examination of Patristic
usage of the two terms is thus very much a desideratum. On the use of Ἑβραῖος in
non-Jewish writers see also Stern (1974–84) 2.160. Lemche's statement (1992) 95
that 'only in the Greco-Roman tradition did Greek *Ebraios* (sic) become the
ordinary way of indicating Jews, and thereafter this tradition was taken over by the
Christian church and became a general way of designing members of the Jewish
people' is in this unnuanced form not correct. According to Kuhn-Gutbrod
(1965) 372 it is rare in Greek literature, but this too is somewhat exaggerated. The
truth lies somewhere in between.

[46] Cf. Kuhn-Gutbrod (1965) 373–375, Arazy (1977) 1.141–158, Tomson (1986)
136–137. On the related (but for us not relevant) issue of the relation between
two terms Ἑβραῖος and Χαλδαῖος see Wong (1992).

the use of the Hebrew language (and especially the intepretation of Pentateuchal names). It occurs very frequently in the *Lives* of Abraham, Joseph and Moses. The only instance where he uses it in a post-biblical context is when he speaks of the Hebrews who came from Jerusalem to translate the Books of Moses (*Mos.* 2.31). Here the term probably indicates that they were speakers of Hebrew. Philo would not have described himself as a 'Hebrew'. On the other hand Ἰουδαῖος is Philo's usual way refering to contemporary Jews in their socio-political situation. It occurs no less than 79 times in his two political treatises. In other treatises it is less common, but always with reference (direct or indirect) to the contemporary situation.[47] Revealingly it is *never* used in the Allegorical Commentary, presumably because this work is written for insiders.[48] Philo would have regarded himself as a *Ioudaios*.[49] A similar usage is encountered in Josephus: '*Ioudaioi* is the regular name for post-biblical Jews'.[50] Surprisingly at the outset of his *Jewish War* he describes himself as γένει Ἑβραῖος (a Hebrew by descent).[51] I agree with Tomson against [16] Gutbrod that Josephus here is exploiting the connotations of ancient prestige that the title connotes.[52]

Against this background there can be little doubt that Eusebius' description of Philo as 'the Hebrew' is deliberate. Philo, who is such a valuable source of information on the beginnings of the Church in Alexandria, belongs to those respected and (relatively) ancient members of the Jewish people who lived before the fall of Jerusalem. Arazy accuses Eusebius of a 'double standard' in his use of appellations: Philo is 'a Hebrew by racial descent', while the people whom he represents and whose troubles he recounts are 'Jewish'.[53] Other Jews who are called Ἑβραῖοι are Josephus and Trypho, the dialogue-partner of Justin Martyr. Arazy concludes: '(1) Any time a positive image of the Jews, contemporary or ancient is to be presented,

---

[47] Rightly observed by Tomson (1986) 137.

[48] Note the reference to Jews (and Egyptians) practising circumcision at *QG* 3.48, which clearly has a contemporary reference.

[49] Cf. King Agrippa's self-description at *Legat.* 278.

[50] Tomson (1986) 138.

[51] There are doubts about the text here, since the oldest ms. and Eusebius delete these words.

[52] Tomson *ibid.*; cf. Kuhn-Gutbrod (1965) 374, who thinks it refers to the fact that he came from a Palestinian family. Cf. also Arazy (1977) 2.10–11, who is not impressed by Josephus' manœuvre.

[53] Arazy (1977) 2.29.

Hebraios is the proper appellation. (2) The appellation *Ioudaios*
should be used in pointing out the negative character of the Jews,
both contemporary and their ancestors.'[54] This statement is no
doubt too clear-cut, and may well need to be qualified by further
research. But it seems on the right track. It is supported by an analysis of the evidence in Origen by De Lange, who concludes that
'*Ioudaios*, in many mouths, was a sneering expression, even perhaps
a term of abuse; *Hebraios*, on the other hand, was a liberal's word,
leaning over backwards to give no offence'.[55]

The positive connotations of the title Ἑβραῖος are confirmed by
our texts. In almost every case the context is non-polemical and, by
implication at least, favourable. Gregory of Nyssa sympathizes with
Philo because his ideas are filched by the heretical Neo-Arian
Eunomius.[56] In the Paschal documents Philo serves as an ancient
authority whose testimony carries weight on account of its antiquity,
and can be used as ammunition against both Christian (or heretical)
opponents and contemporary Jews who follow a different calendar.[57]
To be accredited with the possible authorship of one of the Septuagintal writings, as Julian of Eclanum reports, is surely complimen-
tary. The author of the *Catena* and John of Damascus are pleased to
be able to make use of Philonic [17] exegetical material, even if
caution is required (as John warns his reader). A final example is
more complex. Eusebius of Emesa is pleased to cite Philo the
Hebrew in order to defend a non-literal reading of the LXX text.
But the preceding passage, which points out that the Hebrew text
reads something different than the LXX, is also attributed to 'a Hebrew'.[58] We may suspect a rabbinic exegete or exegetical tradition
here,[59] and the epithet probably implies knowledge of the Hebrew
language. If Philo is deliberately cited as evidence against Jewish
exegesis,[60] then the title, even if it is used on both sides, could still

---

[54] *Ibid.* 2.30–31.
[55] De Lange (1976) 31. See also his comment at 32: 'Origen has thus prepared
the ground for Eusebius' complete repainting of the traditional picture of Jewish
history, which finally redefines *Hebraioi*, so that it can stand in contrast to *Ioudaioi*.'
It is unfortunate for our theme that Origen never gives Philo a title.
[56] See further Runia (1993) 245.
[57] See further *ibid.* 234.
[58] Text at Petit (1991) 135.
[59] Compare the use of Rabbinic material in Origen's exegesis, as sketched in
De Lange (1976) 103–132. Kamesar (1993) 150 n.189 speaks of an 'exegetical
tradition'.
[60] As I argue at Runia (1993) 265.

have a positive connotation in his case. Philo as an ancient Hebrew authority is cited in support of a Greek reading that is disputed by a modern exegete who appeals to the authority of the Hebrew text.

(6) Philo the Jew

In our list a larger number of authors call Philo a Jew than a Hebrew. It takes a while, however, before this practice sets in. Josephus and Anatolius of Alexandria (3rd century) do not actually use Ἰουδαῖος as a title, but Philo's name is closely aligned with references to the 'Jews' in the immediate context. Apart from these texts it is not until the end of the 4th century that we see the title Philo the Jew coming into prominence. Jerome uses it very deliberately in his biographical notice of Philo, and it returns on four other occasions in his writings. Jerome is not, however, our earliest witness. The reference to Philo as 'a Jew' in Theodore of Mopsuestia antedates his use by about 20 years.[61] We may suspect, however, that Theodore's use of the indefinite article indicates that the epithet is not yet being used as a standard title. It is possible that the Anonymous Latin translator uses the title Philo Judaeus at the beginning of his translation of *Contempl.* at about this time.[62] A little later than Jerome we find [18] references to Philo the Jew in Isidore of Pelusium and Ps.Prochorus. Thereafter it becomes the most common way of referring to Philo.[63]

Why does Jerome start his biography so demonstratively with the phrase *Philon Iudaeus*? Since most of the early illustrious men whom he describes were of Jewish descent without this being mentioned, the epithet must refer to something else. Most probable, it seems to me, is that it alludes to Philo's religious allegiance. Philo is a Jew

---

[61] Jerome wrote his *De viris illustribus* in 392–393; cf. Kelly (1975) 174. The mini-treatise 'Against the allegorists' of Theodore is most likely (but not wholly certainly) derived from his *Commentary on the Psalms*; cf. Van Rompay (1982) xlv–xlvii. We know from Theodore's own testimony that this work was his 'debut', written when he was scarcely twenty years of age. Even if allowance is made for some exaggeration, this indicates a date between 370 and 375; see further Vosté (1925) 70–72, Devreesse (1948) 28, Schäublin (1974) 18–19.

[62] The translation is dated to the last quarter of the 4th century by Petit (1977) 1.13. A difficulty is caused by the fact that this title only occurs in the 1527 edition of Sichardus based on the now lost ms. of Lorsch. We cannot be certain that it was not added by the editor himself, although this is unlikely. I would like to thank Mme. Caroline Carlier (Jerusalem) for drawing my attention to this text.

[63] Examples in Cassiodorus, Isidore of Seville, Barḥadbšabba ʿArbaya, Anastasius the Sinaite, Ps.Sophronius, Photius, Arethas, the *Souda*.

who lived during the earliest times of Christianity but remained a Jew. There is, however, not a trace of negative feeling in the use of the title. Jerome is very positive about Philo in this brief report, telling his reader that he places Philo among the ecclesiastical writers because (as Jerome himself believes) he wrote a laudatory account of the early Church in Alexandria. Also, when he calls Philo a 'second or Jewish Plato' the title surely has a positive connotation.

Interpretation of the term *Ioudaios* (or *Iudaeus*) requires more care than the corresponding term *Hebraios* (or *Hebraeus*). As we noted above, it generally refers to contemporary Jews or Jews in the relatively recent past.[64] For Philo and Josephus this means post-exilic Judaism. In Christian terms it means Jews from about the time of Jesus onwards. The word also very often implies a reference to the Jewish religious adherence of the people being described.[65] The reference is by no means necessarily negative, but can easily become such on account of the strong rivalry and frequent antipathy that existed between the two religious groups. Whether *Ioudaios* is used in negative or polemical sense depends entirely on the context. The difference between *Hebraios* and *Ioudaios* in the Christian context may thus be summarized as follows. The use of *Hebraios* may refer to the origins of Christianity in Judaism, but does not imply a contrast between the two religions and their adherents. When *Ioudaios* is used, there is a strong possibility that the author does imply a contrast between Jew and Christian.

If we examine the texts contemporary or later than Jerome in which *Ioudaios* or *Iudaeus* is used, we may conclude that an implicit or explicit contrast with the term *Christianus* is generally present.[66] In Theodore of [19] Mopsuestia the context is strongly polemical: Origen should not have taken over the method of allegorical exegesis from a Jewish author.[67] In the later Syriac author Barḥadb-

---

[64] Cf. Kuhn-Gutbrod (1965) 369–371, Tomson (1986) 136–140 (who emphasizes that it is the name used by Jews in communication with non-Jews, i.e. the outside title in contrast to the inner description Israel). Arazy (1977) *passim* over-emphasizes the negative connotations of *Ioudaios*, which leads him to see a more positive development in the 4th cent., when Julian sees the Jews as allies against the Christians.

[65] And so can perhaps even be used of a pagan adherent to Judaism (but who is not a proselyte); cf. Van der Horst (1991) 68–71.

[66] Exceptions are, I think, the two references to Philo as author of the Wisdom of Solomon in Cassiodorus and Isidore of Seville and the reference to Philo in Arethas, where the term does no more than indicate Philo's ethnic origin.

[67] On this text see further Runia (1993) 264–269.

šabba ᶜArbaya the context is similar, but the tone somewhat less polemical.[68] Isidore of Pelusium in *Ep.* 2.143 praises Philo for reaching some understanding of the doctrine of the trinity 'even though he was a Jew'. Another letter, *Ep.* 3.19, is also interesting. Philo, together with Josephus, is cited in order to refute a Jew (i.e. a contemporary with whom the recipient of the letter has engaged in discussion). Philo and Josephus are described as 'two of your own (i.e. Jewish) writers'.[69] The context in Augustine is overtly, if not aggressively, polemical. In the wholly legendary account in Ps. Prochorus Philo is presented as a typical rabbinical Jew who reads the Law according to the letter and refuses to accept the apostle John's interpretation 'according to the spirit' until he is impressed by a miracle that John performs.[70] The most polemical contexts are to be found in the two late writers Anastasius and Photius, where Ἰουδαῖος has very strong negative overtones indeed.

A final question remains to be answered. Is it significant that towards the end of the 4th century *Ioudaios* starts to replace *Hebraios* as the title most often used for Philo? The answer, to my mind, must be in the affirmative. Through the interventions of Clement, Origen and Eusebius Philo had gained a reasonably comfortable niche within the Christian tradition as a respected Jewish source of historical, exegetical and even theological insight. When this is combined with the legend of Philo Christianus, we may say that he became a Church father *honoris causa*. During the 4th century, however, we observe that the atmosphere changes. It is the time that orthodoxy triumphs over heresy and relations between Jews and Christians deteriorate markedly. The attitude of Ambrose and Augustine towards Philo is ambivalent, that of Theodore of Mopsuestia, as we noted above, decidedly hostile.[71] It should certainly not be concluded that *Hebraios* is always positive and *Ioudaios* always negative. The use of the terms is much less clear-cut. Often it is fairly neutral. But that the increase in the use of *Ioudaios* introduces a new [20] more antithetical and 'tougher' (but by no means always uncomplimentary) attitude to Philo seems to me quite clear.

---

[68] See further *ibid.* 269–270.

[69] Further comments on these texts in *ibid.* 204–209 and Runia (1991).

[70] As Zahn (1880) liv indicates, one cannot be absolutely certain that the author has our Philo in mind, because the incident is situated in Asia Minor.

[71] See my monograph (1993), but I do not pursue the question systematically beyond 400. On Philo and heresy see also Runia (1992).

(7) Philo the Israelite

Israel is the 'inner-Jewish' self-designation, which the Christian church successfully appropriated for itself as the 'New Israel'.[72] It is thus surprising to find one text in which Philo is described as an 'Israelite', namely in the introduction to the Armenian translation of Philo's writings. It is not known who the writer of this text is. It is, as far as I can tell, quite possible that it was the translator himself.[73] The author could just have easily used the Armenian equivalent of *Hebraeus*, but not so easily *Iudaeus*.[74] It is thus a puzzle why he uses the term 'Israelite'. Perhaps it is suggested by his account of the double diaspora of the Jewish people, first at the time of the Old Testament, secondly at the time of the New.[75] The term, we might add, also has a respectable New Testament background, being used there six times, twice in well-known statements of the Apostle Paul about his own lineage (Rom. 11:1, 2 Cor. 11:22).

(8) Philo the Bishop

In one group of Christian documents Philo is endowed with the title ὁ ἐπίσκοπος (the Bishop), namely the *Catena in Genesim* and the *Catena in Exodum*, extensive collections of excerpts from scriptural commentators ordered in the sequence of the biblical text. Philo is quoted on numerous occasions in these works, but the extracts are taken from a limited section of his corpus (only *QG* 1.55–4.228, *QE* 2.1–49, and a few excerpts from *Mos.* 1).[76] Until recently it was thought that these *Catenae* were composite documents that grew by

---

[72] Cf. esp. Tomson (1986) *passim*.
[73] Text at Aucher (1822) vii–xi. Above the text we read 'Outline of the translator or interpreter which precedes the books of Philo on Providence', but this may be simply the surmisal of Aucher the editor, as my colleague J. J. S. Weitenberg informs me. In this case it is also possible that the piece is of much later date. Terian (1981) 6 simply speaks of an 'anonymous scholion'.
[74] According to Weitenberg the Armenian word *hřeaj* (= Jew) is not easily used as a title, whereas for the word *ebrajec‘i* there is no problem.
[75] The account begins by stating that it is not certain from which tribe Philo came. Cf. Jerome's statement that Philo was *de genere sacerdotum*, which according to Schwartz (1984) is not likely to be legendary. The Armenians seem to have been interested in the fate of the Jewish captives. According to the History of the 8th cent. author Moses Khorenats'i one of the leading Armenian families descended from a Jewish captive at the court of Nebuchadnezzar; cf. Thomson (1978) 30.
[76] See the discussion at Royse (1991) 14–25; at 17 n.12 he notes that C-W cite some quotations from *Mos.* 2 from the *Catenae in Numeros*, but he adds that their sources are of doubtful quality (at *Mos.* 1.220 C-W also cite a quote in the *Catena in Psalmos*).

accretion. But recently Françoise Petit [21] has argued that the *Catena in Genesim* at least is basically the work of a single anonymous compiler, and she has commenced on an edition of the entire work in which the excerpts scattered over the various mss. are brought back together in an integral text.[77] Certainly the manner in which Philo is cited offers support to her thesis. The method is utterly consistent: the excerpt is preceded by Philo's name in the genitive, without a title, or with the titles Ἑβραίου or ἐπισκόπου. The third option is the most common, followed by the second, while the name only is relatively infrequent.[78] The provenance of the quotation is never given. (This is in clear contrast to the *Florilegia*,[79] where the location is often told, but Philo is never given a title as far as I know.) In the case of Christian bishops the Catenist sometimes also gives a place-name, e.g. Eusebius bishop of Emesa, Dionysius bishop of Alexandria etc.[80] This is never done in Philo's case. It would seem that the title of Philo the bishop is an idiosyncratic *trouvaille* of the unknown author. It indicates respect (as does the epithet Ἑβραῖος), as well as a complete acceptance of the legend of Philo Christianus. To my mind, however, the usage of the two epithets remains puzzling because they appear to cancel each other out. If Philo is a Hebrew, he is no Bishop, and vice versa.[81]

(9) Philo the Alexandrian

Remarkably, given modern usage, the fact that Philo came from Alexandria is virtually never exploited as an epithet or title in our extant sources. Philo's geographical origin is naturally mentioned in the six biographical accounts that we have (Josephus, Eusebius, Jerome, Ps.Sophronius, Photius, the *Souda*).[82] But elsewhere it is

---

[77] So far she has reached Gen. 11 in two volumes, Petit (1992–93); her hypothesis on the author is presented at (1992) xiv.

[78] A good impression of the complexity of the transmission can be gained by looking at the collection of lemmata from *QG* and *QE* published in Petit (1978). Because the published information is incomplete, I shall give no analysis of the variations in the titles, except to say that the name alone is found mainly in the Leningrad codex.

[79] Also collections of excerpts, but not to be confused with the *Catenae*, cf. Royse (1991) 26–58.

[80] Cf. Petit (1991–93) nos. 237, 225.

[81] Alan Mendelson suggests that Bishop might be used loosely for a eminent religious person, regardless of 'denominational' membership. Compare the way that in the 19th century one spoke of the 'Jewish Church'.

[82] Cf. also the anonymous Armenian translator, who relates Philo to the

only used as a title in two rather late texts, the Armenian translation of Eusebius' *Chronicle* and the chronographic work of George Syncellus. Since both these works make use of the Eusebian chronicle tradition we might wonder [22] whether the title stood in the original Eusebian work (which has not been preserved in Greek). The fact that it is missing in Jerome's translation and reworking of the work, however, argues against this possibility. In this context it is interesting to note the practice of the bibliophile Byzantine Patriarch Photius in his *Bibliotheca*. He regularly cites pagan and Christian authors from Alexandria by means of their name and the epithet Ἀλεξανδρεύς. For example, at *cod.* 49 he records that he has read a book of 'the saintly Cyril the Alexandrian', and at *cod.* 106 (straight after the three chapters devoted to Philo) he mentions the *Hypotyposeis* of 'the blessed Theognostus of Alexandria the exegete', possibly head of the Alexandrian school in the period after Origen. But in the case of Philo he commences (cod. 103) with the usual formula ἀναγνώσθη Φίλωνος Ἰουδαίου (were read of Philo the Jew...), and Philo's Alexandrian origin is mentioned only at the end of *cod.* 105, as part of a brief biographical sketch similar to what is found in Jerome and Ps.Sophronius.[83]

Some conclusions

On the basis of the above discussion the following summary of results can be given.

(1) The titles and descriptions bestowed on Philo concentrate for the most part on two features, his learning and his Jewish descent.

(2) A considerable number of authors express their respect for Philo's learning in general terms, particularly when he is associated with Josephus. If the reference is more specific, then it usually insists on Philo's skill in philosophy. On a number of occasions the phrasing or the context of the reference to Philo's learning or philosophical prowess suggests that it is based on his allegorical exegesis of scripture. The most specific references are those that allude to the proverb comparing Philo with Plato and the title 'Philo the Pythagorean' found in Clement (and taken over in Sozomen).

---

members of the Alexandrian synagogue mentioned in Acts 6:9, and Barḥadbšabba ᶜArbaya, who names Philo as the director of the Alexandrian school.

[83] On this biographical material see Schamps (1987) 460–469.

(3) Two epithets are used to describe Philo's Jewish descent. Until the end of the 4th century *Hebraios* is clearly dominant. Thereafter *Ioudaios* begins to take over, even if it never wholly supplants the other title. Jerome appears to have played an important role in this development, particularly in the West. The reference to 'Philo a Jew' in Theodore of Mopsuestia is most likely earlier than Jerome's description of Philo as *Iudaeus* in his *De viris illustribus*. The title *Hebraios* is in all cases a sign of respect. The interpretation of the term *Ioudaios* is more difficult. Implicit in this term is a contrast with Christianity. It can be meant neutrally, or [23] even have a positive connotation. There are also texts in which the context shows that the reference has a distinct polemical edge.

(4) The title Philo the Bishop, which implies full acceptance of the legend of Philo Christianus, is idiosyncratic, and is only found in the *Catenae*.

(5) Philo's Alexandrian origin is rarely mentioned and never used as a title.

(6) The majority of titles and descriptions used for Philo are positive in content and intent. This reflects the generally positive attitude taken towards him in the Christian tradition.

Finally it is appropriate to end our discussion by drawing some conclusions on *why* titles and epithets are used to describe Philo. Earlier I made a distinction between titles and descriptions. Titles are used to specify who is being talked about, descriptions are used to introduce or bring to mind the figure concerned. There can be no doubt that some of the titles we have discussed (especially *sophos, philosophos, Hebraios, Ioudaios*) are used to indicate which Philo is being talked about. But it seems to me on the basis of our evidence that the titles are not used primarily for the purpose of distinguishing Philo from others who carry the same name. Two arguments support this view. Firstly we recall the fact that Philo is very often cited without any kind of label at all.[84] Secondly it is rather unexpected that *Alexandreus* is never used to identify Philo. It would appear that identificatory labels in Philo's case were not really necessary. Even though there were other Philos with whom some of the more learned members of the Christian community were familiar, these were not of a stature that they could easily be confused with

---

[84] See above p. 29–30.

'our' Philo. Philo is given an epithet mainly in order to tell the reader something about him, and, as we have seen, the epithet is often chosen in relation to the context in which it is used. This has made the subject treated in the present article all the more interesting, because it in fact allows a kind of miniature view of the way that Philo was received in the Christian tradition.

The contrast with our modern situation, mentioned at the outset of the article, is interesting. Today Philo is never called 'the Hebrew' anymore because that title in English, when used of persons, is reserved for the period of the Old Testament or Hebrew Bible.[85] Since the Second World War the title Philo Judaeus too has largely gone out of fashion.[86] [23] The reason for this, I suspect, is that a geographical location is regarded as more neutral than an ethnic origin—an important consideration in our century with its baleful (and alas continuing) history of racial discrimination. Thus we see that today Philo is generally called 'the Alexandrian'. The chief purpose of this practice is to distinguish him from the many other Philos in the Greco–Roman world. This modern habit does not have its roots in antiquity, as far as we can tell from our sources. But even today, of course, it is in certain contexts hardly necessary to identify our hero. In the pages of this Annual, for example.[87] [25]

---

[85] This is different in Italian, where it still occasionally occurs: cf. R-R nos. 6501, 6820.

[86] It was still the preferred title of Goodenough, e.g. in the bibliography that he compiled with Goodhart (1938). Perhaps if his *Introduction to Philo Judaeus* had first been written in 1962 rather than 1940 he might have chosen the alternative title. It seems that the title Philo the Jew is *never* used anymore (not a single example in R-R). For an example of a very deliberate use of the title 'Philo the Jew' in Modern Hebrew see the remark on Rav Hanazir's *Qol Hanevoua* at Neher (1986) 390 n. 6.

[87] Apart from my colleagues Van Rompay and Weitenberg already mentioned in the notes, I would also like to thank Alan Mendelson (Hamilton, Canada), Gerard Mussies (Utrecht), James Royse (San Francisco), David Satran (Jerusalem), and Daniel Schwartz (Jerusalem) for their helpful comments on various draft versions.

Bibliography

A. Arazy, *The Appellations of the Jews (Ioudaios, Hebraios, Israel) in the Literature from Alexander to Justinian* (diss. New York 1977).

J. B. Aucher, *Philonis Iudaei sermones tres hactenus inediti: I. et II. De Providentia et III. De animalibus* (Venice 1822).

J. Bidez and G. C. Hansen, *Sozomenus Kirchengeschichte*, Die griechischen christlichen Schriftsteller (Berlin 1960).

J.-B. Chabot, 'Note sur l'ouvrage syriaque intitulé 'Le Jardin des Délices'', in C. Bezold (ed.), *Orientalische Studien Theodor Nöldeke zum siebzigsten Geburtstag (2. März 1906) gewidmet* (Giessen 1906) 1.487–496.

——, *Anonymi auctoris Chronicon ad annum Christi 1234 pertinens*, Corpus Scriptorum Christianorum Orientalium 109 = Scriptores Syri 56 (Louvain 1952).

R. Devreesse, *Essai sur Théodore de Mopsueste*, Studi e Testi 141 (Vatican City 1948).

C. Duckworth and E. F. Osborn, 'Clement of Alexandria's *Hypotyposeis*: a French Eighteenth-century Sighting', *The Journal of Theological Studies* 36 (1985) 67–83.

J. A. Fabricius, *Bibliotheca Graeca* (Hamburg 1705–28, 1795[4]).

L. H. Feldman, *Jew and Gentile in the Ancient World* (Princeton 1993).

D. Forabaschi, *Onomasticon alterum papyrorum: Supplement al Namenbuch di F. Preisigke*, 2 vols. in 3 (Milan–Varese 1967).

P. M. Fraser, and E. Matthews, *A Lexicon of Greek Personal Names, vol. 1 The Aegean Islands, Cyprus, Cyrenaica* (Oxford 1987).

H. Görgemans, Art. 'Philosophie IIA, Griechische Patristik', *Historische Wörterbuch der Philosophie* 7 (Munich 1989) 616–623.

E. R. Goodenough, *An Introduction to Philo Judaeus* (New Haven 1940, Oxford–New York 1962[2]).

H. L. Goodhart and E. R. Goodenough, 'A General Bibliography of Philo Judaeus', in E. R. Goodenough, *The Politics of Philo Judaeus: Practice and Theory* (New Haven 1938; repr. Hildesheim 1967) 125–321.

B. Grillet, G. Sabbah and A.-J. Festugière, *Sozomène Histoire Ecclésiastique*, Sources Chrétiennes 308 (Paris 1983).

A. van den Hoek, *Clement of Alexandria and his Use of Philo in the* Stromateis: *an Early Christian Reshaping of a Jewish Model*, Supplements to Vigiliae Christianae 3 (Leiden 1988).

W. Horbury and D. Noy, *Jewish Inscriptions of Graeco-Roman Egypt* (Cambridge 1992).

P. W. van der Horst, *Ancient Jewish Epitaphs*, Contributions to Biblical Exegesis and Theology 2 (Kampen 1991).

A. M. Jones, J. R. Martindale, and J. Morris, *The Prosopography of the Later Roman Empire, vol. 1 A.D. 260–395, vol. 2 A.D. 395–527, vol. 3 A.D. 527–641*, 3 vols. in 4 (last two volumes edited by Martindale only) (Cambridge 1971–92).

A. Kamesar, *Jerome, Greek Scholarship, and the Hebrew Bible*, Oxford Classical Monographs (Oxford 1993).

J. N. D. Kelly, *Jerome: his Life, Writings, and Controversies* (London 1975).

K. G. Kuhn and W. Gutbrod, 'Art. Ἰσραήλ κτλ', *Theological Dictionary of the New Testament* 359–391.

R. Kühner and F. Blass, *Ausführliche Grammatik der griechischen Sprache*, 2 volumes in 4 (Hannover 1890–1904[3]).

N. de Lange, *Origen and the Jews: Studies in Jewish-Christian Relations in Third-[26] Century Palestine*, University of Cambridge Oriental Publications 25 (Cambridge 1976).

N. P. Lemche, Art. 'Hebrew', *The Anchor Bible Dictionary* 4 (1992) 95.

A M. MALINGREY, *'Philosophia': étude d'un groupe de mots dans la littérature grecque des Présocratiques au IVe siècle après J.-C.* (Paris 1961).

S. N. MASON, *Flavius Josephus on the Pharisees: a Composition-critical Study*, Studia Postbiblica 39 (Leiden 1991).

G. MUSSIES, 'Jewish Personal Names in some Non-Literary Sources', in J. W. VAN HENTEN and P. W. VAN DER HORST (edd.), *Studies in Early Jewish Epigraphy*, Arbeiten zur Geschichte des antiken Judentums und des Urchristentums 21 (Leiden 1994) 242–276.

A. NEHER, 'Les références à Philon d'Alexandrie dans l'œuvre du Rav Hanazir, disciple du Rav Kook *(Qol Hanevoua, 1970)*', in A. CAQUOT, M. HADAS-LEBEL and J. RIAUD (edd.), *Hellenica et Judaica: hommage à Valentin Nikiprowetzy* (Leuven 1986) 385-390.

V. NIKIPROWETZKY, *Le commentaire de l'Écriture chez Philon d'Alexandrie: son caractère et sa portée; observations philologiques*, Arbeiten zur Literatur und Geschichte des hellenistischen Judentums 11 (Leiden 1977).

W. PAPE and G. BENSELER, *Wörterbuch der griechischen Eigennamen* (Graz 1959, = reprint of 1911[3]).

P. W. PESTMAN *et al.*, *A Guide to the Zenon Papyri (P.L. Bat. 21)*, 2 vols., Papyrologia Lugduno-Batava 21 (Leiden 1981).

F. PETIT, *L'ancienne version latine des Questions sur la Genèse de Philon d'Alexandrie*, 2 vols., Texte und Untersuchungen 113–14 (Berlin 1973).

——, *Quaestiones in Genesim et in Exodum: fragmenta graeca*, PAPM 33 (Paris 1978).

——, *La Chaîne sur la Genèse: Édition intégrale*, 2 vols. (so far), Traditio Exegetica Graeca 1–2 (Louvain 1991–93).

P. PILHOFER, *Presbyteron kreitton: Der Alterbeweis der jüdischen und christlichen Apologeten und seine Vorgeschichte*, Wissenschaftliche Untersuchungen zum Neuen Testament 2.39 (Tübingen 1990).

F. PREISIGKE, *Namenbuch* (Heidelberg 1922).

G. J. REININK, 'Die Textüberlieferung der Gannat Bussame', *Le Muséon* 90 (1977) 103–175.

L. VAN ROMPAY, *Théodore de Mopsueste: Fragments syriaques du Commentaire des Psaumes (Psaume 118 et Psaumes 138–148)*, Corpus Scriptorum Christianorum Orientalium 436 Scriptores Syri 190 (Louvain 1982).

J. R. ROYSE, *The Spurious Texts of Philo of Alexandria: a Study of Textual Transmission and Corruption with Indexes to the Major Collections of Greek Fragments*, Arbeiten zur Literatur und Geschichte des hellenistischen Judentums 22 (Leiden 1991).

D. T. RUNIA, 'Philo of Alexandria in Five Letters of Isidore of Pelusium', in idem, D. M. HAY and D. WINSTON (edd.), *Heirs of the Septuagint. Philo, Hellenistic Judaism and Early Christianity: Festschrift for Earle Hilgert*, Brown Judaic Studies 230 [= *Studia Philonic Annual* 3 (1991)] (Atlanta 1991) 295–319 (= below chapter 9).

——, 'A Note on Philo and Christian Heresy', *SPhA* 4 (1992) 65–74 (= below chapter 8).

——, *Philo in Early Christian Literature: a Survey*, Compendia Rerum Iudaicarum ad Novum Testamentum III 3 (Assen–Minneapolis 1993).

J. SCHAMPS, *Photios historien des lettres: la Bibliothèque et ses notices biographiques*, Bibliothèque de la Faculté de Philosophie et Lettres de l'Université de Liège 248 (Paris 1987). [27]

C. SCHAÜBLIN, *Untersuchungen zu Methode und Herkunft der antiochenischen Exegese*, Theophaneia 23 (Köln–Bonn 1974).

H. SCHRECKENBERG, 'Josephus in Early Christian Literature and Medieval Christian Art, in *idem* and K. SCHUBERT, *Jewish Historiography and Iconography in Early and Medieval Christianity*, Compendia Rerum Iudaicarum ad Novum Testamentum III 1 (Assen–Minneapolis 1992) 1–138.

D. R. SCHWARTZ, 'Philo's Priestly Descent', in F. E. GREENSPAHN, E. HILGERT and B. L. MACK (edd.), *Nourished with Peace: Studies in Hellenistic Judaism in Memory of Samuel Sandmel*, Scholars Press Homage Series 9 (Chico, California 1984) 155-171.

H. SOLIN, *Die griechischen Personennamen in Rom: ein Namenbuch*, 3 vols. (Berlin–New York 1982).

M. STERN, *Greek and Latin Authors on Jews and Judaism*, 3 vols. (Jerusalem 1974-84).

A. TERIAN, *Philonis Alexandrini de Animalibus: the Armenian Text with an Introduction, Translation and Commentary*, Studies in Hellenistic Judaism: Supplements to Studia Philonica 1 (Chico, California 1981).

R. W. THOMSON, *Moses Khorenats'i History of the Armenians* (Cambridge Mass.–London 1978).

P. TOMSON, 'The Names Israel and Jew in Ancient Judaism and in the New Testament', *Bijdragen* 47 (1986) 120–140, 266–289.

B. VANDENHOFF, *Exegesis Psalmorum, imprimis Messianicorum apud Syrios Nestorianos e codice usque adhuc inedito illustrata* (Rheine 1899).

J. M. VOSTÉ, 'La chronologie de l'activité littéraire de Théodore de Mopsueste', *Revue Biblique* 34 (1925) 54–81.

E. A. WALLIS BUDGE, *The Chronography of Gregory Abû'l Faraj, the Son of Aaron, The Hebrew Physician, Commonly Known as Bar Hebraeus, being the First Part of his Political History of the World* (Oxford 1932).

J. WHITTAKER, 'Platonic Philosophy in the Early Centuries of the Empire', *Aufsteig und Niedergang der römischen Welt* II 36.1 (Berlin-New York 1987) 81-123.

C. K. WONG, 'Philo's Use of Chaldaioi', *Studia Philonica Annual* 4 (1992) 1–14.

W. WRIGHT, *Catalogue of Syriac Manuscripts in the British Museum, acquired since the Year 1838, Part II* (London 1871).

T. ZAHN, *Acta Johannis* (Erlangen 1880).

CHAPTER THREE

WHY DOES CLEMENT OF ALEXANDRIA
CALL PHILO 'THE PYTHAGOREAN'?

The evidence and the problem

It is a well-known fact that the massive corpus of writings of Philo of Alexandria only survived because he was taken up in the Christian tradition as a church father *honoris causa*.[1] In our extant sources he is first mentioned by Josephus (*Antiquities* 18.258), who describes him as 'a man respected in every way ... and not unskilled in philosophy'.[2] But this is the last reference to Philo by a Jewish author until the 16th century. We first read about him in a Christian author in the *Stromateis* of Clement of Alexandria (written at the end of the 2nd century A.D.). Clement explicitly refers to Philo on four occasions, but his actual usage of Philonic material is much more extensive. Indeed Clement's handling of Philo is an illuminating example of the way ancient authors were wont to use other authors as a source for their own writing. In her excellent and well-received monograph on the subject Annewies van den Hoek has shown that on at least eight occasions Clement had a copy of Philo on his desk as it were, and that he copied out extensive excerpts in the *Stromateis*, unrolling his scroll as he went along (on one occasion in reverse!).[3]

---

[1] For a full account of this process see my *Philo in Early Christian Literature: a Survey*. Compendia Rerum Iudaicarum ad Novum Testamentum III 3 (Assen-Minneapolis 1993).

[2] ἀνὴρ τὰ πάντα ἔνδοξος... καὶ φιλοσοφίας οὐκ ἄπειρος.

[3] *Clement of Alexandria and his Use of Philo in the* Stromateis: *an Early Christian*

The four passages in which Clement refers to Philo by name are the following:[4]

1.31.1: ἑρμηνεύει δὲ ὁ Φίλων τὴν μὲν Ἅγαρ παροίκησιν ..., τὴν Σάραν δὲ ἀρχήν μου. (Philo interprets Hagar as 'sojourning'..., Sarah as 'my rule'.)

1.72.4: τούτων ἁπάντων πρεσβύτατον μακρῷ τὸ Ἰουδαίων γένος, καὶ τὴν παρ' αὐτοῖς φιλοσοφίαν ἔγγραπτον γενομένην προκατάρξαι τῆς παρ' Ἕλλησι φιλοσοφίας διὰ πολλῶν ὁ Πυθαγόρειος ὑποδείκνυσι Φίλων, οὐ μὴν ἀλλὰ καὶ Ἀριστόβουλος ὁ Περιπατητικὸς καὶ ἄλλοι πλείους, ἵνα μὴ κατ' ὄνομα ἐπιὼν διατρίβω. (That the race of the Jews is by far the oldest of all these (races or cultures) and that their philosophy in a written form commenced prior to that of the Greeks is fully demonstrated by the Pythagorean Philo, as well as by Aristobulus the Peripatetic and many others, a list of whose names I will not bore you with.)

1.152.2: τὴν δὲ ἄλλην ἐγκύκλιον παιδείαν Ἕλληνες ἐδίδασκον ἐν Αἰγύπτῳ, ὡς ἂν [2] βασιλικὸν παιδίον, ᾗ φησι Φίλων ἐν τῷ Μωυσέως βίῳ, προσεμάνθανε δὲ τὰ Ἀσσυρίων γράμματα καὶ τὴν τῶν οὐρανίων ἐπιστήμην παρά τε Χαλδαίων παρά τε Αἰγυπτίων ... (The remainder of the general education Greeks taught him [Moses] in Egypt, as would befit a royal child, an account of which is given by Philo in his *Life of Moses*. In addition he learned Assyrian letters and the science of the heavens from the Chaldeans and from the Egyptians.)

2.100.3: Πλάτων δὲ ὁ φιλόσοφος, εὐδαιμονίαν τέλος τιθέμενος, "ὁμοίω-σιν θεῷ" φησιν αὐτὴν εἶναι "κατὰ τὸ δυνατόν", εἴτε [καὶ] συνδραμών πως τῷ δόγματι τοῦ νόμου ("αἱ γὰρ μεγάλαι φύσεις καὶ γυμναὶ παθῶν εὐστοχοῦσί πως περὶ τὴν ἀλήθειαν", ὥς φησιν ὁ Πυθαγόρειος Φίλων τὰ Μωυσέως ἐξηγούμενος), εἴτε καὶ παρά τινων τότε λογίων ἀναδιδαχθεὶς ἅτε μαθήσεως ἀεὶ διψῶν. (Plato the philosopher posits as the goal of life 'well-being', and says that this is 'becoming like unto God to the extent possible', in this either coinciding somehow or other with the doctrine of the Law (for great natures who are devoid of passions somehow or other hit on the truth, as says the Pythagorean Philo when expounding the works of Moses), or because, as one who was always thirsting for learning, he had been taught it by learned men then living.)

These references deserve further study. In the first, which occurs in the middle of an extensive section that borrows heavily from Philo, the Jewish author is suddenly introduced without any further indication as to who he might be.[5] In the third text both the name and the

---

Reshaping of a Jewish Model, Vigiliae Christianae Supplements 3 (Leiden 1988); see esp. 211–216.
[4] The text used is that of Stählin-Früchtel-Treu (GCS). It is possible that Clement also refers to Philo at *Str.* 1.152.2, but if so, he is mistaken (it should be Philo the Elder, the historian, = RE (46)).
[5] Note how Clement is heavily dependent on a source, but only mentions its name incidentally. This frequent habit of ancient authors was heavily exploited in the method of *Quellenforschung* developed in classical studies in the 19th century,

work used as a source is given. Clement explicitly indicates that he has made use of Philo's account of the life of Moses, no doubt in order to give his own account of the same subject more authority.[6] Here too Philo's name is given without any further description. In the other two passages the situation differs. Clement does add a description that tells us a little more about who this Philo might be. He is twice called 'the Pythagorean'. This epithet is used of Philo in only one other ancient source, namely the historian Sozomen, who informs us that according to 'Philo the Pythagorean' the best of the Hebrews retired to Lake Mareotis and practised philosophy there.[7] A single other text points in a similar direction. When introducing Philo in his *Ecclesiastical History* Eusebius tells us that Philo is recorded as having exceeded his contemporaries in his zeal for the philosophical discipline of Plato and Pythagoras (so I translate τὴν κατὰ Πλάτωνα καὶ Πυθαγόραν ἀγωγήν).[8] This information may be derived from Clement, whom, as we know, Eusebius had read very carefully.[9]

Now in my view the epithet 'Pythagorean' which Clement attaches to Philo is unexpected. It is surely surprising that he does not describe him as 'Philo the Jew' or, as might be more likely, 'Philo the Hebrew'.[10] We would expect that Philo's role as a predecessor in the [3] Jewish-Christian tradition, i.e. the tradition that ascribes authority to the Hebrew scriptures, was more important for Clement than an attachment to a philosophical school of thought. In her monograph Van den Hoek devotes virtually no attention to the matter.[11] Yet it is easy to see that from the historical point of view the issue is not without significance. As we have seen, apart from the

---

an essentially risky procedure because the extent of the dependence can only be determined if the exploited source is still extant (in which case the results of the *Quellenforschung* are generally of much less significance).

[6] Perhaps too because it is an unusual and contestable (since chronologically implausible) piece of information.

[7] *Hist. Eccl.* 1.12.9, referring of course to Philo's account of the Therapeutae.

[8] *Hist. Eccl.* 2.4.3.

[9] For example, at *Praep. Evang.* 9.6.5 he quotes the words of Clement that *immediately follow* the mention of Philo the Pythagorean at *Str.* 1.72.4. Nearly a dozen extracts from *Str.* 1.69–75 are cited throughout books 9 and 10 of *Praep. Evang.* I return to this question later in my paper.

[10] As I have shown in a recent article, Philo is in fact not called 'the Jew' in our sources until the second half of the 4th century. Until then he is 'Philo the Hebrew'; see 'Philonic Nomenclature', *The Studia Philonica Annual* 6 (1994) 1–27, esp. 14–20.

[11] Cf. *op. cit.* (n. 3) 107, 179, 184.

brief notice in Josephus, Clement is the first author to name Philo. It is highly probable that it was through the intervention of the so-called catechetical school of Pantaenus, of which Clement was a member (but of which we know perilously little), that the writings of Philo were rescued from the debris of Jewish-Alexandrian culture after the disastrous happenings in the century after Philo's death.[12] Just as from the textual point of view,[13] so also from the historical perspective the early information supplied by Clement has to be taken very seriously. When he calls Philo a 'Pythagorean', can this mean that in some way or another Philo was a member of the Pythagorean school? Naturally we have to allow for the fact that Clement may have been privy to information that is otherwise lost to us. If this is the case, we cannot check him. But we do have the duty to examine the question of why Clement called Philo 'the Pythagorean' from as many angles as are made available to us by our limited sources. This is the task that I propose to take on myself in the present article.[14]

It is, of course, with Clement that we should start. The answer to our question will be determined primarily by Clement's perception of Philo and other writers like him. The evidence of other contemporary authors is only useful to the extent that it brings Clement's views into sharper relief. I begin, therefore, with the *contexts* of the two passages, since they may well tell us something about why Clement chose to describe Philo in the way that he did. It will be more convenient to take the latter first.

The text at Str. *2.100.3*

After a long passage starting at §78, in which Clement describes how the Greek philosophical doctrine of the various virtues is already

---

[12] See D. Barthélemy, 'Est-ce Hoshaya Rabba qui censura le 'Commentaire Allégorique'? A partir des retouches faites aux citations bibliques, étude sur la tradition textuelle du Commentaire Allégorique de Philon', in *Philon d'Alexandrie: Lyon 11-15 Septembre 1966; colloques nationaux du Centre National de la Recherche Scientifique* (Paris 1967) 60, and also Runia *op. cit.* (n. 1) 22–23.

[13] See P. Wendland, 'Philo und Clemens Alexandrinus', *Hermes* 31 (1896) 435–456, and my 'Underneath Cohn and Colson: the Text of Philo's *De virtutibus*', *Society of Biblical Literature Seminar Papers* 30 (1991) 116–134, esp. 124–127.

[14] Previous research on this question has been limited to scattered observations. See below notes 44 and 71 on the research of R. Radice and D. Winston. I have raised the question without giving an adequate answer at *op. cit.* (n. 1) 136 and in an article 'Was Philo a Middle Platonist? a Difficult Question Revisited', *The Studia Philonic Annual* 5 (1993) 133.

58 CHAPTER THREE

located in the writings of Moses, it is concluded that 'Plato the philosopher' has a doctrine of the *telos* which is the same as that of Moses (see text cited above). The formulation of the *telos* as εὐδαιμονία and ὁμοίωσις θεῷ κατὰ τὸ δυνατόν, derived from *Theaet.* 176b, is of course straight Middle [4] Platonist doctrine.[15] The convergence of doctrine is to be explained either through the fact that great minds can hit on the truth independently of each other, or because Plato, ever thirsting for knowledge, somehow came into contact with learned men who could teach him what was contained in the Mosaic philosophy.[16] The latter alternative recalls the apologetic argument of the 'theft of the philosophers', which is one of the pillars of Clement's argument throughout the entire work.[17]

The first and lesser difficulty posed by the passage is that the quote from Philo which is supposed to support the former alternative is nowhere to be found as such in the Philonic corpus. It is not impossible that Clement has in mind a passage now lost (e.g. in the *Quaestiones* or the *Hypothetica*). But I agree with the editors of Philo, Cohn and Wendland, that he almost certainly has a passage in mind which describes Moses' own education:[18]

---

[15] Cf. Alcinous, *Did.* 2 153.8, 28 181.19 Whittaker, S. R. C. Lilla, *Clement of Alexandria: a Study in Christian Platonism and Gnosticism*, Oxford Theological Monographs (Oxford 1971) 106–110, and for Philo see my *Philo of Alexandria and the* Timaeus *of Plato*, Philosophia Antiqua 44 (Leiden 1986²) 341–343.

[16] So I interpret the phrase παρά τινων τότε λογίων, since the whole context concerns how Greek ethics takes its starting point from Moses. Origen's words at *C. Cels.* 4.39 could be taken as a paraphrase of/commentary on Clement's text: 'It is not quite clear whether Plato happened to hit on these matters by chance, or whether, as some think, on his visit to Egypt he met even with those who interpret the Jews' traditions philosophically, and learnt some ideas from them, some of which he kept, and some of which he slightly altered...' (translation Chadwick). On the entire subject see further the texts assembled by H. Dörrie and M. Baltes, *Der Platonismus in der Antike*, Band 2 Der hellenistischen Rahmen des kaiserzeitlichen Platonismus (Stuttgart 1990), §69–71 (texts at 190–219, commentary at 480ff.).

[17] Cf. D. Wyrwa, *Die christliche Platonaneignung in den Stromateis des Clemens von Alexandrien*, Arbeiten zur Kirchengeschichte 53 (Berlin-New York 1983) 298–316, and for the theme before Clement P. Pilhofer, *Presbyteron kreitton: Der Alterbeweis der jüdischen und christlichen Apologeten und seine Vorgeschichte*, WUNT 2.39 (Tübingen 1990). Wyrwa 148–152 denies its presence in Book II, making a distinction between the claims of theft and of dependence, but this question is not relevant to our present undertaking.

[18] L. Cohn and P. Wendland, *Philonis Alexandrini opera quae supersunt* (Berlin 1896–1915) 4.124 (the work of Cohn); the suggestion was taken over by Stählin-Früchtel in the GCS edition of Clement (2.168).

Philo, *Mos.* 1.22	Clement, *Str.* 2.100.3
πολλὰ γὰρ αἱ μεγάλαι φύσεις	αἱ γὰρ μεγάλαι φύσεις καὶ γυμναὶ
καινοτομοῦσι τῶν εἰς	παθῶν εὐστοχοῦσί πως περὶ τὴν
ἐπιστήμην.	ἀλήθειαν.

It is perhaps better *not* to place Clement's words in quotation marks, since he is giving the gist of Philo's words, not citing them *verbatim*. The context determines the change from ἐπιστήμη (relevant to Moses' natural abilities that came to the fore during his training) to ἀλήθεια (Plato's ethical insights). But then καινοτομοῦσι has to be changed too, for truth (in the ancient conception) is not found through innovation.[19] A further argument in favour of this derivation is that the additional words γυμναὶ παθῶν clearly reflect what Philo says about Moses' asceticism at *Mos.* 1.25–29 (note especially παθῶν at §26). Moreover the cited passage is part of a longer section of Philo's work which Clement adapts at length in book I of the *Stromateis* (he refers to it in the third of the passages cited above in which Philo's name is mentioned).[20] A final consideration is the ambiguity of the phrase τὰ Μωυσέως ἐξηγούμενος which follows the mention of Philo's name. This may mean 'expounding the writings of Moses' (i.e. a very general sense, equivalent to 'in his commentaries on Moses'), or it may mean 'giving an exposition of the facts about Moses', which could then be a reference to the biographical details furnished in abundance in the *De vita Moysis*.[21] The latter view would further support Cohn and Wendland's view. It seems to me, however, that the first interpretation of the phrase is the more likely. [5]

The second interpretative difficulty is that we must try to determine the intent and scope of the reference to Philo. A minimalist view would be that Clement is making an erudite literary allusion to a memorable turn of phrase in Philo. After all the contexts are rather different: in the one case the education of the prodigy Moses, in the other Plato's independent acquisition of a philosophical truth. There is, however, a complication. This particular passage follows on, and can be regarded as the climax of, the passage 2.78.1–

---

[19] As noted by Van den Hoek *op. cit.* (n. 3) 184. The verb εὐστοχέω is in fact not found in our extant Philo.
[20] There are references to Greek teachers at *Mos.* 1.21 and 23, i.e. on either side of the text on natural abilities adapted here!
[21] Cf. the more specific words ἐν τῷ Μωυσέως βίῳ at *Str.* 1.152.2.

101.1, the entire sequence of which is determined by large-scale (but wholly unacknowledged) borrowings from Philo's treatise *De virtutibus*.[22] Is Clement indirectly making amends by naming Philo after the event in the expectation that the attentive reader will make the connection?

The question to be answered, therefore, is whether there is any connection between what we just called the 'erudite literary allusion' and the theme of the passage, i.e. the Platonic *telos*. At this point we should take into account an acute observation made by Dietmar Wyrwa in his analysis of Clement's use of Plato.[23] He points out that Clement's mention of the ὁμοίωσις θεῷ formula is anticipated on two occasions earlier in the passage, i.e. at 80.5 and 97.1, and that both passages are taken straight from Philo (*Virt.* 8 and 168). This means that *if* the formula is now attributed to Plato, at the very least Clement has *implicitly* indicated his recognition that Philo's use of these phrases has a Platonic (as well as a Mosaic) background.[24] It is tempting to connect this observation with Clement's description of Philo as 'the Pythagorean', even if formally and strictly speaking there is no connection between the statement on Plato and the reference to Philo. Whether this interpretation is legitimate has yet to be seen.

The text at Str. *1.72.4*

The context here is less illuminating, and can be dealt with quickly. In this section[25] Clement discusses the relationship between Greek and barbarian philosophy. He argues that (1) many of the first Greek philosophers (e.g. Pythagoras and Thales) were barbarians anyway, (2) Plato recognizes the contribution of barbarian philosophers, (3) many of the Greek philosophers studied with or learnt from barbarian philosophers, and (4) philosophy flourished among the barbarian races before it reached the Greeks. The section ends with a long series of witnesses. The first two are 'Philo the Pythagorean' and 'Aristobulus [6] the Peripatetic', i.e. our text. Thereafter

---

[22] See the lists at A. Méhat, *Études sur les 'Stromates' de Clement d'Alexandrie*, Patristica Sorbonensia 7 (Paris 1966) 238, Van den Hoek *op. cit.* (n. 3) 71–72.

[23] *Op. cit.* (n. 17) 144.

[24] A very similar procedure occurs at *Str.* 5.73, as I pointed out in *op. cit.* (n. 1) 147.

[25] I take section XV = §66–73 as a single unit in the argument.

Clement cites four Greek sources which support his thesis (Megasthenes, anonymi, Herodorus, Hermippus).

There is no text in the extant Philo which explicitly undertakes to prove the antiquity of the Jews and the anteriority of their written philosophy (i.e. the Law). So Clement's statement might be taken as a rhetorical flourish. In most of his extant writings Philo shows little interest in historical details.[26] There can, however, be little doubt that the apologetic motif would have met with his approval. Wendland's suggestion that Clement is referring here to a lost section of the *Hypothetica* cannot be proven, but certainly deserves serious consideration.[27]

Why then is Philo given the epithet 'Pythagorean' in this context? No doubt because it boosts his standing as a witness. There is nothing remarkable about a Jew claiming the antiquity of his own race. Clement does not bother to tell his reader that Philo is Jewish. It does make a difference if he is someone who has an association with the Greek philosophical tradition. Philo's fellow-Alexandrian Aristobulus is also given an epithet that indicates a connection with a philosophical school. It is apparent that Clement's use of such philosophical epithets needs to be examined in closer detail.

Epithets indicating connections with philosophical schools in Clement

Before looking at particular examples, we must first address a preliminary question. What do terms such as 'Pythagorean' and 'Peripatetic' refer to? Here there is an important distinction that needs to be made.

In the first place such terms will very often indicate *membership of* or *affiliation to* a philosophical αἵρεσις, i.e. a philosophical 'school' or, perhaps better, 'school of thought'.[28] In Clement's time, as is

---

[26] Cf. my remarks on his use of the celebrated text *Tim.* 22b on the juvenility of the Greeks compared with the Egyptians at *op. cit.* (n. 15) 77.

[27] 'Die Therapeuten und die philonische Schrift vom beschaulichen Leben', *Jahrbuch für die Philologie* Supplbd 22 (1896) 770, cf. 709–715. Van den Hoek *op. cit.* (n. 3) 179 classifies the text as D, i.e. non-dependence on Philo, but this should be qualified.

[28] There is no need to document what follows in detail. Particularly influential have been the studies of J. Glucker; see esp. his *Antiochus and the Late Academy*, Hypomnemata 56 (Göttingen 1978), esp. 174ff., and 'Cicero's Philosophical Affiliations', in J. M. Dillon and A. A. Long (edd.), *The Question of "Eclecticism"* (Berkeley 1988) 34–69 (where he promotes the terms 'affiliation' and 'membership').

well known, philosophers were generally identified by their
allegiance to one of the rival 'schools' that went back to the earlier
period of the Greek philosophical tradition. These 'schools' scarcely
existed in the institutional sense to which we are accustomed (although in Clement's day there were some municipal chairs for the
various αἱρέσεις, and at Athens even an Imperial endowment).
There was no central body that organized all philosophers who
called themselves Platonists, but no doubt most Platonists would
look up to the occupant of the chair of [7] Platonist philosophy in
Athens.[29] One could be a professional representative of such an
αἵρεσις. Such were the men whom Justin studied with—first a
Στωϊκός, then a Περιπατητικός, then a Πυθαγόρειος, and finally a
prominent Πλατωνικός—before he fell in with the old man by the
sea. One could also be 'affiliated' with such a 'school of thought'
without teaching philosophy professionally. Here we think of men
such as Cicero, who regarded himself as an 'Academic', the 'Platonist' Plutarch, the 'Stoic' Seneca, and so on. Such membership
could be projected into the distant past, e.g. Empedocles could be
called 'the Pythagorean' because he came from Western Greece, was
thought to have been a pupil of Pythagoras, and maintained similar
doctrines (e.g. reincarnation).[30]

It is also possible, however, to use these terms in a different sense,
to indicate not a membership of or an affiliation to a 'school of
thought', but rather an *affinity to the thought* of such an αἵρεσις. One
can be a 'Platonist' if there are elements of Platonic doctrine in
one's writings, even if one does not regard oneself as a 'member' of
that school. The distinction between the two usages is necessarily
somewhat fluid, and cannot always be accurately demarcated. That it
is real can be illustrated if we now turn to some examples found in
Clement himself.

Clement calls various people 'the Pythagorean' if, as he thinks,
they were members of the ancient Pythagorean school, e.g.
Philolaus, Epicharmus, Athamas, Hippodamus, and so on.[31] On two

---

[29] On the public position of philosophers in the 2nd century see now J. Hahn,
*Der Philosoph und die Gesellschaft: Selbstverständnis, öffentliches Auftreten und populäre
Erwartungen in der hohen Kaiserzeit* (Stuttgart 1989), on Athens 118ff.
[30] Cf. texts cited at *Fragmente der Vorsokratiker* 31A11, 82A10 Diels-Kranz, and cf.
J. Mansfeld, *Heresiography in Context: Hippolytus' Elenchos as a Source for Greek
Philosophy*, Philosophia Antiqua 56 (Leiden 1992), esp. chap. 8.
[31] For the references see the useful overview in the GCS edition of Clement
(ed. Stählin-Früchtel-Treu), 4.171–172, s.v. Πυθαγόρειος and Πυθαγορικός.

occasions Clement calls Numa, King of Rome, a 'Pythagorean'. The one text is in the same chapter as the second of the texts analysed above, where it is claimed that Numa learnt from Moses not to allow anthropomorphic images of God.[32] This information Clement derives from Plutarch, who in his biography discusses the possibility that Numa was an intimate of Pythagoras at some length.[33] We note that in this text Clement argues that the Romans were taught in secret that it was only possible 'to have contact with the most excellent principle (ἐφάψασθαι τοῦ βελτίστου)' with the mind alone. The secrecy is Pythagorean, but the philosophy is pure Platonism. Quite different is the case of Pindar. Clement describes him as 'Pythagorean' on account of the first lines of the sixth Nemead, in which the single origin of men and gods is celebrated (i.e. the Pythagorean monad).[34] But there is no association of the Boeotian Pindar with the Pythagorean school.[35] Here we have a clear case of 'affinity of thought' retrospectively attributed.

The only 'modern' Pythagorean whom Clement mentions as such [8] (apart from Philo) is Numenius, in the famous text at *Str.* 1.150.4 where he is recorded as contending that Plato is none other than a Μωυσῆς ἀττικίζων. The text itself does not tell us very much, but we may certainly assume that in Clement's eyes Numenius was a member of (or affiliated with) the Pythagorean αἵρεσις. The more difficult question here is what Numenius' relation to the Platonic school of thought is. After all the pronouncement concerns Plato, not Pythagoras. We shall return to this question below. Strikingly Clement, though himself probably trained in a Platonic school environment, nowhere describes any philosopher as a 'Platonist'.[36]

As for the term Περιπατητικός, it furnishes us with two surprises.

---

[32] *Str.* 1.71.1, cf. 5.8.4.

[33] See esp. Plut. *Numa* 1.2–3, and cf. 8.4–10, 14.2–3, 22.3–4.

[34] *Str.* 5.102.2.

[35] Cf. for example U. von Wilomowitz-Moellendorff, *Pindaros* (Berlin 1922) 251: 'Pythagoreisches läßt sich bei Pindar durchaus nichts nachweisen, es sei denn die Seelenwanderung, die doch in Hintergrunde bleibt'; also E. Thummer, *Die Religiosität Pindars* (Innsbruck 1957) 121–130, W. Burkert, *Greek Religion* (Oxford 1985) 300–301.

[36] The term Πλατωνικός is a late development, emerging towards the end of the 1st cent. AD. See Glucker *op. cit.* (n. 28) 134–137, 206–225; also my 'Philosophical heresiography: evidence in two recently published inscriptions', *Zeitschrift für Papyrologie und Epigraphik* 72 (1988) 243. Clement also does not use the earlier term Ἀκαδημαϊκός; instead he speaks of οἱ ἐκ τῆς Ἀκαδημίας in his long doxography on the *telos* at *Str.* 2.129.8 (the only case).

Firstly Aristotle is once somewhat curiously called 'the Peripatetic',
but there is, one supposes, no good reason for excluding him from
the school that he himself founded.[37] Others given the title be-
longed to the Peripatetic school during Aristotle's lifetime and the
subsequent Hellenistic period: Clearchus, Strato, Lyco, Hieronymus,
Critolaus.[38] Nothing unexpected here. The remaining surprise is, of
course, Philo's fellow Alexandrian Jew Aristobulus, who is called 'the
Peripatetic' in the very same sentence as Philo is called 'the
Pythagorean'. This case requires our closest attention.

Aristobulus the Peripatetic

Much ink has been spilt on Aristobulus, chiefly because he is such
an intriguing figure, about whom we would like to know a lot
more.[39] He is the only one of Philo's Jewish-Alexandrian predecessors whom we know by name. If we take him to have flourished in
the mid-second cent. B.C., then a period of nearly two centuries
separates them. Clement mentions him four times, of which on two
occasions as 'the Peripatetic'. It would appear that Eusebius became
interested in him through his reading of Clement. Whereas Clement
cites only short pieces of text, Eusebius gives us four extended
passages. This means that he must have had access to a copy of
Aristobulus' work, an interpretation of the Jewish Law with an
apologetic orientation. The Eusebian fragments allow a number of
further unnamed borrowings in Clement to be identified.[40]
    Clement's designation of Aristobulus as 'the Peripatetic' is

---

[37] *Str.* 5.88.5 (Clement mentions the title probably in order to emphasize that
four separate schools regard matter as one of the *archai*). At *Str.* 1.63.4 in the
survey of the successions of the philosophers Aristotle is recorded as having
founded the περιπατητικὴ αἵρεσις.
[38] See the list in the GCS edition of Clement (ed. Stählin-Früchtel-Treu),
4.163.
[39] The standard work remains by N. Walter, *Der Thoraausleger Aristobulos: Untersuchungen zu seinen Fragmenten und zu pseudepigraphischen Resten der jüdisch-hellenistischen Literatur*, Texte und Untersuchungen 86 (Berlin 1964). Walter appears to
have succeeded in dispelling the sceptical views of 19th and early 20th century. An
English translation of the fragments by A. Yarbro Collins is found in J. H. Charles-
worth, *The Old Testament Pseudepigrapha* (London 1983–85) 2.837–842. Further
bibliography is given at E. Schürer, G. Vermes *et al.*, *The History of the Jewish people
in the Age of Jesus Christ*, 3 vols. in 4 (Edinburgh 1973–87) 3.587. I have derived
much profit from an unpublished paper by C. R. Holladay, who is about to
publish a new edition and commentary.
[40] Lucid overview at Walter, *op. cit.* 7–9. Presumably a copy was taken by Origen
to Caesarea, as happened in the case of the Philonic corpus.

perhaps even more puzzling that of Philo as 'the Pythagorean', for the extant fragments clearly disclose the conviction—similar to that of Philo—that [9] Greek philosophy is inferior to and indebted to Moses. This of course allows a rather eclectic approach. He in fact mentions Pythagoras and Plato twice, but Aristotle is not mentioned, and the Peripatetics only once. Moreover when discussing the significance of the Sabbath, he clearly indicates that God created the cosmos, a view which is difficult to rhyme with a Peripatetic position.[41] The following hypotheses have been put forward:

(a) that the title 'Peripatetic' is a deduction from his writings, perhaps based on the reference to the αἵρεσις ἡ ἐκ τοῦ περιπάτου in fr. 5, or perhaps based on a more general impression of his apologetic motivation;[42]

(b) that the title does not refer to a philosophical affiliation at all, but rather to a scientific and possibly biographical interest;[43]

(c) the very recent suggestion that Aristobulus may have been acquainted with the pseudo-Aristotelian work *De mundo,* and that this work is his chief point of reference in his orientation towards Greek philosophy, as particularly suggested by his reference to the divine δύναμις.[44]

The assumption of the last two hypotheses is that the title was either a self-designation or handed down through the tradition, e.g. that it was found in the title of Aristobulus' book. It is difficult to argue against this, for there is no hard evidence either way.[45] I assume with Walter that the titles are the work of Clement, or at least have consciously been taken over by him, and so tell us more about his perceptions than about the situation three centuries earlier. From him they pass onto Eusebius, and then further into the tradition.

---

[41] Fr. 5 at Eus. *Praep. Evang.* 13.12.9ff. (which also includes the reference to the Peripatetics). The non-literal interpretation of the creation account, which anticipates Philo's later interpretation, is not the same as denying creation altogether.

[42] Walter *op. cit.* 12, followed by Holladay (see n. 39 above).

[43] M. Hengel, *Judaism and Hellenism: Studies in their Encounter in Palestine during the Early Hellenistic Period,* = Eng. trans. of German 2nd edition, 1973 (London 1974) 164 and n. 373; cf. Schürer *op. cit.* (n. 39) 3.579, where it is suggested that he might have even been a member of the Alexandrian museum.

[44] R. Radice, *La filosofia di Aristobulo e i suoi nessi con il De Mundo attribuito ad Aristotele* (Milan 1994), esp. 29 and 73–95.

[45] There is only evidence from silence. The other independent witnesses to Aristobulus, the author of 2 Macc. and Bishop Anatolius, say nothing about philosophical affiliation, and stress only his Jewishness.

Walter's explanation of the title (i.e. (a) above) is not particularly convincing, for it hardly puts Clement's analysis of Aristobulus' writings in a very favourable light, but we have none better.

Such hypotheses need not delay us any longer, however, for the fragments of Aristobulus himself and their adaptation by Clement give us a sufficient clue. Aristobulus actually speaks of his own 'affiliation' when he says in fr. 4 that 'it is confessed by all philosophers that one should have holy conceptions concerning the deity, which is especially well enjoined by our school of thought (ἡ καθ' ἡμᾶς αἵρεσις)'.[46] Aristobulus aligns himself with Jewish philosophers and particularly Moses. Clement does not allude to this text, but he does cite the passage which according to Eusebius stood a little earlier in Aristobulus' book, that 'Plato followed the lawgiving of our tradition (τῇ καθ' ἡμᾶς [10] νομοθεσίᾳ)' and that 'Pythagoras transferred much from our tradition (τῶν παρ' ἡμῖν) to his own system of thought (δογματοποιία)'.[47] Clement cannot possibly have meant that Aristobulus was a 'member of' or was 'affiliated with' the Peripatetic school. This is the relationship that he had with his own Jewish school of thought. He is called 'the Peripatetic' on account of an *affinity* that he had with Peripatetic thought.[48] Regrettably we are not in a position to determine with any certainty what that affinity in Clement's eyes was.

Philo's affinity with Pythagoreanism

This clear result in the case of Aristobulus will encourage us to undertake an analogous argument for Philo's appellation as 'the Pythagorean'. Philo, we may argue, was in Clement's eyes not a member of the Pythagorean *hairesis*. Such affiliation is reserved for his relationship to Moses.[49] His writings, however, did reveal

---

[46] Fr. 4 = Eus. *Praep. Evang.* 13.12.8.

[47] *Str.* 1.150.1–3.

[48] I prefer this formulation to that of Walter when he says the term indicates Aristobulus' 'Bildung' (and draws the parallel with Philo as Pythagorean). Clement is not concerned with his education (about which he presumably knows nothing), but with the direction of his thought.

[49] Philo himself does not use the phrase ἡ αἵρεσις τοῦ Μωυσέως, but note the very common expression οἱ γνώριμοι τοῦ Μωυσέως (e.g. at *Det.* 86, *Spec.* 1.345 etc.), the reference to the schools (διδασκαλεῖα) where Jews devote themselves on the sabbath to the acquisition of knowledge, and the description of the Therapeutae as having τῆς αἱρέσεως ἀρχηγέται who have shown them the way in allegorical exegesis (*Contempl.* 29).

affinities with Pythagorean thought, and this will have encouraged the use of the epithet. Philo only mentions Pythagoras or his followers explicitly on a limited number of occasions,[50] but Clement's trained eye will have picked up more themes with a Pythagorean origin. What, we may ask, may have induced Clement to regard Philo's thought, and thus Philo himself, as Pythagorean? Let us review four possibilities.

(a) A prominent aspect of Philo's biblical exegesis is his heavy use of number symbolism or arithmology.[51] On a number of occasions he specifically refers to Pythagorean number lore when expounding biblical numbers such as the monad, the triad and the hebdomad.[52] Clement takes over this method. There are at least three significant texts where he takes over substantial material on arithmology from Philo:[53]

(i) *Str.* 2.50–51: on the decad (exeg. Ex. 16:36, cf. *Congr.* 100–106);

(ii) *Str.* 5.93–94: on the six days of creation, cf. *Opif.* 13–14;

(iii) *Str.* 6.139–145: on the hebdomad in relation to the 4th commandment, cf. esp. *Leg.* 1.2–20, and also *Opif.* 89–127.

Moreover the reference to God as beyond the One and the monad at *Paed.* 1.71.2 recalls similar Philonic formulations at *Leg.* 2.3, *Praem.* 40, *QE* 2.68 etc.[54] The possibility has to be considered, therefore, that, when Clement calls Philo 'the Pythagorean', he is specifically thinking of this penchant for arithmologizing exegesis, and also of a connection with a theology of the 'One God'.[55]

(b) Secondly, we need to ask whether there are any other features of [11] Philo's thought that on their own may have been sufficient

---

[50] Nine references in all: *Opif.* 100, *Leg.* 1.15, *QG* 1.17, 1.99, 3.16, 3.49, 4.8, *Prob.* 2, *Aet.* 12. This is a relatively large number if compared with Philo's practice in the case of other Greek philosophers. For example he mentions Plato only 14 times, of which half are in *Aet.*

[51] Best recent treatment in H. R. Moehring, 'Arithmology as an Exegetical Tool in the Writings of Philo of Alexandria', *Society of Biblical Literature Seminar Papers* 13 (1978) 1.191–229; about to be reprinted in J. P. Kenney (ed.), *Moehring Memorial Volume* (Atlanta 1995).

[52] *Opif.* 100 and *Leg.* 1.15 (hebdomad and monad), *QG* 3.49 (thirty-six), 4.8 (triad).

[53] On these texts see further Van den Hoek *op. cit.* (n. 3) 152–160, 196, 205 (she should have included the last passage in her group of 'short sequences' instead of among the 'isolated references').

[54] J. M. Dillon, *The Middle Platonists* (London 1977) 156, regards these statements by Philo as 'an essentially rhetorical flourish', but does see a connection with the Pythagorizing early Middle Platonist Eudorus.

[55] Cf. also Radice *op. cit.* (n. 44) 20.

for Clement to have labelled Philo 'the Pythagorean'. Various
themes come to mind, e.g. Pythagoreanizing esotericism,[56] the goal
of ethics as 'following God',[57] even the doctrine of metempsychosis.[58] It will be agreed, however, that none of these are sufficiently
important in Philo or sufficiently prominent in Clement's borrowings from Philo to explain the epithet.

(c) The third possibility takes us in an entirely different direction.
One of the more obvious features of Philo's writings is their
extensive use of philosophical material from the so-called 'Bible of
the Platonists', Plato's *Timaeus*.[59] As the passage at *Str.* 5.93–94
implicitly shows (Philo's name is not mentioned), Clement was
perfectly aware of this connection.[60] In Clement's day the personage
of Timaeus was regarded as a Pythagorean (in the dialogue he is
described at 20a as coming from Locris in Italy). Moreover a Pseudo-
Pythagorean work, written in Doric and attributed to Timaeus
Locrus, was in circulation and was regarded as the original from
which Plato had taken (or even plagiarized) his doctrines.[61] Clement
refers to the figure of Timaeus (Locrus) twice,[62] but nowhere does
he associate him with Pythagoreanism. For this reason we are not

---

[56] E.g. the injunction 'not to walk on the highways', cited by Philo at *Prob.* 2
and also referred to by Clement at *Str.* 5.31.1, which could be taken in an esoteric
rather than a protreptic sense. At *Str.* 4.3.1 Clement takes over the Platonic
language of the greater and lesser mysteries; cf. Philo *Sacr.* 62 and Van den Hoek
op. cit. (n. 3) 188. This possible interpretation of the epithet 'Pythagorean' for
Philo is suggested by Radice, *op. cit.* (n. 44) 21, who also points to the prominence
of the 'contemplative life' in Pythagorean thought. Note, however, that Pythagoras
or Pythagoreanism are not mentioned at all in Philo's *De vita contemplativa*.

[57] Cf. *Migr.* 128–131, *Abr.* 60, taken over by Clement in *Str.* 2.69.4, cf. 2.100.4.
In the former text Clement brings out the connection with Pythagoras more
clearly than Philo, although he does not mention him by name (τις τῶν παρ'
Ἕλλησι σοφῶν). The latter text follows just a few lines after the mention of Philo
as the Pythagorean (see the text cited at the beginning of the article). But it would
be wrong to see a direct connection with the Pythagorean formula ἕπεσθαι θεῷ,
which Clement does not even mention here, unlike Philo, who refers to it twice at
Migr. 128 and 131.

[58] Referred to by Clement at *Str.* 7.32.8. It is far from clear that Philo subscribes
to the doctrine of metempsychosis (cf. Runia, *op. cit.* (n. 15) 346–349), but there
are a few isolated passages which an interpreter could read in this way if he wished
(cf. esp. *Somn.* 1.139).

[59] As investigated at length in my doctoral dissertation cited above in n. 15.

[60] See n. 53.

[61] See Dörrie–Baltes, *op. cit* (n. 16), texts at 24, commentary 253ff.

[62] *Str.* 1.166.1, 5.114.4. The second text attributes a passage to Timaeus Locrus,
but it is not found in the work under his name still extant; cf. W. Marg, *Timaeus
Locrus De natura mundi et animae*, Philosophia Antiqua 4 (Leiden 1972) 85ff.

justified, I would argue, in concluding that the epithet 'Pythagorean' refers to Philo's fondness for this particular Platonic dialogue.

(d) The final possibility takes us further along the same path. As is well known, during the final century B.C. and the first two centuries A.D. Platonists and (Neo-)Pythagoreans formed two separate αἱρέσεις, but from the doctrinal point of view there were strong connections between them.[63] Indeed Pythagorean doctrine might be described as virtually identical with Platonist philosophy, with the addition of special emphases on the role of numbers (esp. in the doctrine of first principles) and on the contemplative life (together with various practical injunctions). The reason why this was possible is clear enough. Plato was regarded as having 'Pythagorized', not only in the *Timaeus*, but throughout his entire *œuvre*.[64] As the more ancient figure Pythagoras was the creative source, but Plato had worked out his thought in greater philosophical detail. In practice this meant that Pythagoreans could claim Platonist doctrine as an integral part of their αἵρεσις, but had more speculative freedom, because they were less tied to the study of Plato's writings.[65] The best individual example is the philosopher Numenius. As Whittaker remarks, 'in spite of his frequent designation as a [12] Pythagorean, the content of Numenius' surviving fragments is in the main more Platonic than Pythagorean.'[66] Turning to Clement, we see that he on various occasions associates Pythagoras (or Pythagoreans) and Plato.[67] He argues that Plato drew the doctrine of the immortality of the soul from Pythagoras, and even locates a non-existent Pythagorean in one of Plato's dialogues.[68] The suggestion may be made,

---

[63] The last word has not been said on this question. See the comments of J. Whittaker, 'Platonic Philosophy in the Early Empire', *ANRW* 2.36.1 (Berlin-New York 1987) 117–121, J. M. Dillon in Dillon and Long, *op. cit.* (n. 28) 119–125, D. J. O'Meara, *Pythagoras Revived* (Oxford 1989) 9ff. But the question of the 'institutional' relation between the two movements is still far from clear.

[64] Dörrie–Baltes, *op. cit.* 247, who for the phrase ὁ Πλάτων πυθαγορίζει refer to Aëtius 2.6.6 Diels, Numenius fr. 24.57 Des Places, Apuleius *Flor.* 15.

[65] As noted by Whittaker, *art. cit.* (n. 63) 120.

[66] *Ibid.* 119. Cf. also M. Frede, 'Numenius', *ANRW* 2.36.2 (Berlin-New York 1987) 1047, who says of this case: 'Jedenfalls is soviel klar, daß der Ausdruck 'Pythagoreer' selbst für einen Platoniker nicht ausschließt, daß es sich bei der bezeichneten Person um einen Platoniker handelt...' But his observation that mainly Christian authors call Numenius a 'Pythagorean' is a red herring.

[67] *Str.* 1.68.2, 3.12.1, 5.29.3, 5.58.6, 5.88.1 and 89.5 (with Aristotle as well), 5.99.3 (with Socrates, citing Aristobulus).

[68] *Str.* 6.27.2, 1.48.2; on the relation between Pythagoras and Plato in Clement, see further Lilla *op. cit.* (n. 15) 41–45. He points at 43 to the revealing text at

therefore, that when Clement calls Philo 'the Pythagorean', he is indicating that he has recognized not only Pythagorean themes, but also the dominant Platonist element in Philo's thought, for both aspects are covered under the single epithet.

A difficult choice

We are thus left with two alternative answers to our question. It is possible that Clement calls Philo 'the Pythagorean' on account of the role that arithmology or number-symbolism plays in his thought, and especially in his exegesis. It is also possible that the epithet refers to the dominant Platonist strain in his thought. Which of these alternatives deserves our preference? It might be argued that we need not choose, since Clement may have had a plurality of reasons.[69] Nevertheless I think it is useful to determine one's priorities on this issue, and although certainty cannot be attained on this issue, I believe that two arguments support the latter. Firstly, as we said earlier, the context of the two texts in which Philo receives this designation is apologetic rather than exegetical, i.e. the antiquity of the Jews compared with Greek philosophy, and the derivation of the Platonic *telos*-formula from Moses. The second passage is also overtly doxographical (in the broad sense of the term), even if the mention of Philo strictly speaking refers only to a *bon mot*.[70] Clement thus has more to gain from the statement that Philo was well-acquainted with a major direction of Greek thought. A second, admittedly less strong, argument is that Clement nowhere uses the term Πλατωνικός in order to designate a philosopher. This suggests that he may have wanted to avoid the term (for whatever reason), and preferred the more dignified title of Πυθαγόρειος. We thus find ourselves in broad agreement with David Winston when he writes:[71] 'It is thus clear that the expressikon 'Pythagorean' does not preclude one from being a Platonist. Clement's designation of Philo as a 'Pythagorean' was therefore probably not meant to preclude his being a Platonist, but was used [13] only to indicate that both he and Plato had

---

Justin *Dial.* 5.6, where the young Justin, who is studying in a Platonist school (cf. 2.6) is made to say that Plato *and* Pythagoras were 'wise men, who have been a wall and a pillar for philosophy'.

[69] As Prof. Eric Osborn points out to me.

[70] See our discussion of the passage earlier in the article.

[71] At *The Studia Philonica Annual* 5 (1993) 145–6, in response to my article 'Was Philo a Middle Platonist?' at *ibid.* 112–140.

'Pythagorized'.' My proviso would be, however, that we take 'Platonist' here to indicate *affinity to* the thought of an *haeresis*, and not in
the stronger sense of a *membership of* or *affiliation with* such an *haeresis*
(or school of thought). For it would be rash to think that Clement
had overlooked the obvious fact that Philo's loyalty and devotion
were primarily, indeed perhaps even exclusively, to the 'school of
Moses'.[72]

The attitude behind the title

There remains a final question to be discussed in relation to the
epithet that Clement bestows on Philo. We noted at the outset that it
would be more expected that he name him 'Philo the Jew (or
Hebrew)' as an indication of his ethnic and religious provenance.
Does a negative aspect lie concealed in the epithet 'the Pythagorean', that is to say, negative either towards Philo's Jewish background or towards his pagan learning?

It was suggested nearly a century ago by F. C. Conybeare that
Clement may have given Philo this title in order to conceal his
Jewishness:[73]

> If we examine the references to Philo made by Christian writers in
> this earlier time, we find that they were rather ashamed to quote
> Philo; or, if not quite that, at least not inclined to regard him as an
> authority, whose approval of an institution should at once command
> its acceptance by Christians. Let us examine a few of these
> references... Clement of Alexandria in his Stromateis alludes to
> Philo as ὁ Πυθαγόρειος. Did Christians of the late third century (*sic*)
> care for the authority of a Pythagorean?

This approach is not convincing. In fact Clement's writings reveal
surprisingly little contact with the Jewish community of his day
(which may not yet have recovered from the terrible events earlier
in the century), and certainly very little inclination to engage in
open and direct discussion with them.[74] Rather we should argue that

---

[72] On Walter's view that the epithet indicates Philo's 'philosophische Bildung'
see above n. 48. Better is the explanation of D. Wyrwa, *op. cit.* (n. 17) 85, who
argues in passing that it means 'die Gefolgschaft in einer philosophischen
Richtung'.
[73] *Philo about the Contemplative Life* (Oxford 1895, repr. New York 1987) 328–
329. His first example (left out in the quote) is Justin, but the works cited are
pseudonymous.
[74] Cf. my remarks at *op. cit.* (n. 1) 149–150 (with further references). At *Str.*
2.2.1 Clement states that he will use some scripture texts in the hope that 'the Jew

both Clement and Origen had on the whole a relatively neutral, or even sometimes a selectively favourable attitude to contemporary Judaism.[75] It was this 'window of opportunity' presented by the Alexandrian tradition that was in all likelihood responsible for the survival of Philo's writings in the first place.[76] Clement is quite happy to point out that Josephus is a Jew.[77] The reason he does not do so in the case of Philo is presumably because [14] Philo's Jewish origin is obvious enough, and does not need to be underlined. The very first reference to Philo in the *Stromateis* involves the etymology of a biblical name. The reader could be assumed to conclude that Philo as an exegete stood in the Judaeo-Christian tradition. If he was not a Christian, then he had to be a Jew.

The title 'Pythagorean' does not, therefore, conceal Philo's Jewishness, but highlights an aspect of his thought and writings. Is this meant positively or negatively? The answer must surely be the former. Philo stands in the Judaeo-Christian tradition, but he is also a learned man, as expressed in the title, and in the eyes of the 'liberal' Clement this is a positive feature.[78] Admittedly, on one occasion Clement associates Pythagoreanism (and Platonism) with heresy, namely when he argues that Marcion derives his doctrine of the evil nature of matter from that source.[79] But, given Clement's comparatively favourable attitude to the Platonist tradition, we are not surprised to read a few lines later that the heretic has misrepresented the original doctrine. Clement's attitude is brought into clear relief when it is compared with that of his younger contemporary

---

may hear his words and convert from what he believed to the One in whom he did not believe'. As Eric Osborn remarks, ' Clement wanted to convert Jews and to do it quietly. There was traffic in the opposite direction. Clement attacked Judaisers in a separate work (p. 148 in his forthcoming article in *Origeniana Sexta*).' But according to Eusebius *Hist. Eccl.* 6.12.3 this work, entitled Κάνων ἐκκλησιαστικὸς ἢ Πρὸς τοὺς Ἰουδαΐζοντας, was dedicated to Alexander, Bishop of Jerusalem, with whom Clement had close contact after his departure from Alexandria, and so may be the product of a quite different situation than the *Stromateis* written a decade or more earlier.

[75] On Origen see also N. R. M. De Lange, *Origen and the Jews: Studies in Jewish-Christian Relations in Third-Century Palestine* (Cambridge 1976).

[76] See my conclusions at *op. cit.* (n. 1) 344–346.

[77] *Str.* 1.147.2, to my knowledge the only named non-biblical person to be called such in his works.

[78] For the title cf. the splendid description of H. Chadwick, *Early Christian Thought and the Classical Tradition: Studies in Justin, Clement and Origen* (Oxford 1966, 1984²) chap. 2, 'The Liberal Puritan'.

[79] *Str.* 3.12–13; on this text see A. Le Boulluec, *La notion d'hérésie dans la littérature grecque IIe–IIIe siècles*, 2 vols. (Paris 1985) 290.

Hippolytus, for whom the titles Pythagorean and Platonist easily become terms of abuse when brought into connection with heretical thought. Having given a summary of Pythagorean and Platonic doctrine, the latter states that it was 'from this, and not from the gospels, as we shall demonstrate, that Valentinus drew together his *hairesis* (i.e. alternative mode of thought), and so he should rightly be considered a Pythagorean and a Platonist, not a Christian'.[80] The attitude behind calling someone a 'Pythagorean' in this context is the opposite to that involved when Clement gives Philo the same title. What Clement regards positively, Hippolytus views negatively. The same difference is well illustrated by another text, namely the *Sentences of Sextus*. This collection of aphorisms was attributed by some to 'Sextus the Pythagorean'. Jerome in the 4th century strongly polemicizes against it as the work of 'a man without Christ and a heathen', arguing that those who read it take over various pernicious Pythagorean doctrines and so 'drink of the golden cup of Babylon'.[81] But the work in its Christian form, according to Chadwick's reconstruction of the tradition, was probably compiled between 180 and 210 by a writer whose kindred spirit was Clement of Alexandria and whose motto might have been *Pythagoras saepe noster*.[82] This is close to the spirit in which Clement calls Philo 'the Pythagorean', whereas Jerome's attitude is a continuation of what we found in Hippolytus. [15]

Later sources

As noted at the outset two Christian authors subsequent to Clement refer to Philo's Pythagoreanism. By way of an epilogue some brief comments should be made on these texts. If our interpretation of the Clementine title is correct, then it would appear that Eusebius, by describing Philo as 'one who showed zeal for the philosophical

---

[80] *Refutatio* 6.29.1: τοιαύτη τις... ἡ Πυθαγόρου καὶ Πλάτωνος συνέστηκε δόξα, ἀφ᾽ ἧς Οὐαλεντῖνος, οὐκ ἀπὸ τῶν εὐαγγελίων, τὴν αἵρεσιν τὴν ἑαυτοῦ συναγαγών, ὡς ἐπιδείξομεν, δικαίως Πυθαγορικὸς καὶ Πλατωνικός, οὐ Χριστιανὸς λογισθείη. Note how the author both times connects the philosophers with καί, implying that they represent the same 'direction of thought'. On this text and its context see further Mansfeld, *op. cit.* (n. 30) 177–203. Hippolytus takes over this attitude from (his teacher?) Irenaeus, cf. *Adv. haer.* 2.14.6.

[81] Jerome *Ep.* 133.3, cited by H. Chadwick, *The Sentences of Sextus* (Cambridge 1959) 120.

[82] *Ibid.* 160 (with an elegant adaptation of Tertullian's claim *Seneca saepe noster, De anima* 20.1) and *passim*.

discipline of Plato and Pythagoras',[83] reveals a perfect understanding of what Clement will have meant by it. It is uncertain, however, whether Eusebius is here deriving his information from Clement's *Stromateis*. In this text he is embellishing what he read in Josephus, where, as we saw earlier,[84] Philo is described as 'not unskilled in philosophy', a passage which the Church historian cites *verbatim*.[85] But where does he get his extra information from? It is possible that he recalled Clement's epithet.[86] It is equally possible that he drew on his own reading of Philo in the library of Caesarea.[87] Another possibility is that the source that he used for the legend of Philo Christianus contained more information on Philo. This source may have been the *Hypotyposeis*, an important work of Clement now most regrettably lost.[88] The suggestion gains support if we take the other later text into consideration. Sozomen too, as we saw, calls Philo 'the Pythagorean'. Where did he, heavily indebted to earlier sources as he was,[89] get his information from? It has been suggested that the passage in Eusebius just mentioned was his source.[90] This is possible (though why should he choose the school of one philosopher at the expense of that of the other, which was in fact more famous?). But there is also another possibility. A few pages earlier (1.1.12) Sozomen informs his reader that he has written a short account of the history of the Church up to the time of Constantine in two books, in which one of his sources was 'Clement' (in addition to Eusebius). He may mean the *Pseudo-Clementina*,[91] but he may also mean Clement of Alexandria, in which case the lost *Hypotyposeis* would again be a candidate, since we know that it contained much quasi-historical material on the Apostolic age. It is in any case

---

[83] See above n. 8 and text thereto.
[84] See above n. 2 and text thereto.
[85] *Hist. Eccl.* 2.4.3 (description of Philo), 2.5.2–5 (citation of Josephus).
[86] See above n. 9 on his knowledge of the *Stromateis*.
[87] On which his catalogue of Philo's writings in *Hist. Eccl.* 2.18 is based.
[88] As I suggest at *op. cit.* (n. 1) 7.
[89] The extant history shows a great dependence on the earlier work of Socrates Ecclesiasticus. Prof. J. Bremmer suggests to me that Sozomen may have concluded that Philo was a Pythagorean because he drew a connection between the Pythagorean contemplative life and Philo's account of early monasticism (as he read it). I do not know if Sozomen was sophisticated enough to be capable of this. As mentioned above (n. 56), Philo makes no mention of Pythagoreanism in *Contempl.*, but Sozomen most likely had not read this work anyway.
[90] In the note at B. Grillet, G. Sabbah and A.-J. Festugière, *Sozomène Histoire Ecclésiastique*, SC 308 (Paris 1983) 166.
[91] As argued at *ibid.* 116.

probable that Sozomen's description of Philo as 'the Pythagorean' derives from the narrow Alexandrian-Caesarean tradition that we have been investigating.

A final matter of related interest is the *bon mot* on Philo and Plato which began to circulate in the Eastern Church, and which is first recorded in Isidore of Pelusium and Jerome, ἢ Πλάτων φιλωνίζει ἢ Φίλων πλατωνίζει.[92] One wonders whether the expression was not formulated [16] with half an eye on the well-known *dictum* that ὁ Πλάτων πυθαγορίζει.[93] Certainly it was no less true to say from the contemporary Platonist point of view that ἢ Πυθαγόρας πλατωνίζει ἢ Πλάτων πυθαγορίζει than it was for Christians to say that ἢ Πλάτων φιλωνίζει ἢ Φίλων πλατωνίζει.

Summary of results

The argument that we have pursued in this article may be summarized along the following lines. When Clement on two occasions calls Philo 'the Pythagorean', the epithet is surprising because it does not locate him in the Judaeo-Christian tradition where, also for Clement (in the light of his borrowings), he primarily belongs. In both cases the context, though revealing, does not explain the epithet fully. In one of the two passages Philo's name is coupled with that of 'Aristobulus the Peripatetic'. This second title gives us a vital clue, for it can clearly be shown that it must refer not to any kind of 'membership of' or 'affiliation with' the Peripatetic school, but rather an affinity of thought (even if *what* this is remains rather puzzling). For Clement, therefore, Philo shows an affinity of thought with Pythagoreanism. Two plausible explanations can be given for what such an affinity might be, more specifically the role that arithmology plays in his exegesis, or more generally the dominant Platonist strain in his thought (included under the title Pythagorean because it was recognized that 'Plato Pythagorized'). The choice between these two explanations is difficult, but we opt for the second. Clement is not trying to conceal Philo's Jewishness. Given his relatively 'liberal' stance, the title must be seen as a compliment in the direction of his Jewish predecessor. This positive attitude is

---

[92] On this saying see Runia *op. cit.* (n. 1) 4, 208, 313, 319 (where I argue that 'the Greeks' among whom according to Jerome the proverb circulates are likely to be Greek-speaking Church fathers).

[93] On which see above n. 64.

important from the historical point of view, for ultimately it lead to
the survival of Philo's works through the intermediation of the
Episcopal Library of Caesarea.[94]

---

[94] My thanks to the editors of this journal, to my colleagues J. Mansfeld and
A. P. Bos, to Prof. Eric Osborn (Melbourne), and finally to the members of the
Dutch Patristisch Gezelschap for various constructive remarks, which helped me
formulate my views with more precision.
As this article was going to the press Dr. Annewies van den Hoek (Harvard)
kindly drew my attention to an important text that I had overlooked. Codex
Baroccianus gr. 142, fol. 216 records a notice in which the fifth-century Church
historian Philip of Side gives a list of the succession of the heads of the
Alexandrian catechetical school, beginning with Athenagoras and ending with
Rhodon. In this list Pantaenus (who is described as Clement's pupil!) is called an
Athenian and 'a Pythagorean philosopher' (text at G. C. Hansen, *Theodoros
Anagnostes Kirchengeschichte*, GCS (Berlin 1971) 160). This statement contradicts
the report of Eusebius in *HE* 5.10.2, who says that according to tradition
Pantaenus had 'started from the philosophical school of thought (φιλόσοφος
ἀγωγή) of the so-called Stoics'. Philip's statement is too short to interpret with any
confidence. If it has any factual basis, it can be read in a similar way to my interpretation of 'Philo the Pythagorean', i.e. as referring to an affinity of thought. On
the other hand, the formulation of Eusebius' statement suggests it may refer to
Pantaenus' affiliation *before* he turned to Christianity. On the notice of Philip see
now the detailed analysis of B. Pouderon, 'Le témoignage du codex Baroccianus
142 sur Athénagore et les origines du Didaskaleion d'Alexandrie', *Archipel Égéen:
Publication de l'Université de Tours Département d'Études Helléniques*, fascicule 1, 1992,
23–63.

CHAPTER FOUR

UNDERNEATH COHN AND COLSON:
THE TEXT OF PHILO'S *DE VIRTUTIBUS*

1. *Introduction*

Since by now—at least in the country hosting this conference—the vast majority of scholars have discovered the advantages of working with a micro-computer for their scholarly work, allow me to begin with an analogy drawn from the realm of computer technology.[1] When a scholar makes use of a word-processing program, he or she stands at a considerable remove from the workings of the machine itself. Basically the computer 'understands' and responds only to commands it receives in a sequence of zero's and one's, the so-called binary *machine language*. Because such lengthy sequences of numbers are extremely cumbersome and awkward to work with, early computer engineers converted basic sequences into more readable codes which programmers could more easily remember and work with, the so-called *assembly languages*. But even these languages involve the programmer in far too much routine work, so they in turn have been developed into *compilers*, such as Basic or C, which work in something resembling English language, and automatically convert the programmer's intentions into the binary language which formulates the basic commands to which the machine can respond. Through use of such compilers the software developers produce the complex *software programs* which scholars use in their everyday work. These programs, which can only be adapted and manipulated to a

---

[1] For what follows see J. D. Bolter, *Turing's Man: Western Culture in the Computer Age* (Chapel Hill: The University of North Carolina Press, 1984), esp. 127–132.

limited degree, are the final level in a hierarchy which separates the
user from the electronic processes that take place in his machine.

Now consider what happens when the average Philonist studies
the writings and thought of his favourite author. As likely as not, he
or she will consult a translation in a modern language (Colson's
Loeb, Lyon edition, German translation etc.). Hopefully, in the case
of the first two translations, there will be some consultation of Greek
text on the facing page. I surmise, however, that it will only occur
[117] relatively rarely that the scholar turns to the critical edition of
Cohn-Wendland with its full apparatus criticus. As for the original
manuscripts of Philo's writings scattered throughout the libraries of
Europe, these are virtually inaccessible to our scholar and in normal
circumstances will never be consulted. Just as in the case of our computer user, therefore, the Philonist generally *stands at a considerable
remove* from the original text of his author. Where the analogy
breaks down, of course, is in the fact that the computer user can, if
he really wishes, descend to the actual binary code of the program
he is using and this code, furthermore, is essentially unambiguous,
whereas the hapless Philonist can *never be certain* that his text represents the actual words that Philo wrote. This irremoveable constraint
is due to the fifteen centuries of scribal transmission interposed between Philo's autographs and the first printed editions of his works.

This paper has been written as a modest contribution to the team
effort of a group of scholars who are undertaking a fresh examination of the relatively neglected Philonic treatise *De virtutibus*. Its aim
will be to examine the text of the treatise as it appears in the various
texts and translations available to the contemporary Philonist. It will
be important for us to make some judgment on the quality of the
available text, for, as will become clear in the course of our investigation, in this area we remain enormously dependent on the efforts
of previous scholars.

2. *A brief history of the text of* De virtutibus

The Philonic treatise *De virtutibus* as we generally know it today
consists of the following parts:

  a. Περὶ ἀνδρείας, *De fortitudine* (On courage) = §1–50
  b. Περὶ φιλανθρωπίας, *De caritate* (On humane behaviour) = §51–174
  c. Περὶ μετανοίας, *De paenitentia* (On repentance) = §175–186
  d. Περὶ εὐγενείας, *De nobilitate* (On noble birth) = §187–227.

It will perhaps come as a surprise to some readers that the treatise was not published in this form until the edition of Cohn in 1906,[2] and that this particular arrangement occurs in only one single manuscript. It is in fact primarily a scholarly construct, based on a reasoned reconstruction of Philo's intentions in composing his exegetical series which we know as the Exposition of the Law. I shall return to the question of the treatise's contents and title in section 6 below, where I shall argue that Cohn's arrangement is most likely correct. On this assumption we can follow the treatise's special history (i.e. aside from the more general account of the survival of Philo's writings) in the following stages.

a. The treatise is extensively cited and adapted in book II of the *Stromateis* of Clement of Alexandria, who must therefore have had access to a text of the work in Alexandria,[3] in the period before the archetype of all our manuscripts was taken to Caesarea as part of the library of Origen. The remaining *indirect tradition* is very limited in extent. The treatise is not among those translated into Armenian or Latin during the Patristic period. It was neither cited by Eusebius in his [118] *Praeparatio Evangelica*, nor exploited by Ambrose in his exegetical works. Only some brief snippets are found in the *Sacra Parallela* of John of Damascus and other Byzantine anthologists.[4] This indirect tradition will be further discussed below in section 4.

b. The treatise is well represented in the *direct manuscript tradition* of Philo's works, which consists of some 120 manuscripts dating from the 10th to the 16th centuries. As we noted above, however, it is only found once in the reconstructed form with which we are now familiar, and even then there are significant differences (see below section 3(a)). We shall examine this direct tradition, on which our text is primarily based, in greater detail in the following section.

c. The first printed text of *Virt.* is found in the *editio princeps* of

---

[2] *Philonis Alexandrini opera quae supersunt*, 6 vols. (Berlin: Georg Reimer, 1896–1915) 5.266–335 (we refer to this edition henceforth as C-W).

[3] According to the chronology of A. Mehat, *Études sur les 'Stromates' de Clément d'Alexandrie* (Paris: De Seuil, 1966) 42–54, Clement wrote the first six books in Alexandria, before leaving for Jerusalem in 203, where he wrote the 7th book.

[4] See app. crit. to text in C-W at §9, 117, 177, 188. Note also that §212–216 is found as part of the late Byzantine cento *De mundo*, which was the first Philonic text to be printed (by Aldus Manutius in 1497); cf. C-W 2.vi–x and H. L. Goodhart and E. R. Goodenough, *A General Bibliography of Philo* (New Haven: Yale University Press, 1938) 187. This study, which is our chief source of information for the manuscripts and early editions and translations of Philo, will henceforth be referred to as G-G.

Philo published in 1552 by Adrianus Turnebus (1512–1565).[5] The
treatise is split up into three parts: *De caritate* is printed after *Mos.*, *De
fortitudine* after *De iustitia* (= *Spec.* 4.136–237), *De nobilitate* after
Contempl. The brief section of text *De paenitentia* is included, but is
affixed to *De caritate* without any form of break or title. In his edition
Turnebus, following the practice of his time, did little more than set
in print a text based on three (inferior) Parisian manuscripts.[6] He
does try to establish an order for the treatises, basing it (not very
successfully) on Philo's tripartition of the Mosaic writings at *Praem.*
1.[7] This text forms the basis of the so-called Vulgata reprinted in no
less than 4 editions, in each of which the distribution and order of
the parts of *Virt.* remain the same.[8]

    d. The first edition of the text of *Virt.* which can in any sense be
* described as critical is that of Thomas Mangey (1688–1755) in his
famous edition of Philo's *opera omnia* published in 1742.[9] Although
Mangey did not undertake a complete examination of the manuscript tradition, he did recognize the importance of the Seldenianus
manuscript at Oxford, which he used to improve on the vulgate text.
His text also contains a large number of emendations based on a
good knowledge of Greek and a finely developed instinct for Philonic style.[10] The order of his text [119] deviates from Turnebus in that
he groups together *De fortitudine*, *De caritate*, and *De paenitentia*
(which for the first time receives its own separate title), placing
them in their natural position after *Spec.* IV; *De nobilitate*, however, is
placed after *Praem.*[11]

---

    [5] *Philonis Iudaei in libros Mosis, de mundi opificio, historicos, de legibus. Eiusdem libri
singulares ex bibliotheca regis* (Paris 1552), = G-G no. 391. On the distinguished
French scholar Turnebus see J. E. Sandys, *A History of Classical Scholarship*
(Cambridge 1903–08, repr. New York: Hafner 1967) 2.185–186.
    [6] Cf. C-W 1.lxxi, G-G 147, 187–188.
    [7] Cf. C-W *ibid.*
    [8] Editions: Geneva 1613 (= G-G no. 398), Paris 1640 (= G-G no. 402) Frankfurt
1691 (= G-G no. 402), Frankfurt 1729. The last edition is not mentioned by G-G,
but is referred to at C-W 1.lxxiv. A copy of this edition is in my possession. It is of
interest because it adds a notice from the *Bibliotheca Graeca* of the encyclopedist
J. A. Fabricius (1705–28), which remarks on the differing title of *Virt.* in the
Bodleian manuscript (= ms. S). From 1613 onwards a Latin translation by S.
Gelenius (first published in 1554, = G-G 451) is printed beside the Greek.
    [9] *Philonis Judaei opera quae reperiri potuerunt omnia...* 2 vols. (London 1742), G-G
no. 404. On Mangey, a famous English divine, see *Dictionary of National Biography*
(London 1921–22) 12.916.
    [10] Many of these problematic texts are discussed in critical footnotes at the
bottom of the page, which take the place of an apparatus criticus.
    [11] Hence the jump in marginal references to Mangey at C-W 5.324.

e. We now come to a rather curious episode. In 1816 the famous

* classical scholar and prelate A. Mai published a text of *De virtute eius-que partibus* which he claimed to have discovered and places among various *scripta inedita*.[12] It soon emerged, however, that the treatise was neither Philonic nor an *ineditum*, but was rather the (already published) work of the late Byzantine humanist, Gemistus Plethon,[13] as Mai himself had to admit in 1818.[14]

f. The definitive critical edition of *Virt.* was published in 1906 by Leopold Cohn (1856–1915) as part of the great *editio maior* of all Philo's surviving Greek works prepared by him in collaboration with Paul Wendland (1864–1915).[15] This edition is based on a critical comparison of virtually all extant manuscripts, and has formed the basis of all further work on the treatise since the time of its publication. Important ground-work for the edition was laid by Wendland in an article on Philo and Clement of Alexandria.[16] Wendland argued that *De nobilitate* should be appended to *De paenitentia*, which was the sequence adopted by Cohn in his edition[17] and has been standard ever since. The motivations of the editor in choosing his text are further illuminated by an article on problems in the text[18] and by his translation of the treatise that forms part of the German translation of Philo.[19] We shall examine the principles

---

[12] *De Philonis Iudaei et Eusebii Pamphilo scriptis ineditis... dissertatio* (Milan 1816), *Philonis Iudaei de virtute eisusque partibus...* (Milan 1816). Cf. G-G nos. 410–411, where full titles are given (*non vidi*).

[13] Note that two Italian translations appeared in 1817, as reported by G-G nos. 504–505 (*non vidi*). The title of the second as reported by G-G already expresses doubt as to whether the work is by Philo or by Plethon.

[14] The episode is briefly referred to by E. Schürer, *Geschichte des jüdischen Volkes im Zeitalter Jesu Christi* (Leipzig: J. C. Hinrichs, 1909⁴) 3.678 n. 11.

[15] C-W (see above n. 2) = G-G no. 431. Text of *Virt.* at 5.266–335. The two men, the one a Jew, the other the son of a pietistic Lutheran minister, were personal friends. In 1887, at the suggestion of H. Diels, the Prussian Academy of Sciences announced a prize for an edition of Philo's *Opif.* Both men submitted an entry, and both received the prize, the contest thus becoming the starting-point of their joint edition. Both died rather young, within three months of each other, but their great work was as good as finished. See further the necrology of Wendland by M. Pohlenz, *Neue Jahrbücher für das klassische Altertum* 19 (1916) 57–75, and the notice on Cohn in *Encyclopedia Judaica* (New York: Macmillan, 1971) 5.691.

[16] P. Wendland, 'Philo und Clemens Alexandrinus', *Hermes* 31 (1896) 435–456.

[17] Even though the co-editors wanted to change the order of Mangey's edition as little as possible; cf. C-W 5.xxviii.

[18] L. Cohn, 'Neue Beiträge zur Textgeschichte und Kritik der philonischen Schriften', *Hermes* 43 (1908) 177–219, esp. 210–215.

[19] *Philo von Alexandria: Die Werke in deutscher Übersetzung*, herausgegeben von L. Cohn, vol. 2 (Breslau: M. und H. Marcus 1910; repr. Berlin: De Gruyter 1962)

on which Cohn's edition is based at greater length in sections 3 and
5 of this paper.

   g. Finally we should mention more recent printings of the Greek
text of *Virt.* In his English translation of Philo published in the Loeb
Classical Library, F. H. Colson (1857–1943) basically follows the text
of Cohn, giving only a handful of [120] important manuscript
variants in a limited apparatus criticus.[20] But it is clear from his
copious and most invaluable notes that Colson, who had a superb
knowledge of Philo's Greek,[21] critically examined the text while
making his translation, also comparing it with Cohn's own translation. In his preface Colson states:[22]

> I have been startled by the number of times in which I find myself in
> disagreement with him [Cohn], a disagreement extending beyond
> the translation to the text particularly in the cases where he seems to
> me to have printed unjustified emendations. Though it may some-
> times seem disputatious, I have felt bound to record in the footnotes
> or appendix my reasons for differing from him, as what is only due
> to so high an authority.

By way of contrast, the volume devoted to *Virt.* in the French Lyon
edition is a very mediocre piece of work.[23] It prints Cohn's text and
makes one or two isolated comments on it, but is of no value for the
study of the Greek text whatsoever.

3. *The extent and quality of the manuscript tradition*

The direct manuscript tradition of Philo's writings (from which we
exclude excerpts in the Florilegia and *Catenae*) is extremely rich,
consisting of more than 120 manuscripts. As the result of their
extensive investigations Cohn and Wendland divided this mass into
some 20 families, each of which have a single manuscript as chief

---

313–377.
   [20] *Philo in Ten Volumes, with an English Translation by F. H. Colson,* Loeb Classical
Library, volume 8 (London: Heinemann, Cambridge Mass.: Harvard University
Press, 1939) 157–305. On Colson, a Cambridge-trained classicist and headmaster,
see further *Who was Who 1941–1950* (London: A. & C. Black, 1952) 240.
   [21] Of Colson the then editor of the Loeb Classical Library W. H. D. Rouse
(*Philo in Ten Volumes* 10.vii) wrote: 'a translator more careful and more competent
I never worked with'.
   [22] Colson, *Philo* 8.vii.
   [23] *Les Œuvres de Philon d'Alexandrie,* vol. 26, *De virtutibus,* introduction et notes
de R. Arnaldez, traduction de P. Delobre, M. R. Servel, A. M. Verilhac (Paris:
Éditions du CERF, 1962).

progenitor.[24] The text of our treatise is fairly well represented in the manuscripts. There are, however, considerable complexities involved in collecting and assessing this evidence. This is caused by the fact, already noted above, that the treatise is divided into four sections, and these are scattered in various configurations throughout the manuscript tradition. The following table indicates the locations of the various parts in the manuscripts, which are listed in chronological order.

Table 1: manuscripts relevant to the text of *De virtutibus*

ms.	name/location	G-G	date	contents
S	Oxon. Seldenianus 12	107	10–11	1–227
C	Parisinus gr. 435	49	11	51–186, 195–7
V	Vindonensis suppl. gr. 50	113	12	1–50
B	Venetus gr. 42	43	12	1–50
E	Oxon. Lincolniensis 43	76	12–13	1–50 [121]
A	Monacensis gr. 459	35	13	1–50, 51–181
M[25]	Laurentianus plut. X,20	100	13	1–50
P	Petropolitanus XX A 21	104	13–14	51–174, 1–50, 187–227
R	Parisinus gr. 1630	106	14	175–177 (extract only)
O	Laurentianus plut. X,23	102	14	1–50
K	Laur. conv. soppr. 59	96	14	1–46
H	Venetus gr. 40	84	14	51–181, 1–50, 187–227
G	Vaticano-Palatinus gr. 248	83	14–15[26]	51–181 (= G[1]), 1–50, 51–174, 187–227 (= G[2])
N	Neapolitanus II C 32	101	15	187–227
F	Laur. plut. LXXXV.10	80	15–16	1–50, 51–181, 187–225[27]
L	Parisinus gr. 433	99	16	51–181, 1–50, 187–227

A second table shows how the various parts of the treatise are recorded in the chief manuscripts (again presented in order of age).

---

[24] See the analysis in C-W 1.iv–lx and the lucidly presented overview in G-G 139–153. Only in the case of family F is an another manuscript in the same family of any importance (see n. 24 below). There is a large variation in the number of manuscripts in a family. Some 'families' are represented by a single manuscript.

[25] At one time Mediceus, hence the abbeviation.

[26] According to C-W 1.xxxiv 14th century, G-G 147 14–15th century.

[27] For the missing section at the end Cohn used the twin of this manuscript Vaticanus gr. 379 (= G-G 81)

Table 2: record of various parts of *De virtutibus* in the manuscripts

Περὶ ἀνδρείας (§1–50)   S A M P H G F
                                        V B E O K (joined to *Mos.*)
Περὶ φιλανθρωπίας (§51–174)   S C A P H G¹ G² F L
Περὶ μετανοίας (§175–186)   S C G²
                                        A P H G¹ F (break off at §181)
Περὶ εὐγενείας (§187–227)   S G² P H F
                                        C (only §195–7), F (§187–225)

Of these various manuscripts a number are of special interest.
(a) The only manuscript to contain the treatise in the form close to
the way we know it is S. This manuscript, which only contains the
text of *Spec.* 3.37–209, *Spec.* IV and *Virt.*, is among the very oldest
Philonic manuscripts we possess.[28] Although the order of the parts
corresponds to the text presented by Cohn, it differs in the headings
that it gives, not only for these four parts, but also additionally for a
large number of subordinate sections of the treatise.[29] The text that
it offers differs on countless occasions from what is found in all
other manuscripts of Philo. These differences will occupy us at some
length below, but now already we can say that many of these
readings are without doubt authentic and correct, but that there are
also quite a number of very silly readings and patent errors. A
further striking feature of the manuscript is that at the end of *Virt.* it
contains an incomplete commentary on Philo's views on the Decad
of 12 folio pages in length (damaged at the end), which includes
much Pythagoreanizing arithmological material.[30] [122]
(b) The manuscript A, which is one of the fullest and most important Philonic manuscripts, contains especially for §1–50 a number of
independent and generally excellent readings.[31]

---

[28] On this manuscript see L. Cohn, 'Die Philo-Handschriften in Oxford und
Paris', *Philologus* 51 (1892) 266–270. On p. 267 he claims that it is by far the oldest
of Philonic manuscripts. But the palimpsest Vaticanus fr. 316 which he discovered
later is probably older (cf. G-G 150; this manuscript does not contain material
from *Virt.*).
[29] Cf. app. ad §1, 82, 88, 90, 95, 97, 102, 105, 109, 116, 125, 134 (*nota bene*),
145, 148,
[30] Cohn 'Philo-Handschriften' 269f. publishes the first dozen lines. To my
knowledge the remainder is as yet unpublished. One wonders what Philonic
material the commentary is based on (did the author have access to *De numeris?*).
The fragment published by Cohn includes a definition of number drawn from
Nichomachus of Gerasa (2nd century AD), so this part at least is not authentically
Philonic.
[31] Cf. Cohn, 'Neue Beiträge' (n. 18) 211.

(c) V is not the famous Viennese codex derived from the Caesarean archetype (which only contains the first half of *Opif.*).[32] It is an unrelated 12th century manuscript containing *Mos.* I–III,[33] *Virt.* 1–50, *Jos.* This particular placement of Περὶ ἀνδρείας, which gives a eulogy of certain themes in the Mosaic Law, is also found in the manuscripts B E K O. The text of these five manuscripts show many convergences for this section.

The manuscript evidence on our treatise is, therefore, fairly copious but rather chaotically preserved. Although Cohn and Wendland can show that all the evidence in the Greek medieval manuscripts derives from the copies of Philo's works in the Caesarean library, it proved difficult for them to produce anything like a *stemma codicum* which shows the interrelation between the more important manuscripts. In his edition of *Opif.* Cohn divides the manuscript tradition into two distinct families, besides which some single manuscripts are placed,[34] but in the *editio maior* this idea is not further pursued,[35] and in the specific introduction to the treatise *Virt.* a stemmatic analysis of the manuscript tradition is not mentioned at all.

The only other research into the manuscript tradition which is at all comprehensive was carried out by Barthélemy in 1967.[36] He looked above all at two aspects of the evidence. Firstly he observed that certain passages in Philo's writings had been 'retouched' by an interpolator, who was certainly Jewish, and possibly can be identified with the Rabbi Hoshai'a who was the friend of Origen. Remarkably, the only treatise in which he finds this occurring outside the Allegorical Commentary is *Virt.* He notes that in manuscript G at §66 and 69 the name Ἰησοῦς has been changed to Ἰωσοῦα in

---

*

[32] On this codex and its 'cross' recording Εὐζοῖος ἐπίσκοπος ἐν σωματίοις ἀνεώσατο see C-W 1.iii, J. Morris, 'The Jewish philosopher Philo', in E. Schürer, *The History of the Jewish People in the Age of Jesus Christ*, revised and edited by G. Vermes *et al.* (Edinburgh: T. & T. Clark, 1973–87) 3.822.

[33] *Mos.* is always divided into three books in the manuscripts, but this is wrong as *Virt.* 52 shows.

[34] See the stemma at L. Cohn, *Philonis Alexandrini libellus De opificio mundi* (Breslau: G. Koebner, 1889) xxi; also a similar attempt at F. C. Conybeare, *Philo About the Contemplative Life* (Oxford: Clarendon Press 1895) 21.

[35] Cf. the section De codicum auctoritate at C-W 1.xxxvii–xli.

[36] D. Barthélemy, 'Est-ce Hoshaya Rabba qui censura le 'Commentaire Allégorique'? A partir des retouches faites aux citations bibliques, étude sur la tradition textuelle du *Commentaire Allégorique* de Philon', in *Philon d'Alexandrie: Lyon 11–15 Septembre 1966; colloques nationaux du Centre National de la Recherche Scientifique* (Paris 1967) 45–78.

conformity with the Hebraizing Aquilan translation of the Pentateuch.[37] The reason why a Jew should wish to do this in a Christian
setting is obvious. Moreover at §184 it is very likely that the biblical
text of Deut. 26:17 has been altered (this passage will be further
discussed at some length in section 4 below).[38] Secondly Barthélemy
examined the order of the various treatises in the different manuscripts. Combining these two criteria he concludes that there were
[123] two editions of the Allegorical Commentary made at Caesarea.
The first, consisting of two sections (α–β) was tampered with by the
unknown 'retoucher'. The second (ω) was left untouched. The text
of *Virt.*, he claims, formed the hinge between the two sections α–β,
the part Περὶ εὐγενείας coming either at the end of α or at the
beginning of β. This conclusion is based on the fact that Περὶ
εὐγενείας follows on *Conf.* in the manuscripts F and N, and precedes
Fug. in G.[39] In fact Barthélemy's own table shows that the parts of
Virt. are far more often surrounded by works from the Exposition of
the Law (including *Mos.*) than the Allegorical Commentary. Nevertheless the same grouping with allegorical treatises occurs in the
Athenian palimpsest about to be discussed, and, more significantly,
also in the list of writings given by Eusebius.[40] It may be concluded,
therefore, that very early on, in one line of transmission at least, *Virt.*
became separated from its place in the Exposition of Law. But this is
not a fact of great importance for our investigation.

Finally it may be asked whether Cohn omitted to consult or was
unaware of any important manuscript evidence in the preparation
of his text. The manuscripts recorded by G-G as not known to C-W
contain nothing of importance. Of more interest is a palimpsest,
Atheniensis Bibl. Nat. 880. In 1961 P. J. Alexander discovered that
underneath the writing of 13th century Byzantine liturgical text was
an older text containing a collection of Philonic treatises, namely
Sacr. Det. Post. Gig. Deus, Agr. Ebr. Sobr. Conf. Somn. I, *Virt.*[41] The ink

---

[37] Barthélemy, 'Hoshaya Rabba' 47, 57.
[38] Barthélemy, 'Hoshaya Rabba' 50, 53; but the passage is not directly addressed.
[39] See Barthélemy, 'Hoshaya Rabba' 64, and the table at 63.
[40] *HE* 2.18.2, with the sequence *Agr. Ebr. Sobr. Conf. Fug. Congr. Her. Virt.* Περὶ
διαθηκῶν *Migr. Gig.–Deus Somn.*
[41] See the description by P. J. Alexander, 'A Neglected Palimpsest of Philo
Judaeus: Preliminary Remarks *editorum in usum*', in K. Treu (ed.), *Studia Codico-
logica*, Texte und Untersuchungen 124 (Berlin: Akademie Verlag, 1977) 1–15
(contents of manuscript on 13–15).

had been washed off the original manuscript and the folios had been divided in half, so that the original text is not only completely jumbled, but also partly inaccessible on account of the binding of the renewed manuscript. Through a detailed examination of the writing Alexander argues that the original manuscript is to be dated to between 965–1000, which would make it one of the very oldest Philonic manuscripts.[42] For our purposes we note that it contains the text of *Virt.* 175–188, 202–215, 221–227 scattered over no less than 22 pages of the renewed manuscript.[43] This means that most likely it contained only *De paenitate* and *De nobilitate*. We note further that it does not contain any lost parts of the Philonic corpus. Alexander concludes by expressing the hope that the manuscript will be rearranged in order to expose the Philonic material completely and then thoroughly collated. It could then be taken into account in a new edition of Philo.[44]

The papyri evidence on Philo's writings unfortunately contains no textual material from *Virt.* It has been suggested, however, that at least one papyrus fragment may derive from a missing part of the treatise. We return to this question below in section 6. [124]

4. *The value of the indirect tradition*

In his *apparatus testimoniorum* Cohn rightly points out a large number of passages in Josephus' description of the Mosaic πολιτεία in *Ant.* 4.196–302 which are reminiscent of Philo's treatment in *Virt.* These are not close enough to prove direct usage, and are of no value for textual purposes.[45]

Of quite inestimable value, however, is the witness of Clement of Alexandria to our text. In book II, §78–100, Clement makes an extensive and quite fascinating use of *Virt.* in order to expound the

---

[42] See above n. 28.

[43] On the basis of spot checks Alexander finds the text closest to U (Vaticanus gr. 381, = G-G 110; does not contain *Virt.*) and F. The similarity with the contents of F given by Barthélemy, 'Hoshaya Rabba' 64, is striking.

[44] Alexander, 'Palimpsest' 11; especially for *Post.* which is elsewhere only found in U.

[45] Only in the following passages might one be tempted to recognize verbal reminiscence (ignoring parallels caused by reference to the LXX text): §28–30, cf. 4.298 τούς τε νεωστὶ δειμαμένους οἰκίας, φυτεύσαντας, πόθῳ, ἀπόλαυσιν; §96, cf. 4.274 κατ' ἐρημίαν πλανωμένοις; §115, cf. 4.259 ἐμπλησθεὶς τῆς ἐπιθυμίας. These similarities could be explained through coincidence, or just possibly long-distance reminiscence.

virtues of the Mosaic legislation. The borrowing is unacknowledged, and from our modern perspective Clement might stand accused of plagiarism, were it not that right at the end he refers to Philo in connection with another passage as ὁ Πυθαγόρειος Φίλων τὰ Μωυσέως ἐξηγούμενος.[46] This extended passage has been recently studied in depth by Van den Hoek in her study on Clement's use of Philo, but, although she is very alert to the numerous changes and adaptations that Clement makes, textual questions fall completely outside the scope of her study.[47] As she aptly notes, Clement's method can be described as a 'cut and paste technique', for he continually takes small pieces of Philonic material, adapts them to his own language and train of thought, and interweaves them into the text.[48] What we have, therefore, is a rather free paraphrase, with only a limited number of phrases taken word-for-word from Philo's text. But, because we still possess that original text, it is still on many occasions possible to discern the original text that Clement had in front of
* him when he made his adaptation. And this means that we have partial access to the Philonic text at only a century and a half's remove from the original autograph, at least a generation before the archetype of our textual tradition was taken to Caesarea by Origen. Clement's usage was noted by Mangey, but the first scholar to exploit its importance was Wendland, who devoted an entire article to the question.[49]

There are about 40 instances in which Clement's text can be related to significant variants in the textual tradition. First we should note a number of striking examples in which Clement supports the reading of S against the remainder of the manuscript tradition:

> (a) §106: the words based on the biblical text ὅτι πάροικος ἐγένου κατ᾽ Αἴγυπτον are found in Clement 88.2 and added in the margin of S, but are omitted in all other mss.
> (b) §109: S τὰς ἐλεπόλεις ἐφιστάντες (cf. *Spec.* 3.87, 4.222), Clement 88.3 τοῖς τείχεσιν ἐφεστῶτες ὦσιν ἐλεῖν τὴν πόλιν πειρώμενοι, other mss. ταῖς πόλεσιν ἐφιστάντες *vel sim.* [125]

---

* [46] *Str.* 2.100.3; the reference is puzzling because the words attributed to Philo are nowhere found in his extant works.

[47] A. van den Hoek, *Clement of Alexandria and his Use of Philo in the Stromateis: an Early Christian Reshaping of a Jewish Model*, Supplements to Vigiliae Christianae 3 (Leiden: E. J. Brill, 1988) 68–115. For a useful overview of Clement's borrowings see 71–72. The investigation is wholly based on comparison of the texts of C-W for Philo and Stählin-Früchtel for Clement.

[48] Van den Hoek, *Clement* 73.

[49] Wendland, 'Philo und Clemens' (n. 16).

(c) §111: S and Clement 89.1 τρίχας, other mss. χαίτας.

(d) §118: S and Clement 90.2 ἕπεται, ἕψεται G, διέξεισι C, διέξειμι others (!).

(e) §134: S ἄλλο τίθησι διάταγμα συγγενὲς τοῖς προτέροις, ἀπαγορεύων ἡμέρᾳ τῇ αὐτῇ συγκαταθύειν μητέρα καὶ ἔγγονον; Clement 93.2 πάλιν αὖ ὁ χρήσος νόμος ἀπαγορεύει ἡμέρᾳ τῇ αὐτῇ συγκαταθύειν ἔκγονον καὶ μητέρα; G ἄλλο τίθησι διάταγμα συγγενὲς τοῖς προτέροις μὴ καταθύειν ἅμα μητέρα καὶ ἔγγονον; AP ἄλλο τίθησι διάταγμα συγγενὲς τοῖς καταθύειν τολμῶσι μητέρα καὶ ἔγγονον; FL ἄλλο τίθησι διάταγμα συγγενὲς τοῖς καταθύειν μητέρα καὶ ἔγγονον ἐθέλουσι.

It must be conceded that these cases are rather remarkable, and they led Wendland to the conclusion that S should be given the preference over the readings of other manuscripts in all cases where there are no other grounds for decision.[50] It might be suspected, especially on the basis of the marginal notation in (a) that we have here a case of contamination, i.e. that S's text has been altered from Clement. But given the extreme paucity of the Clementine transmission (only a single manuscript survives), this possibility must be ruled out.

On the other hand, Wendland's injunction fails to take into account the fact that on a large number of other—admittedly less spectacular—occasions, Clement agrees with other Philonic manuscripts against S. Again we give some examples:

(f) Clement 78.2 αἴτιον, §34 deleted by S, retained by all other mss.

(g) Clement 81.1 ἀνενδεὲς τὸ θεῖον, §9 ὁ μὲν θεὸς ἀνεπιδεής SAVF etc., ἀνενδεής BEKM.

(h) Clement 81.3 ἀναλαμβάνειν, §18 S ἀλλὰ λαμβάνειν, other mss. as Clement.

(i) Clement 90.1 ἄτμητον, §90 S ἄμητον, CG ἄτμητον, AHP ἀτίμητον.

(j) Clement 94.1 biblical quote beginning with ἀλλ', §142 deleted in SC, retained in G (cf. ἄλλο in remaining mss.).

(k) Clement 95.1 τέμνειν ἐᾷ, §150 S ἀποτέμνειν ἐᾷ, other mss. as Clement.

(l) Clement 95.2 παραβλαστάνον κωλύῃ τὴν αὔξησιν, §156 S παραναβλαστάνῃ τὴν αὔξην κωλῦον, other mss. παραβλαστάνῃ τὴν αὔξησιν κωλῦον vel sim.

In examples (j) and (l)[51] Cohn chooses for S against the combined evidence of Clement and the other manuscripts, which is surely dubious from the methodological point of view. Also the emendation

---

[50] Wendland, 'Philo und Clemens' 456: 'An Stellen, wo innere Gründe die Auswahl unter den Lesarten nicht bestimmen, könnten wir leicht geneigt sein, die weit überwiegende Zahl der Zeugen vor S zu bevorzugen. Indem auch an solchen Stellen das Zeugniss des Clem. zu hinzutreten ist, ergiebt sich der Schluss, dass überhaupt in allen solchen neutralen Fällen S der Vorrang gebührt, dass die Lesart von S, wo keine inneren Gründe gegen sie sprechen, stets als die richtige vorauszusetzen ist.'

[51] For παραναβλαστάνῃ, but not αὔξην .

φιλανθρώπως ὁμοῦ ⟨καὶ στρατηγικῶς⟩ at §28 based on Clement's text is unpersuasive.[52] [126]

These various textual differences may seem to the observer rather trivial, and not of great importance for our understanding of the contents of Philo's work. But this is certainly not always the case, as can be shown from my final Clementine example.

At *Str.* 2.98.2 Clement writes:

καλῶς οὖν ἐπὶ τῶν μετανοούντων εἴρηται τὸ λόγιον ἐκεῖνο· «τὸν θεὸν εἵλου σήμερον εἶναί σου θεόν, καὶ κύριος εἵλετό σε σήμερον γενέσθαι λαὸν αὐτῷ.» τὸν γὰρ σπεύδοντα θεραπεύειν τὸ ὂν ἱκέτην ὄντα ἐξοικειοῦται ὁ θεός. (Excellently, therefore, has this saying been said of the penitents: 'You chose God today to be your God, and the Lord chose you today to become his people.' For the one who hastens to serve the Existent and is a suppliant God makes his own.)

These words are derived in large part from the passage in Περὶ μετανοίας at §184 (I add the relevant manuscript variants):

ὅθεν εὖ καὶ συμφώνως τοῖς εἰρημένοις ἐχρήσθη τὸ λόγιον ἐκεῖνο· «τὸν θεὸν εἵλου σήμερον εἶναί σοι θεόν, καὶ κύριος εἵλατό σε σήμερον γενέσθαι λαὸν αὐτῷ» (Deut. 26:17–18). παγκάλη γε τῆς αἱρέσεως ἡ ἀντίδοσις, σπεύδοντος ἀνθρώπου μὲν θεραπεύειν τὸ ὄν, θεοῦ δὲ ἀνυπερθέτως ἐξοικειοῦσθαι τὸν ἱκέτην καὶ προαπαντᾶν τῷ βουλήματι τοῦ γνησίως καὶ ἀνόθως ἰόντος ἐπὶ τὴν θεραπείαν αὐτοῦ. (Whence well and in full accordance with these words that saying has been pronounced: 'You chose God today to be your God, and the Lord chose you today to become his people.' For the one who hastens to serve the Existent and is a suppliant God makes his own.' Truly excellent is the reciprocation of the choice, when man hastens to serve the Existent, while God hastens without delay to make the suppliant his own and to anticipate the desire of him who genuinely and unfeignedly proceeds to his service.)

Variae lectiones

1.1: τὸν θεόν S, τὸν κύριον CG; εἵλου S, ἀντηλλάξω C, ἀντηλλαξάτω G
1.2: θεόν S, εἰς θεόν CG; εἵλατο S, ἀντηλλάξατο CG; αὐτοῦ S, αὐτῷ CG
1.3: διαιρέσεως S, αἱρέσεως CG   1.4: τὸ ὄν S, θεόν C, θεω G

The differences here are very considerable indeed, and require some kind of special explanation. In all the significant variants S is supported by Clement against the other manuscripts. The variation in the biblical text immediately points to the interposition of the Aquilan translation, as postulated by Barthélemy, and indeed the verb ἀνταλλάσσω is attested for Aquila in Deut. 26:17.[53] Two other

---

[52] Cf. the long note by Colson at *Philo* 8.178f. who suggests, adducing *Spec.* 2.183, that the manuscripts reading φιλανθρωπίαν ὁμοῦ is the result of an incorrect word division and should read φιλανθρωπίᾳ νόμου (the suggestion is described as brilliant by A. D. Nock in his review at *CR* 54 (1940) 170). Only the manuscript A reads φιλανθρώπως.

[53] Cf. J. Reider, *An Index to Aquila* (Leiden: E.J. Brill, 1966) 22. For Barthélemy's

variants in the biblical text may reflect the Aquilan translation: (a) the replacement of θεόν by κύριον at the beginning of 26:17 (since the MT reads two different divine names in this portion of text);[54] (b) the reading εἰς θεόν for the second θεόν in 26:17.[55] But there is more. Going beyond the cited biblical text we find that Philo's description of man as suppliant (ἱκέτης) serving τὸ ὄν (cf. the famous description at *Contempl.* 2) has been changed to θεόν in the same manuscripts that contain the Aquilan variants. The change is most likely motivated by unease at Philo's blatantly philosophical description of God in terms of Platonic being, a discomfort that Clement does not share.[56] The suggestion supports Barthélemy's theory of a Jewish-Rabbinic tamperer, although obviously other explanations [127] are possible.[57] This passage, therefore, discloses various interesting facets of the transmission of Philo's writings. But they can only be discovered by those who care to look at the variants tucked away in Cohn's apparatus.[58]

The indirect tradition, as witnessed by Clement, is also of importance for the vexed question of the original structure and contents of the treatise. We shall return to this subject in section 6 of our paper.

Regrettably Eusebius in his extensive extracts from Philo's writings does not cite any passages from *De virtutibus*. This is all the more a pity because the bishop, unlike Clement, gives *verbatim* quotations of his sources, so that he is an extremely valuable witness to the textual tradition.[59]

---

theory see above at n. 36.

[54] I.e. *Adonai* and *Elohim.* κύριος is only recorded for the LXX in the Ethiopic and Armenian translations. The variant has not been recorded for Aquila, but he may have had a vested interest in giving a literal rendering of the MT because similar otiose repetitions of the divine name were exploited by Christian apologists such as Justin Martyr.

[55] As suggested by Barthélemy, 'Hoshaya Rabba' 53.

[56] Another interesting case of possible tampering is found at §164, where the Platonizing phrase ὅταν θεός, ὁ νοητὸς ἥλιος, ἀνάσχῃ καὶ ἐπιλάμψῃ, as recorded in S, is altered to ὅταν θεοποίητος ἥλιος... in C G (to which variants in other manuscripts appear to be related). Cohn rightly chooses for S.

[57] E.g. a Christian scribe might balk at the description τὸ ὄν. But the proximity to the intruded Aquilan variants gives support to Barthélemy's theory.

[58] It is to be agreed with M. Harl, *Quis rerum divinarum heres sit,* Les Œuvres de Philon d'Alexandrie 15 (Paris: Éditions du CERF, 1966) 159ff., that the textual variants found in the various forms of transmission of Philo's writings should be taken more seriously than is generally the case.

[59] Cf. C-W 1.lxi–lxii. It should be lost out of sight, however, that Eusebius represents part of the *indirect tradition.* He has his own axe to grind, and this can lead to subtle modifications in his recorded texts.

In their monumental edition Cohn and Wendland attempted as best they could to include the remaining indirect tradition located the exegetical *Catenae* and various later Byzantine anthologies.[60] For *Virt.* the harvest was small.[61] The only snippet that is of any real interest is five lines of §117 found in the *Sacra Parallela* of Johannes Damascenus.[62] The text supports S in a number of places, notably in recording παραλιπών (also with Clement) against καταλιπών in all other manuscripts. But it also has some unusual readings of its own (e.g. τελειότατον instead of τιμιώτατον found in all manuscripts). The remaining important pieces of evidence (for our purposes) in the *Sacra Parallela* are the fragments from a lost Περὶ εὐσεβείας found by Pitra and Harris. To these we will return in section 6 below.

5. *An evaluation of the available texts*

As emerged in our brief history of Philo's text, all study and analysis of *Virt.* since 1906 has been based on the critical edition of L. Cohn. Our attention, therefore, must above all be focussed on the merits and failings of this edition. Cohn was certainly well qualified to carry out his task. He was active during the heyday of the German philological tradition. In preparation for his work as an editor he had received not only the customary general training in classical philology, but had also devoted considerable time to learning the technique of collating manuscripts and the various aspects of editorial criticism.[63] His edition has some very obvious merits. Firstly it is extremely conscientious in the recording of manuscript variants. Not seldom the apparatus criticus [128] takes up nearly as much room as the text itself. Secondly Cohn is a careful editor, and may be been considered relatively conservative for his day, if we take into consideration that late 19th century scholarship was much more prone to introduce emendations and conjectures into the body of the text than occurs in modern editorial practice. A few of Mangey's pro-

---

*   [60] Cf. C-W 1.lxiii–lxx, 2.xv–xvii, and esp. L. Cohn, 'Zur indirekten Ueberlieferung Philo's und der älteren Kirchenväter', *Jahrbücher für Protestanische Theologie* 18 (1892) 475–492. See further Morris, 'Jewish philosopher' (n. 32) 3.825. We may be sure that there is more material than that exploited by Cohn and Wendland in their edition.

[61] Cf. above n. 4.

[62] See the apparatus at C-W 5.300–301. The manuscript in which the fragment is located is Vaticanus fr. 1553 (= G-G 52), dated to the 12th century.

[63] Cf. M. Pohlenz's remark in his necrology of Wendland that Cohn 'über eine sichere Editionstechnik verfügte', *Neue Jahrbücher* (see above n. 15) 60.

posed emendations are taken over,[64] but many others are rejected. Cohn adds some of his own, especially if required by accidence or syntax.[65] Quite often, however, he reserves his suspicions of and suggestions for the text for the apparatus, rightly preferring the original text to stand.[66] If there is a weakness, it would be that, as Colson points out on a number of occasions, he is sometimes inclined to give up on a difficult passage too easily and declare it corrupt.[67] Moreover it must recognized that from to time he cannot resist introducing speculative emendations into the text which a modern editor would leave well alone.[68] The temptation here is the desire to improve on the text, i.e. to bring it into line with expectations based on knowledge of Philo's Greek, but also of extraneous factors, such as canons of sound Greek style etc. Of such intrusions the worst I found is at §91, where the readings δικαιότατος (S) and φιλοστοργότατος (other manuscripts) are conflated into φιλοστοργό-τατος καὶ δικαιότατος, a procedure that goes against sound editorial practice. Such attempts, it should be emphasized, occur less often than in most editions from the same period,[69] but nevertheless have to be taken into account by users of the text.

The main difficulty that Cohn encounters, however, is the need to *choose* between the textual variants in the manuscript tradition. The number and divergence of these is quite staggeringly high, and accounts for the unusual length of the apparatus criticus. In §1–50 (Περὶ ἀνδρείας) a larger number of manuscripts preserve the text and there is a fair degree of consensus. But from §51 onwards the role of S (sometimes supported by CG) becomes more and more prominent, and is reinforced by the rather poor quality of the manuscripts outside the group SCG.

S is indeed by all standards a remarkable manuscript. Time after time it preserves readings that are radically different from the rest of

---

[64] E.g. at §25, 31, 34, 45, 216 (which must be correct, since Philo never calls ἐπιστήμη itself an ἀρετή). At §43 Mangey's conjecture is confirmed by A.

[65] E.g. at §47, 53, 110, 123, 203 etc. These kind of emendations are indicated by *scripsi* in the apparatus.

[66] E.g. at §15, 17, 34, 62, 67, 113, 125, 201 (here he adds a safe conjecture into the text and reserves a more daring one for the apparatus).

[67] Cf. §38, 58, 185, 188 and Colson's notes *ad loc.*

[68] E.g. §28, 104 (καὶ ἀγαπῶντος can be retained), 158, 171.

[69] Compare his fellow-editor Wendland, who is much more speculative in his editorial work. Many of the emendations that Wendland suggests in his article cited in n. 16 are *not* taken over; e.g. §109, 209.

the manuscript tradition. As we saw in the previous section, on a number of important occasions these idiosyncratic readings are supported by Clement, and so have every chance of representing the original text. Wendland thus concluded on the basis of these results that S should always be given the benefit of the doubt.[70] Cohn for the most part takes over this advice. On numerous occasions, therefore, he chooses to take the reading of S, even though it is very different from, and sometimes by no means superior to, what is found in the remainder of the tradition. I think it is necessary to place a question mark behind this editorial judgment. It seems to me, on the basis of the collations recorded by Cohn, that S is an extremely *erratic* [129] manuscript. On a large number of occasions the readings it preserves must be right, as in the following examples:[71]

§51: ὁ προφήτης τῶν νόμων S rather than ὁ πατὴρ τῶν νόμων (neither phrase is found in the rest of Philo, but cf. *Mut.* 126, *Decal.* 175, *Legat.* 99).
§89: ῥύσιον S, χρῆσιν G, χρυσὸν other mss. (the context is lending money so the term 'surety' is much better than 'gold').
§160: the sequence is man, animals, plants so ζῴων ἀλόγων S G is obviously superior to ζῴων ἀγόνων (other mss.).
Cf. further §114, 126, 132, 137, 147, 158, 193, 218, 224.

On an equal number of occasions, however, S is very clearly in the wrong:

§69: τὸ φιλάλληλον καὶ φιλοεθνές most mss.; S's φιλόθεον ἐς of course misses the point altogether, since Moses' exhortation to Joshua takes place at the personal–civic level (A reads φιλοκενές).
§102: S reads τῶν μυθικῶν πραγμάτων instead of πλασμάτων.
§145: S reads βοῦν ἀλοῶντα μὴ κημοῦν, the other mss. φιμοῦν. Strangely Cohn adds behind S's reading *fortasse recte*, but this seems to me most unlikely given the presence of the verb φιμοῦν in the biblical text at Deut. 25:4. Cf. also the etymology of Phinehas at *Post.* 182.
Other examples of evident mistakes at §141, 163–4, 165, 175, 180, 203, 212.

How can we explain this erratic nature of our oldest witness? There are certain indications pointing to the fact that we may have to do here with that dangerous phenomenon, an independent and semi-intelligent scribe. To start with, there are the additional section headings which have been systematically added, as well as the commentary on Philo's use of the decad at the end of the manuscript.[72] Furthermore two textual variants are rather suggestive:

---

[70] See quotation in n. 50 and text thereto.
[71] In addition to the correspondences between S and Clement noted above.
[72] See above the notes 29–30.

§139: all the mss. read μὴ ἀποκτείνεσθαι μέχρις ἂν ἀποτέκωσιν *vel. sim.* S's φυλάττεσθαι very much looks like an attempt to circumvent the awkward repetition of two verbs beginning with ἀπο- (which Philo may have introduced as deliberate contrast).

§176: ἀγαθὰ γὰρ προηγούμενα ἐν μὲν σώμασιν ἡ ἄνοσος ὑγεία, ἐν δὲ ναυσὶν ἡ ἀκίνδυνος εὔπλοια, ἐν δὲ ψυχαῖς ἡ ἄληστος μνήμη τῶν ἀξίων μνημονεύεσθαι... It seems that S found the good attributed to the soul somewhat banal, and so records γνῶσις, which *must* be wrong in the context. This forces him two lines later to change καὶ ἡ λήθης ἐκγινομένη ἀνάμνησις to καὶ ἡ ἀληθὴς ἐκγινομένη ἀνάμνησις which surprisingly is also found the brief extract in R (i.e. Parisinus gr. 1630, G-G 106).

We note additionally the interesting text at §58 where Israel is described as a ποίμνη σποράδην [S ἐπ᾿ ὄρους] ἀγελάρχην οὐκ ἔχουσα. As Cohn observes in his article, S's reading adds an allusion to I Kings 22:17. Colson in his note on the passage is correct in pointing out that, since the reading of the other mss. is perfectly acceptable, the question to be answered is whether the allusion was originally inserted by Philo, or is rather the work of the scribe of S. [130]

It seems to me probable, therefore, that S has introduced deliberate alterations into his text, and that some of these will have found their way into Cohn's edition as a result of the strong preference that he shows for the readings of this remarkable manuscript.

Fortunately the English translation of *Virt.* in the Loeb Classical Library furnishes us with a check on the standard German edition. It should be emphasized that Colson takes as his starting point Cohn's text. To his text on the left hand side of the page he appends only a handful of manuscript variants, amounting to a fraction of all manuscript alternatives recorded in Cohn's apparatus. What he checks, therefore, is so much not whether a better text is available, but rather whether the text as it stands makes sense and is consonant with Philonic thought and style. This results in a lengthy series of high-quality notes and observations on Cohn's text which every student of Philo must take into consideration when working on this treatise. At times Colson explicitly approves of Cohn's textual alterations (e.g. at §46, 78 (where an entire paragraph is declared spurious), 183 etc.), and many more are incorporated without comment in his text and translation. In the notes, however, he is very often able to show with considerable conviction that one can understand the Greek text in a different way from that done by Cohn, and that some of the latter's proposals are not without their difficulties. This leads him to remark that in his view Cohn has introduced unjustified emendations into his printed text.[73] At the very least this

---

[73] See the remark cited above at n. 22.

excellent collection of notes squeezed into the uncongenial format
of a Loeb text should serve to remind Philonists that the edition
they use should be not uncritically accepted as a canonical expression of the *ipsa verba Philonis*.[74]

6. *The problem of the treatise's title and its original contents*

Finally we return to the questions of what the original title of *Virt.*
was, and how this title relates to the contents of the treatise as
reconstructed by modern scholars. Much energy and ingenuity has
been devoted to the resolution of the difficulties involved in answer-
ing these questions,[75] and very recently an excellent *status quaestionis*
has been given by J. Morris, which need not be repeated here.[76] We
confine ourselves, therefore, to three observations.

(a) The evidence on the treatise's title amounts to the following:

(1) *direct tradition*

S: Περὶ γ΄ ἀρετῶν ἃς σὺν ἄλλαις ἀνέγραψε Μωυσῆς περὶ ἀνδρείας καὶ φιλανθρωπίας καὶ μετανοίας
other mss.: Περὶ ἀρετῶν ἤτοι περὶ ἀνδρείας καὶ εὐσεβείας καὶ φιλανθρωπίας καὶ
μετανοίας *vel sim.*

(2) *indirect tradition*

Eusebius *HE* 2.2.18.2: Περὶ τριῶν ἀρετῶν ἃς σὺν ἄλλαις ἀνέγραψε Μωυσῆς [131]
Jerome *De vir. ill.* 11: de tribus virtutibus liber unus
Sacra Parallela Codex Rupefucaldinus (= G-G 57) fol. 212ᵛ: ἐκ τοῦ περὶ τριῶν
ἀρετῶν
Sacra Parallela other titles: ἐκ τοῦ περὶ ἀρετῶν.[77]

The agreement between Eusebius and S is striking, but one has to
take into account the very strong possibility of contamination
(Eusebius' *Church History* was a highly popular work in the Byzantine
period). On the other hand, the support for the reading '*three
virtues*' is strong enough to make it probable.[78] The mention of a

---

[74] As regrettably occurs in the French translation of Delobre-Servel-Verilhac.
[75] See esp. E. Schürer, *Geschichte* (n. 11) 3.670–1 and esp. n. 101 (this passage
goes back to the 2nd edition of the work of 1886); L. Massebieau, 'Le classement
des œuvres de Philon', *Bibliothèque de l'École des Hautes Études* 1 (1889) 1–91, esp.
39–41, 49–51; Wendland, 'Philo und Clemens' (n. 16); L. Cohn, 'Einteilung und
Chronologie der Schriften Philos', *Philologus* Supplbd. 7.3 (1899) 387–435, esp.
412–414; Colson, *Philo* 8.xii–xviii, 440–441.
[76] Morris 'Jewish Philosopher' (n. 32) 3.850–853.
[77] The reading at Codex Vaticanus 1553 fol. 73r is difficult, but appears to be
περὶ τῶν ἀρετῶν rather than περὶ γ΄ ἀρετῶν; cf. Wendland, 'Philo und Clemens'
436.
[78] Note that Philo appears to have written another work Περὶ ἀρετῶν, i.e. the

Περὶ εὐσεβείας in the other manuscripts should be explained as a deduction on the basis of the transmitted text, rather than a fossilized reference to a lost part of the treatise. The explanation for this is not, I believe, difficult to give. The words at §51, τὴν δ᾽ εὐσεβείας συγγενεστάτην καὶ ἀδελφὴν καὶ δίδυμον ὄντως ἑξῆς ἐπισκεπτέον φιλανθρωπίαν, can easily be read as referring to a treatment of piety that has just been given. It is important to note that the manuscript G actually goes looking for the section on piety and adds the title Περὶ εὐσεβείας at §34, preceding the account of the seductive Midianite attack on the Israelites.[79] This is not completely foolish, because the theme of piety is specifically mentioned at §42 and 45. The role of εὐσέβεια is in fact prominent in the entire treatise such as we have it. At *Spec.* 4.135, when introducing the theme of the ἀρεταί which still remain to be discussed as an appendix to his Exposition of the Law, Philo refers to piety as the 'queen of the virtues', and adds that he has already discussed her, as well as two other virtues φρόνησις and σωφροσύνη.[80] At §175, the beginning of *De paenitentia*, εὐσέβεια is again mentioned (together with δικαιοσύνη) as the virtue that enables the repentant to join the Mosaic commonwealth, while the section ends with the synonymous term θεοσέβεια. In the examples of true εὐγένεια piety returns on three occasions (§201, 218, 221). Piety, it would seem, is presented by Philo as a kind of super-virtue which stands above the other virtues and is presupposed by them, i.e. if you have δικαιοσύνη, ἀνδρεία, φιλανθρωπία, μετάνοια, εὐγένεια of the kind enjoined by Moses, you will also possess true εὐσέβεια towards God. Schürer is therefore correct, in my view, in concluding that the inclusion of a Περὶ εὐσεβείας was most likely caused by a false inference from Philo's formulation at §51.[81] And this means that there is much to be said for the title printed by Mangey in his edition: Περὶ τριῶν ἀρετῶν ἤτοι περὶ ἀνδρείας καὶ φιλανθρωπίας καὶ μετανοίας.[82]

---

larger work to which *Flacc.* and *Legat.* belong (cf. Morris, 'Jewish Philosopher' 3.863), so there would need to be a way of distinguishing the two works. We note too that *Contempl.* is in some manuscripts called the fourth book of Περὶ ἀρετῶν *vel sim.*

[79] See app. crit. at C-W 5.275.11; noted by Colson *Philo* 8.xiv.

[80] εὐσέβεια is also called ἡγεμονίς at *Decal.* 119 and *Virt.* 95 (here together with φιλανθρωπία).

[81] Schürer, *Geschichte* 3.671 n. 101; cf. Colson, *Philo* 8.xiv.

[82] Mangey, *Philonis* 2.376 (as noted above at n. 11 he does not include Περὶ εὐγενείας in the treatise); cf. Colson *Philo* 8.440, whose criticism of Cohn is quite

(b) If we accept the view that the title referred to three virtues, there is an obvious problem in the case of Περὶ εὐγένειας, since the possibility remains that this section was not part of the original treatise. Here the evidence of Clement surely has great weight indeed. It is safe to deduce from Clement's adaptations [131] that all four sections occurred in sequence in his copy of the treatise, since he makes use of them all in exactly the order given in Cohn's treatise. He had no section Περὶ εὐσεβείας in his copy, but it did include the section Περὶ εὐγένειας. Colson, who finds this last section an unworthy conclusion to the whole work, attempts to circumvent Clement's evidence by suggesting that it was already misplaced in his copy.[83] Such suspicion seems to me unwarranted when it concerns evidence so close to the time of the original autograph. The final section can, in my view, adequately explained as a somewhat polemical development *in contrariam partem* of the final idea of Περὶ μετανοίας, which is based on the biblical text Deut. 26:17–18 cited in §184. If the penitent makes the choice offered in this text, he becomes a true θεραπευτής τε καὶ ἱκέτης and as such is of equal worth to an entire people, i.e. of Israel who made the same choice under Moses (cf. also Deut. 30:19–20). *But*[84] those who do belong to the race of Israel by birth, and rely on that rather than on piety and virtue are making a great mistake, for true εὐγένεια is reserved for the wise man and not those who can boast distinguished ancestors...[85]

(c) How, finally, should we regard the fragments derived from the lost Περὶ εὐσεβείας? Schürer argued that these tell us nothing about the position of the work, in *Virt.* or elsewhere.[86] Philo may have written a work on piety which has nothing to do with our treatise at all. Schürer knew only of the three fragments published by Harris.[87] But since then some fresh evidence has come in, namely

---

justified.

[83] Colson, *Philo* xvii–xviii.

[84] For the text of the opening words of the section in §206 I prefer to read τοῖς δὲ ὑμνοῖσι with the majority of mss, rather than διὸ καὶ τοῖς ὑμνοῖσι (F, preferred by Cohn) or καὶ τοῖς ὑμνοῖσι (S).

[85] In most of *De nobilitate* Philo speaks in rather generalized tones, but that he concretely has Jewish persons in mind is shown by §206, 226.

[86] Schürer, *Geschichte* 3.672 n. 101.

[87] J. Rendel Harris, *Fragments of Philo Judaeus* (Cambridge: University Press, 1886) 10–11. Of these the first is already found in a slightly different version in Mangey, *Philonis* 2.667, while the third was first published by Pitra in 1884.

a fourth fragment. It was first published by Lewy, but in the two manuscripts of the *Sacra Parallela* where he found it no reference was given to the Philonic work from which it was drawn.[88] More recently Royse has shown that the same fragment is found in the manuscript Thessaloniciensis Βλάτεων Monasterii 9,[89] where it is said to come ἐκ τοῦ περὶ εὐσεβείας κεφαλαίου (the same reference given for Harris' third fragment; for the other two the reference is ἐκ τοῦ περὶ εὐσεβείας[90]). Earlier, however, Früchtel had discovered that by an amazing coincidence one of the papyrus scraps of POxy XI 1356 folio 10ʳ contained exactly the same text as the first half of Lewy's fragment.[91] From this Royse concluded that the Philonic co-dex found at Oxyrhynchus probably contained the text of the [133] lost Περὶ εὐσεβείας, and that its length was about 14 pages, which, as he rightly remarks, compares well with two of the parts of *Virt.*[92]

These discoveries, though of great intrinsic interest, are not sufficient to make us revise our views on the contents of *Virt.* The extracts from *Virt.* in the *Sacra Parallela* are labelled ἐκ τοῦ περὶ (τῶν) ἀρετῶν, and do not refer to specific parts of the work.[93] Naturally one is curious to know what the term κεφάλαιον means in the two titles mentioned above. The natural explanation is 'chapter', i.e. part of a larger work. But I have found no parallels in the Philonic fragments found in the *Sacra Parallela* for this designation.[94] Some further interesting evidence is found in a *Catena* on the Pentateuch, where a Philonic extract is entitled Φίλωνος Ἑβραίου ἐν τῷ περὶ εὐσεβείας λόγῳ, but it emerges that the text is from *Spec.* 3.120–124![95] It would appear that these Byzantine attributions are often

*

---

[88] H. Lewy, 'Neue Philontexte in der Überarbeitung des Ambrosius. Mit einem Anhang: neu gefundene griechische Philonfragmente', *Sitzber. preuss. Akad. d. Wiss. phil.-hist. Kl.* 1932 IV (Berlin 1932) 82–83, frag. no. 27.
[89] J. R. Royse, 'The Oxyrhynchus Papyrus of Philo', *Bulletin of the American Society of Papyrologists* 17 (1980) 162.
[90] If I read his cryptic description on p.10 correctly.
[91] L. Früchtel, 'Zum Oxyrhynchus-Papyrus des Philon', *Philologische Wochenschrift* 58 (1938) 1437–39.
[92] Royse, 'Oxyrhynchus Papyrus' 163.
[93] App. test. at C-W 5.268–269, 300. The fragment at C-W 5.321 entitled τοῦ Φίλωνος περὶ μετανοίας has a different background, coming from a manuscript that contains *excerpts* from Philo.
[94] Only a fragment in Paris. Coislinianus 276 (= G-G 50) folio 220ʳ with the title Φίλωνος ἐκ τοῦ περὶ κοσμοποιΐας· γ' κεφαλαίου (actually = *QG* 2.54, cited by F. Petit, *Quaestiones in Genesim et Exodum: fragmenta graeca*, Les Œuvres de Philon d'Alexandrie 33 (Paris: Éditions du CERF, 1978) 110).
[95] *Catena Barbarini* IV 56 (= G-G 183); see app. test. C-W *ad loc.*

rather doubtful, and that it is risky to deduce too much from them.[96]
I am in agreement with Schürer, therefore, that we should not allow
the fragments of Περὶ εὐσεβείας to influence our views on the
contents of *Virt.* such as we know them from the direct and indirect
tradition.

7. *Some concluding remarks*

Philonists may consider themselves fortunate. It is very unlikely, *pace*
Alexander,[97] that the project of new critical edition of Philo's works
will be undertaken again in the foreseeable future. The task would
be vast, as can be gauged from our example of the single treatise *De
virtutibus.* Such a project would have to be carried out by a classicist,
but few are trained to do this work nowadays, and it would not be
placed high on the list of scholarly priorities. It is indeed fortunate,
therefore, that in Cohn's edition of our treatise we possess a solid
foundation for further research. Especially his diligence in recording the manuscipt variants is most valuable. If new discoveries are
made, they will have to be superimposed on his labours. As we have
seen, it is possible to call into question many of his editorial
decisions. But at least the materials for making such evaluations are
readily available. Also in the case of the English translation of
Colson, now fifty years old, fortune has favoured the Philonist.[98]
Colson devoted half a lifetime to an intimate study of Philo's Greek
style, and his rendering points the way to a sound understanding of
a text that is by no means always straightforward. Apart from its
other merits it can serve as a valuable check on the earlier philological work carried out by Cohn and other scholars. [134]
    Nevertheless my hope is that the small piece of research carried
out in this article will shake Philonists out of any kind of complac-
ency they may possess. This was the point of the analogy with
computer programming with which the article commenced. It is
important to bear in mind that both the text and the translations we
use are scholarly products built upon an elaborate sub-structure of

---

[96] There are numerous misattributions in the *Sacra Parallela* and *Catenae*, as a
cursory inspection of the app. test. in C-W and the attributions in Harris and Petit
will confirm.

[97] Cf. the remark cited above at n. 44.

* [98] This applies to the translation work done by Colson himself. In early
volumes he shared the task with G. H. Whitaker, who was considerably less competent. The translation of *Opif.*, for example, contains many serious mistakes.

codicological research and textual criticism. Cohn and Colson can be regarded as sound structures upon which one can build further. But for serious research on Philo's writings the foundations upon which they are built should not remain wholly unexamined. This is not just a matter of a philological purism which attempts to come as close as possible to Philo's original words. The texts that have come down to us are historical products. As we have seen in this article, the survival and transmission of Philo's writings throughout a period of nearly two millenia—from their reception by the early Christians to their treatment at the hands of generations of modern scholars—contain many aspects that should be of intrinsic interest to every student of Philo's writings.

VERBA PHILONICA, 'ΑΓΑΛΜΑΤΟΦΟΡΕΙΝ, AND THE AUTHENTICITY OF THE DE RESURRECTIONE ATTRIBUTED TO ATHENAGORAS

J. C. M. van Winden septuagenario

Already more than a century ago it was recognized that the extensive body of writings of Philo of Alexandria yields important evidence on developments in vocabulary and terminology of Greek as it was written by a well-educated man of letters in the first century AD. In the preface to his study on Philo as interpreter of the Old Testament published in 1875 Siegfried apologized for the fact that his introductory chapter on Philo's 'Gräcität' is disproportionately long (107 pages), but declared his conviction that, by publishing his collections of lexicographical material, he was doing the students of *media et infima graecitas*, as well as future editors of Philo's text, a service.[1] Having given a collection of words in Philo derived from or paralleled in the Platonic corpus, followed by another list of words found both in Philo and in his slightly younger contemporary Plutarch, the industrious German scholar then provides a list of 66 Philonic words which in the *Thesaurus* of Stephanus are marked as ἅπαξ λεγόμενα, to which are added another 42 words which are not found in the great Dictionary at all.[2] Some 14 years later the future editor of Philo, Cohn, in his trial edition of the *De opificio mundi*, draws attention to the same features, giving additional lists of words, taken taken this time only from a single treatise. First we receive *verba Platonica*, then *poetica verba*, followed by *ab Aristotele ... vocabula*. Cohn points out that many words recorded elsewhere earlier are found in Philo with new shades of meaning. Finally he too gives a list of *nova vocabula* which he claims that Philo thought up (*excogitavit*), 38 in *Opif.* alone.[3]

---

[1] C. Siegfried, *Philo von Alexandria als Ausleger des alten Testaments* (Jena 1875) iii; section on Philo's Greek at 31–137.

[2] *Ibid.* 32–47.

[3] L. Cohn, *Philonis Alexandrini libellus de opificio mundi*, Breslauer philologische Abhandlungen 4.4 (Breslau 1889, reprinted Hildesheim 1967) xli–xlvi.

It is worth pointing out that this is a somewhat risky claim. Safer by far is to say that Philo is the first extant author to *record* these words; we cannot be sure that he thought them up. There are some copious [314] Greek authors more or less contemporary with him extant (e.g. Strabo, Dionysius Halicarnassus, Diodorus Siculus, the above-mentioned Plutarch, Josephus), but too much literature has been lost, especially from Philo's native city Alexandria, for us to be sure of Philo's general creativity in this area.

If we examine the lists cited above, it becomes immediately clear that the majority of Philo's ἅπαξ λεγόμενα and first recorded words are compounds. A large number are simple words with one or more prepositional prefixes added to form a new combination, e.g. ἀντιεπίθεσις at *Opif.* 33 etc. Of greater interest from the view of terminology are compounds, in which a noun or adjective or verb or numeral (or also two nouns) have been combined to form a new term (examples are legion, e.g. from Cohn's list πολύβυθος (*Opif.* 29), ἰχνηλατεῖν (*Opif.* 56), ἀνθογραφεῖν (*Opif.* 138) etc.). As is well known, Greek has a great flexibility in the coinage and usage of such compound words.[4] It is also evident that Philo himself had a special predilection for such words, which have the effect of elevating the style or tone of a passage, or, if used excessively, making it high-flown and even bombastic. As an interesting example we might cite the term κοσμοπολίτης, 'citizen of the world', from which the modern word 'cosmopolitan' is derived. According to Diogenes Laertius his namesake, the Cynic Diogenes of Sinope, when asked from whence he came, replied with the single word κοσμοπολίτης. The authenticity of the anecdote is not at issue here. What is interesting is that in the whole of ancient Greek literature there is only a single other example (an insignificant case in the Proclan biography of Homer), except in Philo, who uses it no less than 10 times.[5]

Although a general study of Philo's use of such compound words would certainly be rewarding, it cannot be attempted in this present

---

[4] For discussion and analysis cf. R. Kühner and F. Blass, *Ausführliche Grammatik der griechischen Sprache* (Hannover 1892) 2.311ff., H. Weir Smyth, *Greek Grammar* (Cambridge Mass. 1920, 1974⁹) 247–254.

[5] Diog. Laert. 6.63; *Procli Chrestomathiae Eclogae* (ed. Allen) 99.14; Philo, cf. G. Mayer, *Index Philoneus* (Berlin–New York 1974) 166 (including the phrase κοσμο-πολίτιδες ψυχαί at *Somn.* 1.243). All my statements on the occurrences have been checked against the lexica of Liddell–Scott–Jones and Lampe, and on the 'C' version of the TLG CD-ROM (unfortunately still far from complete).

context. What I wish to do is to draw attention to a much smaller group of compound words, which form a special category and which I would like to give the label *verba Philonica*. These are words taken over or coined by Philo, not merely for stylistic purposes, but especially in order to express particular aspects of his activity as expounder and defender of the Jewish religion. In the case of these words there is a much stronger possibility that Philo himself was the decisive innovator, although we always have to bear in mind the shortcomings of the *argumentum e silentio*. These terms are not used in the particular Philonic sense in pagan literature. Many, however, are taken over from Philo by the Church fathers, some of which indeed become standard terms [315] in Patristic literature. The following list of such *verba Philonica*, given *exempli gratia* and in alphabetical order, is by no means exhaustive:

ἀγαλματοφορεῖν, 'to be an image-bearer': to be discussed below.

ἀνθρωπολογεῖν, 'to speak of God in human terms': found at Philo *Sacr.* 95, *Deus* 60, *Conf.* 135; same usage at Basil *Adv. Eunonium* 5, PG 29.752A, Didymus Alex. *De trinitate* 3.3, PG 39.816C.

ἀνθρωποπαθεῖν, 'to have the feelings of a man': only found at Philo *Leg.* 3.237, *Decal.* 43, *Flacc.* 121.

ἀνθρωποπαθής, 'having human affections', used of the pagan gods or of God: Philo *Sacr.* 95, *Post.* 4, *Deus* 59, *Plant.* 35; frequent in the Patres from Clement and Origen onwards (derived noun in Eusebius *PE* 3.15.2). In pagan authors only late: Hermogenes Rhetor (adverb), Porphyry (noun: *Quaest. Hom. in Iliad* 18.489, not in LSJ); both may be verbally influenced by the Judaeo-Christian tradition.

ἀνθρωποπλάστης, 'moulder of man', i.e. God: found only at Philo *Somn.* 1.210; the equivalent verb found only in Methodius, *Symp.* 2.2, 2.5.

ἑξαήμερος, 'pertaining to the six days of creation': first at Philo *Leg.* 2.12, *Decal.* 100 (if the text is emended), then common in the Patres from Theophilus of Antioch onwards (cf. J. C. M. van Winden, *RAC* 14 (1988) 1256ff.).

ζωοπλαστεῖν, 'to mould into a living being': in the creational sense at Philo *Opif.* 62, 67, *Decal.* 120 (of the womb at *Spec.* 3.33); taken over by Christian writers such as Eusebius, Adamantius, Gregory of Nyssa; in pagan authors only Lycophron (3rd c. BC) in the sense 'make statues' (cf. use in polemical sense by Eusebius *PE* 3.3.17).

ζωοπλάστης, 'moulder of living beings': used 6 times by Philo of God the creator, once polemically of the arrogation of divine power by man (*Spec.* 1.10). Rare among the patres (only Methodius, Nilus), wholly absent in pagan literature.

θεογαμία, 'marriage of gods': only at Philo *Decal.* 156 (with anti-polytheistic intent); not found in extant pagan literature.

θεοπλαστεῖν, 'to mould as a god, deify': used by Philo in a polemical, anti-polytheistic sense in 16 texts; elsewhere only in the pagan author Heliodorus, *Aegyptiaca* 9.9 (on this text see further below); no instances in patristic literature, but cf. the term θεοπλαστία used twice polemically by Athanasius.

θεοπλάστης, 'god-moulder': used of the creator (who creates the cosmos as god and the heavenly bodies as gods) by Philo in a summary of the *Timaeus* at *Aet.* 15; elsewhere no instances in this sense. At fr. 787 of Aristophanes the word θεοπλαστάς is found, presumably referring to the sculpting of statues. Note also texts in Basil and Gregory of Nyssa in which man is described as θεόπλαστος (cf. Gen. 2:7), anticipated earlier in the Hellenistic–Jewish *Oracula Sybillina* 3.8 (but not in the extant Philo).

θεοφράδμων, 'God-interpreting': used three times of Moses by Philo at *Her.* 301, *Mut.* 96, *Mos.* 2.269; not found elsewhere (θεοφραδής found in some pagan texts and Nonnus). [316]

θεόχρηστος, 'divinely inspired': used by Philo of the Jewish scriptures at *Legat.* 210; thereafter only at Didymus *Trin.* 1.18, Photius, *Bibl.* 223, 220b27.

κοσμοπλαστεῖν, 'to mould as a cosmos': only found at Philo *Migr.* 6, *Her.* 166; the equivalent noun κοσμοπλάστης, '[God as] cosmos-moulder' at *Plant.* 3, *Congr.* 48 (also not found elsewhere). On the other hand, Philo's standard terms for creating the cosmos, κοσμοποιεῖν, and for the Mosaic creational account, κοσμοποιΐα, are common in pagan literature, and are taken over by the Patres.

μεγαλόπολις, 'great city' (but adjectival): used of the cosmos five times by Philo (but not at *Flacc.* 163, where it is used of Alexandria in accordance with normal Greek usage); Philo's usage, not found in pagan sources, is taken over by Eusebius, *PE* 7.9.3. The noun μεγαλοπολιτής is also used by Philo at *Opif.* 143 in the sense of citizen of the world.

πρωτόπλαστος, 'first-moulded' (of Adam): one instance in Philo, at Greek fragment of *QG* 1.32; also in Wisdom of Solomon 7:1, 10:1, Apocalypse of Ezra 26.2; thereafter common in Patristic literature, but not found outside the Judaeo-Christian tradition.

σεμνηγορεῖν, 'make solemn pronouncements about', 'worship': used by Philo for pagan deification at *Mos.* 2.195, taken over by Heliodorus, *Aeg.* 9.9 (see further below), and less specifically at *Conf.* 2, *Mos.* 2.130; word not found elsewhere (noun σεμνηγορίη used by 3rd c. BC poet Timon).

σεμνοποιεῖν, 'magnify, extol, worship': rare instances in pagan authors (Lycurgus, Strabo, Harpocration); frequent in Philo (12 instances), some in an anti-polytheistic context (e.g. *Decal.* 4, 71); also one example in Josephus *Ant.* 16.149; found in a few Patristic authors, e.g. Athenagoras, Origen, Gregory of Nazianzen, Gregory of Nyssa etc. The noun σεμνοποιΐα is only found at Philo *Decal.* 80, in an apologetic context.

This list, which—I repeat—is far from exhaustive, reveals a concentration in two areas, (i) the exposition of the Mosaic creation account with its emphasis on God as creator of the entire universe, and (ii) the Jewish apologetic struggle against every form of polytheistic religion. Both concerns are at the centre of Philo's *œuvre*, but they are of course not confined to *his* writings alone. An immediate question that our list poses is whether Philo himself devised the lexical usage it contains, or whether this was shared with a much broader range of Hellenistic Jewish literature. In the case of the term πρωτόπλαστος a wider dissemination is evident (cf. also θεόπλαστος). For the word ἑξαήμερος it is much harder to be certain, since we cannot be sure that the first Patristic witness Theophilus of Antioch had direct access to Philo's writings.[6] In the case of the words θεοπλαστεῖν and σεμνηγορεῖν some interesting evidence points far more clearly to a decisive Philonic role. Both terms are found elsewhere only in the pagan author Heliodorus, in a passage where it is certain that [317] he is paraphrasing Philo's account of Egypt in the *De vita Moysis*.[7] Also in the case of Eusebius' description of the cosmos as a μεγαλόπολις, direct appropriation from Philo is as good as certain. Further investigation will reveal, I am convinced, that Philo's innovative use of certain compound words exercised a considerable influence on the development of Patristic vocabulary, through the mediation of Patres such as Clement, Origen, Gregory of Nyssa, Didymus, whom we know to have made extensive study of Philo's writings. Because Lampe's *Patristic Greek Lexicon*, for regrettable—even if perfectly understandable—reasons, contains scarcely any references to Philo, this important background remains largely obscured.[8]

The term on which I wish to narrow the focus of my article has scarcely been mentioned so far, namely the verb ἀγαλματοφορεῖν. Perhaps the most idiosyncratic of all the *verba Philonica*, Philo uses it 16 times in his preserved writings, more than all the instances in Patristic literature combined (10 known to me[9]), while in extant pagan literature no examples are found at all.[10] The literal meaning

---

[6] The recent articles by J. P. Martín—'La presencia de Filón en el Exámeron de Teófilo de Antioquía', *Salmaticensis* 33 (1986) 147–177, 'La antropologia de Filon y la de Teofilo de Antioquia: sus lecturas de Genesis 2–5', *Salmaticensis* 36 (1989) 23–71, 'Filon Hebreo y Teofilo Cristiano: la continuidad de una teologia natural', *Salmanticensis* 37 (1990) 302–317—contain much valuable parallel material, but are unable prove the direct relation beyond all doubt.

[7] Cf. my discussion of these texts in *The Studia Philonica Annual* 2 (1990) 134–139; I am not convinced by the note of A. Hilhorst in the same journal, 4 (1992) 75–77, which claims that Heliodorus was more likely a Christian than a pagan author. But this question does not affect my present argument.

[8] Cf. the motivation in the preface on p. vii. A happy exception is made in the lemma on ἀγαλματοφορέω.

[9] All recorded in Lampe, checked with the TLG CD-ROM (which so far has no Patristic authors beyond the 4th century).

[10] The 5th–6th century Alexandrian lexicographer Hesychius records the adjective ἀγαλματοφόρος, explaining it as ὡς ἄγαλμα ἐν τῇ ψυχῇ ⟨φέρων⟩ (suppl. Heinsius, Latte prefers κεκτημένος). We cannot know where Hesychius found this

of the compound word is 'to bear a statue or image (as in a shrine)', with reference to the way that a temple or a shrine contains and, from the outside, conceals the statue or image of a god within it.[11] Used in the active voice the verb refers to the person (or thing) bearing the image with him or inside him; in the passive voice, on the other hand, it refers to that which is being carried around like an image. In both cases the implication is that what is carried is something precious, to be carefully looked after, or indeed, if the background of the term is more fully taken into account, to be worshipped.

Philo's use of this idiosyncratic term is rather diverse and complex, but can be analysed along the following lines, with particular attention paid to who/what is doing the carrying, and who/what is being carried (emphasized in bold letters in each case).

(i) When **man** is described as being created according to the image of God (κατ᾽ εἰκόνα θεοῦ, Gen. 1:26), this refers to his *nous*, the director of his soul, which, being in a sense a god, he carries with him as an image (*Opif.* 69). This text is remarkable on account of the explicit identification of what is carried, in this case the *nous*, as 'like a god' (cf. also *Opif.* 137 cited below).[12] Similarly the youthful **Moses** astounded his fellow-pupils, who wondered whether the *nous* which he carried around in his body as an image was human or divine or a mixture of both (*Mos.* 1.27).

(ii) More commonly it is man, or the mind itself, that carries its **thoughts**, whether in general or in particular cases, as ἀγάλματα around with it. In the [318] extended image devised by Philo to illustrate the creation of the intelligible and sense-perceptible worlds, the **architect**, in establishing a new city, stamps his design like in wax in his (rational) soul and bears around as an image an **intelligible city**, which he uses as a model when he executes his plan

---

adjective; there is certainly no indication that it was in a pagan author. For the lemma ἀγαλματοφορεῖσθαι he gives καλλωπίζεσθαι, 'to embellish oneself'.

[11] ἄγαλμα can have a rather general meaning, 'a thing that gives delight or joy', but to my mind it is the more concrete meaning of the statue of a god that is at the word's origin. The question might well be raised whether it was not the carrying of a cult statue of a god in a procession that is at the origin of the image; compare other words containing the root φορ- which refer to similar religious and cultic practices, e.g. κανηφορεῖν 'to carry the sacred basket in a procession', κοσμοφόρος 'one who carries ornaments in a procession', also θυρσοφορεῖν 'to carry the thrysus' and ναρθηκοφορεῖν 'to carry the narthex' in Bacchic rites (see further LSJ *ad locc.*). But it would seem, according to W. Burkert, *Greek Religion* (Oxford 1985) 92, 100, that in classical times at least, the carrying of cult images in a procession was the exception rather than the rule. For Philo the association of the word with the statue in a *temple* is clear.

[12] Discussion of this text at A. Méasson, *Du char ailé de Zeus à l'Arche d'Alliance: Images et mythes platoniciens chez Philon d'Alexandrie* (Paris 1986) 371–377; D. T. Runia, 'God and Man in Philo of Alexandria', *JThS* 39 (1988) 64ff.

(*Opif.* 18). **Man** the microcosm can be called a miniature heaven because he carries **star-like natures** (i.e. thoughts) as ἀγάλματα in himself (*Opif.* 82; the topos derived from Plato *Tim.* 47a-c, cf. also *Opif.* 55 where the stars themselves are ἀγάλματα θεῖα). The same theme is found at *Mos.* 2.135: the **high-priest**, wearing his vestment, carries a **pattern** of the cosmos in his mind, and so is a microcosm. Elsewhere the **fool** carries **idolatrous thoughts** in his mind like an image (*Conf.* 49); the **house of wisdom** (i.e. the mind) bears the **variegator's craft** as a holy image (ἀφίδρυμα) (*Somn.* 1.208);[13] Moses exhorts his **followers** to keep the **memory of God** as an image not to be forgotten (*Virt.* 165); God has established the good among man, finding no temple on earth worthier than his **reason** (λογισμός), which carries the **good** as an image (*Virt.* 188).

(iii) In two texts it is the **body** which carries mind or its thoughts as images. God takes the purest clay (Gen. 2:7) to fashion man's **body** as a holy temple for the **rational soul**, which it was to carry as the most god-like of images (*Opif.* 137). At *Mut.* 21 is the 'somatic and earthly composition' that carries the **mind** as an image. Elsewhere, reporting a controversy concerning the location of the *nous* in the body, Philo refers to some thinkers who consider that it is carried as an image in the **heart** (i.e. the Aristotelian and Stoic view) (*Somn.* 1.32).

(iv) Two texts refer to the Mosaic **laws** as that which is borne as an image, at *Mos.* 2.11 by **Moses** their compiler, at *Legat.* 210 by the **Jews** who regard them as oracles sent by God and to be accordingly venerated.

(v) Finally there are some texts where the word is used even more loosely and appears to means no more than 'to possess something precious': *Mos.* 2.113, of the high-priestly **breastplate** carrying the two **virtues** δήλωσις and ἀλήθεια (i.e. Urim and Thummim) as images; *Mos.* 2.209, of the **hebdomad** stamped on the entire cosmos and carried by **nature** as an image.

It goes without saying that the metaphor involved in this usage of the word ἀγαλματοφορεῖν, derived as it is from Greek religious and cultic practice, is not the invention of Philo. Taken in a literal sense it could not but conflict with the injunction of the second commandment of the Decalogue. Clearly it has a pagan source, and since the prime focus of reference appears to be on the mind and its thoughts,[14] it is surely in philosophical literature that we should look for its origin.[15] In a doxographical report in the so-called *Anonymus Fuchsii*, which may be dependent on the medical writer Soranus (early 2nd century AD), we find a very precise parallel for Philo's idea:[16] ὁ δὲ Ἱπποκράτης τὸν μὲν νοῦν φησιν ἐν τῷ ἐγκεφάλῳ τετάχθαι

---

[13] A difficult passage to interpret: provisionally I take ὁ σοφίας οἶκος as referring to the mind.

[14] I would thus exclude a more general use of the image of ἄγαλμα, e.g. at Plato *Tim.* 37c (of the heaven), *Phdr.* 251a (the beloved).

[15] For what follows see esp. my discussion at *Philo of Alexandria and the* Timaeus *of Plato*, Philosophia Antiqua 44 (Leiden 1986) 332–334, to which I have added some more texts.

[16] *Anon. Fuchsii* (published by R. Fuchs, *Rheinisches Museum* 49 (1894) 540ff.)

καθάπερ τι ἱερὸν ἄγαλμα ἐν ἀκροπόλει τοῦ σώματος. The [319] subject under discussion here is *exactly* that found in Philo *Somn.* 1.32, except that Hippocrates localizes the *nous* in the brain, not the heart. The image of the head as acropolis, going back to Plato *Tim.* 70a, is also regularly found in Philo (but I do not think there is a necessary connection with the metaphor of the shrine or temple).[17] A more general text is found in Epictetus, who with protreptically motivated pathos exclaims, θεὸν περιφέρεις, τάλας, καὶ ἀγνοεῖς... καὶ ἀγάλματος μὲν τοῦ θεοῦ παρόντος οὐκ ἂν τολμήσαις τι τούτων ποιεῖν ὧν ποιεῖς, and proceeds to compare what man would do if he was the statue of Athena or Zeus produced by Phidias.[18] Another text, predating Philo this time, which contains the idea of the mind as an image of a god is found at Cicero, *De legibus* 1.59: nam qui se ipse norit, primum aliquid se habere sentiet divinum ingeniumque in se suum *sicut simulacrum aliquod* dicatum.[19] It is also quite well possible that Plato's comparison of Socrates with images of Silenus containing ἔνδοθεν ἀγάλματα θεῶν (*Symp.* 215b) contributed to the development of the idea.

The *concept* of man or man's *nous* as image-bearer, therefore, has been drawn by Philo from Greek philosophical sources. This does not necessarily mean, however, that also the word ἀγαλματοφορεῖν is taken over from there. As we saw earlier, there is no record of the word in the pagan tradition. I am inclined to agree both with the *Souda*, who notes that the word is Philonic,[20] and the lexicographer Stephanus, who in his *Thesaurus Linguae Graecae* claims that the word itself is *peculiare et proprium* to Philo.[21] All other examples of the word are found in the Patristic tradition, and a brief examination of these

---

1.13; cf. J. Mansfeld's detailed analysis of the doxography of the location of the ἡγεμονικόν in 'Doxography and Dialectic: the *Sitz im Leben* of the 'Placita',' *ANRW* 36.4 (1990) 3092–3108, to which I am indebted for this reference.

[17] Cf. Runia *op. cit.* (n. 14) 306, Mansfeld, *art. cit.* 3105. Further aspects of Philo's use of philosophical sources in his anthropology will not be pursued here

[18] Epictetus 2.8.12, 14, 18, cited by J. Pépin, *Idées grecques sur l'homme et sur Dieu* (Paris 1971) 138 in his discussion of Stoic anthropology.

[19] Cited by P. Boyancé in his rich comments on the sources of Philo's *Opif.*, 'Études Philoniennes', *Revue des Études Grecques* 76 (1963) 109, who in turn cites an earlier 1929 study on the *Somnium Scipionis* by R. Harder.

[20] *S.v.* ἀγαλματοφορούμενος, where the comment is appended: ἀγάλματα ἤτοι τύπους τῶν νοητῶν φέρων ἐν ἑαυτῷ· οὕτως Φίλων. This comment is obviously based on *Opif.* 18.

[21] 1.177, in the edition of Dindorf (Paris 1831–64): this lemma is full of acute observations and interesting quotes from early scholars.

confirms, I believe, the Philonic inspiration. We take the 10 texts in chronological order.

> **Athenagoras**, *De resurrectione* 12.6: God has assigned immortality to those who bear his image as creator in themselves. This would be the oldest text, if indeed this work can be attributed to the Apologist. We shall return to this text directly.
>
> **Origen**, *Commentary on John* 10.39, 215.19 Preusschen: Christ's body as temple (John 2:21) may refer to the body he received from the virgin or to his body the church, for the church is a temple bearing an image, i.e. Christ as first-born of all creation. Note the implicit reference, through the allusion to Col. 1:15 to the Logos as εἰκὼν θεοῦ. Philo describes man's body as an image-bearing temple at *Opif.* 137 (cf. also *Virt.* 188).
>
> **Eusebius** uses the term three times. Two examples occur in an extremely high-flown oration that he puts in his own mouth (*HE* 10.4). The eulogized Paulinus bears as an image in his soul Christ entire, the Logos, Wisdom, the Light, and thus forms a magnificent temple for God the most high (§26).[22] In more general terms he later describes the soul as having an [320] immortal and rational edifice made by the Son in his own image, created so as to be able to bear the heavenly Logos as image (§56). At *Contra Hieroclem* 6, 375.28 Kayser, he describes how a man specially favoured by God has his mind purified and is truly called divine, carrying some great god as an image in his soul (cf. especially Philo *Opif.* 69).
>
> **John Chrysostom**, *Frag. in Prov.* (*e catenis*), PG 64.728.48: through spiritual contemplation the interpreter of scripture will come to know his humanity, so that, bearing an image (i.e. the Logos in him), he will enter paradise.
>
> Three texts in a contemporary of Chrysostom, the monastic writer **Nilus** of Ancyra (PG 79.768A, 829A, 1040C), each concerning the process of acquiring and summoning up thoughts (carried as images) in the memory (an important subject for monks, whose thoughts may go in troublesome areas). The use of ἀγαλματοφορεῖν in these texts may well be inspired by a reading of Philo's description of the architect at *Opif.* 18 (note further verbal parallels, ἀνακαινίζει (Philo ἀνακινήσας) in 768A, εἴδωλα in 1040C).
>
> Finally a 6th century text in **Leontius** of Byzantium, *Contra Nestorem et Eutychem* 2, PG 86.1353A): the Logos did not enter its temple when his body was completed, but while it was still in the womb, so that then already τὸ ἡμέτερον, i.e. the body in human shape, carried the Logos as an image.

It is apparent that these texts stand much closer to the usage of the term ἀγαλματοφορεῖν as developed by Philo than the original application of the metaphor of the ἄγαλμα as found in the pagan philosophical texts. Indeed, except the texts in Nilus, all the passages are directly related to some form of Logos exegesis, either anthropological (exeg. Gen. 1:26) or Christological (e.g. exeg. Gen.

---

[22] Also the comparison in the previous section (§25) with Bezaleel, constructor of the temple, is clearly inspired by Philo; cf. *Leg.* 3.95–96, 102, *Somn.* 1.206–207 (where, as we saw above, the word ἀγαλματοφορεῖν occurs!).

1:26 via Col. 1:15–20) or both. The hypothesis is surely justified that the use of the word ἀγαλματοφορεῖν was taken over from Philo and transmitted to the Patristic tradition through the Alexandrian tradition, where Philo's works were saved from destruction, and where Logos theology played such a prominent role. The first Christian author of whom we can be certain that he read Philo, Clement of Alexandria, does not use the word in his extant works, but he can be said to have prepared the way: in at least four texts he speaks of man having a divine ἄγαλμα of the Logos in his soul or being himself an ἄγαλμα, with in each case Gen. 1:26 lurking in the background.[23]

Further evidence in favour of our hypothesis of a Philonic origin can be found in another example, which is as it were the mirror image of the word we are examining. Just as man can carry in his body the mind as a divine image, so the soul can be forced to carry the body with her around as a corpse. This too is a philosophical theme, going back to [321] Heraclitus and Aristotle's *Protrepticus* and taken up in Platonist tradition, a theme which Philo regularly exploits for exegetical purposes.[24] What is interesting for our purposes is that the verb νεκροφορεῖν, analogous in construction but opposite in meaning to ἀγαλματοφορεῖν, is not found in pagan sources, but occurs some 8 times in Philo, from whom it is taken over in a rather limited way by some Church Fathers.[25]

There is one difficulty confronting our hypothesis, however, and that is the example in Athenagoras. If the treatise *De resurrectione* attributed to him is regarded as authentic, we would have an example that may well pre-date Clement, since Athenagoras' other remaining work, the *Legatio*, is in all likelihood be dated to 176, a few years before Clement arrived in Alexandria (but we know nothing about the date of the Apologist's death).[26] For nearly 40

---

[23] *Protr.* 98.3–4, 121.1, *Str.* 7.29.5–6, 7.52.2–3.

[24] For details see the excellent analysis by J. Mansfeld, 'Heraclitus, Empedocles, and Others in a Middle Platonist Cento in Philo of Alexandria', *VC* 39 (1985) 131–156, esp. 140–141, where he calls the verb νεκροφορεῖν 'expressive'; reprinted in *Studies in Later Greek Philosophy and Gnosticism* (London 1989).

[25] *Leg.* 3.69, 74, *Agr.* 25, *Migr.* 21, *Somn.* 2.237, *Flacc.* 159, *QG* 1.97, 2.12. The verb occurs only in the *De resurrectione* of Methodius (indicating an Origenist position), Epiphanius (reporting Methodius) and in the 9th century Theodorus Studita. Most exx. of νεκροφόρος are not relevant, but note Greg. Naz. *Carm.* 1.1.8.116 (PG 37.455A), 1.2.14.64 (760A).

[26] Taking the chronology of A. Méhat, *Études sur les 'Stromates' de Clement d'Alexandrie*, Patristica Sorbonensia 7 (Paris 1966) 42–47, as our basis for Clement. On the date of the *Legatio* see R. M. Grant, *Greek Apologists of the Second Century*

years now, however, ever since a famous article of Robert Grant, this
* work's authenticity has been the subject of lively scholarly controversy. Grant noted that the attribution was not made until the
10th century, and argued that the work is addressed to a Christian
audience, attacks the position of Origen, and should be dated to the
3rd or 4th century.[27] Schoedel did not find all his arguments equally
convincing, but nevertheless concluded that 'either Athenagoras
anticipated in a remarkable way the theological developments of a
later period, or the treatise is not by Athenagoras'.[28] Gallicet also
concluded that the treatise was inauthentic, but disagreed with the
two previous scholars in preferring to date it before the Origenist
controversy and regarding it as primarily directed, like the works of
the apologists, towards a pagan audience.[29] The majority opinion
appears to remain, however, on the side of those who support the
traditional attribution. Both Barnard and, more recently, Pouderon
have argued vigorously for authenticity, and this view is essential for
the monographs that they have both written on the Apologist.[30] The
article published by the French scholar in this journal is of particular interest to us, because it specifically addresses the question of
the vocabulary and terminology used by the author or authors of the
two works.[31] Outlining his method, Pouderon takes as his starting-
point the index in Schwartz's edition, of which, we are told, 202
words are used only once in either the one of the other treatise, but
not in both. The study of their usage, he claims, cannot be 'révéla-
trice' for a comparative study. On the other hand 98 are used more
than once in either treatise, and 69 are used at least once in both. 30
of these are significant: a brief analysis reveals 'rapprochements ...
frappants', and even if these do not prove the author of [322] both

---

(Philadelphia 1988) 100.

[27] R. M. Grant, 'Athenagoras or Pseudo-Athenagoras', *Harvard Theological Review* 47 (1954) 121–129.

[28] W. R. Schoedel, *Athenagoras Legatio and De Resurrectione*, Oxford Early Christian Texts (Oxford 1972), quote at xxviii.

[29] E. Gallicet, 'Atenagora o Pseudo-Atenagora?', *Rivista di Filologia* 104 (1976) 420–435, 'Ancora sulla Pseudo-Atenagora', *Rivista di Filologia* 105 (1977) 21–42.

[30] L. W. Barnard, *Athenagoras: a Study in Second Century Christian Apologetic*, Théologie Historique 18 (Paris 1972), and also 'Notes on Athenagoras', *Latomus* 31 (1972), esp. 418ff.; B. Pouderon, *Athénagore d'Athènes, philosophe chrétien*, Théologie historique 82 (Paris 1989); see further J.-M. Vernander, 'Celse et l'attribu-tion à Athénagore d'un ouvrage sur la résurrection des morts', *Mélanges de Science Religieuse* 35 (1978) 125–132.

[31] B. Pouderon, 'L'authenticité du Traité sur la Résurrection attribué à l'apolo-giste Athénagore', *VC* 40 (1986) 226–244.

works is the same man, at least they demonstrate that the two works belong to the same epoch and milieu, namely the end of the 2nd century.[32] The methodology here seems basically sound. It is next to impossible to draw hard conclusions about authorship and authenticity through the comparison of vocabulary, as Douglas Young once notoriously demonstrated, when he demolished an attempt to argue for the separate authorship of the *Iliad* and the *Odyssey* by comparing the parallel example of the poems of John Milton.[33] There is, however, an exceptional case. What if we found a Miltonic poem of dubious authorship in which a word such as 'bicycle' or 'software' occurred, i.e. a word that the poet could not have used? Would this not have consequences for the question of authenticity? This is the case that we have to bear in mind for the two Athenagorean works.

We return to the text that is causing the trouble. In *De resurrectione* 12 the author argues that man, as created by the creator, is not made for no good reason, nor for the use of the creator himself or other creatures, but rather for his own sake and through the goodness that is generally revealed in the work of creation. This has consequences for the length of man's life: he is not made to be an ephemeral creature. The text continues (§12.6):[34]

ἑρπετοῖς γὰρ, οἶμαι, καὶ πτηνοῖς καὶ νηκτοῖς ἢ καὶ κοινότερον εἰπεῖν πᾶσι τοῖς ἀλόγοις τὴν τοιαύτην ζωὴν ἀπένειμεν θεός, τοῖς δὲ αὐτὸν ἐν ἑαυτοῖς ἀγαλματοφοροῦσι τὸν ποιητὴν νοῦν τε συνεπιφερομένοις καὶ λογικῆς κρίσεως μεμοιραμένοις τὴν εἰς ἀεὶ διαμονὴν ἀπεκλήρωσεν ὁ ποιήσας, ἵνα γινώσκοντες τὸν ἑαυτῶν ποιητὴν καὶ τὴν τούτου δύναμίν τε καὶ σοφίαν νόμῳ τε συνεπόμενοι καὶ δίκῃ τούτοις συνδιαιωνίζωσιν ἀπόνως, οἷς τὴν προλαβοῦσαν ἐκράτυναν ζωὴν καίπερ ἐν φθαρτοῖς καὶ γηΐνοις ὄντες σώμασιν.

For God has assigned this fleeting form of life, I think, to snakes, birds, and fish, or, to speak more generally, to all irrational creatures; but the Maker has allotted an unending existence to those who bear his image as creator in themselves, are gifted with intelligence, and share the faculty for rational discernment, so that they, knowing their Maker and his power and wisdom and complying with law and justice, might live without distress eternally with the powers by which they governed their former life, even though they were in corruptible and earthly bodies.

In his edition Schoedel see a reference to Gen. 1:26 in the part of

---

[32] *Ibid.* 232–234.

[33] D. Young, 'Miltonic Light on Professor Denys Page's Homeric Theory', in *A Clear Voice: Douglas Young Poet and Polymath* (Loanhead 1975) 107–120 (of which I was reminded by J. Mansfeld).

[34] Translation by W. Schoedel (slightly modified: he omits to translate the words τὸν ποιητὴν which are the predicate of ἀγαλματοφοροῦσι).

the sentence which speaks of man 'bearing the image (ἀγαλματοφοροῦσι) of God as creator in themselves', and this is surely right.[35]
Because man is created κατ' εἰκόνα θεοῦ, he can be said to be or
have the εἰκών of God, and this is effectuated through the gift of
rational thought, through the [323] exercise of which man may en-
sure his never-ending existence. The author does not allude directly
to the Logos theology developed at Alexandria. In fact his statement
is much more reminiscent of Philo's exegesis of Gen. 1:26 at *Opif.* 69
(in spite of the fact that his doctrine of man, with its emphasis on
the reciprocity of body and soul in man, is diametrically opposed to
Philo's view). Precisely here lies the problem.

We have in fact a dilemma. If our hypothesis on the reception of
the *verbum Philonicum* ἀγαλματοφορεῖν is correct, then the author of
this treatise will have derived it directly or indirectly from Philo (the
similarity to *Opif.* 69 suggests the former). Since at the time of
Athenagoras the only access to Philo's works in the Christian tradition was, as far as we can be certain, via the Alexandrian catechetical
school, either Athenagoras gained an acquaintance with the Philonic heritage in Alexandria, or the work is not his. If the work is to be
dated to the 3rd or early 4th century, then there is no problem, for
after Origen's move to Caesarea in 233 Philo's works began to be
more widely circulated, and moreover, as we saw above, the term in
question had begun to circulate in Christian writings themselves.

Now there is a very solid tradition, supported by almost all scholars that Athenagoras hailed from Athens where he presented his
petition to the Emperors (in the title he is called Ἀθηναῖος φιλόσοφος). In his recent monograph Pouderon examines the scanty
evidence available on his life and concludes:[36] 'Ainsi, ce qui paraît
établi avec le plus de certitude reste encore ce qu'Athénagore nous
dit de lui-même dans le titre de la Supplique: athénien d'origine ou
de cœur (pourquoi en douter?), ayant reçu une formation philosophique, puis s'étant converti au christianisme, il a voulu mettre ses
compétences au service de la foi...' On the basis of this position it is
not hard to decide which horn of the dilemma to choose.

There is. however, a tenuous ancient tradition connecting Athenagoras with Alexandria that we must not overlook. The rather unre-
liable 5th century Church historian Philip of Side is reported in a

---

[35] Schoedel *op. cit.* (n. 28) 116.
[36] Pouderon, *op. cit.* (n. 30) 35.

14th century codex to have declared that Athenagoras was the first
* head of the school in Alexandria, flourishing in the times of
Hadrian and Antoninus, to whom he addressed his Embassy. He
embraced Christianity while wearing the garb of a philosopher, and
became the teacher of Clement, whose pupil in turn was Pantaenus.[37] There are two obvious mistakes here. The Embassy is
addressed to Marcus Aurelius [324] and his son Commodus, and we
know from Eusebius that Pantaenus was the teacher of Clement, not
his pupil. This makes one disinclined to give the rest of the report
any credence. One scholar who does take it seriously is Barnard. He
argues that, even if Athenagoras may not have been head of the
school, he may have spent some time in Alexandria.[38] He then continues: 'Another small pointer in the Alexandrian direction is
Athenagoras' use of the Philonic terms ἔνθεον πνεῦμα and ἔκστασις
λογισμοῦ in *Leg.* 9; direct use of Philo by early Christian writers
seems to have been confined to those associated with Alexandria.'
The argument's method is sound, but the parallels, though not without interest, are of insufficient precision and weight to sustain it.[39]
Pouderon is prepared to admit the possibility of a sojourn of
Athenagoras in Alexandria, but purely as a hypothesis, not based on
any proof.[40]

The dilemma therefore does not admit of a straightforward
resolution. But since there is no evidence of any connection with
Alexandrian theology in Athenagoras' *Legatio*, and any connections
of the apologist with the city are entirely speculative, the probability
is, in our view, in favour of the second horn of the dilemma, namely
that the *De resurrectione* is not his and is not to be dated to the second
century, but rather to a later period, when the tradition of Alexandrian theology, decisively influenced by the reception of the
Philonic corpus, spread out from Alexandria to a wider audience in
the early Christian world.[41] This accounts most satisfactorily for its

---

[37] Text at PG 39.229; see further translation at Pouderon *op. cit.* 21–22.

[38] Barnard, *op. cit.* (n. 30) 13–17.

[39] Here one must agree with Pouderon, *op. cit.* 29.

[40] As admitted at *op. cit.* 35. The argument that the *Legatio* reveals a suspiciously
great interest in matters Egyptian (26–29) is tenuous. Literary tourism was common in the ancient world, and even claims to autopsy have to be treated with
caution.

[41] The treatise could be of Alexandrian origin, as suggested by the reference to
camels in 12.2; cf. Barnard, *op. cit.* 15, Pouderon, *op. cit.* 29 (who use this as
evidence for an Alexandrian sojourn of Athenagoras).

use of the idiosyncratic *verbum Philonicum* ἀγαλματοφορεῖν, elsewhere recorded for the first time in the Patristic tradition in Origen.

It so happens that the text cited above from the *De resurrectione* contains another *verbum Philonicum*, namely the verb συνδιαιωνίζειν ('to exist or live eternally together with ...').[42] Not found in pagan
* literature, it occurs four times in Philo (*Mos.* 2.108, *Spec.* 1.31, 76, *Virt.* 71). Pseudo-Athenagoras (as I would prefer) had a fondness for the word, for it occurs no less than three times, in 12.6, 15.8, 25.4). Elsewhere the first recorded instances are in Athanasius, Theodorus of Heraclea and the Cappadocians. Once again the trajectory of Philo–Alexandria–spread of the Alexandrian tradition is plausible, although this word is far less idiosyncratic and less securely coupled to a specific theme than the one that has occupied our attention so far. It lends support to our argument that the *De resurrectione* is not likely to be the work of a second-century author.

This article is dedicated to the editor of this journal on his reaching [325] the Psalmist's milestone of 'three score and ten years'. The author hopes that its modest result will be of interest to a scholar with such an enviable knowledge of both Philo and the Apologetic and Alexandrian traditions of Patristic thought. May he accept it as a token of profound gratitude and admiration.

---

[42] It differs from the exx. given above in that its novelty is determined by the addition of prepositional prefixes.

CHAPTER SIX

PHILO AND ORIGEN: A PRELIMINARY SURVEY

1. The ambitions of this paper are modest. Some time ago I received a request to furnish a volume for the series Compendia Rerum Iudaicarum ad Novum Testamentum. The task entrusted to me was to give a survey of the state of research on the use of Philo in the Christian tradition. Clearly one the most prominent Church Fathers who was well acquainted with Philo was Origen. So I had no choice but to come to grips with the scholarship that has been carried out on the subject of Origen's use of Philo. To my surprise I discovered that, despite the vast amount of literature on both authors, the *status quaestionis* on the relation between them was in fact in a state of some disarray. In my paper I shall say a few words about this, and at the same time give some pointers to what I regard as the more important aspects of the subject.

2. First, however, it is opportune to emphasize how much students of Philo owe to the great master and patron of this colloquium. It can be said beyond all reasonable doubt that the preservation of Philo's writings as we have them today is due to the intervention of Origen himself. Had he not taken copies of Philo's treatises with him when he moved from Alexandria to Caesarea in 233, then these would have gone lost, together with the remainder of the Hellenistic-Jewish literature of Alexandria. Philo had a place in Origen's library. These books were rescued by Pamphilus and consulted by Eusebius when writing his Church history. They were preserved for posterity when Bishop Euzoius of Caesarea had them transferred to parchment in about 375. In a fascinating article presented at the famous Lyon colloque on Philo Father Barthelémy showed that mysterious Rabbinical alterations in a family of medieval Philonic manuscripts could be traced back to surreptitious activity by a Rabbi in Origen's scriptorium, probably to be identified as Origen's friend Rabbi Hoshai'a.[1]

---

[1] *Philon d'Alexandrie: Lyon 11–15 Septembre 1966: colloques nationaux du Centre National de la Recherche Scientifique* (Paris 1967) 45–78

But back to Origen himself. The question that must be posed is why Origen took the trouble to take all those rolls or codices with him. What was Philo doing in his library? This question becomes all the more pressing if we take into account the evidence of Gregory Thaumaturgus, whose letter of thanks informs us about the curriculum of the school at Caesarea.[2] After initial training in dialectic, physics, geometry, astronomy and ethics, the pupil moves on to theology, for which first the texts of ancient philosophers and poets are read, followed by the scriptures. In a beautiful passage Gregory describes how Origen was given the remarkable spiritual gift of penetrating into the meaning of God's prophets (§173–183).[3] But where was the place for Philo in this programme, if Origen moved straight from the philosophers to scripture? [334]

3. But if we want to know more about what Origen did with the Philonic books in his library, first scholarly foundations have to be laid. It must be said that this has been very patchily done, especially when compared to the way that references and allusions to Philo in the Clementine corpus have been dealt with. The annotations in the Origen texts of the GCS and SC series are very incomplete, and also hard to consult because indices are usually lacking. The best list, oddly enough, is probably to be found in Cohn and Wendland's text of Philo, which in the apparatus criticus lists some 99 cross-references to Origen.[4] The necessary tools required in order to make a sound study of the question of Origen's use of and debt to Philo are simply not available. There is thus no chance that the outstanding analysis recently made of Clement's use of Philo in the *Stromateis* could be emulated for Origen at the present moment.[5]

---

*   [2] *In Origenem oratio panegyrica* (= CPG 1763). There is no need here to go into the dispute about whether the work really is Gregory's or not.

[3] Interestingly this very section contains reminiscences of Philonic themes: (1) §176 the concept of friend of God to whom oracles are given or made clear (for Philo the great example being Moses, cf. *Opif.* 5, 8, *Cher.* 49, but also Abraham, *Abr.* 273); (2) §183 the negative interpretation of 'working the soil' (Gen 4:2; cf. *QG* 2.66, *Sacr.* 51, *Agr.* 21; unfortunately the section of the Allegorical Commentary dealing with this text is lost).

*   [4] But these too are not indexed; I hope to supply an index in a forthcoming issue of *The Studia Philonica Annual.*

[5] A. van den Hoek, *Clement of Alexandria and his Use of Philo in the* Stromateis: *an Early Christian Reshaping of a Jewish Model* (Leiden 1988). The analysis is largely based on the apparatus of Stählin and Früchtel in the GCS edition.

Let me illustrate with a couple of interesting examples. In 1952 the Swiss scholar Merki published a useful study on the subject of ὁμοίωσις θεῷ (becoming like unto God) in Gregory of Nyssa and his predecessors. Ten pages are devoted to Philo, fifteen to Clement, but only three to Origen.[6] He concludes that the theme plays only a subordinate role in Origen's thought. Quite rightly Crouzel[7] took him to task for this judgment. In fact this originally Platonic but also quintessentially Philonic theme is of central importance in Origen's theology and anthropology. The reason for the mistake is not far to seek. For Philo Merki could use the indices of Leisegang, for Clement the indices of Stählin, but for Origen he was empty-handed.[8] Similarly we might be inclined to be lenient towards De Lange, whose treatment of Origen's use of Philo in his otherwise fine study on Origen and the Jews is somewhat disappointing. He too hardly had access to tools which could give him a sound start in presenting an adequate discussion. But he does stick his neck out and declare that 'Philo's influence on Origen has been much exaggerated by some recent writers'.[9] This statement seems to me to be premature, given the state of scholarly investigation of the subject.[10]

4. Turning now to our subject proper, the first point I would like to make concerns the direct references to Philo in Origen's works. These occur rather more frequently than is generally thought. I have prepared the following list, the completeness of which cannot be guaranteed, but is certainly more extensive than most scholars hitherto have thought:

---

[6] H. Merki, 'ΟΜΟΙΩΣΙΣ ΘΕΩΙ: von der platonischen Angleichung an Gott zur Gottähnlichkeit bei Gregor von Nyssa (Freiburg in der Schweiz 1952).

[7] H. Crouzel, Théologie de l'image de Dieu chez Origène (Paris 1956) 261.

[8] One modern tool would now be very helpful, i.e. the splendid volume of the Biblia Patristica devoted to Origen.

[9] N. De Lange, Origen on the Jews: Studies in Jewish-Christian Relations in Third-Century Palestine (Cambridge 1976) 16.

[10] But we should make allowance for the fact that he focusses on Origen's contact with living Judaism, to which Philo, of course, does not belong. see ibid. 12.

* *References to Philo in Origen*

Named references

A1. *C. Cels.* 4.51: δοκεῖ δέ μοι καὶ ἀκηκοέναι ὅτι ἐστὶ **συγγράμματα περι-έχοντα τὰς τοῦ νόμου ἀλληγορίας**, ἅπερ εἰ ἀνεγνώκει, οὐκ ἂν ἔλεγεν· αἱ γοῦν δοκοῦσαι περὶ αὐτῶν ἀλληγορίαι γεγράφθαι πολὺ τῶν μύθων αἰσχίους εἰσὶ καὶ ἀτοπώτεραι, τὰ μηδαμῇ μηδαμῶς ἁρμοσθῆναι δυνάμενα θαυμαστῇ τινι καὶ παντάπασιν ἀναισθήτῳ μωρίᾳ συνάπτουσαι. ἔοικε δὲ **περὶ τῶν Φίλωνος συγγραμμάτων** ταῦτα λέγειν ἢ καὶ τῶν ἔτι ἀρχαιοτέρων, ὁποῖά ἐστι τὰ Ἀριστο-βούλου.

A2. *C. Cels.* 6.21: καὶ τὸ ὁδὸν δὲ εἶναι ταῖς ψυχαῖς ἐς γῆν καὶ ἀπὸ γῆς Κέλσος μὲν κατὰ Πλάτωνά φησι γίνεσθαι διὰ τῶν πλανήτων· Μωϋσῆς δέ, ὁ ἀρχαιότατος ἡμῶν προφήτης, ἐν ὄψει τοῦ πατριάρχου ἡμῶν Ἰακὼβ φησιν ἑωρᾶσθαι θεῖον ἐνύπνιον, κλίμακα "εἰς οὐρανὸν" φθάνουσαν καὶ ἀγγέλους "τοῦ θεοῦ" ἀναβαίνοντας καὶ καταβαίνοντας ἐπ' αὐτῆς, τὸν δὲ κύριον ἐπεστηριγμένον ἐπὶ [335] τοῖς ἄκροις αὐτῆς (Gen. 28:12–13), εἴτε ταῦτα εἴτε τινὰ μείζονα τούτων αἰνιττόμενος ἐν τῷ περὶ τῆς κλίμακος λόγῳ· περὶ ἧς **καὶ τῷ Φίλωνι συντέτακται βιβλίον, ἄξιον φρονίμου καὶ συνετῆς παρὰ τοῖς φιλ-αλήθεσιν ἐξετάσεως.**

A3. *Comm. Matt.* XV 3: καὶ **Φίλων δέ, ἐν πολλοῖς τῶν εἰς τὸν Μωυσέως νόμον συντάξεων αὐτοῦ εὐδοκιμῶν καὶ παρὰ συνετοῖς ἀνδράσι, φησὶν ἐν βιβλίῳ ᾧ οὕτως ἐπέγραψεν· Περὶ τοῦ τὸ χεῖρον τῷ κρείττονι φιλεῖν ἐπιτίθεσθαι**, ὅτι 'ἐξευνουχισθῆναι μὲν ἄμεινον ἢ πρὸς συνουσίας ἐκνόμους λυττᾶν' (i.e. *Det.* 176).

Anonymous references

B1. *C. Cels.* 5.55: οὐδὲν ἧττον καὶ περὶ τούτων (i.e. Gen. 6:2) τοῖς δυναμένοις ἀκούειν προφητικοῦ βουλήματος πείσομεν ὅτι **καὶ τῶν πρὸ ἡμῶν τις** ταῦτα ἀνήγαγεν εἰς τὸν περὶ ψυχῶν λόγον, ἐν ἐπιθυμίᾳ γενομένων τοῦ ἐν σώματι ἀνθρώπων βίου, ἅπερ τροπολογῶν ἔφασκε λελέχθαι "θυγατέρας ἀνθρώπων" (cf. *Gig.* 6ff.).

B2. *C. Cels.* 7.20: Φαμὲν τοίνυν ὅτι ὁ νόμος διττός ἐστιν, ὁ μέν τις πρὸς ῥητὸν ὁ δὲ πρὸς διάνοιαν, **ὡς καὶ τῶν πρὸ ἡμῶν τινες ἐδίδαξαν.**

B3. *Sel. Gen.* 27, PG 12.97: "καὶ συνετέλεσεν ὁ θεὸς ἐν τῇ ἡμέρᾳ τῇ ἕκτῃ τὰ ἔργα αὐτοῦ ἃ ἐποίησεν" (Gen. 2:2). ἤδη **τινὲς** ἄτοπον ὑπολαμβάνοντες τὸν θεὸν δίκην οἰκοδόμου μὴ διαρκέσαντος χωρὶς ἡμερῶν πλειόνων πληρῶσαι τὴν οἰκοδομὴν ἐν πλείοσιν ἡμέραις τετελεκέναι τὸν κόσμον, **φασὶν ὑφ' ἓν πάντα** γεγονέναι, καὶ ἐντεῦθεν τοῦτο κατασκευάζουσιν· ἕνεκεν δὲ τάξεως οἴονται τὸν κατάλογον τῶν ἡμερῶν εἰρῆσθαι καὶ τῶν ἐν αὐταῖς γενομένων (cf. *Opif.* 13, 67).

B4. *Sel. Gen.* 44, PG 12.129: **τῶν μὲν πρὸ ἡμῶν ἐτήρησέ τις**, ὅτι ὁ φαῦλός ἐστιν ὁ τὰ γενέσεως ἀγαπῶν πράγματα καὶ τὴν ἡμέραν τῆς γενέσεως αὐτοῦ ἀποδεχόμενος (this text from the Catenae may well be merely a paraphrase B10 cited below).

B5. *Hom. Exod.* II 2: Sed quid dicit Scriptura? *Timebant*, inquit, (Ex. 1:17). Istas obsetrices **dixerunt ante nos quidam** rationabilis eruditionis formam tenere... (cf. *Her.* 128)

B6. *Hom. Lev.* VIII 6: de hoc (Lev. 13:12–14) **quidam etiam ante me dixerunt** colorem vivum indicare rationem vitae, quae in homine est... (cf. *Deus* 125f.)

B7. *Hom. Num.* IX 5: **quidam tamen ex iis, qui ante nos interpretati sunt locum hunc,** memini quod mortuos **dixerunt** eos qui nimietate scelerum in peccatis suis mortui intelleguntur, viventes autem eos qui in operibus vitae permanserint (cf. *Her.* 201, *Somn.* 2.234).

B8. *Hom. Jos.* XVI: etiam **ante nos quidam observantes notarunt in scripturis,** quia presbyteri vel seniores non ex eo appellantur, quod longaevam dixerint vitam, sed pro maturitate sensus et gravitate vitae veneranda hac appellatione decorentur... (cf. *Sobr.* 16ff.).

B9. *Hom. Jer.* XIV 5: **τῶν πρὸ ἐμοῦ δέ** τις ἐπέβαλε τῷ τόπῳ λέγων ὅτι ταῦτα ἔλεγεν οὐ πρὸς τὴν μητέρα τὴν σωματικήν, ἀλλὰ πρὸς τὴν μητέρα τὴν γεννῶσαν προφήτας. τίς δὲ γεννᾷ προφήτας; ἡ σοφία τοῦ θεοῦ. (cf. *Conf.* 49).

B10. *Comm. Matt.* X 22: καὶ ἐν γενεθλίοις δὲ παρανόμου βασιλεύοντος αὐτῶν λόγου ὀρχοῦνται, ὡς ἀρέσκειν ἐκείνῳ τῷ λόγῳ τὰς κινήσεις αὐτῶν. **ἐτήρησε μὲν οὖν** τις **τῶν πρὸ ἡμῶν** τὴν ἀναγεγραμμένην ἐν Γενέσει τοῦ Φαραὼ γενέθλιον (Gen. 40:20) καὶ διηγήσατο ὅτι ὁ φαῦλος τὰ γενέσεως ἀγαπῶν πράγματα ἑορτάζει γενέθλιον. ἡμεῖς δὲ **ἀπ' ἐκείνου ταύτην εὑρόντες ἀφορμὴν** ἐπ' οὐδεμιᾶς γραφῆς εὕρομεν ὑπὸ δικαίου γενέθλιον ἀγομένην (cf. *Ebr.* 208).

B11. *Comm. Matt.* XVII 17: **τῶν μὲν πρὸ ἡμῶν ποιήσας** τις **βιβλία νόμων ἱερῶν ἀλληγορίας,** τὰς ὡσπερεὶ ἀνθρωποπαθῆ παριστάσας λέξεις τὸν θεὸν διηγούμενος καὶ τὰς τὸ θεῖον αὐτοῦ ἐμφαινούσας, ἑνὶ μὲν ῥητῷ ἐχρήσατο περὶ τοῦ ὡς ἄνθρωπον λέγεσθαι εἶναι τὸν θεὸν ἀνθρώπους οἰκονομοῦντα, τῷ 'ἐτροποφόρησέ σε κύριος ὁ θεός σου ὡς εἴ τις τροποφορήσαι ἄνθρωπος τὸν υἱὸν αὐτοῦ' (Deut. 1:31), ἑνὶ δὲ περὶ τοῦ μὴ ὡς ἄνθρωπον εἶναι τὸν θεόν, τῷ 'οὐχ ὡς ἄνθρωπος ὁ θεὸς διαρτηθῆναι' (Num. 23:9, cf. *Deus* 53–54). [336]

B12. *Comm. Matt.* ad 25:30: σκότος δὲ ἐξώτερόν φησιν, ἔνθα οὐδεὶς φωτισμός ἐστιν, τάχα μὲν οὐδὲ σωματικός, πάντως δὲ οὐδεμία ἐπισκοπὴ θείου φωτός... forsitan... forsitan et propter aliam causam (quam nos ignoramus), quoniam **legimus aliquem qui fuit ante nos exponentem** de tenebris abyssi et dicentem quoniam abyssus est extra mundum foris et tenebrae (cf. *Opif.* 32).

B13. *Comm. Joh.* VI 25: ἥντινα κατάβασιν αἰνίσσεσθαί **τινες ὑπειλήφασι** τὴν τῶν ψυχῶν κάθοδον ἐπὶ τὰ σώματα, θυγατέρας ἀνθρώπων τροπικώτερον τὸ γήϊνον σκῆνος λέγεσθαι ὑπειληφότες (cf. *C. Cels.* 5.55 = above B1)

From the list it appears that, though Origen refers to Philo explicitly only three times (once less than Clement does), there are at least 12 or 13 anonymous references.[11] Some of these texts refer to people in the plural, but it is well known that such references in ancient literature often have only a single author in mind.[12] The words

---

[11] Depending on whether we regard B4 as a separate item.
[12] But a vexed question lies concealed here. It is abundantly clear from Philo's

indicated in bold type show how Origen speaks about Philo. It emerges that he regards him above all as a predecessor in the interpretation of scripture. He is described as an interpreter (B7), teacher (B2) and expositor (B12). He is praised for his sharp perception (cf. B8, 11). He supplies the exegete with ideas that can be further pursued (B10). His views are held in respect by intelligent men (A3), among whom Origen is clearly to be included.

It is moreover apparent that nearly all the texts deal directly with scriptural exegesis in one way or another. The only exception is the striking text just referred to (A3), where Origen cites an aphoristic statement by Philo encouraging the drastic act which he himself had carried out many years before. Against Celsus Philo is invoked in general terms on account of his allegorization of scripture (A1). In two other texts (B2, 11) general statements are made about the principles of allegorical interpretation. The remainder of the passages concern specific exegesis of scriptural texts, and in most cases allegorical interpretation of one kind or another is involved (an exception is B12).

5. It is not surprising, therefore, that most scholars have seen Philo's influence on Origen operating predominantly in the area of allegorical exegesis. Especially during the fifties and early sixties this was a lively area of controversy, engaging scholars of the calibre of De Lubac, Wolfson, Daniélou, Hanson, Grant, and Crouzel. The discussions centred on a number of well-known texts in Book IV of the *De principiis*, notably on the triple sense of scripture (2.3) and absurdity of the first chapters of Genesis if taken literally (3.1). The question was: to what extent was Origen dependent on Philo, and if so, to what extent was that influence pernicious in its effect? An interesting division of opinion emerged. Those scholars who regarded Origen primarily as a man of the Church tended to play down his relation to Philonism. Those, on the other hand, who viewed him above all as a systematic theologian or even as a philosopher, regarded the influence as considerable. No consensus was reached, but by way of illustration I briefly mention two views. For

writings that he had numerous exegetical predecessors (and perhaps contemporaries). Would Origen have had access to some of these Judaeo-Alexandrian exegetes? We cannot be sure, but the fact that in A1 he mentions only Philo and Aristobulus, who happen to be the only names we know, is surely suggestive. He may have learnt about Aristobulus from Clement.

Daniélou the heart of Origen's interpretation of scripture lay in its Christocentric emphasis, yielding a typological understanding of the Old Testament. Philo's influence made its presence felt above all in two areas: (1) Origen's desire to read meaning into every single word of scripture; (2) his inclination to revert to allegorical exegesis focusing on the moral life of the soul. Both tendencies Daniélou found dubious and regrettable.[13] Hanson too reached a [337] basically negative conclusion. He saw Philo as in large part responsible for the fact that 'in one important respect Origen's thought remained outside the Bible and never penetrated within it', namely in his failure to appreciate the significance of history.[14]

*   Can further progress be made on this subject? A first step would be, I submit, to go back to the texts and determine more precisely in what ways Origen is indebted to Philo and in what ways not. This will be by no means an easy task, for Origen does not merely cite Philo, but always adapts him to the particular concern of the moment. Moreover he most often relies on his memory, and this is not always exact. For example in text B11, where the conceptuality is perfectly Philonic, he substitutes Deut. 1:31 for the text that Philo always uses, Deut. 8:5. Is this done on purpose because he thinks his own text is better, or does he mistakenly think this was the text present in his source?

6. But it is time to go on to our next question. Is the use of Philo by Origen confined to the area of biblical, and particularly allegorical, interpretation, or does it extend further than that? Or reformulated: is Philonism in Origen something that lies fairly close to the surface, or does it penetrate into the deeper structure of his thought? Most scholars incline to the first position rather than the second, but I wonder whether this is on the right track. Let me illustrate with yet another example.

In the introduction to his monograph, *Théologie de l'image de Dieu chez Origène*, Crouzel affirms:[15]

> The theme of the image of God of which we speak here is found throughout almost all the ancient Christian writers and in them it often occupies a place of considerable importance... The place of

---

[13] Best summary of his position in his article on Origen in *Dictionnaire de la Bible. Supplément*, vol. 6 (Paris 1960) 884–908, esp. 898–902.

[14] R. P. C. Hanson, *Allegory and Event* (London 1959) 363.

[15] *Op. cit.* (n. 7) 11 (my translation).

the theme in the doctrine of Origen is just as central as in his predecessors and successors, and it touches on all the aspects of his personality, exegesis, spirituality and theology. It represents in effect the exegesis of several scriptural texts, especially Col. 1:15 on Christ the Image, and Gen. 1:26–27 on the creation of man according to the image. The account of the participation of man in the image of God, a participation which develops until reaching resemblance in the intimate union with Christ, is bound up with the Alexandrian's entire doctrine of spirituality. Finally the Platonist and Stoic philosophies have played a role in the elaboration of the theme which should not be neglected.

Conspicuous by his absence in this paragraph is Philo. Just like in Gregory's letter the philosophers are mentioned and scripture is given its rightful place at the centre, but there is no room for Philo. This, I submit, is incorrect. The biblical texts are central, I agree, but the Platonism that Origen reads into them is mediated via Philo. From him is derived the singularly important notion that man is not created as the direct image of God, but κατ' εἰκόνα, according to God's image, who is the Logos. And how is this being 'according to the image' to be interpreted? Once again Origen looks to Philo. Man's 'image-relation' to the Logos and ultimately to God exists primarily in respect of his spiritual or intellectual nature. Indeed a closer examination of texts would show that Origen actually sharpens up Philo's emphases on this point in the direction of a thorough-going anti-corporealism.

7. My own position, at present, is that Origen's debt to Philonism should be brought under at least two headings. Firstly, Philo shows him the way to [338] integrate his Platonizing philosophical presuppositions into his reading of scripture. This is done at a general level by means of the spiritual method of reading scripture, and at a particular level in the reading of various, sometimes very important, biblical texts. Secondly, the central focus of Origen's spirituality on the understanding and interpretation of scripture is a direct continuation of Philo's thought. I cannot express this better than it has been done by Andrew Louth:[16] 'As with Philo, the understanding of Scripture is the medium of union with the Word... Understanding Scripture is not for Origen simply an academic exercise but a religious experience'.

---

[16] A. Louth, *The Origins of the Christian Mystical Tradition* (Oxford 1981) 64.

In addition to these two heading, however, I wonder whether a third should still be added. Origen's Platonism, so to speak, is founded on the division between the supra-sensible and corporeal. Its focus, however, is not on the intelligible world or the divine *nous*, but rather on the pre-existent Logos, who took on human form in the guise of the incarnated Christ. The question is whether in the final analysis Origen's thought is Logos-centred or Christ-centred. I realize that a larger question than this can hardly be posed. But if the former *were* the case, would this not encourage us to maximize rather than minimize the impact of Philonism on his thought?

8. In conclusion I want briefly to return to the problem raised earlier on: why was Philo not given an explicit place in the educational programme of Origen's school at Caesarea? One possible answer would be that given by Conybeare nearly a century ago, who argued that Origen was embarrassed to find himself indebted to a Jewish predecessor, and thus concealed the source of his quotations.[17] I am not persuaded by this approach. A vital clue is gained if we look at the way that Origen refers to his predecessor Clement. He never cites him by name, but does refer to him in terms such τις τῶν πρὸ ἡμῶν and *sicut quidam tradunt*.[18] Both times Origen is referring to interpretations of scripture, and the formulae used are precisely the same as those used for Philo (cf. our list above). Apparently Origen sees little need to distinguish between Clement and Philo as honoured predecessors in the task of elucidating scripture.

There was thus also no need to give Philo an explicit place in the school programme. The customary procedure was assumed. When the scriptures were opened and the task of interpretation began, it was a matter of course that the views of earlier interpreters were taken into account. Philo stands as one of a long line of inspired exegetes, a status only a little below that of the prophets themselves. Philo has in fact been adopted as an honorary Church Father. For this reason he had a place in Origen's library, and, as a direct result of this inclusion, his works have survived to this day.

---

[17] F. C. Conybeare, *Philo About the Contemplative Life* (Oxford 1895) 328.
[18] Both examples given by H. Crouzel, *Origène* (Paris 1985) 25, referring to *Comm. Matt.* XIV 2, *Comm. Rom.* I 1.

CHAPTER SEVEN

'WHERE, TELL ME, IS THE JEW...?':
BASIL, PHILO AND ISIDORE OF PELUSIUM

The series of nine homilies which Basil of Caesarea delivered before his congregation, probably during the period of Lent in 378 A.D., represents the first Christian work specifically dedicated to the exegesis of the Mosaic creation account that has survived.[1] As its name indicates, it describes the first six days of creation. No doubt Basil's audience, which at least partly consisted of tradesmen and other humble folk,[2] were dazzled by the display of language and learning which the bishop placed at the service of scriptural interpretation. But in one respect they may have been disappointed. The ninth homily is devoted to the works of the sixth day, but concentrates primarily on the creation of the animals, as its title Περὶ χερσαίων indicates. What about the creation of man, the crown and climax of God's creative work? Basil recognizes the danger. In the final section of the homily he admits that he can imagine a complaint of his listeners along the following lines: 'we have been instructed about the animals that belong to us, but we are still unaware of who we are ourselves' (9.6, 87B). So in this final section he gives a cursory exegesis of the celebrated text Gen. 1:26–27. But not all aspects can be dealt with. The question of how man can said to possess the image of God and to participate in his resemblance will have to be postponed to another time (9.6, 88C). Alas, Basil was already gravely ill when he wrote these words, and he did not live to fulfil his promise.[3]

---

[1] J. C. M. van Winden, Art. 'Hexaemeron', *RAC* 14 (1988) 1260. But note also, prior to Basil, the chapters of Theophilus of Antioch's *Ad Autolycum* 2.10–19 devoted to a literal interpretation of the seven days of creation.

[2] On Basil's audience see now R. Lim, 'The Politics of Interpretation in Basil of Caesarea's *Hexaemeron*', *VC* 44 (1990) 361f.

[3] We assume with the majority of scholars that the two additional homilies *On the origin of man* (*Clavis Patrum Graecorum* 3215–16) are in their present form not the work of Basil himself. As H. Horner (cited *ibid.*) has suggested, they may be based on notes that he left behind. The text at 1.4 shows parallels with our passage, but unlike Basil introduces the doctrine of the trinity. The danger of polytheism is indicated, but there is no mention of Jewish or heretical opponents.

In spite of its brief and somewhat cursory nature, this final section of the *In Hexaemeron* is not without its specific interest, because Basil introduces into his exegesis some brief touches of theological polemic, directed first at a Jewish opponent, and then later at heretical associates in the Christian camp. The aim of our brief article will be to examine some issues to which this polemic gives rise, and to note the response which it evokes in a later author. But first we cite the relevant passage in full (9.6, 87B–88E)[4]: [173]

*   *And God said, let us make man* (Gen. 1:26). Where, tell me, is the Jew, who in the previous sections, even though the light of the doctrine of God was shining forth as if through a window and a second person (of the Trinity) was being disclosed in a secret fashion but was not yet

5   revealed in full clarity, continued to fight against the truth, asserting that God was conversing with himself? For, he says, it was God who spoke and it was God who created: *let there be light, and there was light* (Gen. 1:3). Now the absurdity of their explanation was already quite obvious. Which smith or carpenter or shoemaker, sitting all alone with

10   the tools of his craft, with no one assisting him, says to himself, let us make the knife, or let us assemble the plough, or let us produce the shoe. Surely he completes the action he has undertaken in silence. This is truly a lot of nonsense, that someone should be his own ruler and supervisor, vehemently urging himself on in the manner of a master.

15   But these men do not shrink back from slandering the Lord himself. What would they not say with their tongue trained in the expression of falsehood? The present utterance, however, completely muzzles their mouth: *and God said, let us make man* (Gen. 1:26). You are surely not going to tell me now that the person is still on his own. For it is not

20   written, 'let there be man', but *let us make man*. As long as he who was to be taught (i.e. man) had not appeared, the preaching of the doctrine of God was concealed in deep darkness. When finally the creation of man is imminent, the object of faith is uncovered, and the doctrine of truth is more clearly revealed.

25   *Let us make man.* You hear, fighter against Christ, that he is talking to his companion in the work of creation, *through whom he also made the ages, who bears the universe through his powerful word* (Heb. 1:2–3). But he (i.e. our opponent) does not accept the word of piety (*v.l.* truth) in silence. Just like those wild animals who are most savage towards man-

30   kind, when they have been locked up in cages, bellow forth as they pace around in circles, revealing their resentful and untamed nature, but are unable to consummate their fury, so that race hostile to the truth, the

---

4   My own translation, based on the text in S. Giet, *Basile de Césarée Homélies sur l'Hexaéméron*, SC 26bis (Paris 1968²), and with some reference to his fluent French translation.

Jews, are pushed into a corner and affirm that there is a plurality of
persons whom the word of God addresses. According to them it is to
35   the angels that stand around him that he says, *let us make man*. This is a
Jewish invention, a fiction which reveals their slipperiness. In order not
to have to accept a single addressee, they introduce a multiplicity. In
rejecting the son, they confer on servants the dignity of being counsel-
lors; at the same time they make our fellow-servants masters of our crea-
40   tion. Man when he has achieved perfection is elevated to the rank of
angels (cf. Ps. 8:6). What product of creation can be equal to its creator?

Look also at the words that follow: *according to our image* (Gen. 1:26).
What do you say to this? It is surely not the case that there is a single
image of both God and the angels? But of the son and the father there
45   is every necessity that the form should be the same, the form of course
being understood in a way befitting God, not in terms of bodily shape,
but as the characteristic property of divinity. [174]

Listen, you too from the new circumcision, who advocate Judaism
under the guise of Christianity. To whom does he say, *according to our*
50   *image*? To anyone else than *the radiance of his glory and the imprint of his*
full nature (ὑπόστασις) (Heb. 1:3), who is *the image of God the unseen* (Col.
1:15)? Therefore he speaks to his own living image, who declared, *I and*
the father are one (John 10:30), and *he who has seen me, has seen the Father*
(John 14:9). To this image he says *let us make man according to our image*
55   (Gen. 1:26). When there is a single image, where is the dissimilarity?

And God made man (Gen. 1:27). Not 'they made'. Here he has
avoided the multiplication of persons. In his earlier statement (i.e. Gen.
1:26) he educated the Jew, in these words he blocked off the route to
Hellenism and safely returned to the monad, so that you may both
60   conceive the son together with the father and escape the danger of
polytheism.

In the image of God he made him (cf. Gen. 1:27, 9:6). Once again he
reintroduced the person of the collaborator. For he did not say, 'in his
own image', but *in the image of God*. In which respect man is *according to*
65   *the image*, and how he participates in *the similarity to God* (καθ' ὁμοίωσιν,
cf. Gen. 1:27), will be dealt with in the sequel to this work, if God gives
us the opportunity. For the moment let this only be said: if there is one
image, from where did the intolerable impiety occur to you of saying
that the son is dissimilar to the father? What ingratitude! The resem-
70   blance in which you participate, do you not grant this to your
benefactor? For yourself you consider the gifts of grace as rightfully
yours, but to the son you refuse to concede the resemblance to the
father belonging to him by nature.

But the evening, which long ago escorted the sun on its way to the
75   west, commands us from now on to silence... Let the supporter of
dissimilarity (ἀνόμοιος) be filled with shame, let the Jew turn about, let
the faithful rejoice in the doctrines of the truth, let the Lord be
glorified, to whom be the glory and the power for ever and ever. Amen.

No sooner has Basil commenced his exegesis of Gen. 1:26 than he launches into an attack on an unnamed opponent. Whom does he have in mind? Modern commentators have with varying degrees of confidence identified this opponent with Philo, the Jewish exegete from Alexandria, who more than three centuries earlier wrote the treatise *De opificio mundi* on the first three chapters of Genesis. In 1949 Giet stated that the Jew is, 'selon toute vraisemblance', Philo, adducing two passages: *Opif.* 23, οὐδενὶ δὲ παρακλήτῳ—τίς γὰρ ἦν ἕτερος;—μόνῳ δὲ αὐτῷ χρησάμενος; *Opif.* 72, οὐδενὸς ἐδεήθη τοῦ συνεργήσοντος.[5] In 1967, in an important article on Philo and Gregory of Nyssa, Daniélou claimed that in the part of the *Hexaemeron* which is closely related to Gregory's Περὶ κατασκευῆς ἀνθρώπου there is an 'allusion formelle' to Philo.[6]

> ... Basile discute le: Faisons l'homme..., et il prend explicitement Philon à partie : «Où est le Juif qui naguère, quand la seconde personne paraissait [175] mystérieusement sans se révéler clairement encore, luttait contre la vérité? Il prétend que nombreux sont les personnages auxquels s'adresse la parole divine. C'est aux anges, présents autour de lui, qu'il aurait dit : Faisons l'homme».

Thirdly the most recent translator of the work, Naldini, comments on the words ὁ Ἰουδαῖος that they are 'probably an allusion to Philo', and cross-refers to Giet's citation of the first of his two texts.[7]

At first sight this identification is not without a certain plausibility. Basil had at least some acquaintance with Philo, for he refers to him in one of his letters.[8] It is very likely that, during his preparation for the delivery of the homilies on Genesis 1, he had read or reread Philo's treatise on the same subject. Amand de Mendieta, in a

---

[5] Giet, *op. cit.* 514 n. 3.

[6] J. Daniélou, 'Philon et Grégoire de Nysse', in *Philon d'Alexandrie. Lyon 11–15 Septembre 1966: colloques nationaux du Centre National de la Recherche Scientifique* (Paris 1967) 333–345; quote on 336.

[7] M. Naldini, *Basilio di Cesarea Sulla Genesi* (Omilie sull'Esamerone) (no place indicated, 1990) 401. The reference to *Opif.* 6 is inexact, since Giet had referred to the old numbering used prior to the edition of Cohn and Wendland (it should be 23).

[8] *Ep.* 190, referring to a Philonic interpretation of the nature of manna which is not found in his surviving works, but may have been drawn from a missing section of the *Quaestiones in Exodum*; cf. J. R. Royse, 'The Original Structure of Philo's *Quaestiones*', *Studia Philonica* 4 (1976–77) 58, 61, 76, and now *idem*, *The Spurious Texts of Philo of Alexandria* (Leiden 1991) 34. Interestingly Basil, in describing Philo as ὥσπερ ἐκ παραδόσεώς τινος Ἰουδαϊκῆς δεδιδαγμένος, suggests that he is drawing on a haggadic tradition (cf. L. Ginzberg, *The Legends of the Jews* (Philadelphia 1909–38, 1968¹²) 2.43, 6.17 (but without reference to Basil)).

careful study of the immediate sources of Basil's work, counts Philo's treatise as one of the four 'sources littéraires immédiates que Basile a utilisées au cours de la préparation de l'ensemble des homélies'.[9] It is, moreover, undoubtedly true that Basil's words οὐδενὸς αὐτῷ συνεργοῦντος (line 10), are strongly reminiscent of the second of the Philonic texts cited by Giet, and may well have been been inspired by it.

In spite of these arguments, however, I believe that the identification of Basil's unnamed opponent with Philo cannot be sustained. In order to substantiate this negative conclusion, it will be necessary to take a closer look at some aspects of Basil's text and its exegetical background.

The first sentence in which the Jewish interpreter is summoned, is not at first sight entirely clear. The participle λέγων in the final phrase would appear to refer to the exegesis that the Jew gives of Gen. 1:26, namely that the plural in the biblical verb ποιήσωμεν indicates that God is talking to himself. But the long relative clause that precedes it and begins with the words ἐν τοῖς κατόπιν must refer to the exegesis of the Mosaic text as it has been given in the earlier part of the work.[10] As Giet well observed in a note, in three previous passages Basil argues that the actual wording of the creation gently initiates the reader into awareness of the participation of the son in the act of creation (3.2, 23B; 3.4 26C; 6.2, 51B).[11] Thus, to take one example, in the account of the second day we read first the divine command, γενηθήτω στερέωμα (v.6), followed by a report of the actual act, καὶ ἐποίησεν ὁ θεὸς τὸ στερέωμα (v.7). Basil sees here a distinction between the primary cause (προκαταρκτικὴ αἰτία) which is the father and the executive power (ποιητικὴ καὶ δημιουργικὴ

[9] E. Amand de Mendieta, 'La préparation et la composition des neuf Homélies sur l'Hexaémeron de Basile de Césarée: le problème des sources littéraires immédiates', Studia Patristica 16 (Berlin 1985) 349–367. The evidence on which this assertion was based was to have been presented in a 'commentaire philologique et théologique' on the Homilies, but sadly the author's death intervened. For a list of passages where Basil appears to be dependent on Philo, see Giet op. cit. (n. 4) 50f.

[10] Three times elsewhere in the work Basil uses the phrase ἐν τοῖς κατόπιν (3.5, 26D; 4.2, 34A; 4.5, 37D; the second passage shows that the noun understood is λόγοις). Each time it indicates an internal reference, either to his own exegesis (3.5, 4.2), or in the original Mosaic text (4.5).

[11] Espousing a consciously literal interpretation, however, Basil declines to see in the very opening words ἐν ἀρχῇ a reference to the Logos, as done by Origen before him and Ambrose and Augustine after him; cf. J. C. M. van Winden, 'In the Beginning: Some Observations on the Patristic Interpretation of Genesis 1, 1', VC 17 (1963) 105–121, esp. 121.

δύναμις) which is the son.[12] This background makes clear why in the sentence in which Basil calls forth his Jewish opponent, he first states that the doc[176]trine of a second person has so far (cf. ἐν τοῖς κατόπιν) been hinted at in a concealed way, and then places the text Gen. 1:3 in the mouth of his opponent (cf. φησί). This text is a counter-example to the ones we just cited, for here the command γενηθήτω φῶς is followed by the statement καὶ ἐγένετο φῶς, and there would appear to be no room for reading the presence of the son. So the Jew is made to affirm: it was God who spoke and it was God who made. Basil, as we can see, envisages a kind of running battle between a Christian exegesis of the creation account involving the presence of the Trinity, and the Jewish exegesis with reference to God the creator only. The battle comes to a head in the case of the celebrated plural verb of Gen. 1:26.

For Philo the text had given rise to the exegetical *aporia* of why now for the first time God is envisaged as requiring helpers in his creative work. So far he has created the heaven, the earth and sea without any helpers, and yet in the case of that puny and short-lived creature man he turns to the assistance of others (*Opif.* 72). Philo's answer, expressed with due caution, focuses on the theme of theodicy. God can have no share in evil, so in the case of man he is responsible for creating only the better part that performs good deeds in accordance with reason; the creation of the worse part that perpetrates evil actions is handed over to God's subordinates (*Opif.* 73–75).[13]

It is apparent that this interpretation of the troublesome plural has very little in common with the first explanation ascribed by Basil to his Jewish opponent. The phrase that Basil appears to take over from Philo on God's lack of assistance has a completely different function in the two texts. In Philo it is put forward dialectically. In the rest of the creation account God was in no need of assistance, so why should that be the case for his final creative act? But in fact, according to Philo's theodical interpretation, for man's creation

---

[12] 3.4, 26C. Philo had seen a δύναμις κοσμοποιητική at work in the creation account (*Opif.* 21), but was not of course interested in a distinction of persons.

[13] On this interpretation, ultimately inspired by the role of subordinate creators in Plato's *Timaeus*, see further my *Philo of Alexandria and the* Timaeus *of Plato* (Leiden 1986²) 242–249, and also D. Winston, 'Theodicy and the creation of man in Philo of Alexandria', in A. Caquot, M. Hadas-Lebel, J. Riaud (edd.), *Hellenica et Judaica: hommage à Valentin Nikiprowetzky* (Leuven-Paris 1986) 105–111 (who disagrees with me on some points of interpretation).

God *does* make use of subordinates. The Jewish interpreter in Basil, on the other hand, argues that God does not have any assistants, but rather is talking to himself, an explanation which Basil proceeds to ridicule in a not entirely convincing way.[14]

At this point we should also take strong exception to Daniélou's treatment of Basil's text, which is cavalier in the extreme. The French scholar quotes the text as rendered in Giet's translation, but, without giving any indication to the reader, he in fact joins together two passages which in the original are separated by some twenty lines of text (lines 1–6, 32–34 in our translation above)! In so doing he ignores the fact that Basil by [177] this time is addressing his polemics to a *group* of Jewish interpreters, translating the plural φασίν in the text by the singular 'il prétend', as if Basil still has the same Jew in mind whom he introduced at the beginning of the passage. This makes it seem that the angels mentioned by Basil are inspired by the 'subordinates' introduced by Philo into his exegesis. In actual fact in *Opif.* 72–75 Philo makes no explicit mention of angels at all. I have argued elsewhere that he deliberately avoids making a concrete identification as to who these subordinates are.[15] This does not mean, of course, that it could not happen that subsequent readers, who were acquainted with other exegetical traditions, did interpret Philo's words as referring to angels.

Basil's references to Jewish interpretation of Gen. 1:26 need to be seen against a much broader backcloth than Philo alone. The Rabbis were much occupied with the problem of the plural verb in Gen. 1:26 (and other plurals at Gen. 3:22 and 11:7). The chapter on this text in the Rabbinic compendium *Genesis Rabbah* lists a great variety of solutions to the problem (VIII, 3–9):[16]

1. Rabbi Joshua ben Levi: God took counsel with the works of heaven and earth.

---

[14] Again acutely pointed out by Giet, *op. cit.* (n. 4) 515 n. 4.
[15] Runia, *op. cit.* 247–248, where I note that in parallel passages at *Fug.* 69–72, *Conf.* 168–183, *Mut.* 30–32, *QG* 1.54, the matter is also not settled. J. Dillon, *The Middle Platonists* (London 1977) 172, suggests that Philo may have the planetary gods in mind.
[16] *Midrash Rabbah*, translated by H. Freedman and M. Simon, vol. 1, *Genesis Rabbah* (London 1939) 56–60. The chronological problems involved in using Rabbinic evidence can be ignored here, since the point is to indicate the general exegetical background to Basil's text. For discussion of these and related Rabbinic texts see E. E. Urbach, *The Sages: their Concepts and Beliefs* (Jerusalem 1975) 206–208, Ginzberg *op. cit.* (n. 8) 1.51f., 5.69.

2. Rabbi Samuel ben Naḥman: God took counsel with the works of each day.
3. Rabbi Ammi: God took counsel with His own heart.[17]
4. Rabbi Ḥanina: God took counsel with the ministering angels.
5. Rabbi Joshua of Siknin: God took counsel with the souls of the righteous.
6. Rabbi Hila: there is no taking counsel, but it is a *pluralis maiestatis*.[18]

The same chapter also records comments on the verse which bear some resemblance to the theodical interpretation ventured by Philo:

7. Rabbi Berekiah: God foresaw that righteous and wicked would arise from Adam. So God removed the way of the wicked out of his sight, and associated the quality of mercy with himself (cf. Ps. 1:6).
8. Rabbi Simon: when God came to create Adam the ministering angels met together in groups, some saying 'let him be created', others 'let him not be created' (because they knew that both righteousness and wickedness would proceed from him).
9. Rabbi Huna adds: while the angels were arguing, God created him and then said to the angels, 'what's the use, man has already been made!'.

Finally we note two comments where Rabbis observe that the verse could offer an excuse for heresy: [178]

10. Rabbi Samuel ben Naḥman: when Moses was writing this verse he said to God, 'why do you furnish an excuse for heretics?'.
11. Rabbi Simlai: wherever you find a point supporting the heretics, you find the refutation at its side. What is meant by 'let us make man'? Read what follows, not 'and gods created man', but 'and God created'.

This final remark reappears, as we shall see, in Basil's text when he opposes the tendency to Hellenizing polytheism.

Who are these heretics referred to by the Rabbis? It would be a simplification to identify them with Christians alone. This is shown by an important text in Justin Martyr, *Dial.* 62.1–3, in which the existence of the divine Logos is proven with reference to Gen. 1:26 and 3:22:[19]

---

[17] The Rabbi's further illustration of God's heart with the image of the King and architect appears to go back ultimately to Philo's image in *Opif.* 17–18, through the intervention of Rabbi Hosha'ia, who had contact with the circle of Origen in Caesarea. See further my remarks at *Mnemosyne* 42 (1989) 410–412 (with further references).

[18] It might be thought surprising that *Gen. Rabbah* does not mention the solution that God consults the Torah. This view is found only in very late *midrashim*; cf. Urbach *op. cit.* 779 n. 6.

[19] Text at E. J. Goodspeed, *Die ältesten Apologeten* (Göttingen 1914) 167–168

The same thing, dear friends, the Logos of God also said through
Moses, when he recounted to us that the God whom he made mani-
fest spoke in exactly the same vein at the creation of man in the
following words: (Gen. 1:26–28 is then quoted). You may wish to
change the meaning of the words just cited and give the interpretations of your teachers, either that God spoke to himself the
words 'let us make', just like we very often speak to ourselves when
we are about to do something, or that it was to the elements, i.e. the
earth and the others likewise from which we think man came into
being, that God spoke 'let us make'. To prevent this I shall cite some
more words pronounced by the same Moses, from which we can
draw the indubitable conclusion that he was conversing with someone who was numerically a different and rational being. These are
the words: 'And God said: behold Adam has become like one of us
in knowing good and evil (Gen. 3:22)'. Therefore, in saying 'as one
of us' he has recounted a number referring to beings who are present with each other and the least that number can be is two. For
personally I do not think the explanation is true which the so-called
sect among you declares, nor are the teachers of that sect able to
prove that he spoke to angels or that the human body is the creation
of angels. But this is truly the offspring that was produced from the
father and was present with the father before all creatures (were
created), and it is this (being) that the father addresses...

Two explanations are attributed to the Jews (Justin is engaged in
conversation with Jews, hence the second person plurals) in order to
avoid the conclusion drawn by Christian exegetes: (1) God is talking
to himself, just like we do when are about to make something; (2)
God is talking to the elements out of which he is about to make
man. The first is not found in *Gen. Rabbah*, but is virtually identical
to the solution found in Basil. The second is not found elsewhere,
but is somewhat similar to the first two Rabbinic explanations in
Gen. Rabbah. The explanation that God is talking to his angels is not
given by Justin for [179] Gen. 1:26, but deduced from Gen. 3:22, and
it is attributed to ἡ παρ' ὑμῖν λεγομένη αἵρεσις, which we have to take
as a sectarian group within Judaism. The same two texts are linked
by Tertullian in his treatise *Adversus Praxean* (§12). To his own trinitarian interpretation he opposes the view that God is talking to his
angels, which he attributes without qualification to the Jews (*ut
Iudaei interpretantur*).

The heretics referred to by the Rabbis in various places and by

---

(my translation). But note that this specific Christian exegesis of the plural
ποιήσωμεν is already attested in the *Epistle of Barnabas* 5.5, 6.12, generally dated
between 95 and 130 A.D. Other early christological or trinitarian interpretations
at Theophilus *Ad Aut.* 2.18, Irenaeus *Adv. haer.* 4.20.1.

Justin once cannot, it seems, be reduced to a single group. As Segal has persuasively argued, they may include Christians, sectarian Jews with Gnostic inclination, non-Jewish Gnostics, as well as Pagans. If Justin's evidence is taken seriously, at least one branch represents a Gnosticizing group within Judaism, whose negative attitude to material creation encourages them to introduce angels into the interpretation of the creation account.[20] All this exegetical discussion forms a necessary background for Basil's polemic. But it is important to recognize that, although he makes use of earlier exegetical traditions, his own concerns towards the end of the fourth century are quite different to those of the time of Justin and Tertullian two centuries earlier. It is time to return to Basil's text.

The view attributed to the Jew at the beginning of our passage is not Philonic. It is also not found in this precise form in *Gen. Rabbah*, although it is clearly not far removed from Rabbi Hila's suggestion of a *pluralis maiestatis*. The closest parallel is the Jewish interpretation reported by Justin, as noted above. When Basil considers that this first interpretation is adequately refuted (lines 8–24), he portrays the Jews as pushed into a tight corner and like caged animals making a desperate move in their effort to obviate the truth. Now they suggest that a plurality of persons are involved, i.e. the angels addressed in the word ποιήσωμεν (lines 25–35). This is the solution referred to by Justin and Tertullian, and related to the views of Rabbis Simon and Huna in *Gen. Rabbah*.[21] Basil's refutation is clever. In the same verse God says 'according to *our* image', but this would mean that he and the angels share an image, which on Basil's Platonist assumptions, is quite out of the question (lines 42–47). At the same time he provides himself with a suitable transition to another group of opponents, the Neo-Arian Christian heretics, Aetius and Eunomius. By asserting the essential dissimilarity of the father and the son, the Anomoeans were reverting, in Basil's view, to a form of Judaism. Hence the pejorative description of these men as 'the new circumcision'. Basil has two arguments against [180] them based on the text under exegesis. The first is the corollary of the

---

[20] A. F. *Segal, Two Powers in Heaven: Early Rabbinic Reports about Christianity and Gnosticism* (Leiden 1977) 260–267 and *passim*; cf. also Urbach *op. cit.* (n. 16) 203ff.; more specifically on Justin's text A. Le Boulluec, *La notion d'hérésie dans la littérature grecque IIᵉ–IIIᵉ siècles* (Paris 1985) 77f.

[21] Note also that the dignity of συμβουλία received by the angels reminds us of the formulation of the Rabbi's question: with whom did God take *counsel*.

previous one, that 'our image' must refer to a single image of both father and son (48–55).[22] Secondly he appeals rather briefly to the expression 'in the image of God he (God) made him' (62–64). By implication we are meant to read a reference to the second person in the redundancy of the (implied) double mention of God. In between (lines 56–61) Basil very briefly points out that the wording of Gen. 1:26 also refutes any tendency towards Hellenizing polytheism, for the plural ποιήσωμεν is immediately followed by the singular ἐποίησεν. As noted above, this is exactly the same argument used by Rabbi Simlai against the 'heretics' in *Gen. Rabbah*. But Basil is running out of time. The final few paragraphs of the homily are sketched in very rapidly, and neither the polemic nor the arguments are fully worked out.

We return to our original question. Who is the Jew that Basil summons at the beginning of our passage? Certainly Philo is not meant. A further hint is given in the fact, disregarded by Daniélou, that Basil moves somewhat carelessly between a single opponent and a group of them. He begins with a single figure, ὁ Ἰουδαῖος (line 1). By line 8 he is speaking of 'their' explanation. At line 15 he retains the plural for 'those who do not shrink back from slandering the Lord'. In line 25, however, he returns to the singular χριστομάχος. Soon after it is the Ἰουδαῖοι who are cornered and put forward a new view (line 33). Finally in line 43 we have another singular λέγεις, before Basil moves on to the Anomoeans. In the final sentence the ἀνόμοιος (now singular) and the Ἰουδαῖος stand side by side.

The answer is now clear. Basil does not have any particular Jewish thinker such as Philo in mind in his polemic. The Jew that he invokes is a *collective figure* representing the views of Jewish exegetes opposed to Christian interpretations which read the presence of the Logos or the Trinity into the Mosaic creation account. In presenting these arguments Basil draws on a body of Jewish exegesis with which he is acquainted, whether directly or via earlier reports in Christian authors such as Justin and Origen.

---

[22] In later Greek εἰκών, which Basil in line 45 paraphrases with μορφή, can mean both image and model; cf. Runia *op. cit.* (n. 13) 163, referring to the study by H. Willms, *EIKΩN: eine begriffsgeschichtliche Untersuchung zum Platonismus* (Münster 1935). We note too, how Basil, who so far has concentrated on OT evidence (with the exception of Heb. 1:2–3 cited in line 26), now suddenly cites a salvo of NT texts. The reason is apparent: he has turned to Christian opponents, for whom the NT should be normative.

But our story does not end here. Basil's argument that the truth of Christianity, with its doctrine of the Trinity, stands midway between the falsehoods of Jewish monotheism (or more accurately 'mono-prosopism') and Hellenic polytheism, and that the heretics in their deviations from orthodoxy go astray to either side was a favourite of the Cappa[181]docians.[23] It reappears in many occasions in their works, and was taken over by subsequent ecclesiastical writers. Two further passages are of interest for our theme.

Theodoret of Cyrrhus in his *Quaestiones in Genesim* 19 poses the exegetical question: to whom did God speak the words at Gen. 1:26?[24] He gives the same two unacceptable alternatives as Basil. The first is attributed to some of the δυσώνυμοι αἱρετικοί: God spoke to angels and evil demons. The refutation is exactly the same as Basil's. God and angels, not to speak of evil demons, cannot have the same image, as indicated in the words κατ' εἰκόνα ἡμετέραν. The interpreters who fall into the opposite folly are the Jews, when they assert that God spoke to himself, in imitation of the mighty, for consuls and generals are inclined to use the plural in saying we order, we write, we command etc. Here we have Rabbi Hila's *pluralis maiestatis* in a purer form, though with different examples. It does not seem likely that Theodoret is indebted directly to Basil's discussion in the *In Hexaemeron.*

Far more interesting is a letter of the Egyptian desert monk Isidore of Pelusium, whose correspondence, compiled in the period from about 390 to 430, is still preserved in a corpus of 2000 letters. These letters cover a vast array of subjects, ranging from practical affairs in his community to sometimes quite lengthy exegetical and dogmatic discussions. One of the most interesting is *Ep.* 2.143 on the holy Trinity addressed to a certain Paul (PG 78.585–589). Unfortunately there is no modern edition of the corpus.[25] The text of the

---

[23] Cf. Basil, *Ep.* 210.5, 226.4, *Contra Sabellianos et Arium et Anomoeos* PG 31.600B–C; Gregory of Nyssa, *Oratio Catechetica* Prol. and 1–4, etc. A different variant at Gregory of Nazianzen, *Or.* 2.37, where there are three options: atheism, Judaism, polytheism.

[24] Text at PG 80.100–104. The work was written after 453; cf. J. Quasten, *Patrology*, volume III (Utrecht-Westminster 1960) 539.

[25] According to *Clavis Patrum Graecorum* 5557 it is being prepared by P. Évieux, but there are no signs that its appearance is imminent. The text printed by in Migne PG vol. 78 is a rather curious composite compiled by no less that 5 scholars in the period from 1570 to 1670. It falls far short of modern critical standards, its worst failing being its failure to use the best manuscript, Codex Βα1 of Grottaferrata.

opening passage of this letter is corrupt, but can be restored with
reference to a quotation found in the *Souda*. Elsewhere I have published a revised text, translation and commentary on the letter.[26]

Isidore commences with an eulogy of the truth, praising it for the
force of compulsion that it exercised on the Jew Philo of Alexandria
(585B–C):

*

> I admire the truth for the way in which she has induced the souls of
> intelligent men even to combat the preconceived opinion they have
> of their own doctrines. For the teaching of the truth has embedded
> the concept of the holy Trinity so clearly and lucidly also in the Old
> Testament for those who wish to observe it that Philo, though a Jew
> and a zealous one at that, in the writings which he left behind comes
> into conflict with his own religion. When he examines the words
> spoken by God, 'in the image of God I made man (Gen. 9:6)', he is
> constrained and compelled by the truth also to recognize the divine
> Logos as God. [182]

Even though Philo fails to reach precision in his speaking about the
Logos and God's powers, nevertheless he did achieve some notion
of the three persons of the Trinity, as Isidore proves with a number
of citations and allusions to Philo's writings. This brings him in
proximity to Pauline texts such as 1 Cor. 1:24 and Col. 1:15. He thus
differs from 'the doctrinal position of the uneducated teachers of
the Jews who are held fast in their preconceived opinion (588A)'.
Isidore then proceeds to cite a sequence of eight Old Testament
texts which will have helped Philo develop his view. These begin
with Gen. 1:26, and all involve some kind of περιττολογία, i.e.
stylistically unacceptable pleonasm, which can be interpreted to hint
at the doctrine of the Logos or of the three persons (the same
technique used by Basil in lines 63–64 of our *In Hexaemeron* passage).

In the final part of the letter Isidore demonstrates that the orthodox doctrine of the Trinity, involving three persons and one substance, stands midway between Jewish views of a single person,
followed by the heretic Sabellius, and Greek polytheism, of which
Arius and Eunomius became disciples. To the question why the
doctrine of the Trinity was not made clear from the outset Isidore
replies (589A–B):

---

[26] 'Philo of Alexandria in Five Letters of Isidore of Pelusium', in D. T. Runia,
D. M. Hay, D. Winston (edd.), *Heirs of the Septuagint: Philo, Hellenistic Judaism and
Early Christianity; Festschrift for Earle Hilgert* [= *The Studia Philonica Annual* 3]
(Atlanta 1991) 295–319 [see below Chapter 9 in this collection]. In this article I
do not discuss the connection of *Ep.* 2.143 with Basil's *In Hexaemeron*.

*   ... my answer would be that both as demonstration and as teaching it *was* pellucidly clear to men of intelligence and understanding, as it indeed was to the wise Philo. And if these words have been spoken in an enigmatic fashion, it should be taken into account that Scripture in giving the Law did not think it a good idea to introduce a difference of persons to Jews who showed an inclination to polytheism, lest they should teach that there was also a difference in nature in the hypostases and so plunge headlong into idolatry; but it was better that, having learnt the tenet of divine unicity, they should gradually be taught the doctrine of the hypostases which reverts back again to a unity of nature; thus pronouncements of unity were indicative of the sameness of the divine nature, while statements exceeding the single number revealed the individuality of the hypostases which is contracted into a single being. The assumption of different natures is Hellenic, the assumption of a single person or hypostasis is Judaic. To extend the hypostases to the holy Trinity and contract them into a single being is absolutely true and orthodox doctrine (ὀρθότατον καὶ ἀληθέστατον δόγμα).

The final words form an elegant return to the theme of truth with which the letter began, scriptural truth and orthodox doctrine coming together in a single phrase.

The thematic similarities between Isidore and Basil are unmistakable. But can a closer relation be detected? There are strong grounds for con[183]cluding, I submit, that, although Isidore doubtless was acquainted with other writings of the Cappadocians that deal with the same theme, the direct inspiration of the letter was—at least partially—this final chapter of the *In Hexaemeron*, and particularly the following section (88B–C, 1.56–61 in our translation):

«καὶ ἐποίησεν ὁ θεὸς τὸν ἄνθρωπον». οὐχί, ἐποίησαν. ἔφυγεν ἐνταῦθα τὸν πληθυσμὸν τῶν προσώπων. δι' ἐκείνων μὲν τὸν Ἰουδαῖον παιδεύων, διὰ τούτων δὲ τὸν Ἑλληνισμὸν ἀποκλείων, ἀσφαλῶς ἀνέδραμεν ἐπὶ τὴν μονάδα, ἵνα καὶ υἱὸν νοῇς μετὰ πατρὸς καὶ τῆς πολυθείας ἐκφύγῃς τὸ ἐπικίνδυνον.

That Isidore was well acquainted with Basil's work, and more exactly, this particular homily, can be proven by the fact that in another letter, when presenting the topos[27] that the study of natural science is a waste of time because it makes no contribution to holiness, he gives as an example three doxai on the shape of the earth that *must* come from Basil's passage at 80D.[28] The doxa that the earth is

---

[27] A Christian adaptation of the Socratic topos that φυσιολογία contributes nothing to ἀρετή; parallels at Eusebius *PE* 15.62, Theodoret *CAG* 4.26.

[28] *Ep.* 2.273, PG 78.704. L. Bayer, *Isidors von Pelusium klassische Bildung*, Forschungen zur Christlichen Literatur- und Dogmengeschichte 13.2 (Paderborn

λικνοειδής (fan-shaped) uses a term which is exceedingly rare; in this sense it is probably only found in these two passages.[29]

Apart from the general idea of the interposition of the truth in between the two opposed errors of Judaism and Hellenism, a decisive clue for the dependence of Isidore on Basil lies in the following passage of the letter (*Ep.* 2.143, 585B):[30]

> ὁ λέγων γὰρ ὅτι εἷς ἐστιν ὁ θεός, οὐ πρὸς τὸν ἀριθμὸν κατέδραμε τῆς μονάδος, ἀλλὰ πρὸς τὸ μυστήριον τῆς τριάδος, τὸ τῶν μὲν πάντη διαιρετῶν ἑνικώτερον τῶν δὲ ὄντως μοναδικῶν ἀφθονώτερον. (He who asserted that God is one, did not arrive at the numerical unit of the monad, but rather at the mystery of the Trinity, which is more unified than wholly discrete entities but richer than what is truly monadic.)

When first confronting this passage, I was somewhat puzzled by the choice of the verb κατέδραμε, 'he ran up against' or 'arrived at'. It seems to me now that it is a—probably unconscious—reminiscence of the passage in Basil's text cited above, in which the Mosaic third person singular 'safely returns to the monad' (l. 59). For Isidore, in contrast, Philo in his doctrine of the two divine powers does not 'arrive at the number of the monad', but rather the mystery of the Trinity.

Similarly, in the case of the heretics that Isidore combats, he draws on Basil, but goes his own way. For Isidore it is the modalist monarchianism of Sabellius which represents the 'Judaizing' option, rather [184] than the Anomoeans, as in Basil.[31] As for the opposed tendency, it is Arius and Eunomius (i.e. the chief representative of the Anomoeans) who fall prey to the seductions of Hellenizing polytheism.[32] Isidore regards their differentiation between the first and second hypostasis as tantamount to having two (or more) separate

---

1915) 70, notes the doxographical background, but is unaware of the Basilian provenance.

[29] Lampe *s.v.* gives only these two passages. They are not mentioned in LSJ, which notes only the entries in the *Souda* and Zonaras, where the word is explained by ῥυπαρός (dirty).

[30] But at this point the text in Migne is seriously disturbed; see above n. 26 and text thereto.

[31] Basil associates Sabellius with Judaism in *Ep.* 189.2, 210.3–4 etc., but also with Arius at *Ep.* 226.4 and the Anomoeans at *Ep.* 9.2. In the sermon *Contra Sabellianos et Arium et Anomoeos* PG 31.600ff. the three heresies are grouped together.

[32] Basil gives no heretical representative of this tendency in the passage of the *In Hexameron*. Polytheism is associated with the semi-Arian Marcion at *C. Sabel.* PG 31.605B–C, and with anonymous heretics who sound much like Arians in *Ep.* 243.3. Arius is associated with polytheism by Greg. Naz. *Or.* 2.37.

gods at different levels, which is precisely the charge of polytheism that might be directed at Neoplatonist philosophical theology.[33]

Isidore, we may conclude, has drawn on Basil. But why should *that* be interesting? After all, it is well known that he takes over large amount of material from previous Church Fathers.[34] The interest of the letter seems to me to lie above all in Isidore's attitude to Philo. It is difficult not to conclude that, also in this respect, he is reacting directly to the passage in Basil. The latter had written (lines 1–6):

> καὶ εἶπεν ὁ θεός, ποιήσωμεν ἄνθρωπον. ποῦ μοι ὁ Ἰουδαῖος, ὅς, ἐν τοῖς κατόπιν, ὥσπερ διὰ θυρίδων τινῶν, τοῦ τῆς θεολογίας φωτὸς δια-λάμποντος, καὶ δευτέρου προσώπου τοῦ ὑποδεικνυμένου μὲν μυστικῶς, οὔπω δὲ ἐναργῶς ἐκφανέντος, **πρὸς τὴν ἀλήθειαν ἀπεμάχετο**, αὐτὸν ἑαυτῷ λέγων τὸν θεὸν διαλέγεσθαι;

And a few lines further (lines 32) he describes the Jews as τὸ ἐχθρὸν τῆς ἀληθείας γένος. Isidore too can hardly be accused of a positive view towards Judaism,[35] but he makes an exception for Philo, for in his case the truth exercised a compelling force (585B, translation given above):[36]

> ἄγαμαι τὴν **ἀλήθειαν**, τὴν τῶν συνετῶν τὰς ψυχὰς εἰς τὸ καὶ τῇ τῶν οἰκείων δογμάτων προλήψει μαχήσασθαι περιστήσασαν. οὕτω γὰρ σαφῆ καὶ λαμπρὰν τοῖς βουλομένοις κατοπτεῦσαι τὴν περὶ τῆς ἁγίας τριάδος ἔννοιαν καὶ ἐν τῇ παλαιᾷ διαθήκῃ ἐγκατέσπαρται ἡ διδασκαλία, ὡς καὶ Φίλωνα, καίτοι Ἰουδαῖον ὄντα καὶ ζηλωτήν, δι᾽ ὧν ἀπολέλοιπε συγ-γραμμάτων **ἀπομαχήσασθαι** τῇ οἰκείᾳ θρησκείᾳ. βασανίζων γὰρ τὸ εἰρημένον παρὰ τοῦ θεοῦ, «ἐν εἰκόνι θεοῦ ἐποίησα τὸν ἄνθρωπον», ἠναγκάσθη ὑπὸ τῆς **ἀλήθειας** καὶ ἐξεβιάσθη καὶ τὸν τοῦ θεοῦ λόγον θεολογῆσαι.

Unlike the Jew in Basil's passage, Philo was intelligent enough to pick up the hints given him by the Old Testament, and so developed

---

[33] Similar train of thought at Gregory of Nyssa, *C. Eunomium* 3.2 83.21ff. Jaeger.

[34] Cf. A. M. Ritter, Art. 'S. Isidore de Péluse', *Dictionnaire de Spiritualité* 7.2 (Paris 1971) 2098 who notes debts to John Chrysostom; M. Kertsch, 'Isidor von Pelusion als Nachahmer Gregors von Nazianz', *Jahrbuch der Österreichischen Byzan-tinistik* 35 (1985) 113–122, who rightly points out that almost no research has been carried out on Isidore's debt to the earlier Patristic tradition.

[35] In numerous letters Isidore reveals that he shares the strong anti-Judaic views current in this period. Cf. the remarks of H. A. Niemeyer, *De Isidori Pelusiotae vita scriptis et doctrina commentatio historica theologica* (Halle 1825), printed at PG 78.90–92 and the list of references at PG 78.1743–44. Some strong statements are collected by H. Schreckenberg, *Die christlichen Adversus-Judaeos-Texte und ihr literarisches und historisches Umfeld (1.–11. Jh.)* (Frankfurt-Bern 1982) 365–367.

[36] See above nn. 26 & 30.

some doctrines in his works which anticipate the Christian doctrine of the Trinity.[37]

A further point of interest is the fact that Isidore quotes Gen. 9:6, for in an exegesis of that text Philo had asked the question 'why does Moses, as if speaking about another god, say 'in the image of God I made man', and not 'in his own image'?', and proceeded to develop a view of the Logos as 'second God' which is unique in his writings.[38] This text is, of course, closely related to Gen. 1:26–27 on [185] which Basil concentrates. Indeed, in lines 62–63 Basil had cited Gen. 1:27, but actually in an incorrect form, ἐν εἰκόνι θεοῦ instead of κατ' εἰκόνα θεοῦ, no doubt under the influence of Gen. 9:6. The observation that he makes is exactly the same that inspired Philo's question. Once again the the suggestion might be made that it was Isidore's reading of Basil that induced him to recall the Philonic passage.

There remains one further question to be asked. Why should the fifth century monk Isidore take the trouble to defend the Jew Philo? A broad answer can be given in the fact that from the time of Clement onwards, and especially in Eusebius, Philo had been given a special place in the Christian tradition as a Christian *avant la lettre*, allowing the Fathers to appropriate material and ideas from his works and also solve some puzzles about the beginning of the Alexandrian church.[39] If Philo in his situation could gain some conception of the truth of Christian doctrine, what excuse do contemporary Christians have for rejecting it, when they can draw on the full evidence of revelation and the tradition of the Church? A more specific answer, however, lies in the local conditions in Egypt which form the backdrop to most of Isidore's letters. The letter collection makes it clear that in Isidore's time discussions were taking place between Christians and Jews on religious matters at the local level of

[37] In *Orat. Cat.* 1, 7.5 Srawley, where Gregory is arguing that Christian doctrine avoids the errors of both Hellenism and Judaism, he writes: οὐδὲ γὰρ τοῖς ἔξω τοῦ καθ' ἡμᾶς δόγματος ἄλογον εἶναι τὸ θεῖον ὑπείληπται. As Srawley *ad loc.* points out, Gregory may well be thinking of Philo here. But he does not mention him, and at *C. Eunomium* 3.7 217.20 Jaeger he regards Philo as a source for the heresy of Eunomius.

[38] *QG* 2.62, Greek text cited by Eusebius *PE* 7.13.1, from where Isidore may have derived his information.

[39] See J. E. Bruns, 'Philo Christianus: the debris of a legend', *Harvard Theological Review* 66 (1973) 141–145, and the chapter 'Philo Christianus' in my forthcoming book *Philo in Early Christian Literature*, to be published in the series Compendia Rerum Iudaicarum ad Novum Testamentum.

provincial Egypt. On one occasion Isidore writes to a Jew called Benjamin on how the bread of the Eucharist has replaced the sacrifices
of the Law, while the shewbread in the sanctuary points to Christ
(*Ep.* 1.401). Other letters that give evidence of local discussions are
1.141 (on the incarnation), 2.99 (against a Jew objecting to the
hyperbole in John 21:25) and 3.94 (on the Christological interpretation of Deut. 18:15). Most germane to our context, however, is
Ep. 3.19, in which Isidore gives advice to a fellow-priest involved in a
discussion with a Jew on the validity of non-literal (i.e. allegorical or
typological) interpretation of scripture. This man should be told
that 'the ignorance of you Jews is refuted by two of your own writers
* who lived after the coming of Christ, Philo the master of speculative
thought and Josephus the great historian'. It is downright unfair, he
concludes, that the Jews should reject the testimony of their own
writers.[40] Philo may thus be regarded as a proto-Christian, but at the
same time he is and remains a Jew. As such he can be used as
valuable apologetic ammunition in the contest—dialogue one can
hardly call it—against the Judaism of Isidore's own time.[41]

---

[40] This letter is translated and commented on in the article cited above in n. 26
[see below chapter 9].

[41] I would like to express my thanks to Prof. J. C. M. van Winden who made
valuable sugggestions and saved me from several errors.

CHAPTER EIGHT

A NOTE ON PHILO AND CHRISTIAN HERESY

In an article in the previous volume of this Annual, I presented a text, translation and commentary of five letters of the Desert father Isidore of Pelusium in which Philo plays a significant role. One of the more interesting passages is found in *Ep.* 2.143, in which Isidore argues that Philo, though a Jew, anticipates the doctrine of the Trinity which is already present in the Old Testament:[1]

> With all clarity... the Old Testament... pronounces the rulership, not of one person, but of three hypostases and one substance. Its intention is, on the one hand, to denounce the Jews for having an unsound notion focused on a single person—in whose footsteps also Sabellius followed, possibly encouraged to reach the doctrine of one substance through an excessive regard for the equality of the Son with the Father—, on the other hand to banish the polytheism of the Greeks, whose disciples Arius and Eunomius have been convicted of being, because they fallaciously extended the difference of the hypostases to the aspect of substance.

In a comment on this passage I remarked that 'modern scholars perceive Philo as the 'Father of Arianism,' but to my knowledge he was never accused of such by the Church Fathers themselves.'[2] I now realize that this statement is, if not literally incorrect, certainly misleading. So before any reader corrects me, it is better that I do so myself.

*   The major piece of evidence we have to consider is found in the writings of Gregory of Nyssa, active about a generation before Isidore. Gregory's most significant anti-heretical work is undoubtedly his massive compilation against the heresy of Eunomius, the leader

---

[1] D. T. Runia, 'Philo of Alexandria in Five Letters of Isidore of Pelusium', in D. T. Runia, D. M. Hay and Winston D. (edd.), *Heirs of the Septuagint. Philo, Hellenistic Judaism and Early Christianity: Festschrift for Earle Hilgert,* Brown Judaic Studies 230 [= *The Studia Philonica Annual* 3 (1991)] (Atlanta 1991) 302 [see below chapter 9].

[2] *Ibid.* 306. The scholars cited were Wolfson, Mortley, Williams, to whom can be added C. J. de Vogel, 'Platonism and Christianity: a Mere Antagonism or a Profound Common Ground?', *VC* 39 (1985) 11 (cf. 4).

of the Neo-Arian movement also known as the Anomœans.[3] In this
work (which actually consists of four separate writings[4]) he twice
refers to [66] Philo.[5] In the fifth book of the third work, written
between 381 and 383 he undertakes to refute at great length an
attack of Eunomius on his recently departed brother Basil. A child
of his time, Gregory uses all the rhetorical techniques of invective
and polemic at his disposal. At 3.5.23–25, after quoting some lines
from Basil, he launches into a sharp attack on Eunomius' style
(2.168.5–27):[6]

> These are the words of the great Basil. As for the sagacity that is
> directed against us by the opponent of these words, let those who
> have the leisure to spend their time on unprofitable things learn it
> from the writing of Eunomius himself. For I find it unpleasant to
> insert the sickening nonsense of the rhetor among my own labours
> and to record his ignorance and foolishness through the medium of
> my own words. For he continues with an 'encomium of significant
> arguments which elucidate the underlying subject', and in his usual
> style he compiles and glues together the rag-collection of terms
> tossed away at the crossroads. Then once again the unfortunate
> Isocrates is nibbled at and depilated for words and figures that he
> can use for the composition of his subject. There are also places
> where even Philo the Hebrew suffers the same fate, supplying him
> with terms drawn from his own labours. And not even thus has this
> elaborately stitched and multi-coloured tapestry been completed,
> but every proof and every defence of conceptions and every
> technical exercise collapses of its own accord like bubbles...

Speaking here in quite general terms Gregory accuses Eunomius of
being a plagiarist and a centonist, that is to say, stealing and stitch-
ing together material (a carpet-bag, cento, medley) drawn from
other sources.[7] In his study on Philo and Gregory of Nyssa Daniélou

---

[3] 'Neo-Arians' is the best term according to R. P. C. Hanson, *The Search for the
Christian Doctrine of God* (Edinburgh 1988) 598. The name 'Anomœan' is derived
from the doctrine that the Son is unlike (ἀνόμοιος) the Father.

[4] First disentangled by W. Jaeger in his edition of 1921, reprinted as *Gregorii
Nysseni opera Contra Eunomium libri*, 2 vols. (Leiden 1960²).

[5] We ignore the text in the summary at 1.16.20, since this was added on the
basis of the main body of the text by a later scribe; cf. Jaeger, *op. cit.* 1.3.

[6] My translation (cf. also the English translation by H. A. Wilson in A Select
Library of Nicene and Post-Nicene Fathers, series 2, vol. 5 (Buffalo-New York
1893) 193f.).

[7] Standard polemical procedure, comparable to the accustions made by Hippolytus against the Gnostics, who stitch together centos from Greek philosophers;
cf. the extensive material collected by J. Mansfeld, *Heresiography in Context:
Hippolytus' Elenchos as a Source for Greek Philosophy*, Philosophia Antiqua 56 (Leiden
1992) 153ff.

drew attention to this passage, which he translated and interpreted as follows:[8]

> La première [mention explicite] concerne le style de Philon que Grégoire compare à celui d'Eunome: «(Eunome), suivant son procédé de style habituel, réunit, pour les coudre ensemble, les lambeaux de formules toutes faites (λεξείδια), qui traînent dans les carrefours. Voici le pauvre Isocrate qui se ronge à nouveau, arranchant brin à brin les mots et les figures pour en composer son ouvrage et il arrive aussi que l'Hebreu Philon agisse de même, récoltant pour lui dans ses propres travaux les formules toutes faites». Trois choses ici sont à noter: la mention explicite de Philon d'abord; la connaissance que Grégoire a du style de Philon, ce qui implique la connaissance directe [67] de son œuvre; enfin le jugement sévère à l'égard de Philon. Ce qui paraît ici visé est le rémploi par Philon des mémes formules toutes faites.

Daniélou thinks that Eunomius here is *compared* to Philo, with the implied accusation that Philo, just like Eunomius, repeats himself by drawing on the same formulas used elsewhere. Undoubtedly Philo *is* a repetitious author, but this is *not* what Gregory means here. Daniélou's interpretation is based on an incorrect translation of the text.[9] The point is that the heretic Eunomius is an unoriginal author, who is dependent on other sources. Among these are Isocrates and Philo, who *supply* him with certain terms in his arguments. Gregory does not criticize Philo, but rather feels sorry for him, because his writings are exploited in such an unscrupulous way. On the other hand, the French scholar is certainly correct when he concludes from this remark that Gregory must have been acquainted with the Philonic corpus.

Fortunately some fifty pages later at 3.7.8 Gregory gives an illustration of what he thinks Eunomius filched from Philo (2.217.17–218.5 Jaeger):

---

[8] J. Daniélou, 'Philon et Grégoire de Nysse', in *Philon d'Alexandrie. Lyon 11-15 Septembre 1966: colloques nationaux du Centre National de la Recherche Scientifique* (Paris 1967) 333f., repeated at *L'être et le temps chez Grégoire de Nysse* (Leiden (1970) 86f.

[9] The text reads in Jaeger's edition (2.168.13–18): καὶ διὰ τῆς συνήθους ἑαυτοῦ λέξεως συντίθησι καὶ διακολλᾷ τὰ ἐν τριόδοις ἀπερριμμένα τῶν λεξειδίων ῥακώματα, καὶ πάλιν ὁ τλήμων Ἰσοκράτης περιεσθίεται ῥήματά τε καὶ σχήματα πρὸς τὴν σύνθεσιν τοῦ προκειμένου παρατιλλόμενος, ἔστι δὲ ὅπου καὶ ὁ Ἑβραῖος Φίλων τὰ ἴσα πάσχει, ἐκ τῶν ἰδίων πόνων συνερανίζων αὐτῷ τὰ λεξείδια. For Daniélou's rendering the final sentence would have to read πράττει instead of πάσχει and αὐτῷ instead of αὐτῷ. His interpretation goes back to the 17th century Latin translation by N. Guloni printed at Migne PG 45.747C.

For 'the most eminent God (of his), anterior, he says, to all other beings that are generated, has power over his own *dynamis*'. The statement in its actual wording has been transferred by our literary hack from Philo the Hebrew to his own text, and Eunomius' theft from the actual works compiled by Philo will become as clear as day to whoever is willing to examine them. But I have indicated this in the present context not so much because I reproach our literary hack for the poverty of his own words and thoughts, but rather because I wish to demonstrate to my readers the affinity between Eunomius' doctrines and the texts of the Jews. For the text of Philo in its very wording would not have been suited to his conceptions, if there was not a kinship of thought between the two. Thus is possible to find in Philo the text 'God is anterior to all other beings that are generated', while the following phrase 'has power over his own *dynamis*' has been thrown in from the Neo-Judaic sect. Examination of the text will clearly demonstrate its absurdity...

The passage in the work of Eunomius that Gregory is combatting was ὁ ἐξοχώτατος θεὸς πρὸ τῶν ἄλλων ὅσα γεννητά, τῆς αὐτοῦ κρατεῖ δυνάμεως.[10] Gregory claims that the phrase ὁ θεὸς πρὸ τῶν ἄλλων ὅσα γεννητά is literally taken over from Philo.[11] This claim cannot be substantiated [68] from the Philonic corpus that we still possess. There is a small chance that it may have been located in one of the works of which the original Greek text has been lost, e.g. the *Quaestiones*. It is more likely, however, that Gregory remembered phrases of a similar kind from his reading of Philo and exaggerated the relationship into one of direct dependence. Jaeger pointed to *Leg.* 3.175 ὁ λόγος τοῦ θεοῦ... πρεσβύτατος... τῶν ὅσα γέγονε (but Eunomius is talking about God the Father) and *Migr.* 183 πρὸ παντὸς τοῦ γενητοῦ (sc. ἐστιν ὁ θεός). Another text that Gregory may have called to mind is *Leg.* 3.4 πρὸ γὰρ παντὸς γενητοῦ ὁ θεός ἐστι.[12] Presumably he will also have remembered that Philo often speaks about God's δύναμις or δυνάμεις. The remaining part of the sentence, however,

---

[10] 'From Gregory's rebuttal the work can be partly reconstructed; cf. R. P. Vaggione, *Eunomius The Extant Works* (Oxford 1987), our text at 122.

[11] So not including the phrase ὁ ἐξοχώτατος θεὸς as one might first think. Philo does not use the adjective ἔξοχος, but cf. his expression ὁ ἀνωτάτω θεός at *Sacr.* 60, *Decal.* 53, and also in the text *QG* 2.62, to which we shall pay attention below (see at n. 29).

[12] The last two texts both involve exegesis of Ex. 17:6, so Eunomius might have drawn his quote from the passage in *QE* on that text (cf. also *Somn.* 2.221, with a reference to God's δύναμις). But that is pure speculation. Daniélou *art. cit.* 334 remarks that ὅσα γεννητά is found at *Praem.* 28. This is not strictly correct: ὅσα γενητά occurs at *Plant.* 66, *Mos.* 2.168, *Spec.* 2.166, *Praem.* 28 (for the first and last text a minority of mss. record γεννητά).

is attributed not to Philo, but to the νέα 'Ιουδαϊκή (sc. αἵρεσις). The
reference here becomes clear if we adduce the polemical final
section of Basil's *In Hexaemeron*, where Gregory's great example
* addresses the party of the Anomœans (i.e. Aetius and Eunomius) as
'you from the *new* circumcision, who advocate Judaism under the
guise of Christianity.'[13]

Gregory thus sees a connection between (Neo-)Arianism as
represented by Eunomius and Judaism. On numerous occasions in
the work he refers to the Judaizing tendency of their doctrines. At *C.
Eun.* 1.177 (1.79.9ff. Jaeger), for example, Gregory argues that the
Eunomians in effect propound the Jewish doctrine of God. They
contend that only the being (οὐσία) of God truly (κυρίως) exists,
and reckon the being of the Son and the Holy spirit in effect to
belong to the category of non-existents (ἐν τοῖς μὴ οὖσι). For that
which does not truly (κυρίως) exist is said to be through customary
inexact use of language (καταχρήσει συνηθείας), just like we call a
statue a man, though in fact it is only an image of a man.[14] These
men, it is concluded, should return from the [69] Church to the
synagogues of the Jews.

Gregory also makes it quite clear in the above-cited passage that
part of the Judaizing tendency of the Neo-Arians is their exploitation of Philo's writings. Philo's phraseology encourages Eunomius in
his heretical opinions, because it presents God as ontologically
superior to all other beings that are generated, whereas in Nicene
orthodoxy the Son is generated (γέννητος), but in no respect
ontologically inferior to the Father (for he is ὁμοούσιος, 'of the same
substance'). But Philo's doctrine of the Logos—interpreted as a

---

[13] *Hex.* 9.6, 518.11 Giet (= SC 26bis) (my emphasis). For the theme of God's
δύναμις and the Logos as δύναμις in Arius and Marcellinus of Ancyra, cf. A.
Grillmeier, *Christ in Christian Tradition*, vol. 1 From the Apostolic Age to
Chalcedon (451) (London-Oxford 1975²) 235, 270. The notion of δύναμις
frequently occurs in the remains of Eunomius (Vaggione *op. cit.* 200), and 1 Cor.
1:24 is one of his favourite texts.

[14] For the theological application of the technical term κατάχρησις, which
arguably starts in Philo, see my article, 'Naming and Knowing: Themes in Philonic
Theology with Special Reference to the *De mutatione nominum*', in R. van den
Broek, T. Baarda and J. Mansfeld (edd.), *Knowledge of God in the Graeco-Roman
world*, EPRO 112 (Leiden 1988) 82–89 (reprinted in *Exegesis and Philosophy: Studies
on Philo of Alexandria* (London 1991)). On this same subject see now the further
examination of J. Whittaker, 'Catachresis and Negative Theology: Philo of
Alexandria and Basilides', in S. Gersh and C. Kannengiesser (edd.), *Platonism in
Late Antiquity* (Notre Dame 1992) 61–82.

hypostasis separate from God himself[15]—is implicit rather than explicit in this passage. It will be illuminating, therefore, to adduce one more passage from Gregory, where it is placed more explicitly in the foreground.

At the beginning of the *Oratio catechetica,* Gregory's sketch of a systematic theology, the Cappadocian Father discusses the therapy (or strategy, as we might now say) to be used against systems of thought and belief that differ from Christian orthodoxy, i.e. Hellenism, Judaism and Christian heresy (*Pref.,* 2.11–3.9):[16]

> You will not heal the polytheism of the Greek and the unbelief of the Jew concerning the only begotten God by the same means, nor can you use the same arguments in the case of those among the sects who have gone astray to overturn their deluded doctrinal fairy tales. For the arguments you use to correct the Sabellian will not also benefit the Anomœan, while the struggle against the Manichean will be of no assistance for the Jew, but one should, as I just said, look at the preconceptions that men have and construct the argument against the error located in each opponent, putting forward in each discussion certain principles and reputable propositions, so that through the views admitted on both sides the truth may in consequence be revealed...

The schema that Gregory has in mind is the same used later by Isidore of Pelusium, that the truth of orthodoxy stands midway between the error of Hellenic polytheism and Judaic monotheism, with the Christian heresies deviating to the one or the other side.[17] The parallelism of phrases shows that here too the doctrine of Eunomius and the Anomœans (or Neo-Arians) is associated with Judaizing. In a delightful example of the use of the dialectical method, Gregory [70] proceeds to refute the atheism and polytheism of the Greeks. Then he directs his argument to the Jewish position. Again his method is dialectical, starting from positions held by his opponents (§1, 6.12–7.9):

> But since the doctrine of piety is able to perceive an distinction of hypostases in the unity of the (divine) nature, we must take care that

---

[15] Certain statements of Philo encourage this view, but whether it represents the major thrust of his Logos theology is, to my mind, doubtful. See for example the remarks by D. Winston, *Logos and Mystical Theology in Philo of Alexandria* (Cincinnati 1985) 49–50.

[16] My translation, based on the fine critical edition with commentary of J. H. Srawley, *The Catechetical Oration of Gregory of Nyssa* (Cambridge 1903).

[17] Cf. *Ep.* 2.143, and my comments in *art. cit.* (n. 1) 306. The arbitrariness of the association of heresies with Greek or Jewish thought is shown by the fact that Isidore's schema is exactly the reverse of that of Gregory.

in our combat against the Greeks our argument does not covertly
lapse towards Judaism. So again by means of a systematic distinction
we should correct the error of this view. Now it is accepted by those
outside our doctrine (τοῖς ἔξω καθ᾽ ἡμᾶς δόγματος) that the
Godhead is not without *logos* (ἄλογος). This agreed position of theirs
is sufficient to articulate our argument. For he who agrees that God
is *not without logos* will certainly consent to the view that he who is not
without *logos* in any case *has logos*...

Normally one would expect the phrase 'those outside our doctrine'
to refer to Greek views, but here in the context it must apply to Jews
or Judaizers,[18] and it is to be agreed with Srawley that the prime
example of a Jewish thinker holding the view that God has a *logos*
must be Philo.[19] Here we thus have (by implication) a slightly more
positive view of Philo than in the *Contra Eunomium*, where Philo does
nothing but supply the heretic with erroneous ideas. But we should
not overlook the fact that the context is dialectical. The correct view
that God has a *logos* is only the starting point of the demonstration.
At the end Gregory repeats that 'our doctrine will avoid in equal
measure the absurdity of both positions (i.e. Greek and Jewish),
confessing the living and active and creative Logos of God, which
the Jew will not accept, and that the Logos himself and the One
from which he has his being do not differ in their natures (i.e.
against the Greeks) (§1, 11.16–12.3).' The truth is firmly in possession of the tradition of orthodox Christianity.

Gregory's accusation that Eunomius took over phraseology from
Philo deserves further examination.[20] It is certainly far from impossible that he was acquainted with Philo's work. Prudence dictates,
however, that we make allowance for the possibilities of polemical
distortion. From Justin and Irenaeus onwards it is a standard component of orthodox Christian anti-heretical strategy to accuse heretics
of deriving their erroneous doctrines from sources that fall outside
the scope of divine inspiration or apostolic succession. Thus Hippolytus accuses the Gnostic [71] Christians of taking their doctrines

---

[18] Thus a counter-example to Daniélou *op. cit.* (n. 8) 53, who argues with
regard to the expressions τῶν σοφῶν τις or τῶν ἔξωθέν τινες that 'ces expressions
désignent toujours des philosophes paiens'.
[19] Srawley, *op. cit.* 7. He adds: 'But the belief in a Word as a mediating
influence was not confined to Alexandria. In Palestine it affected the language of
the Targums.' This correct, but does not, I believe, detract from the fact that
Gregory must primarily have Philo in mind; cf. the exploitation of Philo's Logos
doctrine by Eusebius in his *PE*, to which shall return below.
[20] Starting with the texts collected by Vaggione, *op. cit.* (n. 10).

from Pythagoras and Empedocles, the Cappadocians accuse Aetius and Eunomius of learning their futile dialectical arguments from Aristotle, and so on.[21] Philo too stands outside both the biblical and the Christian tradition, and so can be regarded as an extraneous source of error. As we saw, however, Gregory's attitude to him is, in the circumstances, rather mild.

Are there any other sources that reveal that Philo might be regarded as the source of heretical error? We have already referred to the final pages of Basil's *In Hexaemeron*, where, in giving a brief account of the creation of man, Basil attacks both Jews and Anomœans for their erroneous views. Having cited the first words of Gen. 1:26, Basil immediately launches into a strong attack on an unnamed Jew who 'continued to fight against the truth, asserting that God was conversing with himself'.[22] A number of commentators on this text have argued that Philo is the Jew that Basil has in mind.[23] But in a detailed analysis of the passage I have shown that Basil is speaking in quite general terms, and that a Rabbinic tradition of interpretation is alluded to.[24] A close connection is postulated between Judaizing and Christian heresy in this text, but there is no reference to the role of Philo.[25]

Of more relevance is another author, who makes extensive use of both Philo and Basil, Ambrose. Indeed the bishop of Milan is the
* most prolific exploiter of Philonic material in the entire Patristic tradition. In five treatises Ambrose follows Philo so closely that large sections virtually amount to a paraphrase of the original source, even though Philo's name is in fact only mentioned once.[26] In his splendid analysis of these treatises, Savon has shown that, in spite of

---

[21] For Hippolytus see Mansfeld *op. cit.* (n. 7), *passim*; for the Anomœans my article, 'Festugière Revisited: Aristotle in the Greek Patres', *VC* 43 (1989) 23–26.

[22] *In Hex.* 9.6, 514.2 Giet.

[23] Giet at SC 26bis (Paris 1968^2) 514 n. 3, Daniélou, *art. cit.* (n. 8) 336, M. Naldini, *Basilio di Cesarea Sulla Genesi (Omilie sull'Esamerone)* (no place given 1990) 401.

[24] ''Where, tell me, is the Jew...': Basil, Philo and Isidore of Pelusium' (forthcoming in *Vigiliae Christianae*) [= chapter 7 in this volume].

[25] Cf. also Ambrose's adaptation of this passage at *Exam.* 6.7.40, where he polemicizes against both Jews and Arians. But there is no indication that he sees a reference to Philo.

[26] E. Lucchesi, *L'usage de Philon dans l'œuvre exégétique de Saint Ambroise: une 'Quellenforschung' relative aux Commentaires d'Ambroise sur la Genèse*, ALGHJ 9 (Leiden 1977) 7, has estimated that Ambrose uses Philo on some 600 occasions. The single explicit mention is at *De Paradiso* 4.25, where Ambrose criticizes Philo for exegesis that remains on the moral level, and is insufficiently spiritual.

this close relationship, Ambrose is very conscious of the nature of his
source, as is indicated by the subtle corrections that he introduces
into his paraphrases and adaptations. In particular Ambrose is aware
of the fact [72] that Philo is a Jew, and that his opinions may
encourage lapses into Arianism.[27] Two examples are of particular
interest for our theme. In the first both writers give exegesis of Gen.
4:3, where Cain does not give an offering until 'after some days',
whereas the virtuous do this with all speed. Fastest of all is God himself. For purposes of comparison I place the two texts side by side:[28]

Philo, *De sacrificiis* 65	Ambrose, *De Cain et Abel* 1.8.32
For God spoke and acted toge-ther, placing no interval between the two. But if one should put forward a more truly phrased doctrine, his word (λόγος) was his deed (ἔργον).	God gives swiftly, since he spoke, and action took place, he ordered, and creation took place. For the word of God is not, as someone asserts, his product (*opus*), but is in activity (*operans*), as you find written... (citation of John 5:17 follows)

It is apparent that Ambrose has misunderstood the purport of
Philo's words, which intend to say that, because there is no time-
lapse between God's word and its taking place, *word* and *deed* can be
identified. Ambrose thinks that the term ἔργον means 'product', and
so explicitly corrects Philo: the word of God is not an *opus*, but
rather an *operans*, always fully active. The anonymous reference must
be to Philo. As Savon has penetratingly observed, this 'correction'
can only explained if we accept that Ambrose is on the look-out for
expressions in Philo that might give support to Arian doctrine.

The second example is found in *De Noe*, where Ambrose follows
very closely the exegesis of Gen. 6–10 that Philo gives in *QG* 1.87–
2.82. The text that interests us gives exegesis of Gen. 9:6. Again we
place original and derived (but adapted) text side by side:[29]

Philo, *QG* 2.62	Ambrose, *De Noe* 26.99
Why does he say, as if speaking about another god, 'in the image of God I made man' (Gen. 9:6), but not 'in his own image'? Excellently and wisely this oracular utterance is given. For	Many people too are disturbed that he should say 'in the image of God I made man (Gen. 9:6)', and that he did not say 'in my image', since he himself is God. But it should be understood that there is

---

[27] H. Savon, *Saint Ambroise devant l'exégèse de Philon le Juif*, 2 vols. (Paris 1977), esp. 1.118–139.

[28] My translation; texts at Cohn-Wendland 1.228–229, and Schenkl CSEL 32.1.367.

[29] My translation; texts at Petit PAPM 33.116, Schenkl CSEL 32.1.482.

nothing that is mortal can be likened unto the highest God and Father of the universe (πρὸς τὸν ἀνωτάτω καὶ πατέρα τῶν ὅλων), but to the second god (πρὸς τὸν δεύτερον θεόν), who is his Logos. For it was necessary that the rational element in the soul of man should be marked by the divine Logos, since the God anterior to the Logos (ὁ πρὸ τοῦ λόγου θεὸς) transcends every rational nature. It was unlawful that anything that has come into being should be thought a likeness of Him who exists beyond the Logos in the most excellent and transcendent state.

the Father and there is the Son. Although all things are created through the Son, nevertheless we say that the Father made all things and that they are created through the Son, as is written, 'in wisdom you made all things (Ps. 103:24).' If, therefore, it is the Father who speaks, then he created in the image of the Word [73] (ad imaginem verbi); if it is the Son who speaks, then he created in the image of God the Father (ad imaginem dei patris). And so he reveals that man has a nature that is related to and intimate with God, that is of the rational man, according to which we are created in the image of God.

Philo's exegesis, which, in calling the Logos 'the second god' subordinates the Logos to God himself more clearly than anywhere else in his writings, is substantially rewritten by Ambrose. It is to be agreed with Savon that Ambrose's adaptation, with its insistence on the *equivalence* of Father and Son, can be only explained as a deliberate affirmation of Nicene theology in the face of a Philonic text which gives active support to a subordinationalist Logos doctrine.[30] The reason we are able to compare Ambrose's text with the Philonic original is that it has been preserved by Eusebius in his *Praeparatio Evangelica*. Eusebius quotes it because it illustrates the 'Hebrew theology' which he, as a sympathizer with a (moderately) Arianizing theology, finds conducive to his own views.[31] The danger of Philonic influence that Ambrose needs to combat, even while making such extensive use of his writings, was thus very real.

The texts that have been brought forward in this brief note all belong to the period of the 370's and 380's, when Nicene orthodoxy, already gaining the ascendancy, confronted the second wave of Arianism, as propagated by the Anomœans Aetius and Eunomius. To my knowledge—but here too I would be delighted to stand corrected—there are no sources that indicate an explicit connection between Philo and the first wave of Arianism, as initiated by Arius himself.[32] Arius' works are for the most part lost; his great opponent

---

[30] Savon, *op. cit.* 123.

[31] As pointed out by Savon, *op. cit.* 124; the text is found at *PE* 7.13.1–2.

[32] I exclude Eusebius here, because he is operating at a much more general level, attempting to establish historical antecedents for features of Christian

Athanasius never mentions Philo by name. In this light my observation in the article on Isidore was not wholly off the mark. Further investigation, however, may modify this picture.

Finally we should, perhaps, return to the remarks of Isidore which were the starting point of this little piece of research. Clearly Isidore's highly positive attitude towards Philo, as we find in *Ep.* 2.143, contrasts rather sharply with the more negative approach that we find in Gregory and Ambrose. Various explanations can be given. Isidore is writing in Egypt, and perhaps something still lingers of the Alexandrian heritage of Clement, Origen and Didymus, which caused Philo's writings to be [74] preserved in the first place. Moreover circumstances have changed: Isidore is writing a generation later, when the threat to orthodox doctrine was less direct. But we should also not discount the influence of Isidore's own local situation, where he is in contact with Jews who decline to make the move to Christianity. Philo the Alexandrian Jew is put to use as a weapon against Jewish recalcitrance.[33] Such are the curious twists that occur in intellectual history.

---

doctrine, and certainly not specifically linking Philo with Arianism.
[33] See the remarks at *art. cit.* (n. 1) 318.

CHAPTER NINE

PHILO OF ALEXANDRIA IN FIVE LETTERS
OF ISIDORE OF PELUSIUM

1. *Introduction*

One of the more obscure and unusual of the Church Fathers is Isidore of Pelusium, a Saint in both the Eastern and Western ecclesiastical tradition. A weighty tome in Migne's Patrologia Graeca (vol. 78) contains a collection of some 2000 letters from his pen. From these, and from rather scanty reports in other sources, we learn that he was a priest of the church of Pelusium to the east of the Nile delta, just under halfway from Alexandria to Jerusalem.[1] It appears that, appalled at the immorality and corruption of the local clergy, he came into sharp conflict with the bishop Eusebius and his fellow-priests, and decided to retire to the desert. There for many years he lived the ascetic life of a desert monk, probably as a member of a monastic community (κοινόβιον).[2] Through his epistolary activities, however, he maintained contact with a vast array of correspondents, ranging from humble folk in the neighbourhood and local civil and ecclesiastical dignitaries to eminent figures such as the Emperor Theodosius and the Alexandrian Patriarch Cyril.

The dates of his birth and death can be approximately fixed on the evidence of the Letters. He was born, possibly at Alexandria,[3] in about 365–375 AD.[4] We may be fairly certain that it was at Alexandria

---

*   [1] For general accounts, including biographical and bibliographical details, see Schmid (1948) 1–8, Quasten (1960) 180–185, Ritter (1971), and above all Évieux (1975). I have not gained access to Fouksas (1970).

[2] In the tradition he was the Abbot of a monastery, but this is not confirmed by early sources or the evidence of the Letters. Many of these, however, praise the monastic life.

[3] This is affirmed by Ephraem, the 6th century Patriarch of Antioch, according to Quasten (1960) 181 (no reference given).

[4] The traditional date is 365, but Évieux has shown that *Epp.* 1.178, 489 cannot

that he received his not inconsiderable training in classical literature, rhetoric, and (to a lesser extent) Greek philosophy. Here too,
we may surmise that he first gained acquaintance with writers in the
Alexandrian tradition such as Clement and Philo. But there is no
evidence that he came into direct contact with the leading exegete
and scholar of the church in [296] Alexandria, Didymus the blind.[5]
According to some sources he was a pupil of John Chrysostom, but
this must be taken in a spiritual sense. Isidore was a great admirer of
the bishop, and some of his letters are little more than extracts from
the latter's works. In his exegesis and his theological views he reveals
connections with both the Antiochean and the Alexandrian schools.
The date of his death must be placed in about 435 AD, for the last
topical references in the letters are to the Council of Ephesus (431)
and the events that followed it.

In the later Patristic and Byzantine period Isidore was above all
famous for his huge collection of letters. According to Severus of
Antioch (6th century) he wrote almost 3000. But the collection we
have is confined to a round 2000 letters, collected during his lifetime or soon after his death and arranged into a definitive edition
by the monks in the Akoimete monastery in Constantinople between
450 and 550.[6] A selection of 49 letters on mainly christological
subjects was translated into Latin by the Roman deacon Rusticus
during the 6th century and appended to the Acta of the Council of
Ephesus. The Letters were very popular during the Byzantine
period. In the 9th century Photius describes him, together with Basil
and Gregory of Nazianzus, as one of the masters of ancient Christian
epistolography, and also calls him a model of the priestly and ascetic
life.[7]

The corpus of Isidore's letters is not very well known, and has
been scarcely exploited for studies on intellectual life in the early
5th century. The main reason for the inaccessibility is the lack of a

---

have been written to the Praetorian Prefect Rufinus (d. 395), so Isidore may have
been born later.

[5] To the contrary, it has been speculated that he was the fourth member of the
student coterie of Synesius, to whom he writes some letters; cf. Lacombrade
(1951) 54f. But it requires some imagination to see him as a serious student of the
famous Neoplatonist philosopher and teacher Hypatia.

[6] Cf. Quasten (1960) 182. The corpus in the edition in Migne contains 2012
letters in 5 books, among which are 19 doublets. Rusticus tells us that the edition
he used in 566 contained 4 codices, each containing 500 letters.

[7] Ep. 207 Lauordas-Westerink.

modern edition.[8] The text published by Migne is a reprint of the edition of A. Morel dating back to 1638, with various readings added by P. Possinus (1670). But Morel's edition is itself a most curious composite, since it consists of three previous editions bundled together: J. de Billy and J. Chatard (Books I–III), C. Ritterhusius (IV), A. Schottius (V), each of whom contributed a Latin translation and learned notes. P. Évieux has shown that in the process the consistent consecutive numbering of the Letters in the manuscripts has been abandoned, and in the case of the last two [297] books, completely jumbled.[9] The text itself is poor and often confused, and totally fails to meet modern standards. Its greatest defect is the failure to make use of the oldest and by far best of the mss., the Codex Bα 1 of Grottaferrata. It is to be hoped that a critical edition will be available in the not too distant future.[10] Accessibility to the corpus is also hampered by the very imperfect indexing in Migne's reprint.[11]

The aim of this modest contribution is to examine the four letters in the Isidoran corpus in which the Church father makes direct reference to Philo of Alexandria, together with a fifth interesting letter which has hitherto been neglected by modern scholars. It forms part of a research project which aims to illuminate the fate of Philo's writings and thought in the Patristic period. Isidore's letters are interesting and valuable evidence of the way in which the Alexandrian Jew was known and regarded at the beginning of 5th century. It is a very great pleasure to be able to dedicate the article to Earle Hilgert, whose interest in all aspects of Philonic research is so wide-ranging that it will certainly extend to the information supplied by our obscure Egyptian desert Father.[12]

In modern times, after Isidore's testimony was published by Cohn in his great edition in 1896,[13] only two scholarly publications have

---

[8] My account of the various editions is based on Évieux (1975) 45ff.

[9] See Évieux (1975). In anticipation of the definitive edition which will have to revert to the mss. numbering, I have added the mss. numbers as listed by Évieux in brackets to the headings of the five letters dealt with in this article.

[10] According to Geerard (1979) 82 it is being prepared by P. Évieux. Unfortunately, despite repeated efforts, we have been unable to enter into contact with this scholar.

[11] Only an index of addressees and a very imperfect subject index. Most unfortunately there is no index of biblical references. The Letters are also not yet available on the TLG databank.

[12] See the excellent collection of bibliographical information on Philo in the Patristic period collected in Hilgert (1984) 79–81.

[13] C-W 1.cix–cx. The only other references to Isidore given in this edition are

been dedicated to the theme of Philo in Isidore. L. Bayer in a 1915 study on Isidore's classical education devotes a rather unsatisfactory discussion of less than 2 pages to the four main letters.[14] Much more valuable is the contribution of the distinguished German scholar L. Früchtel. In preparing his revised edition of Clement of Alexandria, Früchtel worked his way through the entire corpus looking for traces of usage of Clement and other authors. In two brief articles he not only makes penetrating comments on our 4 letters, but also notes passages in 14 other letters in which Isidore makes anonymous use of Philonic material.[15] [298]

     The method that I shall follow is as follows. For each letter the
* Greek text will be presented, followed by an English translation and a brief commentary. Unfortunately the text will have to be based on the defective textual basis found in Migne. It will be necessary to alter it at various points, as indicated in an *apparatus criticus*, which records only the deviations from Migne.[16] The translation is the first to be made into a modern language.[17] The commentary will be selective, above all focusing on those aspects of the letters which are of relevance to our knowledge of Philo and his presence in the church Fathers. The references in the commentary are to the lines of the Greek text (placed in square brackets in the translation). In some brief concluding remarks various themes that emerge in the letters will be brought together.

     Finally it should be pointed out that there is an important difference between the group of 4 letters in which Philo is actually named, and the other group in which anonymous use is made of Philonic material.[18] In the latter Isidore is simply appropriating ideas as it suits him. In the former Philo is being used *for strategic*

---

to *Ep.* 3.115 at *Jos.* 175, 3.289 at *Virt.* 59.

[14] Bayer (1915) 80–82.

[15] Früchtel (1938). Because the article is rather inaccessible I note the identifications it contains: *Ep.* 2.215 to *Spec.* 3.76; 3.104 to *Somn.* 2.147, *QG* 2.60; 3.160 to *Mos.* 1.31; 3.243 to *QG* 1.28; 3.288 (and 3.179) to *QG* 4.99; 3.356 to *Ios.* 5; 3.362 to *QE* 2.110; 4.87 to *Mos.* 1.141; 4.155 to *Mut.* 3; 5.169 to *Mos.* 2.27; 5.302 to *Anim.* 100. The prevalence of *Mos.* and the *Quaestiones* is notable. A number of these texts, e.g. the last one, are also found as brief *bon mots* in the Florilegia. One wonders whether Isidore took them from an anthology.

[16] The reader should note too that it was necessary to make numerous changes in the punctuation.

[17] I would like to offer my warm thanks to Prof. J. C. M. van Winden (Leiden), with whom I discussed the translation, and who saved me from several errors. Needless to say, responsibility for remaining shortcomings is entirely mine.

[18] As identified by Früchtel (1938); see above n. 15.

purposes, since there is presumably a reason why his name is explicitly mentioned. It is this deliberate use of the Philonic heritage that interests us most in the current article, and that is why I am concentrating on these particular letters. It should be emphasized, however, that this article does not offer a complete treatment of the subject of Philo's presence in this remarkable epistolary corpus. [299]

2. *Five letters: text, translation, commentary*

Ep. 2.143 (= *Ep.* 643 Évieux)

ΠΑΥΛΩΙ

ἄγαμαι τὴν ἀλήθειαν, τὴν τῶν συνετῶν τὰς ψυχὰς εἰς τὸ καὶ τῇ τῶν
οἰκείων δογμάτων προλήψει μαχήσασθαι περιστήσασαν. οὕτω γὰρ
σαφῆ καὶ λαμπρὰν τοῖς βουλομένοις κατοπτεῦσαι τὴν περὶ τῆς ἁγίας
τριάδος ἔννοιαν [οὗ] καὶ ἐν τῇ παλαιᾷ διαθήκῃ ἐγκατέσπαρται ἡ
5 διδασκαλία, ὡς καὶ Φίλωνα, καίτοι Ἰουδαῖον ὄντα καὶ ζηλωτὴν, δι᾽
ὧν ἀπολέλοιπε συγγραμμάτων ἀπομαχήσασθαι τῇ οἰκείᾳ θρησκείᾳ.
βασανίζων γὰρ τὸ εἰρημένον παρὰ τοῦ θεοῦ, «ἐν εἰκόνι θεοῦ ἐποίησα
τὸν ἄνθρωπον», ἠναγκάσθη ὑπὸ τῆς ἀληθείας καὶ ἐξεβιάσθη καὶ τὸν
τοῦ θεοῦ λόγον θεολογῆσαι. τί γάρ; εἰ καὶ δεύτερον τὸν συναΐδιον τῷ
10 πατρὶ, καὶ ἀριθμοῦ καὶ χρόνων ὄντα ἀνώτερον καλεῖ, τῆς ἀκριβείας μὴ
ἐφικνούμενος, ὅμως ἔννοιαν ἔσχε καὶ ἑτέρου προσώπου. καὶ οὐκ
ἐνταῦθα μόνον τοῦτο ἔπαθεν, ἀλλὰ καὶ τὸ θεὸς καὶ κύριος ἑρμηνεῦσαι
πειρώμενος, τῆς βασιλικωτάτης τριάδος ἔννοιαν ἔσχεν. ὁ λέγων γὰρ
ὅτι εἷς ἐστιν ὁ θεός, οὐ πρὸς τὸν ἀριθμὸν κατέδραμε τῆς μονάδος, ἀλλὰ
15 πρὸς τὸ μυστήριον τῆς τριάδος, τὸ τῶν μὲν πάντη διαιρετῶν ἑνικώ-
τερον τῶν δὲ ὄντως μοναδικῶν ἀφθονώτερον· καὶ οὕτως κατὰ κράτος
εἷλεν αὐτοῦ τὴν ψυχὴν, ὡς ἀναγκασθῆναι τοῦτο διαρρήδην καὶ εἰπεῖν
καὶ ἐν συγγράμμασι καταλεῖψαι. δύο γὰρ ἔφησεν εἶναι τὰς τοῦ ὄντος
δυνάμεις, ὧν ἡ μὲν ποιητικὴ καὶ εὐεργετικὴ, φησὶ, καλεῖται θεός· ἡ δὲ
20 βασιλικὴ καὶ τιμωρητικὴ κύριος, οὐ πόρρω βαίνων τοῦ εἰπόντος
«Χριστὸς θεοῦ δύναμις καὶ θεοῦ σοφία·» δύναμις οὐκ ἀνυπόστατος
ἀλλὰ ἐνυπόστατος καὶ παντοδύναμος καὶ ὑποστάσεων δημιουργὸς καὶ
ἰσοσθενὴς ἐκείνου, οὗ δύναμίς ἐστιν. καὶ πάλιν ὁ Φίλων περὶ τοῦ
θεάματος οὗ εἶδε Μωσῆς ἐκφράζων φησί· «θέαμα πληκτικώτατον
25 ὁρᾷ.» εἶτα μετ᾽ ὀλίγα· «κατὰ μέσην δὲ τὴν φλόγα μορφή τις ἦν περι-
καλλεστάτη τῶν ὁρατῶν ἐμφερὴς οὐδενί, θεοειδέστατον ἄγαλμα, φῶς
αὐγοειδέστερον τοῦ πυρὸς ἀπαστράπτουσα, ἣν ἄν τις ὑπετύπωσεν
εἰκόνα τοῦ ὄντος εἶναι.» εἰ δέ τις περὶ τῆς εἰκόνος ἀκριβῶς βούλεται
μαθεῖν, ἀκουέτω φράζοντος Παύλου περὶ τοῦ Χριστοῦ· «ὅς ἐστιν

30   εἰκὼν τοῦ θεοῦ τοῦ ἀοράτου.» οὐκοῦν κἀκεῖνος θεολογίας ὀρθοδόξου
      ἅπτεται. μὴ γὰρ δὴ τὴν ἀκρίβειαν ζήτει παρὰ τοῦ δυνηθέντος ὅλως διὰ
      σύνεσιν εἰλικρινῆ καὶ κατοπτεῦσαι τὴν ἀλήθειαν καὶ τῇ οἰκείᾳ
      θρησκείᾳ ἀπομαχέσασθαι. ἀλλ᾽ ἐκεῖνο ἐννόει, ὅτι εἰς ἓν πρόσωπον οὐ
      συνέκλεισε τὴν θεολογίαν, ὡς οἱ ἀπαίδευτοι τῶν Ἰουδαίων καθηγηταὶ
35   προλήψει τινὶ κατεχόμενοι δογματίζουσιν. οὐκ ἐκ τούτων δὲ μόνον
      πληκτικωτάτων ὄντων εἰς τοσαύτην προσήχθη, ὥς γε ἡγοῦμαι, τὴν
      ἔννοιαν, ἀλλὰ καὶ ἐκ τοῦ «ποιήσωμεν ἄνθρωπον κατὰ εἰκόνα ἡμετέ-
      ραν καὶ κατ᾽ ὁμοίωσιν·» καὶ ἐκ τοῦ «ἔβρεξε κύριος παρὰ κυρίου·» καὶ
      ἐκ τοῦ «ἐκάλεσε κύριος ἐν ὀνόματι κυρίου·» καὶ ἐκ τοῦ «εἶπεν ὁ κύριος
40   τῷ κυρίῳ μου· κάθου ἐκ δεξιῶν μου·» καὶ ἐκ τοῦ «ἐν σοὶ ὁ θεὸς, καὶ σὺ
      εἶ ὁ θεός·» τοὺς γὰρ λέγοντας ὅτι [300] μυριάκις ἐστὶν ἅγιος ὁ θεὸς,
      καὶ τὸ «ἅγιος, ἅγιος ἅγιος κύριος σαβαὼθ» παρερμηνεῦσαι τολμῶντας,
      λαμπρῶς ἐλέγχει τὸ «ἐξεζήτησα τὸ πρόσωπόν σου, τὸ πρόσωπόν σου,
      κύριε, ζητήσω. μὴ ἀποστρέψῃς τὸ πρόσωπον ἀπ᾽ ἐμοῦ.» εἰ μὴ γὰρ τὴν
45   ἁγίαν τριάδα ἀνεκήρυττεν ὁ φράσας, περιττολογίας δίκαιος ἂν εἴη
      ἀπαιτηθῆναι δίκας. οὐ μόνον δὲ ἐν τούτῳ· χρῆναι γὰρ οἶμαι ἐπὶ
      σαφέστερον ὁρμῆσαι ῥητόν· ἀλλὰ καὶ ἐν τῷ «θῦσον τῷ θεῷ θυσίαν
      αἰνέσεως, καὶ ἀπόδος τῷ ὑψίστῳ τὰς εὐχάς σου, καὶ ἐπικάλεσαί με ἐν
      ἡμέρᾳ θλίψεως, καὶ ἐξελοῦμαί σε, καὶ δοξάσεις με.» εἰ μὴ γὰρ ἡ τριὰς
50   ἐνταῦθα σαφῶς ἐκηρύττετο, ἐχρῆν ῥηθῆναι· θῦσον τῷ θεῷ θυσίαν
      αἰνέσεως, καὶ ἀπόδος αὐτῷ τὰς εὐχάς σου, καὶ ἐπικάλεσαι αὐτὸν ἐν
      ἡμέρᾳ θλίψεως σου, καὶ ἐξελεῖταί σε, καὶ δοξάσεις αὐτόν. ἀλλ᾽ οὕτω
      μὲν οὐκ ἐρρέθη· εἴρηται δὲ ὡς εἴρηται. σαφῶς γὰρ καὶ διὰ τούτων καὶ
      δι᾽ ἄλλων πολλῶν [ἅπερ] (ἵνα μὴ μακρὸν ποιήσω τὸν λόγον νῦν
55   παραλείψω τοῖς ἀκούειν δυναμένοις) κηρύττει ἡ παλαιὰ διαθήκη ὅτι
      οὐχ ἑνὸς προσώπου [κηρύττει] δεσποτείας, ἀλλὰ τριῶν μὲν ὑπο-
      στάσεων μιᾶς δὲ οὐσίας· ἵνα καὶ Ἰουδαίων στηλιτεύσῃ τὴν ὡς ἐφ᾽
      ἑνὸς προσώπου οὐχ ὑγιῆ ἔννοιαν, οἷς καὶ Σαβέλλιος ἠκολούθησεν,
      ἴσως ἐκ τῆς ἄγαν τοῦ υἱοῦ πρὸς τὸν πατέρα ἰσότητος εἰς τὸ μίαν
60   ὑπόστασιν δογματίσαι νευρωθείς, καὶ Ἑλλήνων ἐξοστρακίσῃ τὴν
      πολυθείαν, ὧν Ἄρειος καὶ Εὐνόμιος ἑάλωσαν εἶναι φοιταταί, τὴν τῶν
      ὑποστάσεων διαφορὰν εἰς τὴν οὐσίαν παραλόγως ἑλκύσαντες. εἰ δέ τις
      φαίη· διὰ τί γὰρ μὴ σαφῶς καὶ διαρρήδην ἐξ ἀρχῆς ταῦτα κεκήρυκται;
      φαίην ὅτι μάλιστα μὲν τοῖς συνετῶς ἀκούουσι λαμπρά ἐστιν αὕτη καὶ
65   ἀπόδειξις καὶ διδασκαλία, ὡς καὶ τῷ σοφῷ ἔδοξε Φίλωνι. εἰ δὲ καὶ
      συνεσκιασμένως ἐρρέθη, ἐκεῖνο λογίζεσθαι χρή, ὅτι Ἰουδαίοις τοῖς εἰς
      πολυθείαν ῥέπουσι νομοθετῶν οὐκ ἐδοκίμασε διαφορὰν προσώπων
      εἰσαγαγεῖν· ἵνα καὶ μὴ διάφορον φύσιν ἐν ταῖς ὑποστάσεσιν εἶναι
      δογματίσαντες εἰς εἰδωλολατρίαν ἐκκυλισθῶσιν· ἀλλὰ τὸ τῆς μον-

70 αρχίας ἐξ ἀρχῆς μαθόντες μάθημα, κατὰ μικρὸν τὸ τῶν ὑποστάσεων
ἀναδιδαχθῶσι δόγμα, τὸ πάλιν εἰς ἑνότητα φύσεως ἀνατρέχον· ὡς
εἶναι τὰ μὲν ἑνικῶς λεγόμενα τῆς ταυτότητος τῆς φύσεως παρα-
στατικά· τὰ δὲ ὑπερβαίνοντα τὸν ἑνικὸν ἀριθμὸν τῆς τῶν ὑποστάσεων
ἰδιότητος τῆς εἰς μίαν οὐσίαν συναγομένης. τὸ μὲν γὰρ διαφόρους
75 φύσεις ὑποτίθεσθαι Ἑλληνικόν· τὸ δὲ ἓν πρόσωπον ἤγουν μίαν
ὑπόστασιν, Ἰουδαϊκόν. τὸ δὲ πλατύνοντα εἰς τὴν ἁγίαν τριάδα τὰς
ὑποστάσεις εἰς μίαν οὐσίαν συνάγειν ὀρθότατόν ἐστι καὶ ἀληθέστατον δόγμα.

4 Migne (posthac M) per dittographiam legit [οὗ] ἔσχεν. ὁ λέγων γὰρ ὅτι εἷς
ἐστιν ὁ θεός, οὐ πρὸς τὸν ἀριθμὸν κατέδραμε τῆς μονάδος, ἀλλὰ πρὸς τὸ μυστήριον
τῆς τριάδος, quae post τῆς βασιλικωτάτης τριάδος ἔννοιαν (r. 13) transponenda;
cf. Ritterhusii adnotatio ad textum et textus citatus apud Souda s.v. θεός. 7 ἐποίησε
M. 19 M τὰς ὄντως δυνάμεις, ὧν ἡ μὴν ποιητική. 27 ὑπετύπωσεν M. 35 μόνον
πληκτιτωτάτων secl. M perperam. 41 τολμῶντες M. 54 ἅπερ et κήρυττει seclusi. 60
ἐξοστρακίσαι M. 63 σοφῶς M.

To Paul

I admire the truth for the way in which she has induced the souls of
intelligent men even to combat the preconceived opinion they have
of [301] their own doctrines. For the teaching of the truth has
embedded the concept of the holy Trinity so clearly and lucidly also
in the Old Testament for those who wish to observe it that Philo,
though a Jew and a zealous one at that, in the writings which he left
behind comes into conflict with his own religion. When he examines
the words spoken by God, 'in the image of God I made man (Gen.
9:6)', he is constrained and compelled by the truth also to recognize
the divine Logos as God. What is the case? Even if he calls him who
is coeternal with the [10] Father 'second' and 'higher than number
and time', failing therein to reach precision, nevertheless he did
gain a conception of another person. And not only did this happen
to him in this instance, but also when he attempted to interpret the
expression 'God and Lord' he gained a conception of the most royal
(or highest) Trinity. He that asserts that God is one, does not run up
against the numerical unit of the monad, but rather against the
mystery of the Trinity, which is more unified than wholly discrete
entities but richer than what is truly monadic. Indeed this teaching
of the truth took hold of his soul with such force that he was
compelled both to declare it quite explicitly and leave it behind in
his writings. He declared that there were two powers of Him that is,
of which the one, he says, is the creative and beneficent power and is

called God (*theos*), the other is the [20] royal and punitive power and is called Lord (*kurios*). In so doing he moves not very far from the one who said 'Christ the power of God and the wisdom of God (1 Cor. 1:24)', not a unsubstantial power but one with a separate existence, all-powerful, creator of the hypostases, of equal strength to the one whose power he is. In another text Philo, giving an account of the vision that Moses saw, describes him as 'seeing a most startling sight'. Then a few lines later he continues: 'In the middle of the flame was an exceedingly beautiful form, unlike any visible object, a most God-like image, emanating a light more brilliant than that of the fire. One might conjecture it to be an image of He who is.' But if a person wishes to gain more precise knowledge about the image, let him hear Paul's description of Christ, 'who is [30] image of the unseen God (Col. 1:15)'. Thus Philo too comes close to orthodox speaking about God. You should certainly not seek to obtain precision from him who through the sheer purity of his understanding was actually able to gain sight of the truth and even came into conflict with his own religion. But this you should understand, that he did not confine his speaking about God to a single person, as is the doctrinal position of the uneducated teachers of the Jews who are held fast in their preconceived opinion. And it was not only on the basis of these quite startling texts that he developed such an, in my view, advanced position, but also from the text ' let us make man according to our image [302] and likeness (Gen. 1:26)', and from the text 'the Lord rained from the Lord (Gen. 19:24)', and from the text 'the Lord called in the name of the Lord (Ex. 33:19?)', and from the text 'the Lord said [40] to my Lord, sit at my right side (Ps. 109:1), and from the text 'in you is God and you are God (Ps. 24:5?). Those who assert that God is holy a countless number of times, and have the temerity to misinterpret the text 'holy, holy, holy is the Lord Sabaoth (Is. 6:3)' are brilliantly refuted by the text 'I sought your face (person), your face, Lord, I shall seek. Do not turn your face from me' (Ps. 26:8)'. Unless the writer was proclaiming the holy Trinity, he would justly stand accused of superfluous language. This is not only the case here, but—I think I should embark on a clearer verse—in the text 'sacrifice to God a sacrifice of praise, and render your prayers to the most High, and call upon me in a day of trouble, and I shall deliver you, and you shall glorify me (Ps. 49:14–15). If it was not the holy Trinity [50] that was clearly being proclaimed here, what should have been said was: sacrifice to God a sacrifice of praise, and render him your prayers, and call upon him in the day of your trouble, and He will deliver you, and you shall glorify him. But this was not what was said. It was spoken in the way it was spoken. With all clarity, therefore, both through these texts and many others which the Old Testament pronounces—but so as not to unduly lengthen my account I will leave these to those able to understand—, it pronounces the rulership, not of one person, but of three hypostases and one substance. Its intention is, on the one hand, to denounce the Jews for having an unsound notion focussed on a single person —in whose footsteps also Sabellius followed, possibly encouraged to reach the doctrine of one [60] substance through an excessive regard for the equality of the Son with the Father—, on the other hand to banish the polytheism of the Greeks, whose disciples Arius and Eunomius have been convicted of being, because they fallaciously extended the difference of the hypostases to the aspect of substance. If someone should object 'why were these doctrines not proclaimed clearly and explicitly from the very beginning?', my answer would be that both as demonstration and as teaching it *was* pellucidly clear to men of intelligence and understanding, as it indeed was to the wise Philo. And if these words have been spoken in an enigmatic fashion, it should be taken into account that Scripture in giving the Law did not think it a good idea to introduce a difference of persons to Jews who showed an inclination to polytheism, lest they should teach that there was also a difference in nature in the hypostases and so plunge headlong into idolatry; but it was better that, having learnt from the beginning the tenet of divine [70] unicity, they should gradually be taught the doctrine of the hypostases which reverts back again to a unity of nature; thus pronouncements of unity were indicative of the sameness of the divine nature, while statements [303] exceeding the single number revealed the individuality of the hypostases which is contracted into a single being. The assumption of different natures is Hellenic, the assumption of a single person or hypostasis is Judaic. To extend the hypostases to the holy Trinity and contract them into a single being is absolutely true and orthodox doctrine.

COMMENTARY
Theme: The orthodox doctrine of the Trinity, which represents the full truth of Scripture, avoids the excess of divine unity espoused in Judaism

and the excess of divine plurality adhered to by Hellenism. Philo was intelligent enough to perceive something of this truth in his reading of the Old Testament and so came into conflict with his own religion. But you will not find the full orthodox position in his writings.

Addressee. Paul was presumably a layman, since no title is given. From other letters we learn that he was a man with a good deal of intellectual curiosity, who liked to pose Isidore questions on scientific and theological subjects (cf. 2.100, 3.33 etc.). The previous letter (*Ep.* 2.142) is a short statement on the Holy Trinity affirming that one should not compress the divine nature Ἰουδαϊκῶς. Paul must have asked to him to elaborate on this, perhaps posing the question why the Old Testament does not contain the doctrine of the Trinity. He may even have objected that Philo was a Jew and yet had premonitions of Christian doctrine. Isidore proceeds to explain his position in much more detail.

line 1. ἄγαμαι. Isidore is fond of the formula 'I admire'; cf. 3.289, 4.169. The truth is personified, an easy move because it is virtually identified with διδασκαλία (scriptural teaching). We note the somewhat sententious style characteristic of late ancient epistolography. As Isidore writes in 5.133, the letter should be neither ἀκόσμητος nor εἰς θρύψιν κεκοσμημένος ἢ τρυφήν, but rather should have such adornment as suffices both for usefulness and beauty. Sometimes initial phrases of politesse were stripped from letters on publication. In this case, however, Isidore probably prefers to dispense with formalities and launch into a striking beginning.

ll.3–4. τὴν περὶ τῆς ἁγίας τριάδος ἔννοιαν [οὗ]. The text as printed in Migne is seriously corrupt because three lines have been inserted in the second sentence which actually belong about 8 lines further down. Not only does Ritterhusius point out the correct text in a note to Migne, but it is confirmed by an extract in the *Souda*, which most interestingly refers to the Philonic conception of θεὸς καὶ κύριος as summarized by Isidore in its entry for the word θεός (1.698 Adler). C-W 1.cviii fail to print the correct text, even though they mention the Byzantine witness in a footnote. The text as given allows a perfect parallelism between the first sentence, which is quite general, and the second sentence, which gives the particular application to Philo.

l.5. ζηλωτὴν. Philo's zeal presumably refers especially to his efforts on behalf of the Jewish community of Alexandria during the crisis of 38 AD reported by both Josephus and Eusebius. But cf. also Eusebius' statement that he expended much πόνος on τὰ θεῖα καὶ πάτρια γράμματα. Isidore twice (here and in l.18) emphasizes that Philo left behind writings, i.e. that there is concrete documentary evidence of his views. [304]

l.6. «ἐν εἰκόνι θεοῦ... Früchtel (1938) 765 errs in pointing to Gen. 1:26 and *Opif.* 69. The text is Gen. 9:6, as given exegesis in *QG* 2.62 (Greek text at Eus. *PE* 7.13.1, cf. Petit (1978) 116). Philo asks the question why God speaks as if about another God, and not about himself. This is similar to the exegesis practised by Isidore, who looks for oddities of phrasing in the biblical text as hints of the doctrine of the Trinity. The Philonic passage is the only one in which he explicitly describes the Logos as τὸν δεύτερον θεόν, the term which Isidore cites at l.9 (also δεύτερον at *QE* 2.68, but there in a hierarchy of seven, text at PLCL Suppl. 2.256).

l.9. θεολογῆσαι. Not 'theologize about', but rather 'acknowledge as divine or as God'. Numerous exx. in Lampe (1961) s.v. §E. Note esp. an early example in Justin *Dial.* 56.15, εἰ οὖν καὶ ἄλλον τινα θεολογεῖν καὶ κυριολογεῖν τὸ πνεῦμα τὸ ἅγιόν φατε ὑμεῖς παρὰ τὸν πατέρα τῶν ὅλων καὶ τὸν Χρίστον αὐτοῦ..., where the Philonic doctrine of the two divine names seems to lie just under the surface (and with probably a pun meant on κυριολογεῖν).

ll.9–11. The contrast between incipient and fully-fledged Christian terminology is deliberate. συναΐδιος is a specifically Patristic word, not found in Philo or Greek philosophy. πρόσωπον is a *terminus technicus* for persons of the Godhead unknown in this sense to Philo. He speaks sometimes in biblical terms of oracles coming ἐκ προσώπου τοῦ θεοῦ (e.g. *Mut.* 13, 39 etc.). But Isidore will have been especially impressed with *QE* 2.66, in which Philo interprets the *faces* of the Cherubim in terms of the divine powers. For δεύτερος see above on l.9. The phrase ἀριθμοῦ καὶ χρόνων ὄντα ἀνώτερον is problematic. Isidore clearly means it as a quote or paraphrase from Philo's writings. But to my knowledge this phrase is nowhere to be found. There are a number of texts which describe God as above number or time (cf. *Leg.* 2.3, *Praem.* 40 etc.), but it is difficult to apply these to the Logos. A possible solution is that Isidore slightly misread *QE* 2.68, where Philo, giving exegesis of Ex. 25:21b, says of God as ὁ λέγων (and not as λόγος) that he is καὶ ἑνὸς καὶ μονάδος καὶ ἀρχῆς πρεσβύτερος.

l.12. τὸ θεὸς καὶ κύριος. The reference to the divine names only becomes clear in ll.18–20, where Isidore outlines the Philonic doctrine of the powers of God as τὸ ὄν. The coupling of the creative-beneficent and the royal-punitive powers makes it clear that his main source is the exegesis of the Ark of the Covenant that Philo gives at *QE* 2.68 (except that Philo speaks of κολαστήριος instead of τιμωρητική; cf. also *QG* 1.57). But the formulation δύο τὰς τοῦ ὄντος δυνάμεις indicates that he has also read other texts on the powers; cf. esp. *Mos.* 2.99, *Fug.* 94-96. The text *Abr.* 122, cited by Bayer (1915) 81, is less suitable for Isidore, since there Philo regards the divine triad (cf. the three angels in Gen. 18) as constituting the lesser mysteries and a δεύτερος πλοῦς, whereas the vision of the divine unity is the real truth. In *QE* 2.68 Philo interprets the various parts of the Ark in terms of (1) τὸ ὄν (or ὁ ὤν) as ὁ λέγων (cf. Ex. 25:21), (2) the Logos, (3) the creative power, (4) the royal power, (5) the beneficent power, (6) the punitive power, (7) the noetic cosmos. Isidore relates (2)–(6), and perhaps also (1) (see above on ll.9–11), all to Christ the Logos.

ll.18–31. We note how Isidore, who is not averse to repetition, twice follows a sequence of thought with the following steps: (1) introduction of a Philonic text; (2) a parallel text in Paul pointed out; (3) conclusion that Philo does not stand so far removed from orthodox doctrine, i.e. as represented by Paul interpreted in 5th century dogmatic terms. The terms ἀνυπόστατος and ἐνυπό[305]στατος (l.22) are characteristic of the controversies of 4th and 5th centuries; cf. Lampe (1961) s.vv. Both in his Christology and his Trinitarian doctrine Isidore anticipates the formula of the Council of Chalcedon in 451 (ἕνα καὶ τὸν αὐτὸν Χρίστον ἐν δύο φύσεσιν, ἑκατέρας φύσεως εἰς ἓν πρόσωπον καὶ μίαν ὑπόστασιν συντρεχούσης); cf. Schmid (1948) 77–85, Grillmeier (1975) 497.

ll.23–28. Isidore cites *Mos.* 1.65–66 *verbatim*, probably through direct consultation of the text. The variants are minor: both πληκτικώτατον and ὑπετόπασεν are found in certain mss. of Philo (but not ὑπετύπωσεν which Migne reads). Isidore stops at a strategic point, for Philo's next words καλείσθω δὲ ἄγγελος are less suitable for the doctrine of the Trinity.

ll.34–35. We note the present tense used with reference to the 'teachers of the Jews', suggesting an on-going controversy still very much alive at this time.

ll.37–53. The sequence of eight texts used to prove the presence of the doctrine of the Trinity in the Old Testament can conveniently be divided into four groups:

(a) Gen. 1:26. The plural verb indicates plurality in the Godhead. Cf. Philo's exegesis at *Opif.* 72–75, which is not explicit on exactly who God's helpers are. On the Jewish background, both Hellenistic and Rabbinic, cf. Runia (1986) 248, Segal (1977) 122ff. Justin used the text for Christian apologetics against the Jews at *Dial.* 62.1.

(b) Gen. 19:24, Ex. 33:19, Ps. 109:1, Ps. 24:5. In all four texts as quoted by Isidore the name of the Lord or of God is repeated. Only in the third is the LXX followed at all accurately. The identification of the 4th text given in Migne is far from certain, since the LXX text reads: καὶ δίδαξόν με, ὅτι σὺ εἶ ὁ θεὸς ὁ σωτήρ μου. But I cannot find a better text. The texts are clearly traditional in the Christian apologetic tradition; e.g. the 1st and 3rd texts are used by Justin at *Dial.* 56.12–14, 23 (but for the Rabbis Gen. 19:24 was regarded as a potential source of heresy; cf. Segal (1977) 130). Philo does not use them as such, but the same exegetical technique is found at *Somn.* 1.227–228 with reference to Gen. 31:13 (cf. Segal (1977) 159ff.).

(c) Is. 6:3, Ps. 26:8. Two texts in which a single linguistic element is repeated three times, πρόσωπον naturally suggesting the doctrine of the *persons* of the Trinity. μυρίακις suggests Jewish counter-polemic against Christian use of Isaiah's vision to support the doctrine of the Trinity. Philo cites Is. 6:1–2 at *De Deo* 6 and, no doubt identifying the Seraphim with the Cherubim, interprets them as divine powers used in the creation of the cosmos (cf. Siegert (1988) 94ff.). Note also the exegesis in terms of the Trinity by a (converted?) Jew recorded by Origen at *De Princ.* 1.3.4, 4.3.14. But Philo never cites Is. 6:3.

(d) Ps. 49:14–15. The same technique of giving an alternative reading to show what is not meant is used in the next letter we shall discuss. Isidore identifies three persons in θεῷ, τῷ ὑψίστῳ, and με. The text is not used by Philo.

To sum up, the texts and the methods of exegesis have a background in Christian apologetic exegesis, anterior Jewish discussions on God's oneness, and Jewish response to Christian doctrines of the Logos and the Trinity. To all of them the key is what Isidore describes as περιττολογία, i.e pleonasm that is stylistically unacceptable unless the biblical author intended to convey a doctrine through semi-concealment. Isidore assumes that Philo has been influenced by these texts, but he cannot have derived this from his reading of the treatises (except perhaps in the case of Gen. 1:26). Finally we note that in *Ep.* 3.142 Isidore [306] follows a similar procedure, this time using the texts Gen. 1:26, 19:24, Deut. 6:4 (the *Shema!*).

ll.57–62. Both Jewish monotheism and Greek polytheism have had a pernicious influence on some Christian theologians, resulting in heresies of opposed kinds (cf. *Ep.* 1.90 καὶ παρὰ Ἕλλησι μὲν..., καὶ παρὰ Ἰουδαίοις... πολλὰς αἱρέσεις ἔτεκεν ὁ διάβολος). The former seduced Sabellius (early 3rd century) to his 'modal monarchianism', i.e. the differentiation within the Godhead was merely a matter of modes of operation. The latter led to the 'subordinationism' of Arius (d. 336) and Eunomius (d. 396), in which the Son and the Holy Spirit were not co-equal with the Father, but created from Him. Isidore writes many letters on the subjects of the various heresies; e.g. 1.67, 241 (to Synesius), 246–7, 371, 422, 3.141, 149, 334 etc. Note esp. 1.246–7, 3.149 which contain similar themes to our letter (in the latter Sabellius is associated with Judaism). Modern scholars perceive Philo as the 'Father of Arianism' (cf. Wolfson (1956) 585ff., Mortley (1973) 9, Williams (1987) 117–124), but to my knowledge he was never accused of such by the Church Fathers themselves.

ll.65–69. The reason why the doctrine of the Trinity is concealed (cf. l.65 συνεσκιασμένως) in the Old Testament is now disclosed: otherwise the Jews certainly would have inclined to more to polytheism and idolatry than they already did. But the sage Philo (note the epithet) saw through the divine strategy.

ll.69–78. Through comparison with Judaism and Hellenism the orthodox doctrine of the Trinity can be now expressed with quasi-mathematical precision. From the historical perspective, however, Isidore's dialectic surely reminds us of Hegel's view of the history of religion, even if the philosopher does not focus on the aspect of plurality; cf. for example Taylor (1975) 503, 'the incarnate but parochial God [Hellenism] and the absolute but separated God [Judaism] together issue in the supreme God incarnate'.

ll.77–78 ἀληθέστατον δόγμα. Elegant return to the opening theme of the letter, with scriptural truth and orthodox doctrine now combined in a single phrase.

Ep. 2.270 (= *Ep.* 770 Évieux)

ΑΠΟΛΛΩΝΩΙ ΕΠΙΣΚΟΠΩΙ

Πῶς νοητέον τὸ γεγραμμένον· «μήποτε τοῖς ὀφθαλμοῖς αὐτῶν ἴδωσι, καὶ τοῖς ὠσὶν ἀκούσωσι».

ἡ μεταβολὴ τῶν προσώπων τὸν νοῦν τῶν εἰρημένων λαμπρῶς κηρύττει. εἰ μὲν γὰρ πρὸς τὸν λαὸν ἄπαντα ῥηθῆναι ἐχρῆν, οὕτως ἂν ἐρρήθη·
5 πορευθείς, εἶπον τῷ λαῷ τούτῳ· ἀκοῇ ἀκούσετε, καὶ οὐ μὴ συνίητε, καὶ βλέποντες βλέψετε, καὶ οὐ μὴ ἴδητε. ἐπαχύνθη γὰρ ἡ καρδία ὑμῶν, καὶ τοῖς ὠσὶ βαρέως ἠκούσατε, καὶ τοὺς ὀφθαλμοὺς ὑμῶν ἐκαμμύσατε, μή ποτε ἴδητε τοῖς ὀφθαλμοῖς, καὶ τοῖς ὠσὶν ἀκούσητε, καὶ τῇ καρδίᾳ συνῆτε, καὶ ἐπιστρέψητε, καὶ ἰάσωμαι ὑμᾶς. εἰ δ᾽ οὕτω μὲν οὐκ
0 ἐρρήθη, μεταβολὴν δὲ ἐμφαίνει προσώπων τριῶν τὰ λεγόμενα, παρ᾽ οὗ τε καὶ πρὸς ὃν καὶ περὶ οὗ ὁ λόγος, τοιοῦτόν τινα ὠδίνει νοῦν τῶν προκειμένων ἡ δύναμις· «πορευθεὶς εἶπον τῷ λαῷ τούτῳ· ἀκοῇ ἀκούσετε, καὶ οὐ μὴ συνίητε, καὶ βλέποντες βλέψετε, καὶ οὐ μὴ ἴδητε».

εἶτα ὡς τοῦ προφήτου πυθομένου τὴν [307] αἰτίαν, ἢ μὴ πυθομένου
15 μὲν, διδασκομένου δὲ ἐρρήθη· «ἐπαχύνθη γὰρ ἡ καρδία τοῦ λαοῦ τούτου, καὶ τοῖς ὠσὶ βαρέως ἤκουσαν, καὶ τοὺς ὀφθαλμοὺς ἐκάμμυσαν».
εἰ τοίνυν τῇ ἑαυτῶν, ὡς ἄν τις εἴποι, ἀντιπράττουσι σωτηρίᾳ, δι' ἣν
αἰτίαν κηρύξαι με προστάττεις; τάχα πώς φησι· τοῦτο γὰρ ἐνταῦθα
μηνύει τό· «μήποτ' ἴδωσι τοῖς ὀφθαλμοῖς, καὶ τοῖς ὠσὶν ἀκούσωσι, καὶ
20 τῇ καρδίᾳ συνῶσι, καὶ ἐπιστρέψωσι, καὶ ἰάσομαι αὐτούς.» τὸ γὰρ
μήποτε ἐνταῦθα, οὐκ ἀναίρεσιν ἀκοῆς, ἀλλ' ἐλπίδα ἐμφαίνει ὑπακοῆς.
καὶ ὅτι καὶ οὕτως λαμβάνεται, ἄκουσον τῶν ὄχλων τῶν Ἰουδαϊκῶν, τί
φασι περὶ τοῦ Σωτῆρος· «οὐ τοῦτον ἐζήτουν οἱ Φαρισαῖοι ἀποκτεῖναι;
ἰδοὺ παρρησίᾳ λαλεῖ, καὶ οὐδὲν αὐτῷ λέγουσι· μήποτε ἀληθῶς
25 ἔγνωσαν ὅτι οὗτός ἐστιν ὁ Χριστός;» ἔθος δὲ τοῖς σοφοῖς, ὧν εἷς εἶναι
δοκεῖ καὶ Φίλων, τὸ μήποτε ἀντὶ τοῦ ἴσως ἢ ἔσθ' ὅτε τάττειν. τὸ γὰρ
μήποτε, εἰκότως ἀντὶ τοῦ ἴσως, εὐλόγως τάττουσιν. εἰ δὲ καὶ παρὰ
θεοπνεύστου ἀνδρὸς θέλεις τὴν μαρτυρίαν ταύτην λαβεῖν, ἄκουε τοῦ
Παύλου γράφοντος· «δοῦλον δὲ κυρίου οὐ δεῖ μάχεσθαι, ἀλλ' ἤπιον
30 εἶναι πρὸς πάντας, διδακτόν, ἀνεξίκακον, ἐν πραότητι παιδεύοντα
τοὺς ἀντιδιατιθεμένους, μήποτε δώῃ αὐτοῖς ὁ θεὸς ἐπίγνωσιν εἰς
σωτηρίαν.» τὸ γὰρ μήποτε κἀνταῦθα εἴρηται ἀντὶ τοῦ ἔσθ' ὅτε, τάχα,
πως. ἐλπίδα γὰρ μετανοίας ἐμφαίνει, οὐκ ἀναίρεσιν. καὶ ἑτέρωθι δὲ
γέγραπται· «ἔλεγξον φίλον, μήποτε οὐκ ἐποίησεν.» εἰ γὰρ οὕτω νοηθείη
35 τὸ προφητικὸν χωρίον, καὶ τῷ θεῷ τὸ πρέπον φυλαχθείη τὰ αὐτοῦ
πράττειν προῃρημένῳ. σώζεσθαι γὰρ ἐκ παντὸς τρόπου τοὺς εἰς κακίαν
καλινδουμένους βούλεται, καὶ πέμπει τοὺς θεραπεύσοντας, οὐκ
ἀγνοῶν μὲν ὅτι διαφθαρήσονται ὑπὸ τῆς νόσου, τὴν δ' ἀπολογίαν
αὐτῶν ὑποτεμνόμενος. εἰ γὰρ κἀκεῖνοι οὐκ ἀπήνεγκαν ἐκ τῆς μανίας,
40 ἀλλὰ τό γε αὐτὸν τὰ αὐτοῦ πράττειν ἐκ τούτου περιγέγονε. καὶ τῷ θεῷ
τοίνυν τὸ πρέπον φυλαχθείη, καὶ ὁ προφήτης οὐ δόξει μάτην ἀπε-
στάλθαι, οὐδὲ ὕβρεως διάκονος νομισθήσεται, ἀλλὰ θεραπείας καὶ
ἰάσεως ὑπηρέτης εὑρεθήσεται. ἀπεστάλη γὰρ οὐχ ὑβρίσων ἁπλῶς,
ἀλλ' ἐγκαλέσων μὲν τοῖς πλημμελοῦσι, προσοίσων δὲ καὶ δείξων τὰ
45 πταίσματα, καλέσων δὲ εἰς μετάνοιαν, ἐπιστρέφουσι δὲ θεραπείαν
εὐαγγελισόμενος.

26 καὶ om. M. 35 αὐτοῦ M. 39 ἀνήνεγκαν M. 40 αὐτοῦ M.

To the Bishop Apollonius

How are we understand the text μή ποτε τοῖς ὀφθαλμοῖς αὐτῶν
ἴδωσι, καὶ τοῖς ὠσὶν ἀκούσωσι (*mēpote* they see with eyes and hear
with their ears) (Is. 6:10, Matt. 13:15)'?

The change of persons indicates the meaning of the words with full clarity. For if they were meant to be spoken to the entire people, they would have been spoken as follows: Go, say to this people: you will hear very well but not understand at all, and you will see very well but not perceive at all. For your heart has become dull and with your ears you can hardly hear and your eyes you have closed, lest ever you should see with your eyes and hear with your ears and understand with your heart [308] and you should turn to me and I should heal you. If the words are not pronounced in this way [10], but indicate a change involving three different persons, namely the source, the addressee and the subject of the speech, then the force of the proposed text delivers a meaning as follows: 'Go, say to this people: you will actually hear but not understand at all, and you will actually see but not perceive at all.' Then, as if the prophet has inquired as to the reason, or without having inquired has been informed what the reason is, it is said: 'For your heart has become dull and with your ears you can hardly hear and your eyes you have closed.' If therefore they act against, as someone might say, their own salvation, why do you bid me to preach to them?, the prophet maybe says. For this is what is indicated here by the words 'perhaps they might see with their eyes and hear with their ears and understand [20] with their heart and they should turn to me and I should heal them'. For the word *mēpote* here reveals not destruction of hearing, but rather hope of obedience. As evidence that the word indeed is meant in this way, listen to what the crowd of Jews says concerning the Saviour: 'Did not the Pharisees seek to kill him? Behold, he speaks quite openly, and yet they say nothing to him. Is it so the case that they truly recognize that this man is the Christ? (John 7:25-26)' Among the men of wisdom, of which Philo is reputed to be one, it is customary to write down the word *mēpote* instead of *isōs* or *esth'hote*. In doing this they adhere to good style. If you also wish to obtain evidence of this practice from a divinely inspired man, listen to Paul when he writes: 'A servant of the Lord should not fight, but rather be gentle [30] towards all, a good teacher, long-suffering, correcting his opponents with gentleness. God may perhaps (*mēpote*) grant them recognition leading to salvation (2 Tim. 2:24-25)'. Here too the word *mēpote* is used instead of *esth'hote*, *tacha*, *pōs*, for it reveals hope of repentance, not destruction. And elsewhere it is written: 'Examine a friend; he perhaps (*mēpote*) did not do it. (Sirach 19:13)' If the prophetic passage were to be understood in this way, one could preserve what is fitting to God as One who chooses to do what is appropriate to himself. For in every way possible he wishes to save those who succumb to evil, and so sends men with a healing mission. He is quite well aware that the evildoers will be destroyed by their disease, but eliminates the self-defence they might put forward. Even if those men have not turned away from their madness, [40] at least from this course of events it results that God carries out what is appropriate to himself. Thus what is fitting to God will be preserved, while the prophet will not seem to have been sent out for nothing, and he will not be considered an instrument of violence, but will be found to be a servant of care and healing. His mission was not simply to bring about violence, [309] but to rebuke those who have gone astray, to show up and make clear their failings, to invite to repentance, and to promise healing to those who change their ways.

COMMENTARY

Theme: Philo is briefly invoked in support of a bold piece of exegesis. Numerous of Isidore's letters follow this pattern of citing an exegetical *quaestio* in the exordium, and then giving a reasoned reply. For our purposes this letter is the least interesting of the five.

Addressee. A dignitary residing not too far from Isidore, since he twice anticipates meetings (2.31, 3.273). In four other letters he answers exegetical enquiries (2.198, 269, 3.58, 4.189).

ll.1–2. The prophetic text is repeated at length by Jesus at Matt. 13:14–15. The word *mēpote* must be left untranslated in order not to prejudice Isidore's interpretation. With ἴδωσι it would normally mean 'lest they see', but might also be rendered 'perhaps they might see'.

l.3. Isidore refers to a change of persons because in v.9 (and 14) God addresses the people of Israel, but v.10 (and 15) they are referred to in the third person. Isidore thus concludes that in the second verse the prophet must be being addressed.

ll.10–11. Literally prepositional phrases: 'from whom', i.e. God who speaks; 'to whom', i.e. the prophet; 'concerning whom', i.e. the people of Israel.

l.19. The solution to the exegetical conundrum is that *mēpote* means 'perhaps'. This means that the interpretation that God should wish them to remain blind and deaf is rejected. As we learn later (ll.35–39), this would be in conflict with the beneficence that characterizes God's nature.

ll.22–34. Isidore invokes four witnesses for this meaning of *mēpote*: (1) the Jews quoted by John (i.e. taken as a literal reporting of what they said); (2) σοφοί, among whom Philo; (3) Paul; (4) a text from Ben Sirach in the Old
* Testament. By σοφοί he presumably means 'distinguished ancient writers' (in *Ep.* 2.143, 1.65 Philo was also called σοφός). The contrast between Philo as sage and Paul as divinely inspired author (l. 28, θεοπνεύστου, cf. 2 Tim. 3:16) also recalls 2.143 (cf. our note on ll. 18–31).

II.25–26. ὧν εἷς εἶναι δοκεῖ καὶ Φίλων. It is not easy to decide exactly what Isidore means by this phrase. I do not think it expresses doubt. The translation 'is reputed' takes him to mean 'as is reported in Josephus and Eusebius' *vel sim.* If we translate 'seems', then Isidore indicates he is relying on his memory. It is in fact quite correct that μήποτε often means 'perhaps' in Philo. Cf. (in treatises that Isidore probably read) *Abr.* 171, *Mos.* 1.280. If Isidore were thinking of any particular text, it would surely be *Fug.* 94, where the six cities of refuge are interpreted theologically, and the chief metropolis perhaps (μήποτε) would be the divine Logos. But he would find it difficult to find a really suitable parallel for his exegesis here, since Philo almost always uses the word in the phrase μήποτε εἰκότως, or to introduce a possible exegetical interpretation (e.g. *Cher.* 21, *Post.* 91) etc. The exegetical principle used here, however, that no interpretation be given that is unworthy of God, is wholly consonant with the Philonic heritage (cf. *Det.* 13, *Deus* 52 etc.). [310]

I.35. τὸ προφητικὸν χωρίον. Here the author returns to the passage being given exegesis, and explains why he has opted for his bold exegesis.

Ep. 3.19 (= *Ep.* 819 Évieux)

ΑΘΑΝΑΣΙΩΙ ΠΡΕΣΒΥΤΕΡΩΙ

εἰ μηδὲν πλέον τοῦ γράμματος νομίζει τὸν νομοθέτην εἰρηκέναι ὁ πρὸς
σέ, ὡς ἔφης, διενεχθεὶς Ἰουδαῖος, εἰπὲ πρὸς αὐτὸν ὅτι ἐλέγχουσιν ὑμῶν
τὴν ἀπαιδευσίαν οἱ δύο ἄνδρες οἱ μετὰ τὴν τοῦ Χριστοῦ παρουσίαν
συγγραφεῖς παρ᾽ ὑμῖν γεγονότες, Φίλων ὁ θεωρητικώτατος καὶ Ἰώση-
5   πος ὁ ἱστορικώτατος· ὁ μὲν πᾶσαν σχεδὸν τὴν Παλαιὰν εἰς ἀλληγορίαν τρέπων, ὁ δὲ διαρρήδην γράφων, «τὰ μὲν αἰνιττομένου τοῦ
νομοθέτου δεξιῶς τὰ δὲ ἀλληγοροῦντος μετὰ σεμνότητος, ὅσα δ᾽ ἐξ
εὐθείας λέγεσθαι συνέφερε, ταῦτα ῥητῶς ἐμφανίζοντος.» εἰ μὲν γὰρ
προενέγκοιμεν προφητικὰς ῥήσεις τοῦτο ἐγγυωμένας, παρερμηνεῦσαι
10 καὶ παραποιῆσαι οὐκ ὀκνήσουσιν· εἰ δ᾽ ἀποστολικὰς ἀποφάσεις τε καὶ
ἀποδείξεις καὶ ἑρμηνείας, παραγράψασθαι τολμήσουσι δυσσεβῶς·
τὰς δὲ τῶν παρ᾽ αὐτοῖς δοξάντων σοφῶν μαρτυρίας παραγράψασθαι
οὐκ ἂν εἶεν δίκαιοι.

To the Priest Athanasius

If the Jew who according to your report disagreed with you is of the opinion that the lawgiver spoke his words with no more than the literal meaning, tell him that 'the ignorance of you Jews is refuted by two of your own writers who lived after the coming of Christ, Philo the master of speculative thought and Josephus the great historian'. Of these the former turns almost the entire Old Testament into allegory, the latter writes explicitly that 'the lawgiver expresses some matters skilfully in enigmatic language, other matters he presents solemnly through allegory, while those matters which he thought it beneficial to express straightforwardly he reveals in literal speech'. If we were to put forward prophetic utterances which confirm this fact, the Jews will not hesitate to misinterpret [10] and mishandle them. If we were to offer apostolic declarations and proofs and interpretations, they will no doubt irreverently reject them. But if they should reject the testimonies of men who among them have a reputation for wisdom, they would be downright unfair.

COMMENTARY

Theme: Isidore appeals to Philo's practice of allegorical exegesis and Josephus' ascription of allegorizing to Moses in order to refute a Jew who says that the lawgiver only writes at the literal level. Even if the Jews ignore OT prophecy and NT apostolic witness, they can hardly ignore the evidence of men of their own people with such a reputation for wisdom.

Addressee. A priest in the local church of Pelusium, as his association with the [311] detested Zosimus (see next letter) proves (cf. 2.136, 5.536). Isidore often exhorts him to choose the good side against the corrupt clergy, e.g. via exegesis (cf. 4.25, 191), but is sometimes disappointed (e.g. 3.620). *Ep.* 2.46 is a kind of companion piece to this letter, for it commences 'tell the man who disagrees with you and espouses the doctrines of the Greeks...' In *Ep.* 2.81, in response to a request to explain why lepers are excluded from the temple precincts, we learn that Athanasius himself is not in favour of non-literal biblical interpretation.

ll.1–2. ὁ πρὸς σέ ... διενεχθεὶς Ἰουδαῖος. Isidore is responding to a letter in which Athanasius reports a discussion with a Jew. Cf. the similar formula at 3.94, εἰπὲ τῷ πρὸς σὲ διενεχθέντι Ἰουδαίῳ. The Letter collection gives evidence of discussions between Christians and Jews on religious matters at the local level of provincial Egypt. On one occasion Isidore writes to Benjamin the Jew on how the bread of the Eucharist has replaced the sacrifices of the law, while the shewbread in the inner sanctuary points to Christ (*Ep.* 1.401). Other letters giving evidence of local discussions are 1.141 (on the incarnation), 2.99 (against a Jew objecting to the hyperbole in John 21:25), 3.94 (on the Christological interpretation of Deut. 18:15). In these discussions Isidore remains polite enough, but in numerous other letters he reveals that he shares the strong anti-Judaic views current in this period. Cf. the remarks of Niemeyer (1825) 90-92 and the list of references at PG 78.1743–44. Some strong statements are collected by Schreckenberg (1982) 365–367. The Jews are a 'blaspheming and ungrateful people' (*Ep.* 1.18): not only did they ignore the prophecies of Christ's coming during the Old Testament period, but they also rejected him and mistreated him when he did come. They are the murderous tenants of the vineyard in the parable in Matt. 21:33–43 (4.166). On Christian-Jewish relations in Egypt and the Eastern Empire at this time see Simon (1986) 224–233. It will not have gone unnoticed in Pelusium that in 414 at the instigation of the Patriarch Cyril the Jews were expelled from Alexandria and their property confiscated (Socrates *HE* 7.13).

l.1. νομοθέτην. I.e. Moses. The point at issue will no doubt have been typological interpretation of the Old Testament as pointing to the coming of Christ, which would be unacceptable for the Jewish disputant. For a practical example of such a dispute, cf. *Ep.* 3.94 on Joshua and Jesus.

1.3. μετὰ τὴν τοῦ Χριστοῦ παρουσίαν. Isidore thus knows that Philo lived after Jesus' death. A likely source for his information is the *Church History* of Eusebius, although he never refers to this work directly. But the same information is available, if less clearly, in the *Antiquities* of Josephus.

* **1.4. Φίλων ὁ θεωρητικώτατος.** θεωρία not only has the general sense of spiritual contemplation, but Isidore also uses it specifically of non-literal or allegorical interpretation of Scripture (e.g. 2.81, 3.84, both *ad init.*), which makes the corresponding adjective highly appropriate for Philo. Here again Eusebius may be his guide: cf. *HE* 2.18.1, where Philo is described as ὑψηλός τε ὢν καὶ μετέωρος ἐν ταῖς εἰς τὰς θείας γραφὰς θεωρίαις γεγενημένος.

ll.5–6. Isidore is very short on Philo's contribution, perhaps assuming it to be well-known. The word σχέδον hardly gives an idea of Philo's concentration on the Pentateuch. Isidore himself does make use of both allegory and Christological typology in his interpretation of the Old Testament. As an example we may take two letters, *Ep.* 1.192–3. In the former the exegetical *quaestio* is why Jacob [312] during his birth grabs hold of Esau's heel (Gen. 25:26). The answer is that the mind which sees God in purity (this is what Israel interpreted means) trips up the gluttonous passions. The exegesis is not very accurate (Jacob will not be called Israel until
* much later), but clearly is derived from the Alexandrian tradition and ultimately Philo (cf. *QG* 4.163, *Leg.* 3.190, as well as the peculiarly Philonic etymology of Israel). The second letter asks what the kids' skins on Jacob's arms mean (Gen. 27:16). They symbolize (ἠνίξατο) the sinful nature which our Lord and Saviour sinlessly put on (no parallel of any kind in Philo). A third letter we might compare is 2.274, which asks the meaning of the Patriarchs' polygamy, but avoids any allegorical interpretation, in marked contrast to the Alexandrian tradition (even the Pauline θεωρία of Gal. 4:24 is given but the briefest mention at 705C). The Isidoran passages that draw on Philo listed by Früchtel (1938) contain some literal exegesis (2.215, 3.115, 289), but no allegorical themes. On Isidore's exegesis in general we may cite the balanced judgment of Évieux (1976) 335: 'disons qu'Isidore, connaissant les traditions exégétiques alexandrine et antiochienne, commente l'Écriture de la façon la plus propre à se faire comprendre de ses correspondants... Isidore regrette à certains moments de ne pouvoir faire comprendre à ses correspondants le sens allégorique d'un passage scripturaire. Néanmoins, c'est dans l'interprétation littérale qu'on le sent le plus à l'aise, déployant à l'occasion ses talents de grammairien et de philologue. En tous cas... Isidore se montre mesuré, équilibré, ennemi de tout excès.' There is unfortunately no comprehensive study available on Isidore's exegesis of the Old Testament.

1.6. διαρρήδην. The word indicates a *verbatim* quotation, i.e. from Josephus, *Ant.* 1.24, which is very much to the purpose of the letter.
* Isidore refers somewhat more to Josephus than Philo; cf. the collection of passages at Bayer (1915) 78–80, and esp. the eulogy in the next letter.

ll.8–13. Another example of Isidore's carefully formulated and rigorous apologetic logic; cf. the final sentence of *Ep.* 2.143.

Ep. 3.81 (= *Ep.* 881 Évieux)

ΖΩΣΙΜΩΙ ΠΡΕΣΒΥΤΕΡΩΙ

οὐ θαυμάζω εἰ ἐν τοῖς ἄλλοις ἅπασιν ἀπαίδευτος ὤν, κἂν τούτῳ τὴν
ἀμαθίαν τὴν σαυτοῦ ἐπεδείξω. ἀλλὰ τότ᾽ ἂν ἐθαύμασα, εἰ ἐν τοῖς
ἄλλοις πταίων, ἐν τούτῳ οὐ διήμαρτες. τὰ μὲν οὖν αἰσχρὰ πάθη οἶσθα
ἀπὸ σαυτοῦ, καὶ οὐδὲν δεῖ λόγων. ἐπειδὴ δὲ τὰ χρηστὰ καὶ φιλάν-
5 θρωπα ἀγνοεῖς, τοῦτα φράσω. εἰσὶ δὲ ἔλεος, φιλανθρωπία, οἶκτος,
εὐμένεια, καὶ τὰ ἄλλα τὰ τούτων ἀδελφά. εἰ δέ σε ταράττει τὸ καὶ
ταῦτα πάθη λέγεσθαι, καὶ ἐγγυητὰς καὶ μάρτυρας τούτου ἀξιοπίστους
ἄνδρας παρέξομαι. οἶδα μὲν οὖν ὅτι αὐτὸς οὐ παρακολουθήσεις τοῖς
λεγομένοις, ἅτε ἀπαιδευσίας τυγχάνων θρέμμα, ὅμως δ᾽ οὖν αὐτὸς
10 ἐρῶ. Δημοσθένης μὲν οὖν ὁ ῥήτωρ, τὸ τῆς Ἑλλάδος κεφάλαιον, περὶ
τοῦ Φιλίππου λέγων, ὅτε παρεκαλεῖτο δοῦναι τοὺς Ὀλυνθίους
αἰχμαλώτους, ἔφη· «ὥστε τὸν Φίλιππον παθεῖν τι, καὶ δοῦναι τὴν
χάριν.» Ἰώσηππος δέ, ἀνὴρ ἐπὶ παιδεύσει καὶ εἰδήσει λόγων ἐπι-
σημότατος, περὶ τῶν στασιαστῶν τῶν ἐν τῇ ἁλώσει τῆς Ἱερουσαλὴμ
15 ἀκμασάντων γράφων ἔφη· «ὅταν ἀτίθασσος καὶ ἀμείλικτος φύσις
ἄσκησιν τὴν εἰς τὸ ἀνήμερον προσλάβῃ, διχόθεν ἄβατος καὶ
ἀπρόσιτος οἴκτῳ [313] γίνεται, καὶ χρηστῷ πάθει καὶ φιλανθρώπῳ.»
οὐδὲν δὲ οὕτως χρηστὸν πάθος ἀπολώλει, ὡς ἔλεος. καὶ Φίλων δέ,
ἄνθρωπος Πλάτωνος ἢ ὁμιλητὴς ἢ ὑφηγητής τις εἶναι δόξας, διὰ τὸ τῆς
20 φράσεως ὕψος· ἐρρέθη γὰρ περὶ αὐτῶν «ἢ Πλάτων ἐφιλώνισεν, ἢ
Φίλων ἐπλατώνισεν·» ἐγκωμιάσας μὲν τὸν Μωσέα ὡς μισοπόνηρον
ἔφη· «περιπαθήσας δὲ καὶ δικαίας ὀργῆς ἐμπλησθείς, διαβάλλει τινὰς
Αἰγυπτίους, τοὺς ἐργοδιώκτας φημὶ τοῦ Φαραώ.» πάσχει γάρ τι ἡ ψυχή,
καὶ ἢ εἰς ἔλεον, ἢ εἰς εὐμένειαν, ἢ εἰς χρηστότητα, ἢ εἰς μισοπονηρίαν
25 νεύει. εἰ μὴ γὰρ ἐπικλασθείη τις, οὐκ ἂν τὸν ἱκέτην ἐλεήσειεν· εἰ μὴ
ἐπικαμφθείη, οὐκ ἂν τὸν δεόμενον οἰκτείρησειεν· εἰ μὴ πάθοι τι, οὐκ
ἂν τὸν ἐχθρὸν εὐεργετήσειεν· εἰ μὴ νομίσει ἠδικεῖσθαι τὴν δικαιοσύνην, οὐκ ἂν εἰς μισοπονηρίαν τραπείη. τὴν δὲ τροπὴν ταύτην
καὶ πάθος καλοῦσιν. ὥσπερ γὰρ ὁ ἀπὸ τοῦ βελτίονος ἐπὶ τὸ χεῖρον
30 τρεπόμενος πάσχει, οὕτω καὶ ὁ ἀπὸ τῶν χειρόνων ἐπὶ τὸ ἄμεινον
τρεπόμενος πάσχει τι. τροπῆς γάρ ἐστι τὸ πάθος ὄνομα. τοιγαροῦν καὶ
αὐτός, κἂν ὀψέ ποτε τῆς ἡλικίας τὰ αἰσχρὰ φεῦγε πάθη, ἵνα μή ποτε
ἐπαινέσῃς τὴν παραίνεσιν, ὅτε τῶν ἐπαίνων σοι ὄφελος οὐδέν.

To the priest Zosimus

I am not surprised that you, who are uneducated in all other
matters, have also displayed your ignorance in this case. Only then

would I have been surprised if you, while going astray in other matters, in this were not mistaken. As for the evil passions, these you know from you own experience, and there is no need to give an account of them. But since you are ignorant of the good and humane passions, these I will declare. They are mercy, humane feeling, pity, goodwill and other passions related to these. If the fact that these are called passions disturbs you, I shall bring forward men who are trustworthy witnesses and guarantors of this usage. Although I know that you yourself, being a creature of ignorance, will take no notice of what is being said, nevertheless I [10] shall speak. The orator Demosthenes, the champion of Greece, speaking about Philip when he was called upon to hand over the Olythian prisoners, said: 'the result was that Philip was moved and granted the favour'. Josephus, a man highly distinguished for his learning and rhetorical ability, when describing the revolutionaries at their peak during the siege of Jerusalem, wrote: 'when an untamed and unsoftened character reinforces its harshness through practice, on both grounds it becomes impervious and inaccessible to pity, that good and humane passion'. Indeed there is no passion which it destroys as good as mercy. And then there is Philo, a man reputed, on account of the [20] sublimity of his language, to be either the disciple or teacher of Plato, for it has been said concerning them that 'either Plato philonized or Philo platonized'. Singing the praises of Moses as one who hated evil, he said, 'roused to passion and filled with righteous anger, he slandered some [314] Egyptians, I mean the taskmasters of Pharaoh'. Indeed the soul is moved, and in so doing inclines either to mercy or to goodwill or to kindness or to hatred of evil. If a man is not turned back, he would feel no mercy for the suppliant; if he does not experience a change in direction, he would not have pity for the petitioner; if he is not moved, he would not be benevolent towards the enemy; if he does not consider justice to have been violated, he would not be turned to hatred of evil. It is this change of direction which they call passion. Just as the person who turns from the better to the worse [30] is moved, so the same happens to him who turns from the worse to the better. Passion is a term for a change. For this reason you too, even at your advanced age, should flee from your wicked passions, lest you praise my advice at a time when such praise will be of no use to you.

COMMENTARY

Theme. Philo, together with Demosthenes and Josephus, is invoked as a witness for the view that there are not only bad, but also good passions. These involve a turning or change from the worse to the better.

Addressee. Zosimus, priest of the Church of Pelusium and chief confidant of Bishop Eusebius, emerges from the Letters as Isidore's *bête noire*. He is the recipient of numerous letters of advice and reproval, in which Isidore exhorts him in the strongest terms to abstain from corruption and vice. In many other letters we read complaints about the dishonest and worldly practices of Zosimus and his colleagues. Cf. 1.118–120, 3.70, 5.569 etc.

l.1. κᾶν τούτῳ. In the previous letter Isidore accuses Zosimus of offering a broad highway to the wicked and servile passions, while barring the path to those passions that good and free. It is possible that the recipient wrote back, denying the distinction between the two kinds of πάθος (cf. 1.6 ταράττει, which may refer to an actual remark). In any case the theme of this letter concentrates on that distinction.

ll.3–4. The doctrine of the passions (πάθη) on which Isidore's remarks are based will be discussed below in the comments on ll.23–30.

l.9. ἀπαιδευσίας θρέμμα. I have opted for the translation 'creature' on account of the combination with the genitive. But evidently the originally Platonic topos of the wild beast of passion (*Rep.* 588c–590a, *Tim.* 70e), which is also very common in Philo (cf. Runia (1986) 310, 386ff.), is present to Isidore's mind. He works the theme out at greater length in *Ep.* 2.135 (exeg. Ps. 48:13).

ll.10–13. Demothenes is, together with Plato, Isidore's favourite classical author. See the collections of quotations and allusions at Bayer (1915) 19–35. This particular quote is from *De fals. leg.* 195 (cf. Bayer (1915) 33, who notes that Isidore has added the final word χάριν). The operative words are παθεῖν τι, an expression which is notoriously difficult to translate. I have rendered it 'be moved' throughout the letter, but literally it means 'undergo something', and is of course directly related to the term πάθος (literally no more than something that one ondergoes or that happens to one). In this concrete instance the king feels mercy and releases the prisoners. [315]

ll.13–17. The next witness Josephus is this time not praised as a historian (cf. 3.19) but for his learning (παίδευσις as opposed to Zosimus' ἀπαιδευσία, cf. l.1) and knowledge of rhetoric. Bayer (1915) 80 could not identify the quote, but it was brilliantly recognized by Früchtel (1938) 766 as coming not from Josephus, but from Philo's *De Iosepho* 82! Isidore's memory is playing tricks on him. Nevertheless there must have been a passage in Josephus' *De bello Iudaico* of which he was reminded, but for which he substituted the Philonic quote. Perhaps he was thinking of the beginning of Book VI, where Josephus describes the πάθη τῶν Ἱεροσολύμων (did Isidore remember Ἱεροσολυμίτων?) and the pitilessness of the revolutionaries.

ll.18–21. Philo is this time not praised for his knowledge of scripture, but for his literary skills. As in the case of Josephus his Jewishness is not mentioned. The proverb or *bon mot* cited by Isidore is not found in Eusebius, but is first mentioned by Jerome in his brief sketch of Philo's life and

works in *De viris illustribus* 11 (published in 393), who describes it as com-
* monly pronounced 'apud Graecos'. It is subsequently found in Augustine
c. Faust. 12.39, Photius *Bibl.* 105, *Souda* s.v. Φίλων, Theodorus Metochita
Misc. 16 (texts in C-W 1.ciii–xii). Commenting on the various interpretations of the saying, Billings (1919) 2 argues that Isidore belongs to those
who think 'it means a likeness in style only' between Plato and Philo. This
is literally what the text says. Yet the context makes it clear that Philo is
also being invoked for his knowledge of philosophical doctrine.

ll.21–23. Isidore gives the impression of citing Philo *verbatim*, but in actual
fact his text is a collage based on a number of texts from *De vita Moysis* (cf.
Früchtel (1938) 765), i.e. 1.37, 47, 302, 2.271, 279, only the first three of
which are concerned with Moses' righteous anger against the Egyptian
overseers.

ll.23–30. The doctrine of the passions presumed by Isidore's remarks here
must be seen against the background of Greek philosophy, but even so it is
not easy to place. The basic features of the account in the letter are: (1)
the πάθη are divided into good and bad passions; (2) πάθος is identified
with 'turning' (τροπή); (3) good passions occur when one turns from the
worse to the better, e.g. in the case of mercy, from a feeling of anger or
harshness to one of kindness (Isidore speaks of 'bending double or back',
exploiting the common phrase ἐπικλᾶν εἰς οἶκτον, 'move to pity').

For the philosophical background it is important to distinguish between the Stoic and the Platonist position. The Old Stoa associates passion
with turning (τροπή) or change in the *pneuma*, i.e. passion occurs when the
soul loses its proper tension through faulty judgment of the rational
faculty (cf. Diog. Laert. 7.158 (not in SVF 3), Cl. Alex. *Str.* 2.72.1 (= SVF
3.422)—I owe these texts to J. Mansfeld). There are, however, no good
passions, but only εὐπαθεῖαι; the Stoic sage, in attaining the ideal of
ἀπάθεια, does not succumb to feelings of pity or compassion. The turning
can presumably be away from or towards the right tension; in the former
case the passions occur, in the latter they cease. Middle Platonism, taking
its cue from the Posidonian revision of Stoic theory, attribute the passions
to the irrational part of the soul. At Alcinous *Did.* 32.1 πάθος is defined as
κίνησις ἄλογος ψυχῆς ὡς ἐπὶ κακῷ ἢ ὡς ἐπὶ ἀγαθῷ (irrational motion of the
soul as if to something good or to something evil). Moreover the passions
are divided into the tame (pleasure, anger, pity etc.) and the wild [316]
(ridicule, *Schadenfreude*, misanthropy). The ideal in Platonism is most
often, therefore, not ἀπάθεια but μετριοπάθεια, although some Middle
Platonists incline to the more rigorous Stoic view (full discussion at Lilla
(1971) 84ff.). Platonists closer to Isidore's time distinguish between
μετριοπάθεια in the social realm and ἀπάθεια in the contemplative realm
(cf. Porphyry *Sent. ad intell.* 32). Porphyry connects passions with τροπή,
but such turning is a matter of the body (to which the irrational soul is
connected) and not of the incorporeal rational soul (*ibid.* 18).

We may conclude that the neutral conception of τροπή envisaged by
Isidore originally derives from Stoicism, but that his interpretation of the
πάθη is more in line with Platonist views. I can give no precise parallels,
however, for his notion of the good passions as occurring in the change
from the worse to the better. Perhaps the Christian conception of con-
* version has made its influence felt here.

Certainly it is not likely that he derived this notion from Philo, despite his invocation as witness here. For Philo τροπή of the soul is nearly always a purely negative event (cf. *Leg.* 2.33, 83, *Sacr.* 127, *Mut.* 239, but at *Sacr.* 137 τὸ ἡγεμονικὸν πολλὰς πρὸς ἑκάτερον τό τε εὖ καὶ χεῖρον τροπὰς λαμβάνον). Philo generally holds to the doctrine of ἀπάθεια for God and the sage, but is prepared to accommodate 'good' passions such as mercy and hatred of evil. See further the analysis of Winston (1984) 401–405, and esp. the note on 402.

ll.30–33. Isidore applies the results of his exposition of the πάθη to Zosimus' own situation. He too can turn to the better by fleeing from his evil passions. Zosimus appears to have been advanced in years. Cf. *Ep.* 1.140, which announces that the end is near, and recommends a late conversion.

Ep. 4.176 (= *Ep.* 1757 Évieux)

ΕΥΛΟΓΙΩΙ

οὐχ ἱστορίαν ἁπλῶς ψυχαγωγῆσαι δυναμένην ὁ ἱεροφάντης ἔγραψε Μωσῆς· ἀλλ᾽ ἐπειδὴ νομοθετεῖν ἔμελλε, τὸν δημιουργὸν καὶ κριτὴν τοῦ παντὸς προτάττει καὶ τὴν τοῦ κόσμου δημιουργίαν, ἵνα μὴ τοῖς μέρεσι τοῦ κόσμου τὸ σέβας ἀπονέμοιεν· εἶτα τῶν ὁσίων τὰ γέρα καὶ τῶν ἁμαρτωλῶν τὰς κολάσεις προσθείς, οὕτως ἐπὶ τὸ νομοθετεῖν ὥρμησεν, ἵνα ἀπὸ τῶν γεγενημένων καὶ τὰ μέλλοντα πιστωσάμενος, εἰς εὐσέβειαν καὶ δικαιοσύνην τοὺς ὑπηκόους προτρέψειεν.

To Eulogius

The hierophant Moses did not write history simply so that it could offer entertainment, but, as it was his intention to draw up a legal code, he placed at its head the creator and judge of the universe and the creation of the cosmos, so that mankind might not bestow veneration on the parts of the cosmos. Then, when he had added the rewards gained by the pious and the punishments suffered by the sinners, he on this basis embarked on his legislative task, so that, taking the past events as [317] confirmation of what would also happen in the future, he might exhort his subjects to piety and justice.

COMMENTARY

Theme. Philo is clearly Isidore's source for his reflections on the purpose of the creation account and historical sections in the Pentateuch. We include the letter, even though Philo is not explicitly mentioned, on account of its intrinsic interest and because it has been ignored by modern scholars (although the 16th century scholar Ritterhusius recognized the Philonic background; cf. his note at PG 78.1267).

Addressee: A man with an interest in theological questions; cf. 4.89 on striving to gain knowledge of the unknowable (i.e. God), 4.163 (attack on Origen's doctrine of the pre-creational fall of the souls). This letter may simply be an extract from a longer composition.

1.1. ὁ ἱεροφάντης Μωσῆς. The title as often in Philo, e.g. *Spec.* 1.41. In his very positive attitude to Moses (cf. references at PG 78.1753 s.v. Moses) Isidore follows the Alexandrian tradition established since Clement *Str.* I, who drew heavily on Philo's *De vita Moysis* (cf. Van den Hoek (1988) 48–68). But Clement cannot be his direct source for this letter; cp. *Str.* 1.176.1.

1.1. ἁπλῶς ψυχαγωγῆσαι. Derived from Philo *Mos.* 2.48, 'he did not, like any historian make it his business to leave to posterity ancient records for the sake of pleasant but unimproving entertainment (τοῦ ψυχαγωγῆσαι χάριν ἀνωφελῶς), but gave an account of ancient times beginning from the creation of the universe...').

II.2–5. The chief Philonic source for these themes is unquestionably *Mos.* 2.45–53 (*contra* Ritterhusius who thinks he used *Opif.*), but also *Opif.* 1–12, *Abr.* 1–2, *Praem.* 1–3 may have contributed.

1.2. δημιουργὸν καὶ κριτὴν τοῦ παντός. The text in Migne reads κριτήν, but from the Philonic viewpoint one would surely expect κτιστήν, since the context is the creation of the cosmos. I have not changed the text, however, since it appears that Isidore somewhat shifts the emphasis in accordance with Christian eschatology. Whereas for Philo the point of the creational exordium is above all the correspondence between the law of nature and the Mosaic law (God as cosmic lawgiver, *Mos.* 2.48), Isidore stresses rewards and punishments as a guarantee for τὰ μέλλοντα, i.e. the last judgment of God the judge (cf. also the end of *Ep.* 3.81).

1.4. τὸ σέβας ἀπονέμοιεν. The theme of impiously giving honour to the parts of the cosmos is not found in *Mos.* 2.48ff., but cf. *Opif.* 7, *Spec.* 1.13–20.

II.4–5. Rewards and punishments: cf. *Mos.* 2.47 τὸ μὲν περὶ κολάσεως ἀσεβῶν τὸ δ' αὖ τιμῆς δικαίων, but also *Praem.* 2 (note γέρα) and *passim.*

1.6. πιστωσάμενος. The meaning of πίστις as proof, pledge, guarantee shines through. From what happened in ancient times we can be sure of what will happen in the future.

1.7. προτρέψειεν. Theme of exhortation also at *Mos.* 2.51 (τοῦ προτρέ-ψασθαι χάριν μᾶλλον ἢ βιάσασθαι). [318]

3. *Concluding remarks*

The evidence of the five letters we have examined shows that Isidore of Pelusium possessed a more than superficial acquaintance with the thought and writings of Philo, and so stands in the honourable tradition of Clement, Origen, Eusebius and Didymus, the Church Fathers who were instrumental in having Philo's writings saved from destruction. The work he knows best is clearly the *De vita Moysis*, Philo's most popular work during this period. Other writings that he must have read are the *Life of Joseph* and the *Quaestiones*. For some of his

information on Philo he may be dependent on Josephus or on information in the classic works of Eusebius, the *Historia Ecclesiastica* and
Praeparatio Evangelica, but this has not been proven beyond all
doubt.

In two of the letters in which Philo is named (2.270, 3.81) he is
presented as a sage and general authority on literary style and
philosophical knowledge. In the former he is implicitly contrasted
with the scriptural writer Paul, in the latter he is placed beside
Demosthenes and Josephus. But there is no reference to his Jewishness or non-Christian status.

In the other two letters the situation is quite different. In 3.81
Philo is cited precisely because he is a Jew, in order to refute a
contemporary Jew on the admissibility of allegorical interpretation.
In 2.143, the most interesting of the four letters, Philo takes the
centre stage as a Jew who does not espouse the crude monotheism
of his compatriots, but through his penetrating reading of Scripture
has some intimations of the doctrine of the Trinity. Isidore explicitly
refers to three Philonic themes: the Logos, the divine Powers and
the divine names θεός and κύριος. Here too Philo is compared with
Paul, whose description of the Logos is more accurate and corresponds to orthodox theology.

In the long history of Philo's reception in the Patristic tradition
he is sometimes regarded as a Christian *avant la lettre*, at other times
as a devout and learned Jew. Both views can be read into Isidore's
letters, but it seems to me that the latter predominates. Philo is an
effective weapon in the contest—'dialogue' we can hardly call it—
against Jews of his own time, who no longer felt any affinity with the
Hellenistic Judaism that had flourished in the same Egypt centuries
earlier.

Bibliography

L. BAYER, *Isidors von Pelusium klassische Bildung*, Forschungen zur Christlichen
    Literatur- und Dogmengeschichte 13.2 (Paderborn 1915). [319]
T. H. BILLINGS, *The Platonism of Philo Judaeus* (Chicago 1919).
P. ÉVIEUX, 'Isidore de Péluse: la numérotation des lettres dan la tradition
    manuscrite', *Revue d'Histoire des Textes* 5 (1975) 45–72.
P. ÉVIEUX, 'Isidore de Péluse: état des recherches', *Revue des Sciences Religieuses* 64
    (1976) 321–340.
C. M. FOUSKAS, *Saint Isidore of Pelusium: his Life and his Works* (Athens 1970).
L. FRÜCHTEL, 'Neue Quellennachweise zu Isidoros von Pelusion', *Philologische
    Wochenschrift* 58 (1938) 61–64, 764–768.
M. GEERARD, *Clavis Patrum Graecarum*, vol. 3 (Turnhout 1979).

A. GRILLMEIER, *Christ in Christian Tradition*. Vol. 1 From the Apostolic Age to Chalcedon (AD 451) (London 1975²).

E. HILGERT, 'Bibliographia Philoniana 1935–1981' in W. HAASE (ed.), *Hellenistisches Judentum in römischer Zeit: Philon und Josephus, ANRW* II 21.1 (Berlin-New York 1984) 47–97.

A. VAN DEN HOEK, *Clement of Alexandria and his Use of Philo in the* Stromateis: *an Early Christian Reshaping of a Jewish Model,* Supplements to Vigiliae Christianae 3 (Leiden 1988).

C. LACOMBRADE, *Synésios de Cyrène, hellène et chrétien* (Paris 1951).

G. W. H. LAMPE, *A Patristic Greek Lexicon* (Oxford 1961).

S. R. C. LILLA, *Clement of Alexandria: a Study in Christian Platonism and Gnosticism,* Oxford Theological Monographs (Oxford 1971).

R. MORTLEY, *Connaissance religieuse et herméneutique chez Clément d'Alexandrie* (Leiden 1973).

H. A. NIEMEYER, *De Isidori Pelusiotae vita scriptis et doctrina commentatio historica theologica* (Halle 1825), reprinted at PG 78.12–102.

F. PETIT, *Quaestiones in Genesim et in Exodum: fragmenta graeca,* PAPM 33 (Paris 1978).

J. QUASTEN, *Patrology.* Vol 3. The Golden Age of Patristic Literature (Utrecht-Antwerpen 1960).

A. M. RITTER, Art. 'Isidore de Péluse', *Dictionnaire de Spiritualité* 7.2 (1971) 2098–2103.

D. T. RUNIA, *Philo of Alexandria and the* Timaeus *of Plato,* Philosophia Antiqua 44 (Leiden 1986).

A. SCHMID, *Die Christologie Isidors von Pelusium,* Paradosis 2 (Freiburg in der Schweiz 1948).

H. SCHRECKENBERG, *Die christlichen Adversus-Judaeos-Texte und ihr literarisches und historisches Umfeld (1.–11. Jh.),* Europäische Hochschulschriften 23.172 (Frankfurt-Bern 1982).

A. F. SEGAL, *Two Powers in Heaven: Early Rabbinic Reports about Christianity and Gnosticism,* Studies in Judaism in Late Antiquity 25 (Leiden 1977).

F. SIEGERT, *Philon von Alexandrien Über die Gottebezeichnung "wohltätig verzehrendes Feuer" (De Deo),* Wissenschaftliche Untersuchungen zum Neuen Testament 46 (Tübingen 1988).

M. SIMON, *Verus Israel: a Study of the Relations between Christians and Jews in the Roman Empire (135–425)* (Oxford 1986).

C. TAYLOR, *Hegel* (Cambridge 1975).

R. WILLIAMS, *Arius: Heresy and Tradition* (London 1987).

D. WINSTON, 'Philo's ethical theory', in W. HAASE (ed.), *Hellenistisches Judentum in römischer Zeit: Philon und Josephus, ANRW* II 21.1 (Berlin-New York 1984) 372–416.

H. A. WOLFSON, *The Philosophy of the Church Fathers: Faith, Trinity, Incarnation* (Cambridge Mass. 1956, 1970³).

CHAPTER TEN

WITNESS OR PARTICIPANT?
PHILO AND THE NEOPLATONIST TRADITION

It is with some hesitation that I address the subject of Philo and Neoplatonic philosophy. After all, is it not the case that in perhaps the most famous article ever written on the origins of Neoplatonism E. R. Dodds described Philo's thought as the 'eclecticism of the jackdaw rather than the philosopher'?[1] I am sure that what the reader expects is philosophy and not a lesson in ornithology. Without question there was an important Philonic heritage in antiquity, but that heritage is primarily located neither in Greek philosophy nor in later Judaism, but rather in Patristic thought. The use of Philo by the Church Fathers is in fact the area that has engaged my attention in recent years. There are, however, cross-connections between this subject and the question of Philo's place in the development of Platonism, as we shall see. For this reason I have taken the plunge, in spite of the risks involved.

The chief problem I wish to examine is already indicated by the title of my talk. As everyone knows, Philo's writings contain a great amount of evidence on the murky beginnings of Middle Platonism at the beginning of our era, evidence which has been thoroughly exploited by a long succession of scholars. The question is this: is Philo only a *witness*, i.e. someone who happens to furnish us with important information on the above-mentioned developments? *or* did he *participate* in them himself, and so can claim a, no doubt minor, role in the history of Platonism? My paper will fall into three parts. Firstly I provide some orientation by noting various discussions that have taken place on Philo's role in the development towards Neoplatonism. Secondly I will make a bit of a detour and

---

[1] Dodds (1928) 132.

look at the evidence on the fate of Philo's writings. Finally I shall return to philosophical themes and examine one or two examples in the area of theology where one might be inclined to posit Philonic participation in the Platonist tradition. Let me say in self-defence at [37] the outset that, if I fail to reach hard and fast conclusions, this may not just be the result of my vacillating character. There is also the question of evidence to consider, and it has the nasty habit of often leaving us feeling rather frustrated.

1. *Philo and Neoplatonism: state of the question*

An appropriate place to start, I believe, is with the grandiose and idiosyncratic perspective on the history of philosophy developed by the Jewish-American scholar Harry Austryn Wolfson. It is now nearly 50 years ago since it was first presented, and no one has ever subscribed to it in its full form. But it has a kind of archetypal grandeur about it for which I have always, perhaps perversely, had some admiration. Wolfson argued that the history of Western philosophy should be conceived as a mighty triptych, a painting with three panels.[2] In the centre stands the period of a millenium and a half of religious philosophy, initiated by Philo, when the basis of philosophical thought was determined by a number of scriptural presuppositions. Prior to that was the period of pre-religious philosophy inaugurated by the Greeks and dominated by the figure of Plato. Posterior to it was the period of post-religious philosophy, given its vital impulse by Spinoza, when valiant attempts are made to liberate philosophy from its former religious foundations or shackles (whichever way you look at it). The two central figures Philo and Spinoza— it is of course no coincidence that they are both Jews—function as the two hinges between the panels of the triptych.

In my perception Wolfson's theory has at least two merits. It serves as a useful counterweight to views of the history of philosophy such as those of Bertrand Russell, in which the period between Plotinus and Descartes is presented as no more than an unfortunate interlude. Moreover the emphasis that Wolfson more than anyone else placed on the essential unity of the medieval philosophical tradition in its triple guise of Scholastic, Islamic and Jewish philosophy is

---

[2] Wolfson (1947); a summary and evaluation of Wolfson's views on the history of philosophy is given by Runia (1984).

surely helpful. Come to think of it, he no doubt would have strongly approved of the programme put together for the symposium of which this paper is a part.

But to see Philo as the origin of and central figure in this millenium and a half of religious philosophy is another matter altogether. For Wolfson Philo is not just a witness, also not just a participant: he is no less than the star player. But in spite of all his sharp-witted analyses, no one has ever been able to accept this aspect of his theory. One problem we might mention among many others is the anomalous position occupied by the Neoplatonist tradition. The Neopla[38]tonists post-date Philo, yet in their philosophizing they stand in the tradition of pagan philosophy represented above all by Plato and Aristotle.

One of the rare occasions that Wolfson mentions Plotinus in his huge two-volumed study on Philo is in connection with the question of the ineffability and unknowability of God, and this is perhaps an interesting example to look at in a little more detail. Wolfson claims that Philo is the source of these doctrines, and so can be regarded as the father of negative theology. If this view could be granted, then that would certainly make him an important participant in the transition from Platonism to Neoplatonism.

Briefly stated the argument is this.[3] In both Plato and Aristotle we find no statements to the effect that God is unknowable or cannot be spoken of. The doctrine of God's ineffability and unknowability is in fact not found in any philosophical sources prior to Philo. Among the scriptural presuppositions upon which Philo's philosophy is based are the doctrines of God's existence and unity, to which can be added the scriptural principle of the unlikeness of God to created reality. From philosophical sources he took the views that God was incorporeal and simple in his essence. Such simplicity need not exclude a division into genus and species, and hence definition, so would not necessarily lead to the view of indescribability and unknowability. But diverse scriptural texts proclaiming God's unnameability logically led Philo to the view of his indefinability, from where the doctrine of God's unknowability is but a short further step. Philo thus starts off the entire process of speculation on negative divine predicates, which was to be developed to much greater levels of sophistication in the subsequent history of religious

---

[3] Wolfson (1947) 2.110–164; cf. further discussion at Runia (1988) 82–89.

philosophy. Wolfson ends his discussion by outlining doctrines in
Albinus and Plotinus which take over ideas first developed by Philo.

Now it is always risky to base an argument on the fact that
someone is the first to do something. All an opponent has to do is
locate a text that is earlier and the branch upon which one is sitting
is effectively sawn off. In a review of Wolfson's book Henry Chadwick
pointed to a text in Cicero, writing a generation before Philo was
born, where Plato is reported to have said in the *Timaeus* that the
father of this cosmos could not be named.[4] This seemed to strike a
fatal blow against Wolfson's argument, and scholars proceeded to
revert to the comfortable position of using Philo only as a witness
who supplies evidence on various fertile ideas that were already
circulating during his lifetime.

It is time to leave Wolfson, but before we do so we should note
the very strong tendency in his work—and this habit has by no
means died out—to view the history of ideas as consisting of a
number of protagonists engaged in philosophical debate that is all
but raised above the limitations of time and place. Philo is in conversation with Plato and Aristotle before him, while sub[39]sequently
Plotinus, Maimonides and Spinoza respond to his views. Wolfson has
little notion of the slow development of a tradition through a body
of interpreters. The terms Middle Platonism and Neoplatonism are
avoided by him. Nevertheless he is not altogether as naive as one
might think. When summarizing his view that pagan Greek philosophers drew ideas from Philo or Church fathers who had used Philo,
he adds: 'Of course I am aware of the opinion prevailing among
some scholars today that no pagan authors of that time read the
works of Philo. But neither the absence of any mention of his name
nor the absence of any direct quotation from his writings definitely
proves that he was not read, or that those who had read him were
not influenced by some of his ideas.'[5] In this he is, of course, quite
right. The chief question is, however: on whom lies the burden of
proof?

The position diametrically opposed to that of Wolfson has recently been well formulated by the German scholar Matthias Baltes:[6]

---

[4] Chadwick (1949) 63, cited by Mortley (1973) 6.
[5] Wolfson (1947) 2.158. But the appeal to Eusebius in the following words is
specious.
* [6] In an article on the theory of ideas soon to be published in the *Reallexicon für
Antike und Christentum.*

> Da die Erklärungen der Platoniker aus der Zeit des frühen Mittel-
> platonismus weitgehend verloren sind, bietet Philo nicht selten den
> ersten sicheren Beleg für einen Gedanken, woraus man gelegentlich
> zu Unrecht geschlossen hat, Philo sei der Urheber dieses Ge-
> dankens. Wo immer es im Mittelplatonismus Parallelen gibt, ist nicht
> Philo, sondern ein Platoniker als Urheber anzunehmen.

This position would seem to me nowadays to be the *communis opinio*,
though here it is expressed with more than usual rigour. Whereas in
the first four decades of this century a large number of scholars—
the names of Norden, Jonas, Pohlenz, Puech, Bréhier can be mentioned—attempted to investigate the influence of oriental thinking
on Greek philosophy, after the Second World War a strong reaction
set in, which I would particularly associate with the studies of André-
Jean Festugière. In his famous tetralogy *La Révélation d'Hermès
Trismégiste*, which in actual fact is much more about Greek philosophy than the Hermetica, he attempted to show that various later
doctrines, among which the unknowability of God is a prominent
example, are the results of autonomous developments in the history
of Greek philosophy, and that no assumptions of oriental influence
are required to explain them. It would not be exaggerated to say, I
believe, that with these studies the French scholar initiated a paradigm-change which has exerted a powerful influence.[7] Since then it
has been *de rigeur* to explain Greek philosophy on its own terms, at
least until one reaches the theurgical excesses of Iamblichus and his
school.

Allow me to give one more example of this development, this
time focussing on the relation between Philo and Plotinus. In his
monograph with the splendid title *The Architecture of the Intelligible
Universe in the Philosophy of Plotinus*, published in 1940, Hilary Armstrong devoted a chapter to what he calls 'the Great Logos'. Towards
the end of the chapter he concludes:[8] [40]

> If we are to look for a source for the conception... outside Plotinus'
> own thought, it is impossible not to be struck by the resemblance to
> the Logos of Philo. The Philonian Logos, like that of Plotinus, is the
> principle of unity-in-diversity, of the separation and uniting of
> contraries in the material world. It is the universal law, the principle
> of order in the world, distributing to each the lot appropriate to

---

[7] Festugière (1945–54); it is interesting to speculate on what the French priest's
motivations for this change were. One might suspect the influence of Thomism, to
which he was strongly attracted early in his career; see Runia (1989a) 1ff.

[8] Armstrong (1940) 107–108.

him. These resemblances by themselves would not be so striking. They could be explained by the common philosophical heritage of the two thinkers, and especially by their dependence on the Stoic tradition. What seems to bring Plotinus in these treatises very close to Philo is the fact that his Logos is, more than any other hypostasis in the *Enneads*, presented simply as an intermediary between the Divine and the material world. In the same way the Logos of Philo is simply an intermediary between God and the material creation... If we are to look for any external source for the doctrine, it seems that the only resemblance to it in the work of any earlier thinker is to be found in Philo's description of his Logos.

Armstrong, somewhat in the manner of Wolfson, merely observes a similarity between ideas, and does not ask how this might have come about.

John Rist, in his monograph on Plotinus published in 1967, unleashes a powerful attack on Armstrong's position. It is wrong to regard the logos in Plotinus as a kind of fourth hypostasis. *Logos*, Rist emphasizes, is an extraordinarily ambiguous word in antiquity and Armstrong's account of it in Philo leaves too much out. The *logos* of Philo is the place of the forms, corresponding to the Stoic *logos endiathetos*, i.e. more like Plotinus' *Nous* than his *logos*. In Plotinus *logos* occurs at the level of the World soul, whereas in Philo it occurs both transcendently at the level of the nous and immanently as pervading the cosmos.[9]

Of the many things that can be said about this subject, only a few can be mentioned. Rist is wrong in confining *logos* to the level of the Soul-hypostasis in Plotinus. From texts in *Enneads* 3.2 it is clear that *logos* is the 'formative principle' or perhaps activity (*energeia*) of the *nous*, which in its purest form exists only at the level of the *nous*, but also moves downwards into the material realm, where it is responsible, via the activity of the soul, for the rational order of the cosmos.[10] The Logos is for Philo not primarily an intermediate hypostasis, but in the first place the divine activity that is turned towards creation. As such it is located at both the transcendent and immanent level, and is often, but by no means always hypostasized. Plotinus might thus be able to show some understanding for Philo's famous phrase that the *kosmos noētos* is nothing other than the Logos of God in the act of creation (*Opif.* 24). But the Logos is clearly theologized by Philo in a way that Plotinus would find unnecessary.

---

[9] Rist (1967) 100ff.
[10] Texts and interpretation at Boot (1984) 375ff.; cf. also Wallis (1972) 68–69.

Moreover, even though there are some parallels in Middle [41] Platonism for use of the concept of Logos, Philo is, I believe, primarily
moved to employ the term on account of the biblical connotations
of the 'and God said' in Genesis 1.[11]

But we cannot accuse Rist of merely discussing disembodied
ideas. He concludes his brief examination as follows:[12]

> So far the evidence that Plotinus knew Philo is at best inconclusive.
> And there are more general considerations. Who did read Philo in
> antiquity? As far as one can tell, the only people to do so were Jews
> and Christians or at least persons interested in Judaism. Numenius
> *may* have read him; on *a priori* grounds at any rate Plotinus did not.
> And from what we know of Numenius' work, there is nothing to
> suggest that he took over anything which might introduce Plotinus
> to the Philonian *logos*.

It would not be prudent for us to make a conclusive statement on
whether Rist is correct in affirming that 'whatever slight similarities
there are between Philo's *logos* and Plotinus' are almost certainly
accidental', for this would require a much fuller investigation, which
would need to take all the relevant Middle Platonist evidence into
account.

What intrigues me about Rist's conclusion is the remark that we
can be sure on *a priori* grounds that Plotinus did not read Philo.
Surely it is not impolite to ask what these grounds might be. They
are not based on any explicit statement on Plotinus' part, otherwise
they would not be *a priori*. Are they deduced from Porphyry's famous
chapter in the *Vita Plotini* (§16) on Plotinus' altercation with Gnosticizing Christians in his own circle?[13] If so, we might further ask
whether these Gnostics and the ideas they represented can be fairly
compared with Philo and his thought. I would argue not, as will later
become clear. Or are the *a priori* grounds merely a way of indicating
that this conclusion is based on an assumption, or, to put it less
diplomatically, a deep-seated prejudice? Perhaps it is thought
inherently improbable that someone who has drunk from the
limpid font of Greek thought should show any interest in a prolix
and seemingly incoherent author such as Philo. However this may
be, I would argue that Rist has not remained unaffected by the

---

[11] Dillon (1977) 200; Runia (1986) 206, 515.
[12] Rist (1967) 101.
[13] That it is unlikely that Plotinus did not have some contact with Judaism, at
least in semi-religious, semipolitical aspects, is shown by Merlan (1963–64) 15–21.

paradigm-change which we earlier postulated to have been set in motion by Father-Festugière.

In the meantime, however, studies on Philo himself have also not stood still. In his tetralogy Festugière had painted a scathing portrait of Philo, describing him as a perfect example of the *homme moyen cultivé* produced by the dozen in the Hellenistic schools, a man whose entire writings one could read without coming across a single original thought.[14] Since then it has been decisively shown by Valentin Nikiprowetzky and others that such a portrait only emerges if one treats him as systematic philosopher rather than what he himself clearly regarded himself as being, namely an exegete of scripture who drew on the Greek philoso[42]phical tradition to unfold and expound the hidden wisdom of Mosaic philosophy.[15] In his expository task Philo exploits the ideas of various philosophical traditions, but most of all Platonism, which has led some scholars to call him a Middle Platonist, a label I can understand but would personally resist. Philo's originality lies in the creative way in which he relates the Greek intellectual tradition to the—for him authoritative—biblical tradition. This, above all, is what he bequeathed to later Patristic thought. To the extent that medieval philosophy depends on this convergence of Greek and biblical thought, there is some truth in Wolfson's claim that Philo stands at its cradle.

All of this, I would argue, should induce us to refine our original question somewhat. We started off with the dilemma witness *or* participant. The metaphor presupposed here is no doubt that of the sporting fixture. One is either part of the action, in the ring, on the field etc., or one is a spectator on the sidelines, looking on. Our image is respectable enough. Was it not reportedly used by Pythagoras to describe the role of the philosopher? But we mean it differently than he did, for in our case it is the philosophers who are in the ring, while Philo, if a witness, might be compared to a sporting journalist, sitting in the stadium and giving reports on the action that occurs before his eyes.

But if Philo, as an exegete of Mosaic scripture, is doing his own thing, and is only secondarily concerned with philosophy, we will have to come up with a better image. I have racked my brains and

---

[14] See esp. Festugière (1945–54) 2.519–585.

[15] Cf. Nikiprowetzky (1977), Winston (1985), Runia (1986), Reale-Radice (1987).

thought up the following. Since the philosophers have already been rubbed in the dirt, why don't we now compare them to politicians, politics of course being a rather special kind of game. There they are on the floor of the Parliament, engaged in the thrust and parry of party politics, debating issues of national and international importance. The journalists are sitting on the gallery, but we are not likely to find Philo there. Why don't we compare him to an academic, a professor of political science, say, or even of religion if you like, since we know that politics and religion are always closely entwined. Philo does his own thing, not directly concerned with the events in Parliament, but following them at a distance. Naturally if all other information about political happenings should be lost, then he might still be able to supply us with some material. But is it not the also case that the politicians too might be to some degree interested in what he is doing, and that this might be of some influence on their activities? Of course my image hits a bottleneck here, for politicians are on the whole far too busy to do much reading, while most philosophers hardly resemble politicians. All the same, I hope I have been able to make my point clear. [43]

2. *Detour: a brief glance at the fate of Philo's writings*

Since I have made a few pointed remarks about scholars who play around with disembodied ideas, I would now like to make a little detour and tell the tale of the survival and dissemination of Philo's writings. It is, to my mind, a fascinating story, which is not as well known as it should be, mainly for the reason, perhaps, that no readily accessible account of it has ever been given.[16] All I can do is give the bare outlines; otherwise it would distract us too much from our theme. Its direct relevance, however, will become clear towards the end. The story will be more easily followed if the reader consults the diagram on the facing page.

Philo must have died about 50 AD, and one might have expected his writings, just like the rest of Hellenistic-Jewish literature to have been lost during the series of disastrous events that overcame the community of Alexandrian Jews during the next hundred years. About a generation after Philo's death the Jewish historian Josephus

---

[16] Most information at Morris (1987). I hope to give a full account in the near future.

refers to Philo and appears to have made some use of his writings in the composition of his *Antiquities*.[17] After that there is silence for nearly a hundred years. The first Christian author to refer to Philo is Clement of Alexandria writing between 180 and 200 AD. His rather extensive use of Philo's works has recently been investigated in a fine study by Annewies van den Hoek.[18]

How did Philo survive this early watershed? It is very likely that this happened in the so-called Catechetical school of the Christian diocese of Alexandria, perhaps through the special efforts of its first 'director'—(to use a modern term)—Pantaenus. At any rate Philo's fate will from then on be intimately associated with that of the more intellectually inclined Church Fathers. Origen took a complete set of Philo's writings with him when he left Alexandria for Caesarea in Palestine in 233. We know that these copies were still there in the days of Eusebius nearly a century later, for he dutifully records them in a catalogue in his *Church History* (2.18). It is not entirely true, as is often said, that all the writings that we possess are on his list. Nevertheless it is probable that Origen's library is the archetype from which our manuscripts are derived. One of our manuscripts informs us that in the 370's Bishop Euzoius had the works transferred to parchment, which no doubt ensured their further survival.

At the same time copies of Philo's works will have continued to circulate in Alexandria. This is proven by the extensive use made of them by Didymus, the blind exegete and theologian of the Alexandrian church whose long life spans nearly the entire fourth century. At Coptos and Oxyrhynchus two fine 3rd century codices of treatises from the Allegorical Commentary were found in Christian homes—from the spine of one of them some very old [44] Gospel papyri were extracted.[19] So we know that Philo must have penetrated to the provinces. If copies were mainly available via the Catechetical school, one might be inclined to surmise that Plotinus, for example, would not have easily gained access to them while he was a student of Ammonius Saccas. But if these were available in the provinces, then probably it was not so difficult to get hold of a copy in Alexandria if one made some effort.

---

[17] Cf. *Ant.* 18.257–260. The extent of Josephus' use of Philo is somewhat controversial; cf. Feldman (1984) 410–418, and now Schwartz (1990) 40–43, 51–54.

[18] Van den Hoek (1988).

[19] For the fascinating details, see Roberts (1963).

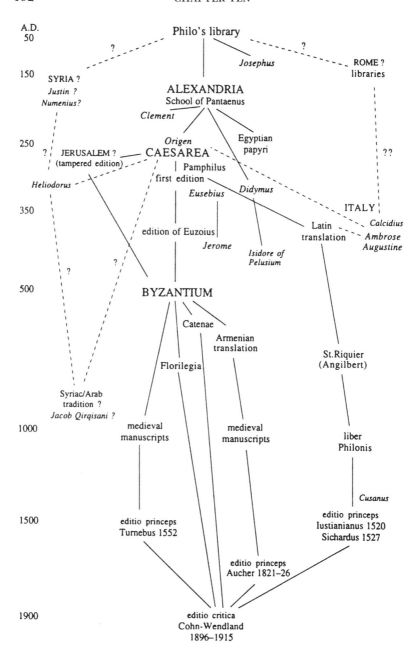

Schematic representation of the history of the transmission of the
Philonic corpus

Sometimes it is possible to trace the spread of Philo's writings with greater accuracy. I came across an interesting case when studying Van den Hoek's results. It struck me that Clement refers extensively to Philo's writings in the first five books of the *Stromateis*, but that in books 6 & 7 he only appears to make direct use of the *Quaestiones*. This fits in remarkably well with the chronology established by Méhat, who has suggested that these last two books were written after Clement left Alexandria, and started working for the bishop of Jerusalem.[20] Presumably he took a copy of the *Quaestiones* with him (this, together with the *De vita Moysis*, was the most popular work of Philo in antiquity), but had no access to the remainder of the corpus outside Alexandria.

About fifty years later it seems that Bishop Alexander of Jerusalem did want copies of Philo in the library he had established. So he sent word to Origen that he would like copies made of various treatises, and these were duly prepared in the scriptorium at Caesarea. Remarkably, as Father Barthelémy has suggested in a fascinating article,[21] it would appear that while the copies were being produced, they were tampered with by a Jew, who at a number of significant places in the corpus substituted the text of Aquila's translation for the Septuagintal text that Philo had written. Barthelémy has made a good case for identifying this Jew with Rabbi Hoshai'a, a contemporary and friend of Origen. One particular saying of this Rabbi in the *Genesis Rabbah* so closely resembles Philo's famous image of the king and the architect in the *De opificio mundi* that direct acquaintance with Philo's writings must be assumed.[22] This, however, is just about the only unambiguous example of use of Philo in the Rabbinic tradition. It would appear that the Rabbis decided that the name and work of their compatriot, who had found so much favour in the eyes of the Christians, should be consigned to oblivion.

Translations of Philonic writings were made into at least two other languages. In the late sixth century a substantial selection was translated into Armenian, including 9 treatises which are no longer extant in Greek and have only come down to us via this route.[23] Earlier, in the fourth century, two treatises had been translated into

---

[20] Méhat (1966) 42–54.
[21] Barthelémy (1967); the theory is somewhat speculative, but has not been refuted.
[22] Cf. Runia (1989b) 410ff.
[23] On the Armenian corpus see now Siegert (1989).

a very eccentric late Latin by an unknown translator. These, together with the Wisdom of Solomon, formed the basis of a slender *liber
Philonis*, which enjoyed a modest popularity in the Medieval west
and is referred to by, among others, Nicholas Cusanus.[24] Whether
there were Syriac or Arabic translations of Phi[46]lo is still an open
question. References to 'an Alexandrian' in the tenth century
Karaite writer Jacob Qirqisani are thought by some to refer to
Philo.[25] It would be highly desirable if experts in the area of Medieval Jewish and Arabic literature could determine with more precision the fate of Philo's writings and thought during this period.

But the curious tale of the fate of Philo's writings is not yet ended.
In his notice on Philo in the *Church History* (2.18.8) Eusebius
remarks that Philo's public appearances in Rome during the reigns
of Gaius and Claudius made such an impression that copies of his
treatises were deposited in Roman libraries. This report, of course,
does not sound as if we should take it very seriously. In a detailed
study, however, Enzo Lucchesi has attempted to show that the text
presupposed by Ambrose's extensive borrowings from Philo cannot
be reduced to the Caesarean tradition of the manuscripts or to the
papyri.[26] He suggests that the bishop of Milan may have gained
access to the Roman copies through the intermediation of the priest
Simplicianus, who also introduced him to Origen. Lucchesi's thesis
sounds a little far-fetched, but it has so far not been decisively
disproven.[27]

Finally I want to return to the very early period of the dissemination of Philo's writings, and so gradually make my way back to the
philosophical side of things. The often stated contention that there
is no evidence that any pagan author had ever read Philo is simply
not true. It is incontrovertible that the author of the novel *Aethiopica*,
Heliodorus, drew on Philo's *De vita Moysis* in his description of the
Egyptian worship of the Nile.[28] Heliodorus was a pagan who hailed
from Emesa in Syria, and probably lived in the early fourth century.

---

[24] On the translations Petit (1973), and the medieval transmission Wilpert (1960).
[25] Most recent discussion in Fossum (1987).
[26] Lucchesi (1977); unfortunately not discussed in Morris (1987).
[27] Polemical but not decisive remarks in Savon (1984).
[28] Proven in Runia (1990) 135ff. Rist (1967) 256 cites Goodenough (1962) 96: 'There is not a single pagan author who is remotely to be suspected of ever having read Philo.' Goodenough should have known better, since he mentions Helio-dorus at Goodhart-Goodenough (1938) 250 n.1.

Emesa is not so far from Caesarea, and the novelist may easily have gained access to this Philonic work, which itself has novelistic features, via the Caesarean route. Nevertheless I am intrigued whether Philonic material may have circulated in Syria at an earlier period, i.e. in the second century, before Origen came to Palestine.

The three names involved here are Justin, Numenius and Bardaisan. The relation of the first two to Philo has long been hotly debated. I am convinced that no passage in Justin's extant works can be adduced to prove direct use of Philo. One particular theme, however, is most intriguing, namely the interpretation of the divine theophanies in the Old Testament. Justin's christological interpretations are uncannily similar to Philo, yet differ at crucial points.[29] Generally this is explained through Justin's use of other Hellenistic-Jewish literature now lost. I would suggest an alternative hypothesis which I cannot prove. Justin studied Philo's works while still in Palestine (or possibly Syria). Later he moved to Rome where he no longer had access to the original texts, and so when he wrote the *Dialogue with Trypho* years later he had to rely on his memory and introduced modifications. This reconstruction would explain [47] the similarities and the differences, but, as I just said, cannot be proven. Two generations later Bardaisan lived in Edessa, somewhat further away. Han Drijvers has noted that the intriguing correspondences between Philo's dialogue *De Providentia* and Bardaisan's *Dialogue on Fate* raise the possibility that Philo's works were also
* known rather early in Edessa.[30]

This leaves us with the figure of Numenius, who came from Apamea, equidistant from Edessa and the hometown of his contemporary Justin, Flavia Neapolis (now Nablous). With Numenius we finally end our detour, and come to the third part of my paper. We return, therefore, to the philosophical tradition of Middle Platonism and Neoplatonism.

3. *Theological themes in Numenius and Plotinus*

It has long been recognized that, if there is to be participation of Hellenistic Jewish and specifically Philonic ideas in the development of Neoplatonism, then Numenius is its ideal vehicle. The two near-

---

[29] Cf. the analysis of Skarsaune (1987) 410ff.
[30] Drijvers (1970) 25.

contemporaries Celsus and Numenius, though both affiliated with the Platonist tradition, seem to be at the opposite ends of the spectrum. Celsus is evidently acquainted with Jewish allegorization of the scriptures, but he argues that the allegories are even more absurd than the myths they try to excuse, 'since with an astounding and quite senseless stupidity they join up ideas which in no way can be made to fit' (quoted at Origen *c. Cels.* 4.51). How different, Origen retorts, is the attitude of Numenius, who in many places comments on the ideas of Moses and the prophets and interprets them figuratively in a not unpersuasive way. Origen cites four works in which this happens. One has the title Περὶ ἀριθμῶν, which is intriguing because Philo wrote a treatise with the same name. Did Numenius include arithmological material from the Septuagint, e.g. on the numbers 1 and 7, taking his cue from Philo?[31] At any rate the sympathy that Numenius had for Jewish ideas is well attested, not only by Christian authors, who might be thought to be biased, but also, as it happens, by the (in this respect) quite unimpeachable Porphyry.[32] Such sympathy, it should be noted, cannot be gained merely through a superficial acquaintance with the Bible. In order to allegorize some form of more concentrated reading is required. Numenius apparently made the effort to do this; Celsus thought it a waste of time.[33]

The other side of the coin is that it definitely cannot be said that Numenius was a minor figure in the development of Platonism. Both Porphyry and Proclus attest to his importance, Porphyry telling

---

[31] Contrast Celsus' objection to the scheme of the creation in days as being 'very silly' (*ap.* Or. *c. Cels.* 6.49–50).

[32] Collected, with valuable comments, by Stern (1974–84) 2.206–216.

[33] Cf. the recent remarks on Porphyry by Jerphagnon (1990) 50f. which can be applied to Celsus. Note how some scholars go to absurd lengths to restrict Numenius' interest in Judaism. Here are two examples focussing on the famous *Moysēs attikizōn* remark. Dodds (1957) 6: 'If it were safe to generalise from this single example [of allegorization], we might urge that instead describing Plato as "Moses talking Attic" Numenius *ought* to have described Moses as "Plato talking Greek" (his emphasis).' Merlan (1967) 100: 'When we now ask which aspect of Plato's philosophy Numenius had in mind when he compared him to Moses, it is perhaps a fair guess that it was *only* the way in which Plato, in connection with introducing the artificer, used the term *to on aei* on one side and the phrase reading in the Septuagint "I am he who is" on the other (my emphasis).' I am not convinced by the latest attempt by Edwards (1990), published just after I presented my paper. It is true that the Numenian material in Eusebius is not very illuminating. But he was no doubt limited to the books that he could find in the Episcopal library.

us not only that Numenius' works were studied in Plotinus' school but also, quite remarkably, that the founder of Neoplatonism was accused of plagiarizing material from him (*Vita* [48] *Plot.* 14, 17). If such an accusation seems hard to believe in the light of the fragmentary material still remaining, then this no doubt tells us a lot about the state of our evidence.

Numerous footnotes and short discussions have been devoted to the possible acquaintance of Numenius with Philo. This, as John Dillon says,[34] 'would be an important fact, could it be proved'. I think it unlikely that this *can* be decisively proven one way or another, unless fresh evidence comes along. In the meantime the question will remain a matter of exercising judgment on the basis of frustratingly limited evidence.

In taking my final example from the area of Numenius' theology, I will not concentrate on the question of whether in fr. 13 Des Places he may have described his highest god with the Septuagintal and eminently Philonic epithet *ho ōn*. Ever since this possibility was first raised, it has been a source of lively dispute. Some scholars, most notably John Whittaker, defend the notion that Numenius used the Jewish phrase, regarding it as easily absorbed in a Platonizing context; others disagree, proposing conjectures or preferring to read the passage in another way.[35]

The subject I want to examine in more detail is one that Professor Waszink already some time ago in one of his learned footnotes described as 'besonders wichtig', namely Numenius' designation of his highest god as *hestōs*, 'standing'.[36] Before I proceed on this subject, I should say that it has much wider ramifications than I can possibly discuss here. These are not only philosophical but also 'religionsgeschichtlich', and include developments in both Gnostic and Islamic studies.[37]

---

[34] Dillon (1977) 144.

* [35] Pro the Judaizing reading: Festugière (1945–54) 3.44, Whittaker (1967, 1978), Des Places (1973) 55, Tarrant (1979). Proposing or accepting emendations Dodds (1957) 15, Thillet *ap.* des Places (1973) 55, Baltes (1975) 262, Dillon (1977) 368. Now Edwards (1989) proposes to retain the text, but regard ὤν merely as a participle with σπέρμα. His discussion, however, fails to take the articles of Baltes (1975), Whittaker (1978), Tarrant (1979) into account.

[36] Waszink (1964) 51.

* [37] Drs. Pieter Goedendorp (University of Groningen) is preparing a wide-ranging dissertation on the subject, to a first draft of which I am partially indebted. It may, however, still be a little while before the results of his investigations can be made public. See also the discussion in the context of Gnostic thought in Williams

The chief text in which Numenius calls his first god *hestōs* is fr. 15 (= Eusebius *PE* 11.18.20–21). I give an unpretentious literal translation:

> These are the lives of the first god and of the second god respectively, that is to say, the first god will be standing (*hestos*), the second god by way of contrast is in motion. The first god is concerned with the intelligibles, the second god with the intelligibles and the sense-perceptible things. Do not be surprised at this statement of mine, for you will hear something much more remarkable. Instead of the motion that belongs to the second god, I pronounce that the stability belonging to the first god is an innate motion, from which both the cosmos' order and eternal permanence and salvation are poured forth onto the universe.

Numenius' hieratic and somewhat pompous tone emerges clearly in this fragment. This is the only place where he calls god *hestōs*. But elsewhere the verb *hestēke* and the participle *hestēkos* are used very emphatically of *to asōmaton* and *to on*, i.e. god in his noetic aspect (fr. 4a, 5, 8). Standing and stability are clearly emphatic Numenian themes. [49]

The first response one might have to this emphasis is to look for help in the Greek philosophical tradition. Aristotle's Unmoved mover, emphatically taken over by the Middle Platonist Alcinous (*Did.* 10.2), comes to mind. Numenius should then have written *akinētos*, but his emphasis is different. Platonic texts are more important. Stability and permanence, we need hardly stress, are an essential feature of the realm of Platonic ideas. But at a certain period of career, Plato began to stress that the contrast between an unchanging noetic world and an material world in permanent flux could lead to misapprehensions. In the second hypothesis of the *Parmenides* both standing and moving are attributed to the One (146a, with twice *hestos*). A more important text, however, is the discussion in the *Sophist.* Plato is concerned that we should not take too static a view of being in its fullest sense. Whether 'being' (*to pantelōs on*) here is meant to the refer to the intelligible realm only or rather is being expanded to a wider range of things is highly controversial.[38] Numenius will, needless to say, have, adhered to the former view. 'Should we really be persuaded, Plato writes (248e ff.),

---

(1985), esp. 44f.

[38] For two opposed interpretations see Cornford (1935) 246, De Vogel (1969) 176ff.

that motion and life and soul and understanding are not present to being in the complete sense, and also not being alive and thinking, but that it is solemn and holy, without intelligence, unmoved (*akinēton*) and stable (*hestos*).'[39] And a few pages later he argues that the ideas of both motion and stability occur among the *megista genē* and that they both interrelate with being.

It seems to me highly likely that Numenius has in mind in our text the notion of spiritual motion, *kinēsis akinētos*, which was developed at great length in later Platonism on the basis of this Platonic text.[40] Nevertheless some oddities remain. The emphasis on standing is stronger in Numenius, particularly if we add the emphatic application of stability to *to on* in the other texts mentioned above. Here it is not abstract being but god who is called *hestōs* in a way that is supposed to jolt the reader.

At this point we might turn to Philo. The notion that God is *ho hestōs*, the stable or immobile one, a pillar of support for the whole of creation, is one of the more striking theological conceptions that Philo develops. It is found in so many texts throughout the Allegorical commentary that it is certainly a theme that would be picked up even by a fairly casual reader. There are at least fifteen texts in which God or the wise man are described as *ho hestōs* or *hestōs*. In each of these passages Philo brings the theme in relation to certain Pentateuchal texts, of which the most important are:

> Gen. 18:22: 'and Abraham was standing (the LXX has *hestēkōs*, but Philo cites as *hestōs*) before the Lord and he drew nigh and spoke';
> Ex. 17:6 (God speaking): 'here I am standing (*hestēka*) before you were there on the rock in Horeb';
> Deut. 5:31 (God speaking to Moses): 'but you stand (*stēthi*) here with me'. [50]

Mostly God's stability is contrasted with the mutability of created things in a relatively straightforward way, and the theme is transferred to the wise man *par excellence*, Moses (or Abraham), who cleaves to God and achieves the same stability of thought and purpose.[41] Undoubtedly the most impressive passage, which was also

---

[39] *Soph.* 248e–249a.

[40] Cf. Gersh (1973) on Proclus, but he does not discuss precursors except Plotinus.

[41] The more important passages, together with the biblical texts cited, are: *Cher.* 18–19 (Gen. 18:22), *Post.* 19–30 (Gen. 18:22, Deut. 5:31), *Gig.* 48–49 (Num. 14:44, Deut. 5:31), *Conf.* 30–32 (Deut. 5:31, Ex. 7:15), *Somn.* 1.241 (Gen. 31:13, Ex. 17:6), *Somn.* 2.221–230 (Ex. 17:6, 24:10, Gen. 18:22, Deut. 5:31, 5:5). See further

exploited at some length by Clement of Alexandria,[42] is in *De posteritate Caini* 12–31, where exegesis is given of the text 'Cain went out from the face of God and dwelt in the land of Naid.' Cain is the archetypal foolish man, and he goes to live in a land, the name of which is etymologized as 'tossing' or 'tottering'. So the contrast with Moses is easily made; hence too the relevance of the theme of God as *ho hestōs*. One little passage in this larger context struck me as particularly interesting in relation to our Numenian text. Just as earthly things would appear to stand still compared with the speed of the heavenly bodies, Philo declares, so God, who made all things, must be faster still. The strangest thing is, however, that God who outstrips even the heavenly bodies, himself stands still.[43]

Philo brings out the paradox in a way that reminds us quite plainly of the later Numenian passage. Admittely the theme of spiritual motion which we have sought behind Numenius' theology is not drawn out in Philo, even though it can easily be read in. I would not wish to claim that this passage proves Philonic influence on Numenius. Nevertheless I am convinced that that we can say that the philosopher would certainly have been attracted not only to Philo's ideas on the theme of divine stability, but also to the way in which these were derived from the Mosaic oracles. The process of allegorization is certainly in the case of this theme by no means as forced as we often find elsewhere. Numenius, so Origen tells us, allegorized the Jewish scriptures. We may surmise that the above-mentioned texts, to which attention was drawn through a reading of Philo, were among those which attracted him. Certainly it is justified, in my view, to put forward this background as an explanation for his choice of the striking epithet *hestōs* applied to the first god in fr. 15.[44]

It is with Plotinus that we should end. If Philo is to be seen as not just as a witness, but also a participant in the development of Neoplatonism, then, as we saw, this would most likely occur through the influence that Numenius exerted on Plotinus. This I regard as

---

Winston-Dillon (1983) 261f., Runia (1986) 434 (where the emphasis on Aristotelianism I would now regard as one-sided).

[42] *Str.* 2.51–52, on which see Van den Hoek (1988) 161ff.

[43] Philo, *Post.* 19. The passage is much more complicated than my paraphrase, but I cannot dwell on the other themes that are compressed together in this passage.

[44] Note that the theme of God as ἑστώς also occurs in the Hermetica; cf. *CH* 2.12, *Ascl.* 31.

more plausible than that Plotinus should have studied Philo himself, although the possibility certainly should not be excluded on *a priori* grounds. One point should at least be clear: Plotinus could not have condemned Philo on the grounds for which he attacks the Gnosticizing thinkers in *Enneads* 2.9, since these ideas are not present in his writings. Philo's practice of teasing wisdom out of ancient texts will have elicited more respect from Plotinus than the 'melodramas' (Armstrong's felicitous translation) that he disliked so much in the case of the Gnostics.[45] [51]

There are a number of texts where the theme of standing occurs in a theological context, that it to say, when Plotinus is discussing the three hypostases and our knowledge of them. All that I have time for now is to briefly indicate two passages located in the final
* treatise of the *Enneads*, 6.9.

The first is in §3, where the One is described as neither something, nor quality, not quantity, nor mind, nor soul, nor in motion, nor standing (*hestōs*), nor in place, nor time etc. (lines 41–42).[46] Henry and Schwyzer rightly point to the first hypothesis of the *Parmenides*. Nevertheless I wonder whether Plotinus has not deliberately included the various epithets in this particular form to make quite plain that in this respect his highest hypostasis differs from the first god of his predecessor Numenius.

The second interesting locus involving *hestōs* occurs in the well-known final chapter. An outpouring of terms, phrases, images, is all that the philosopher can give when trying to describe what happens in the union with the One. He is 'as if snatched up or possessed by a god, in quiet solitude and a state of calm, not turning away anywhere in his being and not turning about himself, altogether at rest (*hestōs pantē*) and having become like rest (*stasis*) itself' (11.13–15).[47] It is perhaps not contemplation, Plotinus continues, but another kind of seeing, both *ekstasis* and *stasis*, 'standing outside oneself', yet also 'standing', as well as a number of other terms, piled up in order to express what cannot be expressed (23–24). Remarkably Plotinus

---

[45] *Enneads* 2.9.13.7; cf. also the stimulating remarks of Puech (1934) 765f., but these do not apply to Philonic thought.

[46] 6.9.3.40–45. γεννητικὴ γὰρ ἡ τοῦ ἑνὸς φύσις οὖσα τῶν πάντων οὐδέν ἐστιν αὐτῶν. οὔτε οὖν τι οὔτε ποιὸν οὔτε ποσὸν οὔτε νοῦν οὔτε ψυχήν· οὐδὲ κινούμενον οὐδ᾽ αὖ ἑστώς, οὐκ ἐν τόπῳ, οὐκ ἐν χρόνῳ, ἀλλ᾽ αὐτὸ καθ᾽ αὐτὸ μονο-ειδές, μᾶλλον δὲ ἀνείδεον πρὸ εἴδους ὂν παντός, πρὸ κινήσεως, πρὸ στάσεως· ταῦτα γὰρ περὶ τὸ ὄν, ἃ πολλὰ αὐτὸ ποιεῖ.

[47] My translation based on Armstrong (1966–88) 7.343.

even refers with approval to the wise among the prophets who express in riddles how god is seen. This noteworthy emphasis on standing and stability I would regard as Numenian, and it is perhaps no coincidence that the chapter's famous final words, φυγὴ μόνου πρὸς μόνον (flight of the alone to the alone), take over and deepen a Numenian phrase.[48] These texts cannot, of course, prove that Plotinus had read Philo. They do become more comprehensible if the Philonic background is taken into account, as passed through Numenius. It need not, therefore, be a mirage, if we were to perceive far in the distance behind the word *hestōs*—but perhaps also the word *ekstasis*—the figure of the Patriarch Abraham, i.e. Pentateuchal texts as expounded by Philo, even if Plotinus may not have been conscious of these texts when he wrote his treatise.[49]

4. *Conclusion*

In conclusion I would sum up my paper in two theses.

(1) It seems to me very unlikely that the question of whether Philonic ideas exerted any influence on the development of Platonism can be definitely sett[52]led one way or another. The evidence is simply too fragmentary and has come down to us in too arbitrary a way.

(2) In such a situation the question of the *burden of proof* becomes all important. Ever since Festugière this has been assumed to lie with those who affirm that Greek philosophy was not a self-contained tradition. My inclination is to opt for the reverse. The contacts between philosophers and other religious traditions in the second and third centuries were more extensive than has often been thought. If any interest was shown in writings of Philo, then I would argue that it will have occurred on his own terms, i.e. as an expositor of ancient and venerable scriptures, even if not all the claims that he made for those writings were acceptable to philosophers, who had their own set of interests and priorities.

---

[48] Cf. Dodds (1957) 16–17, who to my mind plays down the debt to Numenius too much.

[49] Especially Gen. 18:22, Gen. 15:12 (see exegesis at *Her.* 249–267, *QG* 3.9). The comments of Arnou (1967²) 260–271 are still well worth reading.

Bibliography

A. H. ARMSTRONG, *The Architecture of the Intelligible Universe in the Philosophy of Plotinus*, Cambridge Classical Studies 6 (Cambridge 1940).

A. H. ARMSTRONG, *Plotinus*, 7 vols., Loeb Classical Library (Cambr. Mass. 1966–88).

R. ARNOU, *Le désir de Dieu dans la philosophie de Plotin* (Rome 1921, 1967²).

M. BALTES, 'Numenios von Apamea und der platonische Timaios', *VC* 29 (1975) 240–270.

D. BARTHÉLEMY, 'Est-ce Hoshaya Rabba qui censura le 'Commentaire Allégorique'? A partir des retouches faites aux citations bibliques, étude sur la tradition textuelle du *Commentaire Allégorique* de Philon', in *Philon d'Alexandrie Lyon 11–15 Septembre 1966: colloques nationaux du Centre National de la Recherche Scientifique* (Paris 1967) 45–78.

P. BOOT, *Plotinus, Over de Voorzienigheid (Enneade III 2–3 [47–48]): inleiding – commentaar – essays* (diss. Amsterdam 1984).

H. CHADWICK, Review of H. A. Wolfson *Philo, Classical Quarterly* 63 (1949) 24–25.

F. M. CORNFORD, *Plato's Theory of Knowledge* (London 1935).

J. DILLON, *The Middle Platonists: a Study of Platonism 80 B.C. to A.D. 220* (London 1977).

E. R. DODDS, 'The *Parmenides* of Plato and the Origin of the Neoplatonic One', *Classical Quarterly* 22 (1928) 129–142.

E. R. DODDS, 'Numenius and Ammonius', in *Les Sources de Plotin*, Entretiens Hardt 5 (Vandœuvres-Geneva 1957) 3–61.

H. J. W. DRIJVERS, 'Edessa und das jüdische Christentum', *VC* 24 (1970) 4–33; reprinted in *East of Antioch* (London 1984).

M. J. EDWARDS, 'Numenius, fr. 13 (Des Places): a Note on Interpretation', *Mnemosyne* 42 (1989) 478–483.

M. J. EDWARDS, 'Atticizing Moses? Numenius, the Fathers and the Jews', *VC* 44 (1990) 64–75.

L. H. FELDMAN, *Josephus and Modern Scholarship (1937–1980)* (Berlin-New York 1984).

A. J. FESTUGIÈRE, *La révélation d'Hermès Trismégiste*, 4 vols. (Paris 1945–54).

J. FOSSUM, 'The Magharians: a Pre-Christian Jewish Sect and its Significance for the Study of Judaism and Christianity', *Henoch* 9 (1987) 303–344.

S. GERSH, *ΚΙΝΗΣΙΣ ΑΚΙΝΗΤΟΣ: a Study of Spiritual Motion in the Philosophy of Proclus*, Philosophia Antiqua 26 (Leiden 1973).

E. R. GOODENOUGH, *An Introduction to Philo Judaeus* (Oxford 1962).

H. L. GOODHART and E. R. GOODENOUGH, 'A General Bibliography of Philo Judaeus', in E. R. GOODENOUGH, *The Politics of Philo Judaeus: Practice and Theory* (New Haven 1938, repr. 1967²) 125–321.

A. VAN DEN HOEK, *Clement of Alexandria and his Use of Philo in the* Stromateis: *an Early Christian Reshaping of a Jewish Model*, Supplements to Vigiliae Christianae 3 (Leiden 1988).

L. JERPHAGNON, 'Les sous-entendus anti-chrétiens de la Vita Plotini ou l'évangile de Plotin selon Porphyre', *Museum Helveticum* 47 (1990) 41–52.

E. LUCCHESI, *L'usage de Philon dans l'œuvre exégétique de Saint Ambroise: une 'Quellenforschung' relative aux Commentaires d'Ambroise sur la Genèse*, ALGHJ 9 (Leiden 1977).

A. MÉHAT, *Études sur les 'Stromateis' de Clement d'Alexandrie* (Paris 1966).

P. MERLAN, 'Religion and Philosophy from Plato's *Phaedo* to the Chaldean Oracles, with an Appendix on Plotinus and the Jews', *Journal of the History of Philosophy* 1–2 (1963–64) 163–76, 15–21; reprinted in *Kleine Schriften* (Hildesheim 1976) 358–378.

P. MERLAN, 'Greek Philosophy from Plato to Plotinus', in A. H. ARMSTRONG (ed.), *The Cambridge History of Later Greek and Early Medieval History* (Cambridge 1967) 14–132.

J. MORRIS, 'Philo the Jewish Philosopher', in E. SCHÜRER, *The History of the Jewish People in the Age of Jesus Christ* (175 B.C. – A.D. 135), a new English version revised and edited by G. VERMES *et al.*, vol. 3 part 2 (Edinburgh 1987) 809–889.

R. MORTLEY, *Connaissance religieuse et herméneutique chez Clément d'Alexandrie* (Leiden 1973).

V. NIKIPROWETZKY, *Le commentaire de l'Écriture chez Philon d'Alexandrie: son caractère et sa portée; observations philologiques*, ALGHJ 11 (Leiden 1977).

F. PETIT, *L'ancienne version latine des Questions sur la Genèse de Philon d'Alexandrie*, volume I édition critique, volume II Commentaire, Texte und Untersuchungen 113–114 (Berlin 1973).

E. DES PLACES, *Numénius Fragments* (Paris 1973).

H.-C. PUECH, 'Numénius d'Apamée et les théologies orientales au second siècle', in *Mélanges Bidez [Annuaire de l'institut de philologie et d'histoire orientales 2 (1934)]* (Bruxelles 1934) 745–778.

G. REALE and R. RADICE, 'La genesi e la natura della "filosofia mosaica": struttura, metodo e fondamenti del pensiero filosofico e teologico di Filone di Alessandria', in C. KRAUS REGGIANI, R. RADICE. and G. REALE, *La filosofia mosaica* (Milan 1987) vii–cxli.

J. M. RIST, *Plotinus: the Road to Reality* (Cambridge 1967).

C. ROBERTS, *Buried Books in Antiquity*, Arundell Esdaile Memorial Lecture for 1962 (London 1963).

D. T. RUNIA, 'History in the Grand Manner: the Achievement of H. A. Wolfson', *Philosophia Reformata* 49 (1984) 112–133; reprinted in Runia (1991).

D. T. RUNIA, *Philo of Alexandria and the* Timaeus *of Plato*, Philosophia Antiqua 44 (Leiden 1986).

D. T. RUNIA, Naming and Knowing: Themes in Philonic Theology with Special Reference to the *De mutatione nominum*', in R. VAN DEN BROEK, T. BAARDA, and J. MANSFELD (edd.), *Knowledge of God in the Graeco-Roman world*, EPRO 112 (Leiden 1988) 69–91; reprinted in Runia (1991).

D. T. RUNIA (1989a), Festugière revisited: Aristotle in the Greek Patres', *VC* 43 (1989) 1–34.

D. T. RUNIA (1989b), 'Polis and megalopolis: Philo and the founding of Alexandria' *Mnemosyne* 42 (1989) 398–412; reprinted in Runia (1991).

D. T. RUNIA, 'How to search Philo', *The Studia Philonica Annual* 2 (1990) 106–139.

D. T. RUNIA, *Exegesis and Philosophy: Studies on Philo of Alexandria*, Variorum Reprints Collected Studies (London 1991).

S. SCHWARTZ, *Josephus and Judaean Politics*, Columbia Studies in the Classical Tradition 18 (1990 Leiden).

F. SIEGERT, 'Der armenische Philon: Textbestand, Editionen, Forschungsgeschichte', *Zeitschrift für Kirchengeschichte* 100 (1989) 353–369.

O. SKARSAUNE, *The Proof from Prophecy: a Study in Justin Martyr's Proof-text Tradition; Text-type, Provenance, Theological Profile*, Supplements to Novum Testamentum 56 (Leiden 1987).

M. STERN, *Greek and Latin Authors on Jews and Judaism*, 3 vols. (Jerusalem 1974–84).

H. A. S. TARRANT, 'Numenius Fr. 13 and Plato's *Timaeus*', *Antichthon* 13 (1979) 19–29.

C. J. DE VOGEL, *Philosophia: Studies in Greek Philosophy* (Assen 1969).

R. T. WALLIS, *Neoplatonism* (London 1972).

J. H. WASZINK, 'Bemerkungen zu Justins Lehre vom Logos Spermatikos', in *Mullus: Festschrift T. Klauser* (Münster 1964) 380–390.

J. WHITTAKER, 'Moses Atticizing', *Phoenix* 21 (1967) 196–201; reprinted in Whittaker (1984).

J. WHITTAKER, 'Numenius and Alcinous on the First Principle', *Phoenix* 32 (1978) 144–154; reprinted in Whittaker (1984).

J. WHITTAKER, *Studies in Platonism and Patristic Thought*, Variorum Reprints Collected Studies (London 1984).

M. A. WILLIAMS, *The Immovable Race*, Nag Hammadi Studies 29 (Leiden 1985).

P. WILPERT, 'Philon bei Nikolaus von Kues', in *idem* (ed.), *Antike und Orient im Mittelalter: Vorträge der Kölner Mediaevistentagungen 1956–1959*, Miscellanea Mediaevalia 1 (Berlin 1962) 69–79.

D. WINSTON, *Logos and Mystical Theology in Philo of Alexandria* (Cincinatti 1985).

D. WINSTON and J. DILLON, *Two Treatises of Philo of Alexandria: a Commentary on De Gigantibus and Quod Deus Sit Immutabilis*, Brown Judaic Studies 25 (Chico, California 1983).

H. A. WOLFSON, *Philo, Foundations of Religious Philosophy in Judaism, Christianity and Islam*, 2 vols. (Cambridge Mass. 1947, 1968[4]).

POSTSCRIPT: In this article I was unable to take into account the radical thesis of R. Radice, in which he argues that Jewish-Alexandrian philosophy made a vital contribution to the development of Middle Platonism, namely through the doctrine of the ideas as thoughts of God. See R. Radice, *Platonismo e creazionismo in Filone di Alessandrie*, Pubblicazione del Centro die Recerche di Metafisica: sezione die Metafysica del Platonismo nel suo sviluppo storico e nella filosofia patristica. Studi e testi 7, Milan 1989, and a convenient summary of his thesis in English by the author in 'Observations on the Theory of the Ideas as the Thoughts of God in Philo of Alexandria', in D. T. Runia, D. M. Hay and D. Winston (edd.), *Heirs of the Septuagint. Philo, Hellenistic Judaism and Early Christianity: Festschrift for Earle Hilgert*, BJS 230 [= *The Studia Philonica Annual* 3 (1991)] 126–134. Further discussion by J. P. Martín, 'Filon y la historia del platonismo: un dialogo con R. Radice', *Methexis* 3 (1990), 119–127.

CHAPTER ELEVEN

GOD OF THE PHILOSOPHERS, GOD OF THE PATRIARCHS: EXEGETICAL BACKGROUNDS IN PHILO OF ALEXANDRIA

1. *Introduction*

Fire
God of Abraham, God of Isaac, God of Jacob,
not of philosophers and scholars.
Certainty, certainty, heartfelt, joy, peace.
God of Jesus Christ...

Through the centuries the *Mémorial* of Blaise Pascal, found sown into his clothing after his death, has been a source of inspiration for those who reflect on the God of the Jewish and Christian traditions. Also in our time interest in this statement has not abated.[1] The precise dating of the document—23rd November 1654, 10:30 till 12.30 in the evening—indicates that it records an intense religious experience. But we should not overlook that it also reflects a biblical theology. In its totality the *Mémorial* is a tissue of references to and echoes of biblical texts. In this brief contribution I wish to examine a small aspect of the biblical and exegetical background of Pascal's antithesis between the 'God of Abraham, God of Isaac, God of Jacob' and the 'God of philosophers and scholars'. As Emmanuel Levinas has pointed out, this antithesis was already in part anticipated by the medieval Jewish philosopher Judah Halevi.[2] In his

---

[1] I am thinking here particularly of the recent study by, Th de Boer, *De God van de filosofen en de God van Pascal: over het grensgebied van filosofie en theologie* (The Hague 1989), which has received much attention in this country.
[2] E. Levinas, *God en de filosofie, vertaald, ingeleid en van aantekeningen voorzien door Th. de Boer* (The Hague 1990) p. 13. I thank Prof. de Boer for pointing out this reference to me.

Kuzari he makes the king of the Khazars exclaim:[3] 'Now I understand the difference between God and the Lord and I see how great is the difference between the God of Abraham and the God of Aristotle.' In contrast to Halevi Pascal incorporates an identifiable biblical text into his antithesis. An examination of the biblical and exegetical background will show that the theme of God of the philosophers and God of the Patriarchs has an anterior exegetical background that goes all the way back to the first Jewish philosopher, Philo of Alexandria. Because this antecedent background has seldom to my knowledge been noticed or studied, it would seem appropriate to examine it in a little more detail, as a small χαριστή-ριον to a theologian who has contributed so much to our understanding of the theme of the God of Israel in the long tradition of Jewish and Christian theology and philosophy.

2. *Biblical background*

Pascal's words 'God of Abraham, God of Isaac, God of Jacob' allude to a scriptural text. In Exodus 3:6 God is recorded as saying to Moses:[4] 'I am the God of your father, the God of Abraham, the God of Isaac, the God of Jacob.' In the same chapter the words are repeated. When Moses asks God what name he should [14] report to the children of Israel, the reply we read in Exodus 3:14–15 is: 'I AM WHO I AM. Say this to the people of Israel, I AM has sent me to you.' But immediately the words are added: 'The Lord the God of your fathers, the God of Abraham, the God of Isaac, the God of Jacob, has sent me to you.' In the following chapter, when Moses appears before Pharaoh, the same phrase recurs. God instructs Moses to catch the rod turned snake by the tail 'that they may believe that Lord the God of your fathers, the God of Abraham, the God of Isaac, the God of Jacob, has appeared to you.' Remarkable as it might seem, Pascal's phrase recurs nowhere else in the Hebrew Bible. It is specifically tied to the role of Moses in the Exodus from Egypt.

In the New Testament, however, the words of God to Moses are found again. All three synoptic Gospels record how Jesus cites the

---

[3] *Kuzari* 4.16. I cite the translation of I. Heineman in *Three Jewish Philosophers* (New York 1969).

[4] For biblical passages in this section, referring to the original Hebrew and Greek texts, I have used the Revised Standard Version.

text in order to respond to the trick question of the Sadducees about a life after death. I cite the version at Luke 20:37:[5] 'But that the dead are raised, even Moses showed, in the passage about the bush, where he calls the Lord the God of Abraham and the God of Isaac and the God of Jacob. Now he is not God of the dead, but of the living; for all live to him.' The Evangelist repeats the phrase twice in a shortened form in the Acts of the Apostles. In Peter's speech to the 'men of Israel' in 3:13 he declares that 'the God of Abraham and of Isaac and of Jacob, the God of our Fathers, glorified his servant Jesus, whom you delivered up and denied in the presence of Pilate.' In the speech of Stephen before the Sanhedrin the words look back more directly to the incident of Exodus (Acts 7.31–32). When Moses saw the wonder of the burning bush and drew near to look, 'the voice of the Lord came, I am the God of your fathers, the God of Abraham and Isaac and Jacob.' For the Christian Pascal, therefore, the New Testament not only places the words cited in the *Mémorial* in the mouth of the Saviour, but also elsewhere refers explicitly to their original place in the Exodus story.

3. *Three passages in Philo of Alexandria*

We turn now to the writings of the precise contemporary of Jesus and Stephen, Philo of Alexandria. While the Apostles were beginning to spread the Gospel beyond the confines of Palestine, Philo was engaged in the defence of his beleaguered fellow-Jews in Alexandria and Rome, but also found time to write his numerous commentaries on the Pentateuch. We shall briefly examine three passages in which Philo meditates on the words spoken by God to Moses in Exodus 3:14–15. As is almost always the case in Philo, these passages can only be properly understood if we look at the context of the work in which they occur.

The first passage occurs in the *Life of Moses*, in which Philo presents a portrait of the great leader of the Israelite nation. Although in the form of a biography, the work is systematically organized. Philo first portrays Moses as king and leader, then as law-giver, priest and prophet. The incident on Mount Horeb has to do with his task as leader. God speaks to Moses and declares to him that [15] He is a God of mercy, kindly by nature and merciful to those who supplicate

---

[5] Similar texts at Matthew 22:32, Mark 12:26.

Him. Moses' task is to go to the king of Egypt and speak on behalf of his people. Philo then continues (*De vita Moysis* 1.74–76):[6]

> Moses, knowing full well that his fellow-countrymen and all the others would disbelieve his words, said: 'If they should ask the name of him who sent me, and I myself am unable to tell them, will I not make the impression of a deceiver?' God replied: 'Tell them in the first place that I am the Existent (ὁ ὤν), that they may learn the difference between being (ὄντος) and non-being (μὴ ὄντος), and also the further lesson that no name (ὄνομα) at all can properly be used of Me (κυριολογεῖται), to Whom alone Being (τὸ εἶναι) belongs. But if, being rather weak by nature, they should seek some title (πρόσρησις) to use, reveal to them not only that I am God (θεός), but also the God of the three men whose names express their excellence (ἀρετή), God of Abraham and God of Isaac and God of Jacob, the first the exemplar of wisdom gained by teaching, the second of wisdom possessed by nature, the third of wisdom gained by practice.

Philo, as the first in a long succession, interprets the divine pronouncement in Exodus 3:14 in terms of the Platonic doctrine of Being, as encouraged by the Septuagint translation on which he bases his commentary. God alone is the Existent (or the One Who is)—in contrast to non-being, i.e. created reality. No name can be properly spoken of Being. We are not told why this is so. But, as the context has already told us, God is a God of mercy, and so takes cognizance of human weakness. A distinction is made between a name and a title. Man receives a title for the Existent, i.e. God, but not the bare title alone. God is God of Abraham, Isaac and Jacob. Why this further specification, we may ask. Philo does not tell his reader what his biblical text says, that these names represent the 'Fathers' of the Israelite people. Instead they commemorate exemplars or canons of excellence, i.e. the standard allegorical interpretation of the Patriarchs in terms of the three ways of gaining wisdom. The reader cannot help but be struck by the fact that the philosophical and allegorical interpretation of the text fails to cohere with the context of Mosaic leadership and rescue from oppression. It looks very much like a fixed exegetical schema that has been imposed on the narrative.

The second passage occurs in another treatise that combines biblical exposition with biography, the *Life of Abraham*. At its outset,

---

[6] The quotes from Philo's writings in this article are given in a considerably modified version of Colson's Loeb transation.

before embarking on an account of the life of the Patriarch, Philo outlines two trinities of men favoured by God, Enos–Enoch–Noah and Abraham–Isaac–Jacob. Of these the [16] second is greater than the first. Again we cite the text (*De Abrahamo* 50–52):

> It is the case that these three were all of one house and one race—the last was son of the second and grandson of the first. All alike were God-lovers and God-beloved, and their devotion to the true God was returned by Him, Who in recognition of their high and life-long excellences considered them worthy, as the oracles reveal, to be made partners in His own title (προσρήσεως). For He joined and united His special name (ἴδιον ὄνομα) to theirs, calling Himself by an appellation (κλῆσις) that was a combination of the three. 'For this,' He said, 'is my age-long name (ὄνομα αἰώνιον)—the God of Abraham, the God of Isaac and the God of Jacob,' relative (πρός τι) instead of absolute (καθάπαξ). This statement is surely reasonable. God indeed needs no name; nevertheless, though He did not need it, He bequeathed to the race of mankind an appropriate name, so that men might be able to take refuge in prayers and supplications and not be deprived of good hope. These words do indeed appear to be spoken in the case of holy men, but they are also statements about an order of things, which is less apparent, but far superior to the sense-perceptible realm. For the holy word appears to be searching into types of soul, all of them of high worth, one which pursues the good through teaching, one through nature, and one through practice...

Although the general resemblance to the previous passage is clear, there are some new shades of emphasis. The Patriarchs are now without doubt real people, 'men of holy life', who have entered into a special relationship with the Deity. They receive this honour not because they are the object of divine election, but on account of the excellence of their way of life. At the end of the passage Philo reverts to the allegorical interpretation, which clearly has his preference. Because of the passage's encomiastic emphasis, Philo is primarily interested in the text Exodus 3:15, and this results in a quite different interpretation. The metaphysics of Being appears to be set aside. Philo no longer objects to the idea that God has a name.[7] He does not need it, but graciously bequeathes it to mankind. For if

---

[7] Note, however, that Philo does not speak of 'God' as a 'proper' name (κύριον ὄνομα), but rather as a 'special' or 'particular' name (ἴδιον ὄνομα). This may reflect the Aristotelian view that properties (ἴδια) of a substance do not represent its essence (i.e. parts of its definition), but rather characteristics in consequence of its essence. At *De mutatione nominum* 14, however, ἴδιον and κύριον are simply placed in parallel.

mankind did not have a name for God, it would lack a focal point for its hopes and supplications. But this name is not given in absolute terms, i.e. just as 'God'. It is brought in relation to the three Patriarchs, as a mark of honour and reward for their excellence. The text Exodus 3:14 is thus not explicitly mentioned. One may suspect, however, that [17] it remains implicit in the statement that (for Himself) God does not need a name.

Our third Philonic passage is found in a strictly allegorical work, *On the change of names*, and is far more complex and demanding than the previous two. Indeed it is so complicated that a full examination of its difficulties would extend us beyond the confines of this article.[8] The following discussion will thus concentrate on essentials.

In the opening passage of the treatise, Philo cites his main biblical text which he wishes to expound, Genesis 17:1: 'Abraham became ninety-nine years of age, and the Lord was seen by Abraham, and He said to him, I am your God'. Hundred is the number of perfection (when Isaac is born). Abraham, on reaching ninety-nine is making good progress towards that goal. The vision of the Lord happens to him not through the eyes of the body, but through the illumination of the mind. Philo's exegetical eye falls on the two divine names, Lord and God, which the passage appears to juxtapose. Moreover the statement 'I am your God (ἐγώ εἰμι ὁ θεός σου)' can hardly fail to remind him of the other more famous text, 'I am the Existent (ἐγώ εἰμι ὁ ὤν). So he continues (*De mutatione nominum* 7):

> Do not however think that the Existent (τὸ ὄν), that which truly exists, can be comprehended by any human being; for we have in us no organ by which we can envisage It, neither sense-perception, for It is not perceptible by sense, nor mind. Thus Moses the explorer of nature which lies beyond our vision, who, as the divine oracles tell us, entered into the darkness (Exodus 20:21), by which figure they indicate the invisible and incorporeal realm of being, searched everywhere and into everything in his desire to see clearly and plainly Him, the object of intense yearning, Who alone is good.

---

[8] I have discussed various aspects of this passage in my article, 'Naming and Knowing: Themes in Philonic Theology with Special Reference to the *De mutatione nominum*', in R. van den Broek, T. Baarda and J. Mansfeld (edd.), *Knowledge of God in the Graeco-Roman World* (Leiden 1988) 69-91. Some points in my interpretation are disputed by J. Whittaker, 'Catachresis and Negative Theology: Philo of Alexandria and Basilides', in S. Gersh and C. Kannengiesser, edd., *Platonism in Late Antiquity* (Notre Dame 1992) 61–82. At vital points the text is obscure. I adopt the readings of Colson.

But even the great prophet is thwarted in his quest and can only see what is behind the Deity—Philo cites Exodus 33:13—i.e. those things that are 'after the Existent' (μετὰ τὸ ὄν). We then read (*De mutatione nominum* 11–14):

> It is therefore consistent [with the doctrine of divine unknowability] that not even a proper name (ὄνομα κύριον) can be pronounced for the truly Existent. Do you not see that when the prophet desires to know what he must answer to those who ask about His name He says [18] 'I am the Existent (Exodus 3:14)', which is equivalent to 'my nature is to be, not to be spoken'? But lest the human race be altogether deprived of a title (προσρήσεως) for the supremely Good, He allows them to use by licence of language, as though it were His proper name, the title of Lord God of the three natures, teaching, perfection, practice, of which Abraham, Isaac and Jacob are recorded as symbols. For, He says, 'this is my age-long name (Exodus 3:15),' as if subject to examination in the age of human existence, not in the realm prior to that existence (ἐν τῷ πρὸ αἰῶνος), and 'a memorial,' that is, not set beyond memory or apprehension, and again 'for generations', not for beings that never came into being. Those who are born into mortality are in need of some substitute for the divine name, so that even if they may not approach the reality [of the Existent], they may at least be equipped with the best (substitute) name for It. This is also shown by the oracle proclaimed from the mouth of the Ruler of all in which He says that no proper name of Him has been revealed to any person. 'I was seen,' He says, 'in relation to (πρός) Abraham, Isaac and Jacob, being their God, and My name 'Lord' (τὸ ὄνομά μου κύριον) I did not reveal to them (Exodus 6:3).' For when the transposition (lit. *hyperbaton*) is re-established in the proper order the declaration would be, 'My proper name (ὄνομά μου τὸ κύριον) I did not reveal to them,' but only the substitute name for the reasons already mentioned.

We see here that Exodus 3:14–15 and 6:3 are added as secondary biblical lemmata in order to elucidate the primary exegetical text, Genesis 17:1, which is Philo's main concern. The doctrine of Being, in terms of which Exodus 3:14 is interpreted, is taken to mean that God is unknowable in his essence, and so also unnameable. But the Existent does have names, most notably 'God' and 'Lord'. These, Philo argues are not proper names, i.e. descriptive of the essence, but are substitutionary or catachrestic names, i.e. involving licence of language. The ever gracious Deity grants the human race the title of 'Lord God of Abraham, Isaac and Jacob'. Some terms in Exodus 3:15 are looked at more closely and interpreted to mean that the name is meant for that form of existence that is subject to time and generation, in opposition to the realm of unchanging being that characterizes the Existent. As final proof Philo embarks on a daring interpretation of Exodus 6:3, seemingly not shrinking back from an emendation of the sacred text.[9] God says not that 'He did not reveal his name Lord (i.e. Κύριος, translating the tetragrammaton) to the Patriarchs', [19] but rather that he did not reveal his proper name (ὄνομα κύριον) to them. What is revealed to the man of progress is not the Deity as He really is, but rather in the guise of his powers. Abraham has seen the Deity as Lord, and now he is offered the revelation of Him as God. Philo's philosophical speculations on the naming of God are dovetailed into the anagogic allegory of the soul making progress in her quest for the goal of perfection, as realized in the intimate knowledge and experience of the Deity.

4. *Some comments on Philo's interpretation*

Although the contexts of the three passages differ and there are a number of divergencies and discrepancies between them—e.g. whether God actually has a name or only a title—, the convergence is sufficient to suggest that Philo has given the text Exodus 3:14–15 a unified interpretation.[10] Our task is now to reflect on its significance.

It cannot, in the first place, be said that Philo totally dehistoricizes God's revelation to Moses and his relation to the Patriarchs. There is no doubt in his mind that Abraham, Isaac, Jacob, and later Moses were real, if clearly exceptional, men. The situation of the children of Israel, their need for a God to whom they could direct their supplications and hopes, their need also for an inspired leader, is recognized. On the other hand Philo does not interpret the text as indicating that God embarks on a special relationship with the people of Israel. The declaration that He is the God of Abraham, Isaac and Jacob is not taken to mean the reaffirmation of a covenant earlier established or the fulfilment of a promise earlier given. The Patriarchs are honoured on account of the excellence of their lives.

---

[9] If the text indeed did read ΚΥΡΙΟΣ. But recently James Royse has made a strong case for the assumption that Philo's Bible text actually contained the tetragrammaton in paleo-Hebrew or Aramaic letters; see 'Philo, Κύριος, and the Tetragrammaton', in D. T. Runia, D. M. Hay and D. Winston, edd., *Heirs of the Septuagint. Philo, Hellenistic Judaism and Early Christianity: Festschrift for Earle Hilgert* [= *The Studia Philonica Annual* 3 (1991)] (Atlanta 1991) 167–183.

[10] I set to one side the question of the extent to which Philo may in this be indebted to an earlier Alexandrian tradition.

It is no coincidence, perhaps, that two of the passages occur in biographies. The tendency of Philo's reading is clearly towards a more general understanding in terms of an allegorical or symbolic reading. Moses represents the soul in search of God's being, the Patriarchs are symbols of the anagogic path to perfection. Such perfection is expressed in terms of the Greek philosophical theory of the excellences (ἀρεταί). We should note, however, that it is risky to assume that what Philo means by these necessarily corresponds to what they mean in Plato, Aristotle, or Plotinus.

The key, in my view, to Philo's reading is that he sees a *distinction* between the two verses and the two divine pronouncements that they contain. When God describes himself as 'the Existent' in Exodus 3:14, he is speaking of Himself as He truly is, in and for himself. Man can take note, but not fully grasp. Between this statement and the one that follows Philo places the small but crucial adversative 'but'. The pronouncement that God is the God of the Patriarchs in Exodus 3:15 is interpreted as relational and accommodatory. The title 'God (θεός)' is in itself an indication of His creative power responsible [20] for the derivative existence of created reality.[11] The addition of the names of the Patriarchs accentuate the relation to mankind further. Man has an object towards which he can direct his supplications and aspirations.

It would be wrong, however, to overinterpret this distinction and read it as an *antithesis*.[12] We cannot read into his text the kind of opposition envisaged by Pascal between a God of the philosophers and a God of the Patriarchs, the former (vainly) approached by reason, the latter through belief and prophetic experience. Although distinguishing between the two texts, Philo nevertheless regards them as *complementary*. Philosophy, properly understood as the path to an understanding of the wisdom embodied in the Law, reveals the meaning of both, the former as indicating what passes beyond the mind's reach, the latter as disclosing what can be attained. For this reason, as we saw above, the names of the Patriarchs are primarily interpreted in terms of an allegorical (and basically philosophical) schema. Nowhere in Philo's writings do we find polemic against the

---

[11] The relationality of the title God is further emphasized at *De mutatione nominum* 27–28. The question of how to interpret Philo's theology of the divine Powers must also be left aside in our present context.

[12] My Utrecht inaugural lecture cited below in n. 16 was insufficiently clear on this point.

'God of the philosophers', but rather against the 'gods' of mis-
guided thinkers, who fail to recognize the utter uniqueness of the
First and only true cause. Let me cite one particularly optimistic
statement of this position, when Philo describes Israel as the nation
who is the special suppliant of Him who truly exists, maker and
father of all (*De virtutibus* 65):[13]

> For what philosophy with its high reputation grants to its disciples,
> the Jews receive from their laws and customs, namely knowledge of
> the highest and most ancient Cause, thereby rejecting the delusion
> of created gods. For no being that has come into being is truly a god,
> but only in men's fancies, since it is deprived of that most necessary
> attribute, eternity.

The emphasis on a universalist viewpoint is typically Philonic. Yet it
would be foolish to overlook the context which is in its emphasis on
the special status of the people of Israel is quite particularist.

The distinction that Philo reads into the two divine pronouncements in Exodus 3:14–15 centres on the difference between what
God is *in se*, with regard to His own Being, and what God is *in
relation*, i.e. with reference to the whole of created reality that is
dependent on him.[14] Philosophically this position cannot be denied
consistency. God's fulness of Being can only be [21] known to himself. If man could attain to it, he would be on an equal footing with
God, but this cannot be the case, for man's place is firmly fixed as an
(admittedly privileged) part of created reality. But, we must further
ask, is Philo *justified* in reading these views into his text? At this point
we must bear in mind that it is the Greek text that he is interpreting
as the divinely inspired Word. In his Alexandrian context it would
be asking rather a lot of him to demand that he refrain from
reading this text in ontological terms. It may well be that this is
exactly what the translators intended. If the text of Exodus 3:14–15
contained no more than the two statements that Philo concentrates
on, we would have to admit that his reading is at least defensible.
But this conclusion would be too hasty, for it is clear that the interpreter has engaged in a sleight of hand. Not only is there no 'but'
between the verses, such as he introduces into his interpretation. Far
more serious is the fact that he deletes a vital part of Exodus 3:14
altogether. The two verses in fact contain three separate statements:

---

[13] Cf. also the similar text at *De specialibus legibus* 2.165.
[14] See again the further passage in *De mutatione nominum* 27–28, and also the
further developments of the theme in Augustine to be discussed below.

v. 14:   I am the Existent.
         Thus you will speak to the sons of Israel, the Existent has
         sent me to you.

v. 15:   Thus you will speak to the sons of Israel, the Lord God of
         your Fathers, the God of Abraham and the God of Isaac
         and the God of Jacob has sent me to you.

Two conclusions are clear. Verse 15 stands in parallel to verse 14.
Like in a psalm couplet, the second verse is intended to say the same
as the first verse but in a different formulation: the Existent *is*
precisely the God of the Fathers. And if this is not yet clear enough,
we should note that in verse 14 the first statement records the
Existent standing apparently in splendid isolation, but in the second
He is the subject of the verb 'has sent' and so enters, as the Existent,
in salvific relation to His people, to whom he sends Moses as leader
and prophet. It is only by deleting this second statement from his
exegesis that Philo can make his philosophical interpretation work.

Inspired by Greek philosophy and an ontologizing Bible translation, Philo makes a distinction between God as He is in himself and
God as he stands in relation to his people which cannot be sustained
in the light of the biblical text itself. Biblical thought does not
encourage a down-playing of the relational aspect in favour of
ontological self-sufficiency, even if the subject is God in all His
majesty and power. In fairness to Philo, however, we should not
overlook the other side of the picture. The distinction does not
become an unbridgeable chasm. In all three passages echoes can be
heard of the doctrine of grace that is so central in Philo's thought.[15]
God listens to the supplications of his people. Knowing man's
natural limitations, he graciously bestows the [22] means whereby
the recipient can draw nigh to the Giver. This is possible through
the title 'God of the Abraham, God of Isaac, God of Jacob.'

5. *Postscript: historical connections?*

One further aspect might still be mentioned. As we noted at the
beginning of our article, Pascal famously refers to the words 'God of
Abraham, God of Isaac, God of Jacob' in his *Mémorial*. It is surely not
a coincidence that the very word 'memorial' is found in the text of

---

[15] On this theme see now D. Zeller, *Charis bei Philon und Paulus* (Stuttgart
1990).

Exodus 3:15: μνημόσυνον in Philo's Greek Septuagint, *memoriale* in Pascal's Latin Vulgate. At the same time Pascal's allusion can hardly fail to remind us of Philo's use of the same text. But as scholars we find it equally difficult to resist asking a further question and speculating on whether there might be a *historical* connection between the two thinkers. Is there a historical link that joins them together, whether directly or indirectly?

Philo's route to survival lay via the Christian tradition. Because the Rabbis neglected him, whether wilfully or out of a lack of interest, medieval Jewish thinkers remained unaware of his existence. Halevi cannot have thought of Philo when he made his antithesis between the God of Abraham and the God of Aristotle and his distinction between the names God and Lord, for the simple reason that Philo's interpretations were unknown to him. It is also not likely that Pascal will have read the three Philonic passages that we have discussed. By the middle of the 17th century Philo's complete works were available in a Greek edition and a Latin translation, and were the subject of some controversies on the doctrine of the Trinity. But it is not likely that Philo was part of Pascal's classical or theological erudition.

There remains, however, a possible route from Philo to Pascal. It passes via the greatest of the Latin Church fathers, Augustine. There are some five passages in Augustine's writings, three in his *Commentary on the Psalms*, two in his *Sermons*, in which a distinction very similar to that of Philo is made between the two statements in Exodus 3:14 and 3:15. God's true and eternal name is the great *Est* (HE IS). But how can man participate in such transcendence. Do not despair, human fragility. God also reveals that he is God of Abraham and God of Isaac and God of Jacob. This is given as God's temporal name, but it can also be called *in aeternum* (Exodus 3:15), because it leads man to eternal life.[16]

It is something of a mystery how this Philonic theme finds a place in the writings of Augustine. The Church Father mentions the Jewish thinker once in a rather critical vein. He knows one or two of the latter's works, but there is no direct evidence that he knew the treatises in which the three passages analysed above were contained.

---

[16] For references to and further discussion of these texts see my inaugural lecture, *Platonisme, Philonisme en het begin van het christelijk denken* (Utrecht 1992), esp. p. 5–7 [see above chapter 1, p. 2–3].

Verbal parallels are suggestive, but the fact that [23] differing languages are involved robs them of any demonstrative force. The more I study the respective passages, the more I am convinced that there is a link between Philo and Augustine. But I cannot prove it beyond all doubt. Even less am I able to prove that Pascal knew the particular writings of Augustine in which his exegesis of Exodus 3:14–15 occurs. This lack of proof explains the modesty of the title of this contribution. I prefer to speak of the 'backgrounds' to rather than the 'origins' of Pascal's theme.

The following necessarily speculative reconstruction thus suggests itself. Pascal knew the biblical expression 'God of Abraham, God of Isaac, God of Jacob' from the words of Jesus and Stephen in the New Testament, but was also aware that its origins lie in the revelation to Moses on Mount Horeb. The same biblical passage also contained the chief text used to read a philosophical theology into the Bible. Augustine, and before him Philo (although Pascal did not know this), had focused precisely on this text to indicate a distinction between a 'higher' and a 'lower' way of naming God, the former disclosing God as He is for Himself, the latter making him known to mankind as God of the Fathers. Pascal repudiates such an interpretation entirely. He wants nothing to do with a God of the philosophers, whether He (or It) be read into a biblical text or discovered through the endeavours of pure reason. The God of the Bible is none other than the God of the Fathers, who is also the God of Jesus Christ. The distinction speculatively delineated by Philo and Augustine is thus dismantled and rebuilt into a powerful antithesis. In so doing Pascal radically undermines the project of philosophical theology on which Philo, and after him Augustine, had embarked.

CHAPTER TWELVE

CONFRONTING THE AUGEAN STABLES:
ROYSE'S *FRAGMENTA SPURIA PHILONICA*

Although Philo's extant works occupy an impressive amount of space on the bookshelf, it would be quite wrong to think that they represent all that he ever wrote. This emerges from the following table, which lists those works, or sections thereof, that are known to have perished (the asterisks will be explained below):[1]

1.   Three complete books of *Quaestiones in Exodum*, plus the remainder of Book I, and also some missing parts of *Quaestiones in Genesim*.
2.   Some parts of the *Legum allegoriae*, perhaps amounting to two books.
3.   Another book *De ebrietate* (probably preceding the extant treatise).
4.   A book Περὶ μισθῶν mentioned at *Her.* 1.*
5.   Two books Περὶ διαθηκῶν referred to at *Mut.* 53.*
6.   The rest of the work of which *De Deo* is a fragment.
7.   Three additional books *De somniis*.
8.   Lives of the patriarchs Isaac and Jacob referred to at *Ios.* 1.*
9.   A work or a section of a work entitled Περὶ εὐσεβείας.
10.   The complementary work to *Prob.* mentioned at *Prob.* 1.*
11.   The complementary work to *Contempl.* mentioned at *Contempl.* 1.*
12.   The remaining part of *Aet.* announced at *Aet.* 150.*
13.   Some further historical-apologetic treatises in addition to *Flacc.* and *Legat.*
14.   The remainder of the *Hypothetica*, parts of which are quoted by Eusebius.
15.   A work Περὶ ἀριθμῶν, to which Philo refers at *Opif.* 52.

The list adds up to about 20–25 books, equivalent to almost half of Philo's extant corpus (50 treatises[2]). This means that what we have now amounts to no more than about two-thirds of what Philo

---

[1] Based on, but not identical with, the list compiled by J. Morris in E. Schürer, *The History of the Jewish People in the Age of Jesus Christ*, revised edition by G. Vermes *et al.* (Edinburgh 1973–87) 3.868. I delete those items of which there is no reasonable probability that they were written, e.g. a work of *Quaestiones* on the remaining books of the Pentateuch. I also cannot deal with the multitude of difficulties surrounding these lost works, for which the reader is referred to Morris' excellent discussions (which take over much from Schürer's original handbook).

[2] *QG* should be counted as 6 books; see below n. 4.

actually wrote. Some readers will no doubt feel that what we have is
more than enough. Others are greedy, however, and like to savour
every available snippet. It is this second category of scholars who are
likely to be interested in the subject of Philo's fragments.[79]

It is of the greatest importance to recognize that the works
contained in the table above need to be divided into two categories.
The first, marked in each case by an asterisk, are those works which
did not survive the double watershed in the transmission of Philo's
writings, the Library of the Catechetical school in Alexandria, and
the Episcopal Library of Caesarea. These writings were lost at an
early stage, and it is impossible—barring a miracle—that fragments
should ever be found. The second group consists of those works
which were available to Origen, Eusebius and subsequent ancient
readers, but since then have disappeared from circulation. Of these
works a number of fragments have survived, scattered throughout a
variety of sources.

There is, however, a third category of works which also needs to
be taken into consideration when we tackle the subject of Philo's
fragments. As nearly all students of Philo know, a number of his
writings survive in a secondary form: the original Greek text has
been lost, but the contents have been preserved in an Armenian
translation (and in the case of one treatise, in a Latin version).
These works are the following:[3]

1. 6 books of the *Quaestiones in Genesim*.[4]
2. 2 books (the first incomplete) of the *Quaestiones in Exodum*.
3. 2 books of *De providentia*.
4. 1 book *De animalibus*.
5. A fragment entitled *De Deo* by the first editor, Aucher.
6. Possibly a fragment from the work Περὶ ἀριθμῶν.[5]

Of these works too small sections of Greek text have been indirectly
preserved in other sources.[6] These may also be considered fragments of Philo. In fact in the case of the *Quaestiones*, on account of

---

[3] Useful overview of the 'Armenian Philo' now by F. Siegert in *Zeitschrift für
Kirchengeschichte* 100 (1989) 353–369.

[4] That *QG* as preserved actually consists of 6 books, but that these are not
entirely complete has been shown by J. R. Royse, 'The original structure of Philo's
Quaestiones' *SPh* 4 (1976–77) 41–78.

[5] As suggested by its editor, A. Terian, 'A Philonic Fragment on the Decad', in
F. E. Greenspahn, E. Hilgert, B. L. Mack (edd.), *Nourished with Peace: Studies in
Hellenistic Judaism in Memory of Samuel Sandmel*, (Chico, California 1984) 173–182.

[6] Only two small sections have been preserved in a direct ms. tradition: *QG* 2.1–
7 (recently published by J. Paramelle); *QE* 2.62–68 (discovered by Cardinal Mai).

the vagaries of transmission to be discussed below, the group of such fragments is much larger than those from the first list of writings mentioned above. If this list of lost works is added to the previous one, we obtain a result that may surprise many readers of Philo: the extant Greek corpus published in the critical edition of Cohn-Wendland amounts to just over half of what we know Philo originally to have written (38 out of 70–75 treatises). [79]

The first scholar to collect and publish fragments of Philo's lost works was Thomas Mangey in his celebrated edition of 1742, a collection that is still sometimes referred to.[7] The second important collection was by J. R. Harris, who brought together most of the fragments published by previous scholars and added some new ones of his own discovery.[8] Since then various other fragments have been published in a large number of different publications, many of which are hard to obtain.[9] The fragments of the *Quaestiones* only have been brought together by Marcus and Petit.[10] But no complete corpus of fragments has as yet been assembled. The collection prepared by Ludwig Früchtel was left unfinished at the time of his death in 1963. What is required is a definitive collection of fragments, based on thorough research of the manuscript tradition, which could take its rightful place as volume VIII of the edition of Cohn–Wendland. Only then, after nearly one hundred years, would there be a critical edition of *all* that Philo wrote which has been preserved in the original Greek. In 1977 James Royse announced that he had embarked on this project.[11] As a *preliminary* piece of research necessary for the completion of this huge task he has now nearly fifteen years later published a monograph entitled *The Spurious Texts of Philo of Alexandria: a Study of Textual Transmission and Corruption with Indexes to the Major Collections of Greek Fragments*.[12] In the remainder of this review article I wish briefly to outline and evaluate the important material contained in this study.

---

[7] T. Mangey, *Philonis Judaei opera quae reperiri potuerunt omnia*, 2 vols. (London 1742) 2.625–680.

[8] J. R. Harris, *Fragments of Philo Judaeus* (Cambridge 1886).

[9] For an overview see R. Radice and D. T. Runia, *Philo of Alexandria: an Annotated Bibliography* (Leiden 1988) nos. 1800–1822.

[10] R. Marcus, in PLCL Supplement II (1953) 179–275; F. Petit in PAPM 33 (1978).

[11] *Art. cit.* (n. 4) 65; cf. also *Studia Philonica* 5 (1978) 138–139.

[12] Arbeiten zur Literatur und Geschichte des Hellenistischen Judentums 22 (Leiden 1991) (referred to in the rest of this article as Royse *ST*).

A text may be regarded as a fragment of Philo if it satisfies three conditions: (a) it is attributed to him in the source where it is located (otherwise we would not know it was Philonic); (b) the text cannot be found in Philo's extant Greek works; (c) the text cannot be shown to be indubitably non-Philonic.[13] For condition (a) it has been necessary to scour the sources where such material is located, the *Catenae*, the Florilegia, and—more uncommonly—late ancient Christian authors. Most of this work [81] has been done, although, until there are definitive editions of all these sources, it is possible that more texts will emerge. Condition (b) has involved a lot of labour in the past. It can now be done very efficiently through the use of lexica and computer analysis.[14] Condition (c) has given rise to the subject of Royse's monograph. A considerable number of texts which are attributed to Philo in the ancient sources and have found their way into modern collections can be shown with certainty not to be Philonic. These 'spurious texts' have to be removed before the definitive corpus of Philonic fragments can be established.

Royse's research proceeds in two main steps. First he examines the two chief sources in which the fragments are located. These need be dealt with separately, since they involve differing sets of
* problems. The exegetical *Catenae* are collections of excerpts from authors in the Judaeo-Christian tradition (including Philo and Josephus) which comment on the biblical text.[15] The excerpts very often are preceded by a lemma which indicates the author. Obviously the attribution may or may not be correct, depending on the vicissitudes of transmission. Royse demonstrates that in the *Catenae on the Octateuch* only excerpts from *QG*, *QE* and *Mos.* 1 are represented. This allows a certain amount of discrimination, for if the *Catenae* attribute a text to Philo on a passage in Genesis or Exodus which is covered by the extant Armenian version but the fragment is

---

[13] Two further possibilities remain: (1) that unattributed fragments could be found, e.g. in papyri, where the language or thought resembles Philo so closely that it may be conjectured to be his (the risk involved is illustrated by the controversy aroused by the 'Stahlschmidt papyrus' discussed by Royse *ST* 139–140); (2) that an anonymous text is discovered to be a Philonic text because it coincides with preserved translations (this occurs on a few occasions, cf. Royse *ST* 15, n. 7).

[14] Finding the location of unidentified fragments in the *Quaestiones*, however, can still involve much labour. Many identifications have been made by Harris, Früchtel, Petit and Royse himself.

[15] Royse *ST* 14–25.

cannot be located there, it will in all likelihood be spurious.[16] Royse notes some 18 non-Philonic glosses found in Harris, Wendland and Marcus, which can be removed through this reasoning. It is perhaps worth emphasizing more than Royse does, however, that the validity of the procedure is dependent on the reliability of the Armenian text, which will have undergone vicissitudes of its own.[17]

A more fertile supply of spuria is furnished by the other main source, the Florilegia. Royse gently and lucidly introduces the reader to the extremely complex subject of these late ancient and byzantine anthologies [82] of excerpts from Judaeo-Christian and pagan authors.[18] The chief sources are the *Sacra Parallela* of Johannes Damascenus and the florilegia of Maximus the Confessor, Antonius Melissa and two others. Since these works do not exist in modern editions, Royse has been forced to examine the mss. themselves. Philo is cited very often in these works: in the *Sacra Parallela,* for example, he is the third most frequently cited author, behind Gregory of Nazianzus and Basil. Most spurious fragments occur once again because of misattribution in the lemmata indicating the author's name. This takes place most commonly when a Philonic excerpt is followed by one from a different source. If the lemma naming the second author becomes misplaced, then both fragments become attributed to Philo, the second erroneously. Needless to say there are many other sources of error, discussed in loving detail by Royse. One methodological dispute with Petit on the *Quaestiones* is of particular interest. Royse notes that when the Florilegia give a definite location for the excerpt, errors are comparatively rare. In fact none of the fragments explicitly assigned to the *Quaestiones* can be shown to be spurious. This raises the question of what to do with the approximately 50 fragments recorded in one or more mss. as deriving from *QG* and *QE*, but no longer traceable in the Armenian or Latin translations. Petit is sceptical about the provenance of such fragments, but Royse argues that the text of these works used by the

---

[16] The situation is more difficult when the text is not found in those chapters dealt with in the *Quaestiones*, since we do not have these complete, and we cannot in all cases be sure what they originally covered.

[17] Cf. Royse *ST* 16–18. No critical edition has been prepared of the Armenian text of the *Quaestiones*. The unreliability of the Armenian text has been claimed, not in entirely convincing fashion, by E. Lucchesi, *L'usage de Philon dans l'œuvre exégétique de Saint Ambroise: une 'Quellenforschung' relative aux Commentaires d'Ambroise sur la Genèse*, ALGHJ 9 (Leiden 1977) 104–105, 121.

[18] Royse *ST* 26–58.

first excerptors may well have been more extensive than that used by
the translators.[19] Many fragments are also transmitted under the
name Philo without further reference (as in the *Catenae*). Most of
these can be identified with extant texts, whether in Greek, Armenian or Latin. Royse argues persuasively against Harris that those
texts that remain unidentified, although they should be regarded
with due scepticism, should not be ignored altogether, since there is
always a chance that they can still be identified or may derive from a
Philonic work now lost.[20]

The second main part of Royse's study consists of a collection of
61 'spurious fragments', i.e. texts that we know have been erroneously attributed to Philo because they can be assigned with certainty to another author. Royse incorporates the findings of previous
scholars (esp. Harris and Früchtel), but has also engaged in exciting
detective work of his own. In recent years he has been able to make
use of the TLG data bank of Greek electronic texts, which helped
him to identify 9 texts. The texts are presented in four categories—
hellenica, biblica, judaica, patristica–[83]byzantina—and within each
in chronological order. Lovers of textual curiosities will be fasci-
nated and delighted by Royse's discussions of these spuria. Particularly deserving of attention are Fr. sp. 7 (ps.Aristotle), Fr. sp. 18
(attributed to Philo's wife!), Fr. sp. 25 (a fragment of ps.Philo *De
Sampsone*, revealing how ancient the pseudonymous attribution is),
Fr. sp. 50–56 (Agapetus' *Capita admonitoria*, a popular 6th century
work on political theory[21]).

The main body of the monograph has been discussed, but Royse's
largesse is not yet exhausted. In a brief chapter, included 'for the
sake of completeness' as he tells us, he discusses those entire works
that have been spuriously attributed to Philo, both in ancient and
modern times.[22] Once again many interesting details are furnished,
although not in all cases will our curiosity be satisfied. For example,
Royse mentions the cento *De mundo* which was actually the first work
to be printed under Philo's name. It would be interesting to know
more about the historical background and likely provenance of this
work. His confidence that the place of the *De aeternitate mundi* in the
Philonic corpus is secure at present is perhaps unjustified. In Sand-

---

[19] Royse *ST* 34–36, arguing against Petit PAPM 33.28.
[20] Royse *ST* 37–41.
[21] Royse's most remarkable discovery; see the extended discussion at 46–58.
[22] Royse *ST* 134–147.

mel's widely read introductory work on Philo its authenticity is regarded as dubious,[23] and recently R. Skarsten defended a thesis in Bergen which claims to prove its inauthenticity by means of advanced techniques of computer analysis.[24]

Finally Royse includes a lengthy appendix in which he lists all the Philonic fragments that have been included in the eleven major collections from Mangey to Petit, and also the Philonic excerpts in the four main Florilegia.[25] He hopes that these will offer some guidance through the labyrinth of the various collections. Certainly scholars who have occasion to refer to or use these fragments will be advised to consult these lists. In one respect they fall short of completeness. The indices only work in one direction, from source to original or unidentified Philonic text, not in the reverse direction. If the reader wishes to know all the texts from, say, *Legum allegoriae*, that are located in the florilegia or the fragment collections, he or she must work through the whole appendix. Such a reverse index could be conveniently supplied in the Instrumenta section of this

*   Annual. [84]

What should be our evaluation of this highly specialized and complicated monograph? In a sense the final result of the entire exercise is slight, a corpus of 61 texts that do *not* belong to Philo. It would be easy to see its value above all in *negative* terms, as a definitive attempt to purge Philonic studies of a number of *Fremdkörper*. The actual collection of spurious fragments can only serve a negative purpose. The study, however, also proclaims a salutary warning: beware when using fragments attributed to Philo, do not accept their attribution at face value. Royse shows how a number of scholars have been caught off-guard. The most conspicuous offender here is undoubtedly E. R. Goodenough. In his study of Philo's politics he cites a fragment from Antonius Melissa which he claims best expresses Philo's attitude to kingship, and this fragment is similarly referred to in several subsequent studies by other scholars.[26] But it emerges that

---

[23] S. Sandmel, *Philo of Alexandria: an Introduction* (New York-Oxford 1979) 76.

*   [24] According to my informants the Norwegian version of the thesis was defended in 1990, and is currently being translated into English.

[25] See list at 149–150 (where the date for Petit should be 1978); occasional reference is made to 10 other smaller collections. The appendix occupies *ST* 152–223.

[26] Royse *ST* 122 n.112, alluding to *The Politics of Philo Judaeus: Practice and Theory* (New Haven 1938) 99; further usage not mentioned by Royse by G. F. Chesnut at *ANRW* 2.16.2 (Berlin 1978), F. Trisoglio at *ANRW* 2.21.1 (Berlin 1984) 617 etc. Fr.

the text comes from the 6th century author Agapetus. In his quiet
way Royse points out further disquieting deficiencies in standard
works of Philonic scholarship. Cohn-Wendland's sources 'are far
from the best'; Goodhart-Goodenough 'supply some useful information, which must, however, be used with caution'; Marcus' collection
of the Greek fragments was 'apparently compiled in some haste'
and 'should be viewed with considerable caution'; even Petit, who
'improves greatly on her predecessors', leaves out fragments or
includes some which have since then been identified.[27]

But this monograph, although only a preliminary study, also has a
more *positive* aspect. It shows in the clearest fashion how the survival
of the Philonic corpus is intimately tied to its reception by Christians
in the late ancient and byzantine era. Aside from the more general
introductions to the problematics of the catenae and the florilegia,
Royse's study gives numerous fascinating *aperçus* into the details of
this history. A warning is in order here. This history *is* complex,
involving forays into areas far from the mainstream of classical,
judaic and even patristic scholarship. From time to time Royse
attempts to soften the impact of this esoteric material (e.g. in his
presentation of the Florilegia), but the reader will find much of the
detail hard going. What is missed most of all is a *status quaestionis* on
the scholarly research done on Philo's frag[85]ments in general, or
on the *Catenae* and Florilegia in particular. This exercise would
certainly have exceeded the bounds of what Royse has set himself to
do, but also means that considerable knowledge is assumed on the
part of the reader.

There is in my view remarkably little to criticize in the volume
under review. The author has presented his material as camera-
ready copy with great care. Typographical purists will not like the
fact that the footnotes are in the same size font as the main text, but
it does make all the details contained in them easier to read. Also
the Greek font used is aesthetically deficient. On the other hand,
Royse's attention to accuracy of detail is quite astounding: the book
is almost totally devoid of misprints and incorrect numerical and
cross-references. Certain indications reveal that it has been some

---

sp. 30, which is obviously Christian, and was recognized as such by many scholars
until its Origenian origin was identified by Wendland, is cited as Philonic by
Goodenough in *op. cit.* 72 (cf. Royse *ST* 97 n. 72).

[27] Cohn-Wendland, cf. Royse *ST* 17; Goodhart-Goodenough, 14, 26; Marcus,
218; Petit, 149, 221.

time in preparation, and is not wholly up to date in its use of standard reference works. For example, Winston's study on the Wisdom of Solomon (1979) is described as recent (the reference on p.134 is inaccurate and should be p. 68 n. 86). Royse does not refer to Gigon's new edition of Aristotle's fragments (1987), nor to the revision of Radice's Philo bibliography (Radice-Runia, 1988). From the methodological point of view a query might also be raised about the method of identifying spurious fragments. Royse only includes those which can *definitely* be attributed to other authors. In my study of the relation between God and man in Philo, published some years ago,[28] I rejected the evidence of Fr. sp. 51 (the 'Goodenough fragment') because I noted the phrases εἰκόνι θεϊκῇ and κόνει χοϊκῇ were non-Philonic. Little did I know that the text actually belongs to the 6th century, as Royse has shown. He himself points out that the word χοϊκός first occurs in Paul's 1 Cor. 15:47–49, and is only found in Christian texts.[29] In Fr. sp. 61 the word σπανιάκις is non-Philonic (the text is from Theophylactus, the 11th century archbishop of Ohrid). One wonders whether lexical and linguistic techniques might be used to show that other fragments attributed to Philo cannot be drawn from his lost writings. Naturally there will be a margin for error here, whereas the spurious fragments contained in this volume are all cut and dried cases.

All Philonists interested in the history and extent of the Philonic corpus will be deeply grateful for the research that Royse has distilled into this study. But he will not be offended if we say that it should above all be regarded as an *appetizer*. The main course has yet to be served, the complete collection of the fragments of Philo, now divested of the spurious elements hitherto included among them. It would be marvellous if [86] this could appear in 1996, to mark the centenary of the first volume of Cohn and Wendland's great critical edition of the Greek Philo. And it is fervently to be hoped that this edition of Philo's Fragments will be an incentive to further work on an even greater project, a detailed investigation of the fate of the Philonic corpus from Alexandria to the present day. The Augean stables of the Philonic fragments are not quite as cluttered as they were hitherto. But much of the Herculean task remains to be done.

---

[28] D. T. Runia, 'God and man in Philo of Alexandria', *Journal of Theological Studies* 39 (1988) 48–75.

[29] Royse *ST* 55 and n.136.

CHAPTER THIRTEEN

REFERENCES TO PHILO
FROM JOSEPHUS UP TO 1000 AD

From the very first edition of Philo's complete works it has been customary to include a list of ancient witnesses to Philo that can be gathered from the remains of ancient and early medieval literature. The editions of Mangey and Cohn-Wendland both give quite lengthy lists of passages in which reference was made to Philo.[1] The first of these witnesses is the Jewish author Josephus. The remainder are all Christian sources, for, as we all know, it was in the Christian tradition that Philo was preserved and transmitted. Various additional references are also given in the monographs of Siegfried and Conybeare, and there is a rather undigested complilation of relevant material in the bibliography of Goodhart and Goodenough.[2] So far, however, there has never been an attempt to compile a *complete* list of references to Philo in the ancient and medieval sources. In my recent monograph on *Philo in Early Christian Literature* I decided to include such a list in an Appendix.[3] This list contained a number of omissions and errors. So it seemed worthwhile to publish a second, corrected version of the list as an instrument of research for readers of this Annual.

This list contains all those passages in which Philo is referred to by name. In addition references are also given to texts in which Philo is referred to in anonymous terms, in phrases such as 'some say' or 'one of my predecessors said' (these occur rather frequently in Patristic exegesis). Inclusion of these anonymous references is necessary somewhat arbitrary and incomplete. Such references are marked by a dagger (†). Full details on the texts where the reference

---

[1] References below on p. 112.

[2] C. Siegfried, *Philo von Alexandria als Ausleger des alten Testaments* (Jena 1875); F. C. Conybeare, *Philo about the Contemplative Life* (Oxford 1895, repr. New York 1987); H. L. Goodhart and E. R. Goodenough, 'A General Bibliography of Philo Judaeus', in E. R. Goodenough, *The Politics of Philo Judaeus: Practice and Theory* (New Haven 1938, repr. Hildesheim 1967).

[3] *Philo in Early Christian Literature: a Survey*, CRINT III 3 (Assen–Minneapolis 1993) 348–356.

is found are not given, but these [112] can be easily found through consultation of various reference works.[4] I have tried in each case to use the most recent edition available. A very brief summary of the contents of the reference is given (it would take up too much space to include the texts entire). The authors included in the list are presented in approximate chronological order. Some attempt has been made to include references to Philo outside the Latin and Greek tradition, notably in works preserved in Syriac and Armenian.[5] Cut-off point is the date 1000 AD. This date is of course quite arbitrary, and there are a considerable number of subsequent references to Philo in Byzantine and Medieval Latin literature. But we have to stop somewhere, and the competence of the compiler is already being stretched to the limit.

Finally I indicate in square brackets behind each reference if it has been included in earlier lists of testimonia. The lists of Mangey and Cohn are still useful because they print the texts involved (though often in outdated versions). The key used to indicate earlier lists is as follows:

T   = A. TURNEBUS, *Philonis Iudaei in libros Mosis, de mundi opificio, historicos, de legibus; eiusdem libri singulares* (Paris 1552): Περὶ τοῦ Φίλωνος (pages unnumbered)

V   = Vulgate edition (TURNEBUS–HOESCHELIUS–GELENIUS), *Philonis Ioudaei omnia quae extant opera,* published in various forms in 1613, 1640, 1691, 1729: Illustrium et praecellentium scriptorum de Philone testimonia (pages unnumbered).

M   = T. MANGEY, *Philonis Judaei opera quae reperiri potuerunt omnia,* 2 vols. (London 1742): Veterum testimonia de Philone Judaeo (xxi–xxix).

C   = L. COHN and P. WENDLAND, *Philonis Alexandrini opera quae supersunt,* 6 vols. (Berlin 1896–1915): Testimonia de Philone eiusque scriptis (1.lxxxxv–cxiii, compiled by Cohn).

Since the sources that refer to Philo are widely scattered throughout

---

[4] Esp. the *TLG Canon* (edd. L. Berkowitz and K. A. Squitier), and for Patristic sources the *Clavis Patrum Graecorum* (ed. M. Geerard) and the *Clavis Patrum Latinorum* (ed. E. Dekkers); see further also in general the study cited in the previous note.

[5] The reception of Philo in these traditions has not yet been thoroughly investigated. I have included all the references to Philo in the Syriac tradition which I know, relying here on the assistance of my colleague L. van Rompay. The references to the Armenian tradition are given *exempli gratia.* In both cases the cut-off point of 1000 AD does not make very good sense.

diverse linguistic and literary traditions, the present list no doubt
contains omissions and in due course will have to be supplemented
by new discoveries. For the present time, however, it is as complete
as I can make it, except in the case of the Armenian tradition. [113]

LIST OF REFERENCES

JOSEPHUS (37– c. 100)
> *Antiquitates Iudaeorum* 18.8.257–260, 4.186 Niese: Philo, leader of
> the Embassy of Alexandrian Jews to the Emperor Gaius [VMC]

CLEMENT OF ALEXANDRIA (c. 150– c. 215)
> *Stromateis* 1.31.1, 20.5 Stählin: etymologies of Hagar and Sarah
> [MC]
> *Str.* 1.72.4, 46.17: Philo the Pythagorean gives many proofs that
> Jewish philosophy is more ancient than Greek philosophy
> [MC]
> *Str.* 1.141.3, 87.25: on the kings of Judah (mistaken reference[6])
> [C]
> *Str.* 1.152.2, 95.16: on the education of Moses as reported in the
> *De vita Moysis* [MC]
> *Str.* 2.100.3, 168.2: on great natures hitting on the truth [C]

CANON MURATORIANUS (c. 160–200)
> fol. 2a.7–9, = lines 69–71: Wisdom of Solomon written by Philo (if
> Tregelles' emendation is accepted)

ORIGEN (c. 185–254)
> *Contra Celsum* 4.51, 314.30 Borret SC[7]: Origen's opponent Celsus
> must be referring to the allegories of Philo and Aristobulus
> [MC]
> *C. Celsum* 5.55, 152.18: allegorical exegesis of daughters of men
> (Gen. 6:2) in terms of souls desirous of bodies†
> *C. Celsum* 6.21, 232.17: Philo composed a book about Jacob's
> ladder (i.e. *Somn.*) [MC]
> *C. Celsum* 7.20, 60.5: the Law as two-fold, literal and figurative†
> *Selecta in Genesim* 27, PG 12.97C: the six days in creation account
> for the sake of order (cf. *Opif.* 13, 26–28)†

---

[6] On this mistaken reference see further above p. 28.
[7] Line number on page, not of chapter.

Sel. in Genesim 44, PG 12.129D: on Pharaoh the φαῦλος who,
attached to *genesis*, celebrates his birthday (cf. *Ebr.* 208)†
(perhaps paraphrase of *Comm. in Matt.* 10.22)

Homiliae in Exodum 2.2, 74.3ff. Borret SC: on the Jewish midwives,
exegesis Ex. 1:17 (cf. *Her.* 128)†

Hom. in Leviticum 8.6, 34.9ff. Borret SC: on the colour of the
leper, exegesis Lev. 13:14–15 (cf. *Deus* 125)†

Hom. in Numeros 9.5, 61.8 Baehrens: ethical interpretation of the
alive and the dead, exegesis Num. 17:13 (cf. *Her.* 201)†

Hom. in Josua 16.1, 358.1 Jaubert SC: presbyters in scripture
determined not by length of years (cf. *Sobr.* 17)† [114]

Hom. in Jeremiam 14.5, 74.26 Nautin SC: the wise man complains
to Sophia, exegesis Jer. 15:10 (cf. *Conf.* 49)†

Commentarii in Matt. 10.22, 10.30.5 Klostermann-Benz: on
Pharaoh the φαῦλος who, attached to *genesis*, celebrates his
birthday (cf. *Ebr.* 208)†

Comm. in Matt. 15.3, 10.354.30 : according to Philo it is better to
be a eunuch than to rage after sexual intercourse (citation of
Det. 176) [MC]

Comm. in Matt. 17.17, 10.635.16: on the principles of
anthropomorphic language concerning God† [MC]

Comm. in Matt. frag. *ad* 25:31–34, 11.163.16: on the exegesis of
Gen. 1:2 (cf. *Opif.* 32ff.)†

Comm. in Joh. 6.42.217, 151.16 Preuschen: on the descent of souls
into bodies, exegesis Gen. 6:2†

PSEUDO-JUSTIN *Cohortatio ad Graecos* (between 220 and 300)
§9.2, 34.21 Marcovich: the 'most wise historians' Philo and
Josephus on Moses as ancient ruler of the Jews [MC]
§10.1, 36.8: Philo and Josephus on the life of Moses [MC]
§13.4, 41.29: translation of the LXX is no myth, the author has
seen the translators' cells himself and is corroborated by Philo
and Josephus [MC]

ANATOLIUS of Alexandria, bishop of Laodicaea (died c. 280)
cited at Eusebius *HE* 7.32.16: evidence of Philo on the date of
Easter [C]

PETER, bishop of Alexandria (*sedit* 300–311) and his opponent, the
Montanist TRICENTIUS
cited at *Chronicon Paschale* PG 92.73B-C, 76B: appeal to ancient
Hebrew sages on the Paschal question†

EUSEBIUS of Caesarea (c. 260–339)[8]

> *Chronicon ad Ol.* 203, 213 Karst: Philo of Alexandria, a learned man, was prominent
>
> *Chr. ad Ol.* 203, 213 Karst, 176.15–18 Helm: Sejanus attempts to destroy the Jewish people, as recorded in Philo's *Legat.*
>
> *Chr. ad Ol.* 204, 214 Karst, 177.18 – 178.3 Helm: Flaccus descrates the Jewish synagagues at Alexandria, impelling Philo to undertake the embassy [MC]
>
> *Chr. ad Ol.* 204, 214 Karst 178.17–20 Helm: statues of Gaius placed in synagagues, as Philo and Josephus report
>
> *Historia Ecclesiastica* preface to book 2, 100.20 Schwartz: this book put together from writings of Clement, Tertullian, Josephus, Philo [115]
>
> *HE* 2.4.2–6.4 : Philo introduced and then used as a source for events during the reign of Caligula [TVMC]
>
> *HE* 2.16.2–18.8: Philo as a source for the first Christians in Egypt, as witness in his *De vita contemplativa*; inventory of Philo's writings [TVMC]
>
> *HE* 6.13.7: Clement refers to Philo in his *Stromateis*
>
> *HE* 7.32.16: extract from Canons of Anatolius on the date of Easter, referring to the evidence of Philo and other Jewish authors (see also above under Anatolius) [C]
>
> *Praeparatio Evangelica* 1.9.20 Mras: Eusebius indicates that he means Philo of Byblus, not 'the Hebrew'
>
> *PE* 7.12.14—13.7: texts from Philo quoted to prove biblical basis for the 'theology of the second cause' [M]
>
> *PE* 7.17.4–18.3: again Philonic text used to interpret biblical doctrine, this time on the nature of man
>
> *PE* 7.20.9–21.5: Philo quoted on the subject that matter is not uncreated (ἀγένητος)
>
> *PE* 8.5.11–7.21: quotes from Philo's *Hypothetica* on the flight from Egypt and the Mosaic constitution [M]
>
> *PE* 8.10.19–12.20: quote from same work and *Prob.* on the Jewish ascetic way of life exemplified by the Essenes [M]
>
> *PE* 8.12.21–14.72: extracts from *Opif.* on creation and *Prov.* 2 on providence to illustrate Jewish theology [M]

---

[8] I have not included the references to Philo in the summaries preceding the books of *HE* and *PE*, except the significant remark at the end of the summary of *HE* book 2.

PE 11.14.10–15.7: repetition of Philonic material on the second cause [M]

PE 11.23.12–24.12: quotes from *Opif.* on the Mosaic (and Platonic) theory of ideas

PE 13.18.12–16: quotes from *Spec.* 1 on the Mosaic injunction not to worship the heavenly bodies

Demonstratio evangelica 8.2.123, 390.5 Heikel: Philo's evidence on Pilate and the episode of the Golden shields (*Legat.* 299) [M]

EUSEBIUS of Emesa (c. 300–359)

Frag. in *Catena in Genesim ad* Gen. 2:6, no. 194 Petit: citation of fragment from *QG* 1.3 on how 'spring' can be understood collectively

DIDYMUS THE BLIND (313–398)

Commentarii in Genesin 118.24, 119.2, 19 Nautin SC: exegesis Gen. 4:1–2, allegorization of Cain and Abel

Comm. in Gen. 139.12: exegesis Gen. 4:18, Philo is invoked as useful source of information for etymologies (cf. *Post.* 66–75)

Comm. in Gen. 147.17: exegesis Gen. 5:3–5, Philo again useful source if one wants a μυστικὸς λόγος for names and numbers

Comm. in Gen. 235.28, 236.8: exegesis Gen. 16, Philo gives a different allegorical interpretation than Paul for Sarah and Hagar [116]

Commentarii in Ecclesiasten 276.19–22 Gronewald: exegesis of Eccl. 9:9a recalls Philo's interpretation of Hagar in Gen. 16

Comm. in Eccl. 300.15 Gronewald: exegesis Eccl. 10:7–8, citing Philo's life of Moses on philosophers as kings (cf. *Mos.* 2.2)

Comm. in Eccl. 356.10–14 Binder-Liesenborghs: exeg. Eccl. 12:5 on the special nature of the almond tree (cf. *Mos.* 2.186)†

Commentarii in Zacchariam 320.6–9 Doutreleau: sword in Zach. 11:17 recalls oracle to Abraham in Gen. 12:1, which is given an allegorical interpretation†

EPIPHANIUS (c. 315–403)

Panarion (*Adv. Haer.*) 1.29.5.1–3 Holl: One may learn more about the Iessaioi from the historical writings of Philo, who visited the early Christians at Lake Mareotis [MC]

BASIL OF CAESAREA (c. 330–379)

Ep. 3.190, 74.23 Deferrari LCL: Philo interprets manna as if drawing on a Jewish tradition [MC]

GREGORY OF NYSSA (c. 338– c. 395)

> *Contra Eunomium* cap. 9.1, 1.16.20 Jaeger[9]: Eunomius' doctrine of
> God draws on Philo
> *C. Eun.* 3.5.24, 2.168.17: Eunomius glues together a rag-bag of
> statements, for which Philo supplies some material
> *C. Eun.* 3.7.8–9, 2.217.19–218.3: further explanation of Eunomius'
> theft from Philo
> *De vita Mosis* 2.113, 67.22 Musurillo: a literal justification of the
> *spoliatio Egyptiorum* is rejected†
> *Vita Mos.* 2.191, 98.15: some predecessors have regarded the blue
> of the high priest's tunic as symbolizing the air†
> *De infantibus praemature abreptis* 77.23–78.23 Horner: man created
> so that the earth would not be bereft of intelligence†

CALCIDIUS (*floruit* 350 (?))

> *Commentarius Timaei* 278, 282.8 Waszink: Philo interprets the hea-
> ven and earth in Gen. 1:1 in terms of ideas and compares them
> with the creation of archetypal man before corporeal man

PS. CHRYSOSTOM (homily dated 387)

> *In sanctum Pascha sermo* 7.2, PG 59.748: the Hebrew sages Philo
> and Josephus assure us that Easter must take place after the
> spring equinox [MC] [117]

AMBROSE (339–397)[10]

> *De Paradiso* 2.11, 271.8–272.2 Schenkl: exegesis of Adam and Eve
> in terms of νοῦς and αἴσθησις†
> *Par.* 4.25, 281.19–282.5: exegesis Gen. 2:15, man's double task in
> Paradise; Philo as a Jew only gives a moral interpretation [MC]
> *De Cain et Abel* 8.32, 367.2 Schenkl: the Word is not God's
> product (*opus*) (cf. Philo), but is himself producing (*operans*)†
> *De Noe* 13.43–44, 441.8–21 Schenkl: exegesis Gen. 7:4, rain for
> forty days and nights refers allegorically to man and woman†
> *Noe* 14.47, 445.9–16: exegesis Gen. 7:15, the double divine name†
> *Noe* 15.52, 449.26: our predecessors on the 15 cubits of Gen.
> 7:20†
> *Noe* 17.63, 459.1–6: exegesis Gen. 8:15, water as the force of the
> passions†

---

[9] The summary was probably added by a later hand, as noted by Jaeger in his edition.

[10] The list of anonymous references in Ambrose is necessarily incomplete.

Noe 26.99, 482.17: on the exegesis of the repetition of 'God' in
Gen. 9:6†

De Abrahamo 2.11.83, 634.14 Schenkl: a question raised by the
seemingly excessive death sentence in Gen. 17:14†

De fuga saeculi 4.20, 180.12 Schenkl: the etymology of Bethuel†

RUFINUS (c. 345– c. 410)

Historia Ecclesiastica 2.4–6, 2.16–18 Mommsen: Latin translation
of Eusebius' work (see above)

JEROME (347–420)

Adversus Iovinianum 2.14, PL 23.317A: Philo has written a book
on the Essenes

Chronicle, translation of Eusebius: see above under Eusebius

Commentarius in Amos 2.9 CCL 76.238.314: etymology of Esau as
meaning 'oak'

Comm. in Amos 3.6, CCL 76.304.182: on the seven ages of life (cf.
Opif. 103ff.)

Commentarius in Danielem 1.1.4a, CCL 75A.779.60: Philo thinks
the language of Hebrews was Chaldean [MC]

Commentarius in Hiezechielem 4.10b, CCL 75.171.1160: Philo on the
hyacinth of the high-priestly robes (cf. also 8.7, 75.362.850)

De viris illustribus 11, 96.5 Ceresa-Gastaldo: brief biographical
notice, together with list of writings (Philo also briefly
mentioned in §8.4 on the apostle Mark, §13.2 on Apion)
[VMC]

Dialogus adversus Pelagianos 3.6.62, CCL 80.106.62: on the seven
ages of life

Epistulae 22.35.8, CSEL 54.1.200.7: Philo reports on sober meals
of the Essenes at Pentecost [M] [118]

Ep. 29.7.1, CSEL 54.1.241.17: Philo as interpreter of the high
priestly vestments [M]

Ep. 70.3.3, CSEL 54.1.704.12: Philo, whom critics call the Jewish
Plato, cited in discussion of sound usage of pagan learning [M]

Liber interpretationis Hebraicorum nominum, praefatio, CCL 72.1.59.1–
60.3 Philo according to Origen author of a book of Hebrew
etymologies (incompletely cited in C-W) [MC]

Prefatio in librum Iob PL 28.1141A: Philo as one of the witnesses to
fact that Hebrews composed poetry (cf. *Contempl.* 80) [MC]

Praefatio in libros Salomonis, PL 28.1308A: some consider Philo to
be the author of the Wisdom of Solomon [M]

Hebraicae Quaestiones in Genesim 17:15, CCL 72.21: Sarah's name-
change by doubling the R is erroneous†[11]

THEODORE OF MOPSUESTIA (c. 350–428)
Treatise against the Allegorists, CSCO.SS 190, p. 14.27–16.5 Van
Rompay: Origen goes astray in learning the allegorical
method from the Jew Philo

AUGUSTINE (354–430)
Contra Faustum 12.39, CSEL 25.366, PL 42.274: Philo goes astray
in his allegorical exegesis of Noah's ark because he does not
take Christ into account [MC]

ISIDORE OF PELUSIUM (c. 370– c. 435)
Epistulae 2.143, PG 78.585–589: unlike other Jews Philo was
moved by the Truth to gain some idea of the orthodox
doctrine of God as one substance and three hypostases [MC]
Ep. 2.270, PG 78.700C: Philo one of the sages who use μήποτε in
the sense of ἴσως or ἔσθ' ὅτε [MC]
Ep. 3.19, PG 78.746A–B: the Jewish affirmation that the lawgiver
only spoke literally is refuted by Philo who converts nearly the
entire Old Testament into allegory [C]
Ep. 3.81, PG 78.788C–D: quotation from Philo proves that there
are beneficent passions [MC]

OROSIUS (c. 378– after 418)
Historiae adversus paganos 7.5.6–7, 445.12 Zangemeister: Philo's
embassy before Caligula fails

MARUTA OF MAIPHERKAT (*flor.* c. 410)
Canons III, CSCO.SS 192 p. 9 Vööbus: order of monks had
different name in Old Covenant, as testified in Letters
prepared by Philo for James, brother of the Lord [119]

PSEUDO-PROCHORUS (*flor.* 400–450)
Acta Johannis 110.6–112.11 Zahn: Philo has an altercation with
the Apostle John, but is converted after John heals his wife
from leprosy

JULIAN OF ECLANUM (386– c. 454)
at Augustine *Contra secundam Juliani responsionem opus imperfectum*
4.123, PL 45.1420: unless one should think that the Hebrews

---

[11] Other anonymous criticisms of Philonic etymologies at Siegfried *op. cit.* (n.
2) 396.

Sirach or Philo, who are thought to be authors of the Wisdom
of Solomon, are Manichees

* THEODORET OF CYRRHUS (c. 393– c. 466)
Quaestiones in Exodum 24 PG 80.251A: Philo interprets Pascha as
crossings (διαβατήρια) [MC]

SALAMINIUS HERMIAS SOZOMEN (c. 400– c. 460)
Ecclesiastical History 1.12.9–11, 26.4, 18 Bidez-Hansen: Philo
describes the beginnings of the monastic movement [MC]
Eccl. Hist. 7.18.7, 328.11 Bidez-Hansen: Anatolius on Philo on the
Easter question (taken over from Eusebius *HE* 7.32.16, see
above)

CATENA IN GENESIM, CATENA IN EXODUM (end 5th century)
Numerous exegetical extracts from Philo under the headings
Φίλωνος ἐπισκόπου, Φίλωνος Ἑβραίου, Φίλωνος.[12]

PROCOPIUS OF GAZA (c. 465– c. 529)
Extensive, always anonymously presented exegetical extracts from
QG and *QE* in *Commentary on the Octateuch,* PG 87†

CASSIODORUS (487– c. 580)
Institutiones divinarum litterarum PL 70.1117B: Jerome right in
attributing the Wisdom of Solomon to Philo [M]

JOHANNES LYDUS (490– c. 565)
De mensibus 4.47 103.14–104.1 Wuensch: Philo in his *Life of Moses*
writes of his Chaldean origin and the fact that his books were
written in Hebrew

ANONYMOUS ARMENIAN TRANSLATOR OF PHILO'S WRITINGS (c. 550)
Praefatio in libris Philonis De providentia, p. vii–xi Aucher: lengthy
notice on Philo's life and description of translated works [C]

ISIDORE OF SEVILLE (c. 570– 636)
Etymologiae 6.2.30: Philo and the Wisdom of Solomon [120]

BARHADBŠABBA ᶜARBAYA, bishop of Ḥalwan (c. 600)
Cause of the Foundation of the Schools, 375.6–376.4 Scher: Philo the
Jew was Director of the School of biblical exegesis in
Alexandria[13]

---

[12] In the apparatus to *Mos.* C-W also cite extracts from the *Catena in Numeros*
and the *Catena in Psalmos.*
[13] This rather inaccessible text is printed at Runia *op. cit.* (n. 3) 269–270.

ANASTASIUS SINAÏTA (c. 610– c. 700)
  Duae Viae 13.10.1–96, CCG 8.251 Uthemann: cites Ammonius of
  Alexandria who cites a dialogue between Philo and Mnason, in
  which Philo attacks the divinity of Christ [C]

CHRONICON PASCHALE (c. 650)
  PG 92.69A: quotes *Mos.* 2.222–224 on the vernal equinox and the
  Passover feast [M]

ANANIAS SHIRAKATZI (c. 650)
  Armenian Easter treatise, containing extensive reference to
  Philo's interpretation of Ex. 12:2, p. 126–127 Strobel[14]

Ps.SOPHRONIUS (7th century)
  Ἱερωνύμου ἐπιστολὴ πρὸς Δέξτρον (= Greek translation of Jerome,
  De viris illustribus) 12, 21, 23 von Gebhardt [C]

JOHN OF DAMASCUS (c. 675– c. 750)
  Prol. in Sacra Parallela, PG 95.1040B, 1044B: Philo (and Josephus)
  are cited, even though they are Jews, because they can make a
  valuable contribution [MC]

BEDA VENERABILIS (c. 673–735)
  In Marci evangelium praefatio, CCL 120.431: citation from Jerome
  on the beginnings of the church of Alexandria

GEORGE SYNCELLUS (died after 810)
  Ecloga chronographica 399.5, 402.14, 19 Mosshammer: Philo on the
  reign of Gaius (taken from Eusebius) [M]

ANONYMOUS Syrian commentator of the works of Gregory of
  Nazianzus (8th–9th century)
  ms. London, Brit. Libr. Add. 17,147, fol. 98a and 144a: some
  quotations are found from other writers, among them two
  quotations from 'Philo the Hebrew'

IŠO'DAD DE MERV (c. 850)
  Commentary on Exodus 23:19, 56.5 van den Eynde: Philo is cited on
  the injunction not to boil a lamb in its mother's milk (cf. *Virt.*
  143–144)
  Commentary on Numbers 7:11, 120.28 van den Eynde: on the phases
  on the moon and the ten sacrifices (cf. *Spec.* 1.177–178) [121]

---

[14] Further references to Philo in the Armenian tradition are not recorded in
our list.

FRECULPHUS, Bishop of Lisieux from c. 825 to 851
  Chronicon 2.1.11, PL 106.1126: On Philo and the fate of the Jews under Gaius [M]

PHOTIUS, bishop of Constantinople (c. 820–891)
  Bibliotheca 103–105, 2.71–72 Henry: record of Philonic works read, with critical comments added, to which a biographical notice is appended [VMC]

GEORGE THE SINNER (OR THE MONK) (c. 830– c. 890)
  Chronicon 9.4 1.324.17 de Boor: in the reign of Gaius Philo and Josephus, the Hebrew sages, were prominent

ANASTASIUS INCERTUS (9th century)
  In hexaemeron 7, PG 89.961D: Philo among those Church fathers who allegorized paradise in terms of the Church [C]

ARETHAS, archbishop of Caesarea (c. 850– c. 940)
  Commentary on the Apocalypse 1, PG 106.504D: on the Hebdomad [MC]

ANONYMOUS COMPILER of Nestorian exegesis (10th century (?))
  Exegesis Psalmorum 29.1 Vandenhoff: Philo as 'spiritual philosopher' in a long list of exegetes

SOUDA (c. 1000)
  1.10.14 Adler: s.v. Ἀβραάμ, Philo's book on the life of the πολιτικός will testify to Joseph [M]
  1.18.32: on the term ἀγαλματοφορούμενος [M]
  1.472.3: on the term βίος (reference mistaken, actually Eusebius, *Suppl. min. ad quaest. ad Marinum* PG 22.1008)
  2.146.9: s.v. δύναμις, two powers enter into every soul [M]
  2.655.3: in the notice on Josephus it is mentioned that Apion accused Philo
  2.698.27: s.v. θεός, an extract from Isidore of Pelusium *Ep.* 2.143 on Philo's doctrine of God (see above under Isidore) [M]
  2.705.29: s.v. θεραπευταί, Philo's account mentioned and name explained [M]
  4.737–8: s. v. Φίλων, biographical notice. with list of writings [TVCM][15]

---

[15] Other Byzantine references printed by Mangey and Cohn and also two intriguing Jewish texts in Mangey are later than 1000 AD.

CHAPTER FOURTEEN

AN INDEX TO COHN–WENDLAND'S
APPARATUS TESTIMONIORUM

The final volume of the great critical edition of Philo's writings preserved in Greek was published by Leopold Cohn and Paul Wendland in 1915, the same year in which both editors died within three months of each other. The task of preparing indices was taken over by Hans Leisegang, who in 1926–30 published the familiar two volumes containing an *index nominum*, an *index locorum veteris testamenti*, and the remarkable *index verborum*.¹ Leisegang's handling of the material recorded in the second apparatus to the text poses some problems. In this apparatus the editors had recorded both *sources* used by Philo in his writings (or sometimes mere parallels) and *witnesses* to the Philonic text in later Patristic writings. The sources were collected by Leisegang and combined—in a rather unsatisfactory fashion—with his *index nominum*. The witnesses, however, were not collected, and so remain rather inaccessible for scholars wishing to consult the edition. This is greatly to be regretted, for, as Hervé Savon has pointed out,² this *apparatus testimoniorum* is a highly precious instrument for all those studying the Patristic reception of the Philonic corpus.

In this index I have collected all the references to later patristic writings found in the apparatus of Cohn–Wendland's 6 volumes. No attempt has been made to check the accuracy of the references or bring them up to date (except in the case of Clement, where the editors themselves were inconsistent in their method of citation). Readers should note that occasionally references were added by the editors as *addenda* (see esp. volume 1, pp. lxxxx–lxxxxiv); these have been marked by an asterisk. I have not included references in the apparatus to the *Catenae* or the *Sacra Parallela*. This task I leave to those who are better acquainted than I with these recondite areas of the transmission of the Philonic corpus. [87]

---

¹ On this index see my remarks at *SPhA* 2 (1990) 107–110.
² *Saint Ambroise devant l'exégèse de Philon le Juif* (Paris 1977) 2.13 n. 23.

2.11	*Opif.* 165	45.16	*Opif.* 142*
2.11	*Leg.* 1.90	64.2	*Fug.* 137–139
3.14	*Leg.* 1.63	65.2	*Her.* 182
3.15	*Leg.* 1.74	65.5	*Her.* 185
3.16	*Leg.* 1.68	67.3-4, cf. 6	*Fug.* 157–158
3.17	*Leg.* 1.69	67.5-6	*Fug.* 158–161
3.18	*Leg.* 1.72		

Exameron

Epistulae

		1.2.6	*Mos.* 1.20
2.20	*Ios.* 42	3.6.27	*Opif.* 45
8.2-6, cf. 10	*Fug.* 132–139	3.9.40	*Aet.* 128
8.8-9	*Fug.* 140–141	4.1.3	*Opif.* 45
8.11	*Fug.* 143–144	5.14.45	*Opif.* 63
8.12-13	*Fug.* 168–170		
8.14	*Fug.* 172		
27.2-6	*Fug.* 18–20		
27.5–8	*Fug.* 14–16	**AMMIANUS MARCELLINUS**	
27.10	*Fug.* 44		
27.11–12	*Fug.* 21–22	*History*	
37.12	*Prob.* 38	17.7.13	*Aet.* 120, 140
37.13	*Prob.* 37, 40		
37.19	*Prob.* 59		
37.20	*Prob.* 60		
37.24	*Prob.* 17	**ARISTIDES**	
37.28	*Prob.* 19		
37.30	*Prob.* 21–22	*Apology*	
37.32	*Prob.* 46	p. 107 Harris	*Contempl.* 8
37.34-5	*Prob.* 94–6		
38.8	*Fug.* 16		
43.3	*Opif.* 78*		
43.7	*Opif.* 82*	**AUGUSTINE**	
43.10–11	*Opif.* 77*		
43.14	*Opif.* 83*	*Locutiones*	
43.15	*Opif.* 69*	1.81	*Post.* 133
43.16	*Opif.* 84*	3.59	*Gig.* 33
43.17	*Opif.* 85–86*		
43.19	*Opif.* 147*	*Locutiones in Heptateuch*	
44.1	*Opif.* 8–12*	I *ad* Gen. 31:13	*Somn.* 1.229
44.2	*Opif.* 13*		
44.4	*Opif.* 117*	*Quaestiones*	
44.4	*Opif.* 119*	1.1	*Post.* 49
44.10	*Opif.* 105*	1.50	*Ebr.* 208
44.11	*Opif.* 104*	1.156	*Conf.* 76
44.13	*Opif.* 118*	4.55	*Gig.* 25 [90]
45.7	*Opif.* 154*		
45.9	*Opif.* 155*		
45.10	*Opif.* 157*		
45.14	*Opif.* 141*		

BASIL

Hexaemeron

4.1	*Opif.* 149

CHALCIDIUS

In Platonis Timaeus

276	*Opif.* 26
278	*Opif.* 16
278	*Opif.* 134

CLEMENT OF ALEXANDRIA

Paedagogus

1.4	*Agr.* 178
1.5	*Agr.* 175
1.21-22	*Plant.* 169
1.97	*Plant.* 106
2.8	*Mos.* 1.65
2.10	*Contempl.* 38
2.15	*Det.* 60
2.22	*Contempl.* 45
2.29	*Contempl.* 37
2.35	*Contempl.* 49
3.1	*Virt.* 9
3.3	*Prob.* 123
3.8	*Abr.* 133
3.11	*Prob.* 37
3.27	*Ebr.* 26
3.39	*Her.* 31
3.53–54	*Plant.* 110–111
3.93	*Fug.* 157–158

Protrepticus

10	*Virt.* 183
12	*Plant.* 148
25	*Migr.* 69
69	*Somn.* 2.193–4*

Quis Dives

8	*Post.* 71

Stromateis

1.1.12	*Gig.* 25
1.5.29	*Congr.* 77
1.5.30-31	*Congr.* 20
1.5.30	*Congr.* 14
1.5.30	*Congr.* 79–80
1.5.30	*Leg.* 3.244
1.5.31	*Congr.* 2
1.5.31	*Congr.* 34
1.5.31	*Congr.* 124
1.5.31	*Ebr.* 82
1.5.32	*Congr.* 153–154
1.5.32	*Congr.* 158
1.5.32	*Congr.* 177
1.22	*Mos.* 1.2
1.23	*Mos.* 1.141
1.23	*Mos.* 1.146
1.23	*Mos.* 1.23
1.23	*Mos.* 1.5–12
1.23	*Mos.* 1.60
1.24	*Mos.* 1.164
1.26	*Mos.* 1.162
2.1.5	*Conf.* 137
2.1.6	*Post.* 14
2.6.28	*Plant.* 106
2.10.46	*Congr.* 86
2.10.47	*Congr.* 83
2.11	*Cher.* 12
2.11.50	*Congr.* 100
2.11.51	*Post.* 22
2.11.51	*Congr.* 102–105
2.11.51–52	*Post.* 27
2.15.69–70	*Migr.* 127
2.16.72	*Deus* 52
2.16.72	*Migr.* 47
2.18	*Virt.* 34
2.18	*Virt.* 9
2.18	*Virt.* 18
2.18	*Virt.* 28
2.18	*Virt.* 45
2.18	*Virt.* 82
2.18	*Virt.* 88–89
2.18	*Virt.* 90–91
2.18	*Virt.* 95–96
2.18	*Virt.* 97–99
2.18	*Virt.* 103
2.18	*Virt.* 106
2.18	*Virt.* 109 [91]
2.18	*Virt.* 110

2.18	*Virt.* 115	6.16.134–136	*Her.* 167
2.18	*Virt.* 116–117	6.16	*Opif.* 104
2.18	*Virt.* 122	7.9.53	*Deus* 65
2.18	*Virt.* 124		
2.18	*Virt.* 126		
2.18	*Virt.* 129		
2.18	*Virt.* 131		**CYRIL OF ALEXANDRIA**
2.18	*Virt.* 134		
2.18	*Virt.* 137	*Contra Julianum*	
2.18	*Virt.* 139–140		
2.18	*Virt.* 143	p. 134	*Conf.* 4
2.18	*Virt.* 145–146		
2.18	*Virt.* 148		
2.18	*Virt.* 156		**DIONYSIUS OF ALEXANDRIA**
2.18	*Virt.* 165–166		
2.19	*Virt.* 168	*ap.* Eus. *PE* 14.23.2	*Aet.* 8
2.19	*Virt.* 171		
2.19	*Virt.* 183		
2.19	*Virt.* 184		**ELIAS OF CRETE**
2.19	*Virt.* 201		
2.19	*Virt.* 205	*Commentarius in Gregorium Nazianum*	
2.19	*Virt.* 207		
2.19	*Virt.* 216	36.912	*Mut.* 187*
2.19	*Mos.* 1.22		
2.19.100–101	*Migr.* 127		
2.20	*Spec.* 4.101		**EUSEBIUS**
4.7	*Prob.* 22		
4.7	*Prob.* 96	*Demonstratio Evangelica*	
4.7	*Prob.* 108		
4.25.161	*Post.* 133	8.123	*Legat.* 299
5.4.22	*Contempl.* 16		
5.5	*Prob.* 2	*Historia Ecclesiastica*	
5.5	*Cher.* 4*		
5.5	*Cher.* 7*	2.5.7	*Flacc.* 1*
5.6	*Mos.* 2.118	2.6.1	*Legat.* 8*
5.6	*Mos.* 2.98–99	2.6.2	*Legat.* 346
5.6	*Mos.* 2.101–104	2.17.3	*Contempl.* 2
5.6	*Mos.* 2.122	2.17.5	*Contempl.* 13
5.8.52	*Agr.* 82	2.17.5	*Contempl.* 20
5.11	*Sacr.* 82	2.17.7	*Contempl.* 21–22
5.11	*Sacr.* 95–96	2.17.9	*Contempl.* 25
5.11	*Sacr.* 98	2.17.10	*Contempl.* 28
5.11.69	*Somn.* 1.235	2.17.12-13	*Contempl.* 29
5.11.72	*Post.* 14	2.17.14-15	*Contempl.* 37–38
5.11.74	*Somn.* 1.63	2.17.17-19	*Contempl.* 68
5.12.78	*Post.* 14	2.17.20	*Contempl.* 78 [92]
5.12	*Sacr.* 60	2.17.21-24	*Contempl.* 83
5.14.95-96	*Migr.* 127		
6.3.34	*Migr.* 47		

3.226–227	*Spec.* 1.198	4.228	*Spec.* 4.208
3.227	*Spec.* 1.289	4.228	*Spec.* 4.212
3.228–229	*Spec.* 1.212	4.228	*Virt.* 146
3.229	*Spec.* 1.220	4.228–229	*Spec.* 4.203
3.230–232	*Spec.* 1.226	4.231	*Virt.* 90
3.232	*Spec.* 1.235	4.233	*Virt.* 145
3.236	*Virt.* 126, 134	4.241	*Spec.* 2.216
3.237	*Spec.* 1.169	4.246–248	*Spec.* 3.80
3.238	*Spec.* 1.177	4.249–250	*Spec.* 2.136
3.239	*Spec.* 1.180	4.250–252	*Spec.* 2.175–76
3.240–243	*Spec.* 1.186	4.251	*Spec.* 3.72
3.246–247	*Spec.* 1.189	4.252	*Spec.* 3.69
3.249	*Spec.* 1.181	4.253	*Spec.* 3.30
3.252	*Spec.* 2.179	4.257ff.	*Virt.* 110
3.252–253	*Spec.* 1.183	4.259	*Virt.* 115
3.255–256	*Spec.* 1.172	4.260	*Spec.* 2.232
3.257	*Spec.* 1.256	4.268	*Virt.* 89
3.270–273	*Spec.* 3.53	4.270	*Spec.* 3.204
3.274	*Spec.* 3.11	4.271	*Spec.* 4.2
3.274	*Spec.* 3.26	4.271	*Spec.* 4.7
3.275	*Spec.* 3.32	4.271	*Spec.* 4.19
3.275	*Spec.* 3.39	4.272	*Spec.* 4.3
3.275	*Spec.* 3.39	4.272	*Spec.* 4.11
3.276	*Spec.* 1.108	4.274	*Virt.* 96
3.277	*Spec.* 1.101	4.275	*Spec.* 3.32
3.277	*Spec.* 1.105	4.275	*Virt.* 116
3.277	*Spec.* 1.110–113	4.277	*Spec.* 3.106
3.278	*Spec.* 1.80	4.278	*Spec.* 3.108
3.278	*Spec.* 1.117	4.279	*Spec.* 3.94
3.279	*Spec.* 1.98	4.281	*Spec.* 3.144
3.281	*Spec.* 2.86	4.283–284	*Spec.* 3.148
3.281	*Virt.* 97	4.287	*Spec.* 4.34
3.282	*Spec.* 2.122	4.288	*Virt.* 88
3.283–284	*Spec.* 2.111	4.289	*Spec.* 3.153
3.285	*Spec.* 2.116	4.296–297	*Virt.* 109
4.67–69	*Spec.* 1.157–158	4.298	*Virt.* 28
4.70–71	*Spec.* 1.135	4.301	*Virt.* 18
4.71	*Spec.* 1.132	8.191–192	*Spec.* 3.29
4.72	*Spec.* 1.247	14.71–72	*Spec.* 1.72
4.74	*Spec.* 1.147	18.19–20	*Prob.* 75
4.79-80	*Spec.* 1.268	18.20	*Prob.* 86
4.81	*Spec.* 1.262		
4.126	*Mos.* 1.294		
4.174–175	*Spec.* 2.126	*Bellum Judaicum*	
4.200, 203	*Spec.* 1.68	2.122	*Prob.* 86
4.207	*Mos.* 2.205	2.124	*Prob.* 85
4.218	*Spec.* 4.190	4.483-4	*Abr.* 140 [94]
4.226	*Virt.* 156	5.212	*Mos.* 2.88
4.227	*Virt.* 159	5.217	*Mos.* 2.102

Contra Apionem

1.30-31	*Spec.* 1.101
1.30-31	*Spec.* 1.110. 112
1.42	*Mos.* 2.13
1.284	*Spec.* 1.117
1.286	*Mos.* 1.17
2.193	*Spec.* 1.68
2.199	*Spec.* 3.39
2.202	*Spec.* 3.110
2.203	*Spec.* 3.63
2.206	*Spec.* 2.235
2.209	*Virt.* 103
2.237	*Mos.* 2.205
2.277–278	*Mos.* 2.13
2.280, 282	*Mos.* 2.19

LACTANTIUS

Institutiones Divinae

3.23	*Contempl.* 14

NEMESIUS

De natura hominis

1.44	*Opif.* 77
2 107	*Aet.* 42

ONOMASTICA

Ed. Lagarde

51.3	*Post.* 63
58.29	*Post.* 63
179.14	*Post.* 56
197.27	*Post.* 56
199.80	*Post.* 63

ORIGEN

Commentarius in Johannem

2.23, 80	*Post.* 14

6.10, 119	*Her.* 14
6.25, 142	*Gig.* 12

Commentarius in Matthaeum

10.22, 471	*Ebr.* 208
15.3, 3.331	*Det.* 176
15.5, 656	*Ebr.* 212
17.17, 795	*Somn.* 1.237
17.17, 795	*Deus* 52

Commentarius in Psalmos

88, 776	*Fug.* 58

Contra Celsum

2.72	*Migr.* 47
2.84	*Contempl.* 14
3.23	*Plant.* 148
4.21	*Conf.* 4
4.43	*Fug.* 9
4.44	*Fug.* 200
4.44	*Somn.* 1.6
4.45	*Fug.* 121
4.45	*Somn.* 1.247
4.71-72	*Deus* 52
4.71-72	*Somn.* 1.237
5.30	*Conf.* 68
5.55	*Gig.* 12
6.16	*Agr.* 131
6.17	*Post.* 14
6.21	*Somn.* 1.1
6.21	*Somn.* 1.133
6.62	*Migr.* 47
6.64	*Post.* 28
6.70	*Gig.* 25
7.34	*Migr.* 131

De oratione

27	*Fug.* 57
27	*Leg.* 3.25

De principiis

1.1.7	*Opif.* 62
4.16	*Leg.* 1.43
4.16	*Post.* 2
4.16	*Somn.* 1.235 [95]

ADDENDA ET CORRIGENDA

In this section I indicate the place where the studies collected together in this volume were first published, make a few remarks about what prompted me to write them in the first place, and add brief comments about specific passages (marked with asterisks in the margin of the text). These comments include corrections, occasional changes of mind and pointers to supplementary research that has been carried out since the studies were published.

CHAPTER ONE
Platonism, Philonism, and the Beginnings of Christian Thought
Translated from the Dutch original, entitled *Platonisme, Philonisme, en het begin van het christelijk denken*, Quaestiones Infinitae: Publications of the Department of Philosophy Utrecht University no. 2 (Utrecht 1992).

The circumstances of the lecture are indicated in the asterisked footnote on p. 1. The genre of the inaugural lecture is difficult. I decided to present some of the more accessible results of my research on Philo and the Church fathers, outlined in bold strokes, with emphasis on philosophical and theological aspects of the theme, and naturally with special focus on the contribution of the famous Dutch scholar who endowed the chair.

p. 2: In the original I spoke of a 'contrast', but I am persuaded after a conversation with Prof. Th. de Boer (Amsterdam) that this is too strong. See further the remark below at p. 214 n. 12.
p. 4 n. 14: The Ps.Justinian work has now been tentatively attributed to the 4th century author Marcellus of Ancyra: see C. Riedweg, *Ps.-Justin (Markell von Ankyra?) Ad Graecos De vera religione (bisher "Cohortatio ad Graecos"): Einleitung und Kommentar*, 2 vols., Schweizerische Beiträge zur Altertumswissenschaft 25 (Basel 1994), on this passage 380.
pp. 5–7: On Philo in Jerome and Augustine see now Chapter 15 in *Philo and Early Christian Literature*.

p. 8, n. 29: See below 190–195, but now wholly superseded by Chapter 1 of *Philo and Early Christian Literature.*

p. 9, n. 35: See now *Philo and Early Christian Literature* 47–58. It should be emphasized that these remarks do not represent Osborn's final word on the subject. Two further contributions are in the press.

p. 11, n. 41: See especially the conclusions presented in Chapter 16 of that work.

p. 12: This suggestion has proved controversial; see *Philo and Early Christian Literature* 340 n. 3.

p. 21: I return to this question in Chapter 11 below, where after some further reflection I am somewhat more positive on the direct relation between Philo and Augustine, and also connect their common exegesis to the *Mémorial* of Pascal.

CHAPTER TWO
Philonic Nomenclature
Originally published in *The Studia Philonica Annual* 6 (1994) 1–27.

The occasion that prompted me to write this paper is given in the first footnote. A shortened version was presented at the symposium Facets of Philo, held in honour of David Winston at the Center of Jewish Studies, Graduate Theological Union Berkeley, on 23 November 1994. The paper is largely based on material collected for *Philo in Early Christian Literature* (see also below chapter 13), but examines its subject from an angle that is not systematically dealt with in that study.

p. 30: On Ps.Justin see the remark in this chapter above on p. 4.

p. 32. There is a second reference to Philo as τῷ σοφῷ Φίλωνι (the wise Philo) towards the end of the letter.

p. 35. Isidore's use of the epithet mentioned in the previous note should have been noted here.

p. 37 n. 29: See now chapter three.

p. 50 n. 86: This practice is continued by Rav Hanazir's daughter-in-law in the title of her very recent monograph: N. G. Cohen, *Philo Judaeus: his Universe of Discourse,* Beiträge zur Erforschung des Alten Testaments und des Antiken Judentums 24 (Frankfurt 1995).

CHAPTER THREE
Why does Clement of Alexandria call Philo 'the Pythagorean'?
Originally published in *Vigiliae Christianae* 49 (1995) 1–22.

This question intrigued me for some time. In *Philo in Early Christian Literature* 136 I wrote that I found the epithet that Clement gives Philo 'rather puzzling'. See also brief comments at *The Studia Philonica Annual* 5 (1993) 133 (to which David Winston replied at 145), and 6 (1994) 11–12 (= p. 37 above). So clearly it was time to reach a more definitive verdict.

CHAPTER FOUR
Underneath Cohn and Colson: the Text of Philo's De virtutibus
Originally published in E. H. Lovering Jr. (ed.), *Society of Biblical Literature 1991 Seminar Papers*, Society of Biblical Literature Seminar Papers Series 30 (Atlanta, Georgia 1991) 116–134.

This paper was prepared for a meeting of the Philo Seminar, which took place at the 127th Annual meeting of the Society of Biblical Literature, Kansas City, on November 24th 1991. As in the case of meetings of the Seminar in earlier years, one session was devoted to the detailed examination of a Philonic treatise, in this case *De virtutibus*. The task I was set was to look at the text of the treatise. At the same time I tried to broaden the theme somewhat and also take into account the questions of what we are doing when we read a Greek Philonic text and what we should think of the texts that we have at our disposal. My paper shows a certain amount of overlap with the paper presented by Earle Hilgert at the same session, 'A Review of Previous Research on Philo's *De virtutibus*', published on pp. 103–115 of the same volume. Although concentrating somewhat more on Philo's own writings than other papers in this collection, it did fit in well with my research on Philo and the Church Fathers, because work on the Philonic text needs to take into account the transmission of Philo's works in the Patristic period, as is demonstrated at some length in the course of the argument.

As the paper was going to press Prof. James Royse (San Francisco) kindly sent me a number of comments on a draft version, which I was no longer able to take into account before the paper was published. Extracts from these will be cited in the additional notes below.

p. 77: Royse writes: 'Your analogy... is, I think, slightly skewed at one point. Basic and C are not compilers, but are, rather, what are called high-level languages, in contrast to machine or assembly languages. The distinction is as you say: they look more like English (at least like structured, technical English), and in particular they permit the programmer to ignore the internal workings of the particular machine involved. (This latter point is sometimes put in terms of portability: a C program on one machine may look exactly the same as a C program on another machine. The machine or assembly language program will look completely different.) What the compiler does is to convert a program in the high-level language into the machine language for the particular machine involved. (Usually a compiler will also produce assembly language, give messages on syntax errors, etc.) So each high-level language on each (type of) machine will have a compiler.

p. 80: Mangey's text is the one on which C. D. Yonge's English translation of 1854–55 is based on, recently republished as *The Works of Philo Complete and Unabridged* (Peabody, Mass. 1993). See also the note below on p. 100.

p. 81: More details on this episode now in J. R. Royse, *The Spurious Texts of Philo of Alexandria: a Study of Textual Transmission and Corruption with Indexes to the Major Collections of Greek Fragments*, ALGHJ 22 (Leiden 1991) 136–138.

p. 85, n. 32: See now my further discussion in *Philo in Early Christian Literature* 21 and plate opposite.

p. 88: This can be seen by following the italicized passages in the translation of the passage offered by Van den Hoek on p. 71–106 of the study cited in n. 47.

p. 88, n. 46: On the mention of Philo's name, the immediate context and the words attributed to him, see further above p. 57–60.

p. 90: I have added a translation of the two Greek texts.

p. 92 n. 60: On these sources see now the excellent chapters in the study of James Royse cited in the note on p. 81 above, p. 14–58.

p. 99: On the presence of Philo in the *Catenae* and the title 'Hebrew' see above p. 46–47 (where I missed this exceptional reference). According to the contents of the ms. given by G-G no. 183 the extract is from the *Catena in Numeros*.

p. 100, n. 98: This is not to say that a new English translation of Philo's works is not highly desirable. See my review of the reprint of Yonge's 1854–55 translation in *The Studia Philonica Annual* 6 (1994) 171–182, esp. 181.

CHAPTER FIVE

Verba Philonica, Ἀγαλματοφορεῖν, *and the Authenticity of the* De Resurrectione *Attributed to Athenagoras.*
Originally published in *Vigiliae Christianae* 46 (1992) 313–327, in a special fascicle containing two articles dedicated to Prof. J. C. M. van Winden on his 70th birthday (the other by J. Mansfeld).

The main purpose of the article was to draw attention to influence that Philo's language had on Patristic terminology. The chief example used was the case of ἀγαλματοφορέω, and this had a possible consequence for the debate on the authenticity of the treatise attributed to the apologist Athenagoras. Unbeknown to me Philo's usage of the same term was analysed in an Italian article by P. Graffigna, 'Un hapax di Filone d'Alessandria: ἀγαλματοφορεῖν', *Maia* 43 (1991) 143–148. She does not examine the patristic usage dependent on Philo.

p. 103: The case in Proclus is perhaps not as insignificant as I thought. Homer is called a κοσμοπολίτης because he does not indicate his parents of place of birth, and numerous cities have claimed him as his own. The implication is that Homer's status transcends particular interests and is truly universal.

p. 103 n. 5: The new 'D' version reveals one more text, Didymus of Alexandria, *Commentary on the Psalms* 186.18. Didymus was well acquainted with Philo's writings; cf. *Philo and Early Christian Literature* 197–204.

p. 106 n. 9: The new 'D' version of the TLG reveals two additional texts in Didymus of Alexandria, *Commentary on Zacharias*, 5.149.7, 5.150.5 (exegesis Zach. 14:15, the soul symbolized by an ass is freed from irrationality and goes up to the spiritual Jerusalem, just as Jesus was ἀγαλματοφορούμενος on an ass). The editor L. Doutreleau, SC 85 (Paris 1962) 3.1055, notes that the word is strange because ἄγαλμα usually refers to an idol. But he has not taken the Philonic background into account and the fact that the term must be placed in the context of Logos theology/epistemology (cf. the other patristic texts discussed below at p. 110). The same disk also gives two texts from the Byzantine historian Nicephorus Gregoras, *Historia Romana* 2.894.14, 3.544.5.

p. 112: The debate recorded here has been continued by the two main scholars representing the positions against and for authenticity:

—H. E. Lona, 'Bemerkungen zu Athenagoras und Pseudo-Athenagoras', *VC* 42 (1988) 352–363 (not cited in the original article); 'Die dem Apologeten Athenagoras zugeschriebene Schrift «De resurrectione mortuorum» und die altchristliche Auferstehungsapologetik', *Salesianum* 52 (1990) 525–578; *Über die Auferstehung des Fleisches: Studien zur frühchristlichen Eschatologie,* Beihefte zur Zeitschrift für de neutestamentliche Wissenschaft 66 (Berlin-New York 1993), esp. 127–129.

—B. Pouderon, 'La chair et le sang: encore sur l'authenticité du traité d'Athénagore', *VC* 44 (1990) 1–5 (also not cited in the original article); *Athénagore. Supplique au sujet des Chrétiens, Sur la résurrection des morts,* SC 379 (Paris 1992), esp. 33–34; 'Apologetica. Encore sur l'authenticité du «De Resurrectione» d'Athenagore (= part one)', *Revue des Sciences Religieuses* 67 (1993) 23–40 (the part in which he replies to my position has not yet been published).

It should be observed that these two authors approach the question from two completely different viewpoints. Lona is above all concerned with the doctrine of the resurrection of the body, Pouderon with the *œuvre* of the apologist Athenagoras. Finally we note that according to J. Pepin in R. Goulet (ed.) *Dictionnaire des philosophes antiques,* vol. 1 (Paris 1989) 642, 'il est impossible d'arriver à une certitude' in this question.

p. 115: Pouderon has returned at great length to this question in the article cited above on p. 76.

p. 116: It goes without saying that this second term is not present in the *Legatio* (otherwise my argument would lose its force), but I should perhaps have stated this explicitly. This term too occurs twice in Didymus of Alexandria, *Fragmenta in Psalmos* 893, 1071 Mühlenberg.

CHAPTER SIX
Philo and Origen: a Preliminary Survey
Originally published in R. J. Daly (ed.), *Origeniana Quinta: Papers of the 5th International Origen Congress Boston College 14 18 August 1989*, Bibliotheca Ephemeridum Theologicarum Lovaniensium 105 (Leuven 1992) 333–339.

This brief study on Origen's debt to Philo forms a preparatory study for chapter 9 in *Philo and Early Christian Literature*. It goes into much less detail, because it was presented as a workshop paper at the fifth International Origen Congress. It is worth reprinting because it offers a succinct and useful *status quaestionis* of the subject.

p. 118 n. 2: Further details in *Philo and Early Christian Literature* 158 n. 6.

p. 118 n. 4: See below chapter 14.

p. 120: Translations of these passages are found in *Philo and Early Christian Literature* 160–162.

p. 122: Further discussion of these controversies in *Philo and Early Christian Literature* 163–171.

p. 123. I. e. if a study parallel to that of Van den Hoek, cited in n. 5, were to be achieved, it would require extensive reading of and research on the vast, chaotically preserved *corpus Origenianum*. I am not persuaded by the argument of C. Blönnigen, *Der griechische Ursprung der jüdisch-hellenistischen Allegorese und ihre Rezeption in der alexandrinischen Patristik*, Europaische Hochschulshcriften Reihe XV: Klassische Sprachen und Literaturen 59 (Frankfurt etc. 1992), esp. 265, that Origen deliberately avoids direct usage of Philonic themes. More research needs to be done first.

CHAPTER SEVEN
'Where, tell me, is the Jew...?': Basil, Philo and Isidore of Pelusium
Originally published in *Vigiliae Christianae* 46 (1992) 172–189.

Various themes connecting Basil of Caesarea and Isidore of Pelusium with Philo are brought together in this article. Of particular interest is the fact that both church fathers are concerned to combat Judaism (as well as heresy), but that Isidore undertakes to defend

Philo from the general indictment given by Basil in his sermon on the sixth day of creation. A reason for this strategy is suggested at the end of the article. On the relation between Philo and heresy see further chapter eight below. On Basil's knowledge and use of Philo see also *Philo and Early Christian Literature* 235–241. The chapter builds on the results of chapter 9 below, but I have retained the chronological order of the church fathers involved.

p. 127: The numbering of the lines in the long quotation differs slightly from that in the original. References to these lines below have been adjusted accordingly.

p. 129 n. 8: Prof. A. Kamesar (Hebrew Union College, Cincinatti) is about to publish an article in the Italian journal *Henoch*, in which he very plausibly argues that Basil may have in mind the passage in Wisdom of Solomon 16:20–21, which is attributed to Philo because he was regarded as the author of this work (as noted in *Philo and Early Christian Literature* 277, 319, 331–2, but not in relation to this particular text discussed at 236).

p. 138 & 139: The Greek text of the entire letter is given below in chapter 9.

p. 142 n. 37: See the further examination of Philo's relation to heresy in chapter 8 below.

p. 142 n. 39: See now *Philo and Early Christian Literature* 1–33.

p. 143: On these titles see chapter 2 above, and esp. p. 36, 39.

CHAPTER EIGHT
A Note on Philo and Christian Heresy
Originally published in *The Studia Philonica Annual* 4 (1992) 65–74.

As indicated in the opening words of the article, its subject was a direct result of researches on the role of Philo in the Letters of Isidore of Pelusium (see chapter 9). The question of Philo's purported relation to Christian heresy required a separate treatment.

p. 144: On Gregory's knowledge and use of Philo see further *Philo and Early Christian Literature* 243–261.

p. 145: On the epithet 'the Hebrew' that Gregory uses to describe Philo here see further above p. 40.

p. 148: Basil's text is further discussed above in chapter 7; see esp. p. 135–137.

p. 151: On Ambrose's knowledge and use of Philo see further *Philo and Early Christian Literature* 291–311.

p. 152: Cf. also exegesis of Gen. 9:6 by Basil and Isidore mentioned above at p. 142.

CHAPTER NINE

Philo of Alexandria in Five Letters of Isidore of Pelusium
Originally published in D. T. Runia, D. M. Hay and D. Winston (edd.), *Heirs of the Septuagint. Philo, Hellenistic Judaism and Early Christianity: Festschrift for Earle Hilgert,* Brown Judaic Studies 230 [= *The Studia Philonica Annual* 3 (1991)] (Atlanta 1991) 295–311.

The presence of Philo's writings in the Letter-collection of Isidore of Pelusium remains an almost wholly unexplored subject. Further work is hampered by the lack of a sound critical edition. There is no evidence to suggest that this situation will improve in the near future.

p. 155 n. 1: An important survey article on Isidore is about to be published by U. Treu in the *Reallexikon für Antike und Christentum.*

p. 158: The line numbering differs somewhat from that in the original publication. All references have been modified accordingly.

p. 167: 'Modern scholars...' This remark prompted my later article on Philo and Christian heresy (see above chapter 8).

p. 167: 'Epithet'. See the remarks in this chapter above on p. 32 and 35.

p. 170: See above p. 34–35.

p. 173. ὁ θεωρητικώτατος. On the epithet see further above p. 39.

p. 173. Jacob and Israel. On this theme in Philo see now the monograph by E. Birnbaum, *The Place of Judaism in Philo's Thought: Israel, Jews, and Proselytes,* Brown Judaic Studies (Atlanta 1995).

p. 173: Josephus in Isidore. See now also the brief discussion in H. Schreckenberg, 'Josephus in Early Christian Literature and Medieval Christian Art', in H. Schreckenberg and K. Schubert (edd.), *Jewish Historiography and Iconography in Early and Medieval Christianity,* CRINT III 1 (Assen 1992) 79–80.

p. 177: Jerome. On this text see further *Philo and Early Christian Literature* 314, 319.

p. 177. Isidore on the passions. Further investigation needs to be made of patristic evidence on this theme. For example Gregory of Nyssa, who upholds the ideal of ἀπάθεια, states at *Dial. de anim. et res.* 61A that the passions as κινήματα τῆς ψυχῆς are ἀρετῆς ἢ κακίας ὄργανα depending on the use made of them in the rational choice (προαίρεσις). But Gregory does not focus on the aspect of turning or change.

CHAPTER TEN
Witness or Participant? Philo and the Neoplatonic Tradition
Originally published in A. Vanderjagt and D. Pätzold (edd.), *The Neoplatonic Tradition: Jewish, Christian and Islamic Themes*, Dialectica Minora 3 (Köln 1991) 36–56.

This article was written in response to the invitation of Dr. A. Vanderjagt to give a paper at a symposium on the Neoplatonic tradition on the occasion of the 25th anniversary of the Faculty of Philosophy, University of Groningen, as a separate faculty. I used the opportunity to prepare a preliminary study for part of the contents of chapter one of *Philo and Early Christian Literature*, in which I trace the history of the survival of the Philonic corpus. The middle section of the paper is a brief summary of my findings. I have included the paper because in the first section it gives a useful *status quaestionis* on the question of the relation between Philonic thought and Neoplatonism, and in the third section it discusses an interesting and important theological theme common to Philo, Numenius and Plotinus. Clearly, however, much research still needs to be carried on the main subject of the article before any more definitive results can be reached.

p. 185 n. 6: Now published in Band XVII 213–246, quote on 236.
p. 192. I have replaced the diagram presented in the original article with the updated version published in *Philo and Early Christian Literature* 18 (with the permission of the publisher Van Gorcum).
p. 194: I hold on to this view, and remain unconvinced by the objection of A. Hilhorst that Heliodorus may have been a Christian; see A. Hilhorst, 'Was Philo Read by Pagans? The Statement on Heliodorus in Socrates *Hist. Eccl.* 5.22', *SPhA* 4 (1992) 75–77.
p. 195: Prof. Drijvers now thinks that Alexander of Aphrodisias was Bardaisan's chief Greek source.

p. 197 n. 35: The question remains controversial. In a paper presented to the Leiden Seminar for Ancient and Medieval Philosophy in May 1994 John Whittaker disclosed that he has changed his mind, and no longer supports the 'Judaizing' interpretation of fr. 13.

p. 197 n. 37: The dissertation has still not been completed.

p. 201. Two important commentaries on *Ennead* 6.9 have since appeared: P. A. Meijer, *Plotinus On the Good or the One (Enneads VI, 9)*, Amsterdam Classical Monographs 1 (Amsterdam 1992); P. Hadot, *Plotin Traité 9 VI, 9* (Paris 1994). Neither devote any attention to the theme of the 'standing god' and the relation to Numenius or Philo).

CHAPTER ELEVEN
God of the Philosophers, God of the Patriarchs: Exegetical Backgrounds in Philo of Alexandria
Originally published in F. J. Hoogewoud and R. Munk (edd.), *Joodse Filosofie tussen Rede en Traditie: Feestbundel ter ere van de tachtigste verjaardag van Prof. dr. H. J. Heering* (Kampen 1993) 13–23.

The first part of the Festschrift in honour of Professor Heering, Emeritus Professor of the Philosophy of Religion at the University of Leiden, consists of twelve essays exploring the relation between the God of the philosophers and the God of Abraham, Isaac, and Jacob. Its purpose was to serve as an example of how philosophy and Jewish tradition have co-existed and can fruitfully interact with each other. My task was to start the ball rolling by examining Philo's contribution. Certain themes of my Utrecht inaugural lecture return here [= above chapter one] and are further developed. In this collection I publish the original version of my article as submitted. In the published version the beginning was altered so that it would fit in with the book's Introduction.

CHAPTER TWELVE
Confronting the Augean Stables: Royse's Fragmenta Spuria Philonica
Originally published in *The Studia Philonica Annual* 4 (1992) 78–86.

As noted on p. 226, the subject of Philo's fragments is intimately connected with the transmission of his writings in the Patristic period. Royse's long-awaited edition of the complete Greek fragments of Philo has not yet appeared, but on the basis of this and other research we may safely predict that, when it is finally published, it will have been worth the wait.

p. 222: On the *Catena in Genesim* see further the remarks above at p. 46–47, and also my review of volume 1 of F. Petit's edition at *SPhA* 5 (1993) 229–232.

p. 225: The additional reverse index suggested here was published by Royse in *SPhA* 5 (1993) 156–179.

p. 225, n. 24: Skarsten's dissertation is still not yet available in English. But for further information on may consult see his article 'Some Applications of Computers to the Study of Ancient Greek Texts: a Progress Report', *Symbolae Osloenses* 66 (1991) 203–220.

CHAPTER THIRTEEN
References to Philo from Josephus up to 1000 AD
Originally published in *The Studia Philonica Annual* 6 (1994) 111-121.

The list is as complete as I have been able to make it within the limits indicated in the preliminary remarks, with the exception of one additional reference listed below.

p. 237: Theodoret makes another reference to Philo at *Curatio affectionum Graecarum* 2.94 61.19 Raeder, where before citing Philo of Byblus, he repeats Eusebius' assertion that οὐχ ὁ Ἐβραῖος ἀλλ᾽ ὁ Βύβλιος is meant. Cf. Eusebius *PE* 1.9.20 cited below at p. 232, and also my remarks on this text above at p. 28.

CHAPTER FOURTEEN
An Index to Cohn-Wendland's Apparatus Testimoniorum
Originally published in *The Studia Philonica Annual* 6 (1994) 111-121.

After some deliberation I have decided to reprint this index. It gives access to a large amount of Patristic material relevant to Philonic studies which has scarcely been noted because it has been tucked away by the two editors in the apparatus and addenda of their great critical edition.

INDICES

1. *Index of biblical passages*

2. *Index of Philonic passages*

3. Index of ancient authors

4. *Index of modern authors*